A
Country Schoolmaster

JAMES SHAW
TYNRON, DUMFRIESSHIRE

EDITED BY

ROBERT WALLACE
PROFESSOR OF AGRICULTURE AND RURAL ECONOMY IN EDINBURGH UNIVERSITY

With a Portrait of the Author and Eight full-page Plates

"Full many a flower is born to blush unseen,
And waste its sweetness on the desert air."

EDINBURGH
OLIVER AND BOYD
LONDON: SIMPKIN MARSHALL, HAMILTON, KENT & CO., LTD.

1899

Publishing Statement:

This important reprint was made from an old and scarce book.

Therefore, it may have defects such as missing pages, erroneous pagination, blurred pages, missing text, poor pictures, markings, marginalia and other issues beyond our control.

Because this is such an important and rare work, we believe it is best to reproduce this book regardless of its original condition.

Thank you for your understanding and enjoy this unique book!

Dedicated by permission

TO HER GRACE

THE DUCHESS OF BUCCLEUCH AND QUEENSBERRY

EDITOR'S PREFACE

In May 1898 I sent the following letter to the editors of the *Educational News*, Edinburgh, the *Dumfries Standard*, and the *Dumfries Courier and Herald* :—

LITERARY REMAINS OF JAMES SHAW.

Sir,—I suggested to the late James Shaw of Tynron Parish School, a few months before his death, that he ought to write his autobiography and incorporate with it a selection from the contributions he had made to literature. With this object in view he had collected a number of papers, but he had done very little in the matter of selection or arrangement. The papers have come into my possession, and it is suggested that a book of about 300 pages 8vo should be issued, containing a brief historical sketch of Shaw's life and work, and a selection from his voluminous writings on a great variety of scientific, antiquarian, and popular subjects.

A book of this kind would be a suitable tribute to the memory of one who possessed in a conspicuous manner literary instincts of an exceptionally brilliant order, which, had they been turned in any one direction, would have made for him a highly distinguished name in the world of letters.

His literary work, though excellent, was in its subject-matter somewhat too diversified in character, yet it was worthy of the appreciation it received, and Shaw was highly esteemed by those who had the privilege of his personal acquaintance.

By all he is remembered not only as an interesting contributor to current prose literature, but as a poet, a man of science, an antiquarian, and a most enjoyable and engaging companion. Many of his descriptions of local places and districts are not only interesting, but also unique historical records. His collections of folklore and quaint words and phrases in the Dumfriesshire dialect, and his instructive records of the manners and customs of a people who are rapidly changing owing to better means of education and a much higher standard of worldly prosperity, will, as years pass by, become of greater and greater value.

If a sufficient number of subscribers are forthcoming at 5s (cash price) the book will be prepared, and published in due course by Oliver & Boyd, Edinburgh. Intending purchasers are requested, with your gracious permission, to communicate with me without delay. I am pleased to do my share of the work as a labour of love, but as there are no funds to defray expenses, it is essential that 250 subscribers should be secured before any further development is possible.—Yours, &c., ROBERT WALLACE.

THE UNIVERSITY,
EDINBURGH.

By means of the publicity thus made to my proposal, and by the hearty co-operation of a number of Shaw's friends, the subscribers asked for were secured. On the first perusal of the material in my possession I gave way to the temptation to include a greater number of articles than was at first contemplated, and the volume swelled to one of 492 pages. I also added a frontispiece, reproduced from an excellent photograph of the author, and eight full-page process plates, showing selected views of the district dealt with. For the use of the original negatives from which the plates were produced I am indebted to Miss Clark-Couper for two specially taken for the purpose, to John Bell, photographer, Barrhead, nephew of the late author, and to John Douglas, Barber, Thornhill, who lent negatives which belonged to his late father, Thomas Douglas. I have in addition to acknowledge much hearty and ready assistance rendered by those to whom it was necessary to apply for detailed information during the progress of the work.

I have endeavoured to the best of my ability to pick out from a large unassorted pile of manuscript and printed extracts from newspapers and magazines those productions of our author which seemed to combine the qualities of being representative of his literary style in at least one of its many phases, and of possessing an interest to the reader, and concomitantly some literary or scientific value.

I by no means exhausted the material which was worthy of incorporation. It is to be regretted that space was not available for the publication of the whole of the exhaustive epic poem on the Expulsion, and a number of his shorter metrical productions, or for two long meritorious essays on Sir Walter Scott and John Knox, besides other early written articles in prose, such as 'Recollections of Old Sermons,' 'The Adventures of a Dancing Master,' and 'Sketches of Obscure Persons—the Tailor, the Sweep,' etc.—all of which, with others enumerated in Appendix C, may be seen in Dr Grierson's Museum, Thornhill. Ample evidence exists of the fact that the papers which came to me *en masse* and those which I succeeded in finding otherwise, formed but a small fraction of the product of our author's busy pen.

As editor, it was necessary to allow myself a free hand. In quoting poetry from memory our author sometimes adopts a liberal rendering which it did not seem desirable to alter.

To his spelling of local names I have generally adhered, although in a number of cases his mode is a little antiquated, and inspired by what he believed to be more in accord with the etymology of the words than with the modern pronunciation and spelling.

I have excised the courtesy title of 'Mr' in the belief that it would have been out of place in a work of this kind, although for the information of future readers it may be worth recording that, following the custom of the country, Shaw adopted the almost invariable practice of writing of living authors or preachers who at the time had no claim to a higher title, as Mr So-and-so, *e.g.*, Mr Carlyle and Mr Gilfillan.

The work has been to me most interesting and instructive, and that I have the satisfaction of knowing that I have done something to keep alive the treasured memory of a worthy friend is no mean reward for the labour it has entailed.

My intimacy with Shaw was of the closest and most agreeable kind. As a boy in my early teens I attended his school; I was for three years a member of his School Board, and during that period undertook his duties for a time while he suffered from a severe attack of ophthalmia. I played chess almost weekly with him for a number of years, and to him I shall ever be gratefully indebted for my initiation in the mysteries and delights of field botany, in which we revelled during many a Saturday and many an evening ramble.

William Stewart Ross writing of him says :—' He was a large man, fated to play out his life-drama on a small and dimly-lighted stage'; and I cannot but feel that, had he been destined to mix with men whose literary instincts approximated more closely to his, the humble efforts I have made to perpetuate his memory would have been unnecessary. ROBERT WALLACE.

UNIVERSITY, EDINBURGH,
  May 1899.

N.B.—The specimen of closely reasoned 'Biblical Criticism' in Appendix D (page 384)—a letter to the Reverend David Morrison on the *Epistle to the Hebrews*—would have occupied a more prominent position had it been in my possession at an earlier date.

CONTENTS

LIST OF PLATES

BIOGRAPHICAL SKETCH OF JAMES SHAW.

JAMES SHAW, the writer of the 'Literary Extracts' contained
in this memorial volume, was born in the Renfrewshire
village of Barrhead on 22nd April 1826. No notice of
his early boyhood is to be found, except the reference by
himself, which appears at page 146 of this volume. While
still very young—probably not thirteen years of age—
he was sent by his parents to Glasgow for about two
years to learn pattern-designing, under the tutelage of
Peter M'Arthur, who had gone from Barrhead. He
boarded with Mrs John Stewart, who, with her husband,
hailed from Perth. In the confidence of this kindly
couple Shaw spent a very agreeable and evidently profit-
able time. M'Arthur (1805 to 1881), a very old and intimate friend of the family, had been groomsman at the
wedding of James Shaw's parents. To the distinction of
occupying 'a leading place in his profession,' he added the
cultured amusements of painting and of versification in
the native doric. As the author of *Amusements of Minstrelsy*,
he occupies a creditable place among Scottish Poets.
Such a congenial companion and instructor could not fail

b

to exercise a healthy moral influence upon young Shaw's
career, which was even then in process of development.
From Glasgow, at about the age of fifteen, he removed to
Gateside Printworks, which are still to be seen a mile to
the west of Barrhead; and with Glen & Macindoe he under-
went a seven years' apprenticeship as a pattern designer.
After the termination of this engagement, and while
suffering from a troublesome form of dyspepsia, he took
employment for two or three years with J. & R. Melville,
at Roebank Printworks, Beith.   There he did clerking
work and some designing in the special line of silk handkerchiefs, and there, too, he completely recovered his
normal state of good health.   The next great though un-
successful step in his career, was to begin business as a
master printer in partnership with five others, at Crossmill,
three-quarters of a mile east of Barrhead.   At page 147
a good idea of the mode of life experienced by those
engaged in the calico-printing trade is given by himself,
while the ruin which overtook this once flourishing branch
of industry and the village, now razed to the ground, are also
referred to.   The force of adverse circumstances led, after
the brief period of two years, to his deserting the
commercial and industrial life which was repugnant to his
nature, and taking up, when nearly thirty years of age,
the profession of schoolmaster, in which he found more
congenial employment, and also time to practise those
intellectual pursuits which made life so bright and interesting to himself, and the fruits of which have so often
delighted those with whom he came in contact.   He spent
the session of 1855-56 in the Established Church Training
College, Glasgow, and left it in July 1856, with a first-
class certificate of merit.   It would appear, although
there is no accurate information as to dates, that he first,
through an advertisement, secured for a year a position
as assistant in a private school in Melrose.   The succeed-

ing period of three or four years, till after 1860, was
spent as an assistant in West Kilbride, a delightful rural
village not far from the Ayrshire coast. Before taking
up his final position as Parish Schoolmaster of Tynron,
Dumfriesshire, in October 1862, he was employed for
a short time in Dovecothall School, situated in the lower
part of Abbey Parish, Barrhead.

One of his oldest and most esteemed friends, John
Broom, who died in 1899, communicated the following
interesting sketch of Shaw's early life and work :—

Broom's Statement

'My acquaintanceship with James Shaw began at
Barrhead about 1847. He was then a young man of
twenty-one years of age—about two years older than
myself. He was a member of a respectable family which
was in rather a better position than is usual amongst
tradesmen—his father, Archibald Shaw, being a master
joiner and the owner of property in the village. He must
have been a very apt pupil and a most enthusiastic
reader, as the knowledge he had acquired, and the
readiness he early displayed in English composition
were far beyond that of his fellows. Even before he
was twenty years of age his acquirements were looked
upon by people of the district as quite phenomenal. He
had a wonderful facility in versification, a faculty which
grew with him and continued to the end. The first time
I saw him was at a gathering of perhaps a dozen people,
and I recollect how astonished I was at his power of im-
provising. He began at one end of the company and
devoted a stanza to each member of it. It was evidently
an impromptu performance, for some of those present he
had never seen before, and many of the allusions had
reference to the sayings and doings of the evening, and
though, no doubt, the verses would hardly have been fit

for publication, it seemed to me a very wonderful gift that the author possessed.

'He had by that time begun to learn pattern-designing for shawls and dresses, a trade at which he continued for probably ten or twelve years. About the year 1853 he started business in the trade of shawl and calico printing. It was a flourishing industry at the time, but a change of fashion in dress shortly afterwards set in, and that venture was stranded. With the loss of what must have been to him and his family a very considerable sum of money, he was now adrift at about thirty years of age, with no trade to which he could turn, nor perhaps much commercial aptitude. He then thought of teaching as a profession. He was at all times an insatiable reader, with a singularly retentive memory, but I do not think he ever was what is called a very exact scholar.

'After he went to Dumfriesshire I met him but rarely, probably once or twice a year. For the last dozen years or so, as his holidays came round, he invariably spent some time in making a tour amongst his old associates, and, amongst others, I had the happiness of having him as a guest for a few days. On several of these holiday occasions he indulged in a Continental tour, and so had an opportunity of getting a knowledge of the scenery of at least France, Switzerland, Italy, and Germany.

'As the population of Tynron was very small, he had abundance of time on his hands, and being always of great mental activity, he took enthusiastically to the study of field botany, in which he became quite an adept, and that led him further into a familiarity with most of the recent literature connected with evolution. Indeed, his interest in this subject became so engrossing, that his former enjoyment of general literature seemed to diminish greatly, or to become at least of secondary moment.

'In youth he never was much interested in the usual
sports or enjoyments of people of his own age. From his
boyhood literature and speculation on political or social
science seemed to suffice for his mental activity. At an
early period—I think he could not have been more than
twenty years old—he had written a tragedy of the usual
five acts in length.* I have heard it read, but memory
does not serve me sufficiently well to enable me to say
much regarding it. Possibly I was too young to enjoy or
appreciate it then, and the subject, which was a classical
one, did not interest me much. It never was printed,
and in later life he never referred to it. In middle life
he wrote verse with great ease, and dealt at times with
lofty themes. His most ambitious effort in that direction
was a continuation of "Paradise Lost," [referred to in
Chapter X] which appeared in successive numbers of
the *Dumfries Herald* in 1878. For some years his chief
literary work was in this direction, but he did not seem
to be ambitious of publication. Possibly he did not receive
sufficient encouragement, and he was always doubtful of
himself; for though his poetry was distinctly his own, and,
with the exception of the Miltonic continuation, in no
sense an echo of previous writers, yet it was not strikingly
novel, and often seemed to belong to an older age of
thought and reflection than the present. His knowledge
of English poetry in all its range was simply wonderful, and his rapid apprehension of latent beauty in works

---

* *Carinus and Rienzi*, a tragedy in five acts, although a first
effort, is not one of which the author had cause to be ashamed. It
gave ample promise of the development in literary taste and style
which was subsequently realised. The tale relates to a conspiracy
against a corrupt and tyrannous 'Emperor of the West,' named
Carinus, and although the plot was discovered and all the leading
participants, male and female, put in prison, everything ends
happily with the repentance and death of the monarch. The story
is an exciting one, and the interest of the reader is maintained
throughout.

of literary art almost remarkable. That probably added
also to his diffidence in the matter of publication.

'From my earliest intimacy with him I was most deeply
impressed with the fact that very early in life he must
have got beyond the influence of all ordinary formulas,
as he was so untrammelled by early education or beliefs,
and so determined to get back to first principles as a
basis for opinions. Yet he never seemed to care much
for purely metaphysical writers, and, I think, esteemed
them but slightly. Herbert Spencer he had studied very
fully, more so than any one else with whom I have been
acquainted. He was for a great many years a pronounced
Positivist, but in later life his views seemed to change, and,
to use a phrase which was much in his mouth, he often
"went back to the fountains that had nourished his boyhood."

'Though an abundantly kind man, yet his feelings were
more intellectual than emotional. With ready and
helpful sympathy, he was yet not affected, as most people
are, by tales of suffering. I remember his telling me that
he did not recollect ever having once been moved to tears
over a book, except when reading Emerson's *Essay on
the Oversoul*. Though a strange statement, I have no
doubt it was truthful; it was certainly characteristic.
His mind was always more affected by meeting with great
and unexpected thoughts, than by accounts, however brilliantly narrated, of any human experiences. At times
after or during the perusal of such works as that of Sir
Robert Ball on *Astronomy*, or some account of the later
speculations or discoveries in physics or cosmic motion, he
became quite excited, and seemed lost, as no doubt he was,
in another world, and yet he had a deep interest in the
history of humanity. For instance, he had mastered the
great work of Gibbon on the *History of the Decline and
Fall of the Roman Empire*—a work which many are ac-

quainted with, but which few have thoroughly perused; indeed, he was familiar with the works of all the great historians.'

The following valuable contribution to the biography of our author, from the pen of John Laurie—perhaps his most intimate friend during the later and riper period of his literary career—requires no introduction or preliminary explanation:—

LAURIE'S STATEMENT

'James Shaw and I first met in the early winter of 1863. About a year before he had entered on his duties as teacher of the " Parish School" of Tynron, while that year I had taken charge of the "Endowed School," which forms part of the hamlet of Tynronkirk. The Parish School is located two miles further up the Shinnel Water, where the Glen is narrow, the hills higher, and the population, chiefly pastoral, sparser. From local exigencies we lodged for twelve months in the neighbouring village of Moniaive, where we "forgathered" nearly every evening. Although unaccustomed to a country life, he speedily mastered the conditions of his environment and learned to love his quiet restful home among the Dumfriesshire hills—a home whose unexciting surroundings admirably suited a man of greedy appetite where literature was concerned, which lent its influence in securing the honourable literary position attained by "the picturesque schoolmaster of Tynron," as the Dumfries *Standard* once jokingly styled him. It had at once been recognised that Shaw was no ordinary pedagogue, but a man of bright intelligence and splendid powers of memory, with a guileless simplicity of character and ways all his own. At that time he was thirty-six years of age, rather diffident in

manners, dark-haired, and with a smack of West Country
dialect in his speech.   The friendship we then formed
remained close and unbroken during the thirty-three
years we were brother teachers.   I have thrown together
a few jottings, without regard to time or sequence, that
may assist the readers of the following Literary Extracts to
form some conception of the writer and his ways.   Thus
may I add a stone to the memorial cairn of a man who for
one-third of a century was a strong personality in Tynron
and Dumfriesshire, and whose name was known in literary
circles of much wider area.   To the mysteries of the
science of botany I had the privilege of introducing my
friend.   He at once became enthusiastic in the subject,
and soon out-distanced his preceptor.   Perhaps in no
other branch of science was Shaw so much a specialist as
in botany, and its charms were to him an abiding joy
until the very close of life.   Nor did his enjoyment end
there ; for he further inspired a little band of enthusiasts,
who became excellent botanists.   Among my most treasured books are two volumes of Bentham's *Handbook of
the British Flora*, which were used by him.   They are
liberally pencilled in the well-known character, and
those notes on the habitats of the rarer plants are
interesting and instructive.   As Secretary to the Barrhead Mechanics Institute prior to 1862, he corresponded
with a number of prominent men, such as the Duke of
Argyll, Professor Tyndall, and Charles Kingsley, whose
letters he treasured.

'To James Shaw all Nature was replete with charm,
whether she spoke to him in the floweret of the field,
the fern in the bosky dell or on the craggy hillside, in
the song of mavis or merle or scarlet-breasted robin,
whose varied notes told to his discriminating ear who it
was that piped or sang so lustily.   He delighted to
register the time of the first appearance of the hardy little

flowers as they emerged from the lap of earth in the months of spring. He revelled in the glory of summer, and rejoiced in the tints of autumn and the snow-crystals of winter. All were scanned with admiring eye or touched with reverent hand. The life of the stately foxglove on the roadside was dear to him, and his entreaties averted the sickle of the surfaceman. Nor did the studious teacher decline the humblest channels of knowledge—he would give and take with "all sorts and conditions of men." The man who gloried in the sublimity of the starry heavens did not disdain to examine the nests of his little feathered friends. It was a pleasant sight to see the teacher accompanying his pupils as they started for their moor-land homes, they pointing out the nests to him, and he discoursing lucidly on the names and qualities of the plants they culled. Doubtless the influence of these walks and talks on their young minds was far-reaching in awakening closer habits of observation, a deeper tenderness for all living things and a stronger love of Nature and the Author of Nature. This education he had the knack of quickening by his quotation of a great variety of verses, lines, or phrases apposite to his themes— verses which were likely to be remembered. His modes of eliciting information from his scholars were entirely his own, and sometimes greatly amused visitors to the school. When a youth one day, in his little essay, described an ass as "a wee horse with *a tail like a cow's*," he was happy, for was not his teaching bearing the fruit he sought?

'It was also a pleasant sight to see the "old philosopher," as we latterly sometimes called him, feeding his pet animals and talking to them in a language they seemed well to understand. It might be a Darwinian lecture on development, but it was kindness itself.

'The school-house garden was of the recognised legal extent, viz., one-fourth of a Scotch acre, or about fifty

poles imperial. In the course of years he accumulated an
excellent collection of plants, chiefly of the herbaceous or
perennial class. The style of arrangement was peculiarly
his own. There was hardly a straight line in the garden.
The walks ran anyhow, and were covered with 'pebbles'
(his title for *gravel*), which sometimes formed the text
of a little geological lecture. His currant and goose-
berry bushes were not planted with any rigid regard to
regularity. (I often wondered at this in a man who had
been trained as a pattern-cutter.) Noble delphinium,
giant helianthus, and stately phlox, were there interspersed
with lowly pansy, mignonette, or lobelia. Art could not
certainly be said to have supplied his models, for he
evidently copied Nature, who rears her giants and her
pigmies so often side by side. When I would recommend
gradation among his plants he listened respectfully, but
continued his flowery jungle. In addition to the more
strictly garden flowers, he had collected many of the rarer
wild plants, such as the greater celandine, fool's parsley,
butcher's broom, and teasel. He had also a fondness for
flowering shrubs, which he planted promiscuously. A
golden juniper he prized, transplanted by friendly hands,
is now growing by " the master's " grave in Tynron Churchyard. In the earlier years of our acquaintance, my
recollection is that Shaw's strength lay in general literature, history, poetry, biography, and travel. Later on he
began to feel the allurements and fascinations of science
and archæology.

'For years we read together the *Athenæum*, but by-and-
bye *Nature* and *Knowledge* displaced for him the critical
journal. Early in his career he had taken to the pen, and
to the close of life he continued to write on every conceivable subject, most of his contributions appearing in
the newspaper press. All the little excitements of our
parish, lunar rainbows, meteors, freaks of nature, etc.,

 [*Face page* xxvi.

II.—James Shaw's Grave in Tynron Churchyard.

facility); his strange facial "contortions," as we may call
them; his head moving horizontally—were all in marked
individuality.

'As an after-dinner speaker he was first-rate, full of
illustration, hard-hitting, or humour that "set the table
in a roar." Many of these speeches deserved more than
the ephemeral applause of such occasions. As a reciter,
Shaw chiefly relied on such *morceaux* in his repertoire as
"Daniel O'Connell," "The English Curate," "The Aul'
Farran' Wean," * "Aye Dram-drammin'," "The Bashful
Man," or "The Barber o' Dunse." In no way could he be
said to be a finished elocutionist, in the ordinary sense.
Taking the first-named piece for example, his mastery of
the Irish brogue was very defective; yet all were rendered
with such verve and pawkiness that they never failed to
score, even with those who had heard them times and
again. In his "Daniel O'Connell," an imitation of the

* In the *Tynron Curling Song*, composed by the same writer,
John Laurie, and first sung by him in November 1870, to the tune
'My name, it is Gorilla,' at the annual business and social gathering of the curlers of the parish, apt and highly appreciated reference is made to Shaw, his recitations, and to the title of 'Doctor,'
as Colonel Lane Fox dubbed him at a meeting of the British
Association.

> 'An' there's a lad, aye welcome here,
>   A chiel o' sense an' brain,
> Wi' heidfu' rhymes an' stories queer,
>   An aul' "aul' farran' WEAN."
>
> *Chorus.*—Then let us sing, till rafters ring,
>   The game we a' adore!
> May ilka chiel be true as steel,
>   T' uphaud aul' Tynron Core!
>
> Hoo aft we've sat beneath the spell,
>   As Time were at a stan',
> An' listened tae the words that fell
>   Frae glorious 'DEAR OULD DAN!'
>   Then let us sing, etc.
>
> A lot o' swells in Glesky toun
>   Were cluster'd in its College;
> Ilk big-wig glower'd and claw'd his croun
>   Tae hear oor "DOCTOR'S" knowledge.'
>   Then let us sing, etc.

great Irish orator and repealer, he was so ready in adapting himself to the varying circumstances of his audience that no one ever heard it twice in the same words. He was not musical, and this deficiency of ear is discernible in his poems. Yet he had a wonderful knowledge of songs, and could, I verily believe, have repeated or chanted nearly every song that Burns ever wrote—not that he was a blind unquestioning worshipper of our national bard. Of Sir Walter Scott he had no praise strong enough. His appetite for standard books (including novels) was simply wonderful. For many years he acted as secretary to the "Upper Nithsdale Teachers' Association," writing minutes and reading papers with a sincerity worthy of Carlyle. Many of his circulars calling the meetings were couched in rhyme, often doggerel, but always amusing. His minute book was characteristic, and had *Shaw* 'writ large' on every page. His résumés of papers were excellent, and never failed to do justice to a brother teacher.

'His social qualities were undoubtedly of a high order. He was a capital conversationalist—at all times fresh, and abounding in information, humour, or satire, as occasion demanded.

'As a companion in an outing, such as we schoolmasters had to Mitchellslacks and Queensberry, renowned in Covenanting story, Shaw was simply admirable, and his newspaper account of the trip is a delightful bit of reading. Much good-natured banter had "the master" to endure over his confirmed bachelorhood. I well remember on one occasion a professional brother pointedly alluding to the fact when speaking to the toast of "Our Permanent Secretary." Up sprang Shaw in his best form, and delivered a telling little lecture on development, arguing that as animals ascend in the scale of creation their progeny decreases in number. The cod-fish, he

said, perpetuated his kind by millions, the noble sagacious
elephant by one or two, while that glorious king of in-
tellects and of bachelors, Sir Isaac Newton, left *not even
one* to bear his name. It was an effective reply.

'I cannot do better than sum up these rambling reminiscences by quoting the substance of a short article
contributed by me to the *Dumfries Courier and Herald*
at the time of Shaw's death on 15th July 1896 :—

' " In the course of the thirty-four years during which he
laboured in Tynron, he made himself many friends, and
few, if any, enemies. With old and young alike he was
a general favourite—with the old, because of his ability
and his transparent honesty, and with the young, because
of his freshness and the zest with which he entered into
their amusements. It might be said that freshness and
sterling honesty were his outstanding characteristics. He
was always strikingly original, and bubbling over with a
pawky humour. His memory was most retentive, and
this, combined with his wide and varied reading, made
him an excellent conversationalist, a ready speaker, if
not an orator, and, in short, the best company under any
circumstances. . . . He was essentially a generalist as
opposed to the specialist; but of all the studies he took up,
he had a great deal more than a smattering of knowledge ;
in several branches of science, indeed, he was a recognised
authority. His literary tastes were for the classic writers,
and his almost phenomenal memory enabled him to repeat
by heart whole pages of Burns, Shakespeare, Shelley, or
Morris, for he was equally at home with any of these
poets. Carlyle, perhaps, was his favourite author ; and,
indeed, it may almost be said that the 'Sage of Chelsea'
coloured his writings, and possibly to some extent his
opinions. In addition to reading, however, he wrote
many sketches, giving evidence of talent almost amounting
to genius, while his poems frequently found their way

into print. He was a good botanist, and of astronomy and geology he had a fair knowledge. In antiquarian matters, especially of the district in which he lived, he took a great interest. Folklore, especially, he made peculiarly his own. He wrote racy and interesting sketches * of the parishes within a few miles of which he spent so large a portion of his threescore years and ten. In history, ancient and modern, he was 'well up,' and this information was made use of in connection with his Continental tours. . . . His genial presence will be missed by a wide circle of friends and acquaintances, his deserved popularity extending far beyond the bounds of the parish in which his lot was cast." '

Robert Service, a recent but intimate associate of Shaw, formerly Secretary of the Dumfriesshire and Galloway Natural History and Antiquarian Society, writing from Maxwelltown, Dumfries, supplements the foregoing statements by the following notes :—

SERVICE'S STATEMENT

'It was not till 1876 that I became acquainted with James Shaw, when I first saw him at one of the meetings of the then newly resuscitated Dumfriesshire and Galloway Natural History and Antiquarian Society. His frank, open-hearted manner, cheery smile, and merry form of conversation, were most attractive. From that time till his death we were firm friends, although belonging to different "schools" of naturalists,—for "he was steeped to the lips" in Darwinism, while I never hesitated to tell him that the great hypothesis which has so distinguished the present century was never intended by its illustrious author to form the be-all and end-all of natural history studies, as so many of his disciples, almost his devotees,

* Reproduced in this work.

I may say, have made it. I believe Shaw never looked
at the slightest incident in natural history, at the unfolding of a flower, the flight of a bird, or, indeed, anything
and everything that may be classed within the study,
except with the thought of its possible part in, or bearing
upon the theory of, evolution. Next to natural history
in all its provisions, he was much interested in philology,
and published from time to time some valuable papers on
his local studies in this science.

'There was a curious vein of superstition, or regard for
the pseudo-supernatural in his disposition, very rare
indeed in the man of science, who of necessity deals with
such hard facts as to gradually eliminate all sense of
"Borderland" fancies and psychic manifestations from
his mind. I believe Shaw fostered these notions entirely
against his own consciousness—he did not seem to be able
to help it. And similarly in his antiquarian researches, he
seemed almost willing to believe what was pure and crass
superstition rather than the reality. He wrote many notes
on an Adder Bead,* for instance, that came into his possession, and, reading them, one became convinced that
Shaw was extremely unwilling to believe that this ancient
relic of a pre-historic burial was anything else than the
product of some orgy upon a fairy knoll of a writhing
mass of serpents! Similarly he had a very particular predilection for old-fashioned tales of the uses and origins of
plants, and half mythical stories concerning birds and
animals, together with a kind of awestruck admiration for
weird and unusual manifestations of natural phenomena.
And yet for all that, as I have said, he was an out and out
Darwinian—an omnivorous swallower of every word of
that creed—a curious paradox.

'Welcomed and appreciated by all classes of the community, he was the life and soul of a small tea-party, the

* *Vide* Appendix B.

leading figure at a dinner-table after the ladies had retired, and a conversationalist of superior talent.'

Joseph Laing Waugh * adds to the vividness of the
mental picture which should be forming in the reader's
mind by the following interesting and characteristic
notes.

WAUGH'S STATEMENT

'As a lecturer and reciter, James Shaw had few equals
in the locality. In Scotch pieces he was particularly
happy and entertaining. He possessed a keen sense of
the humorous, and when giving one of his choice selec-
tions, by the introduction of a little local colouring, and
by allusion to some recent event, he would bring his
subject into touch with the home life of the district, and
keep his hearers in roars of laughter.

'Occasionally he would lower his voice to what sounded
like a forced grating monotone, and in doing so, he
brought into clearer evidence a delightful burr, which,
although pronounced, was more pleasing than otherwise.
He seemed to be fully conscious of this, for at these times
he never seemed at a loss for words which contained the
letter "r," and he rolled them out one after another in
delightful alliteration.

'Happy memories of many pleasant evenings spent
with him are with me still, but none perhaps more vivid
and clear than that of the Burnhead U. P. Soiree.

'The Church had been renovated, and had undergone
some little external improvement, and the worthy
minister had made it an occasion of jubilation. A row
of ministers representing the different denominations
filled the temporary platform, and in the centre sat the

* Who was present as reporter to a Dumfries paper, and to
whom reference is made in Shaw's correspondence at page lxxxvi.

only lay speaker—James Shaw. Anthem or hymn had followed each sermonette until at last the chairman called on our worthy friend. The congregation cheered lustily as James Shaw rose to his feet, and after much "hostin'" and shuffling, settled down in great expectation. His appearance that evening was so striking that it yet remains pictured to my mind's eye. There was an irresistible smile on his animated face, and an ease and confidence in his actions which betokened a thorough grip of the subject in hand.

'Before saying a word, he leisurely unbuttoned his coat and put the tips of his fingers in his waistcoat pockets. This was a favourite pose, and having assumed it, he gravely announced that "never in all his life had he felt so much like a fish out of water," with that strong burr on the last letter of never and water. "Ministers," he said, "to right of him, ministers to left of him, ministers behind him had 'volleyed and thundered,' and among all these big cannons he felt a very small gun indeed."

'A sermonette on the lines followed by the reverend gentlemen who had preceded him was not in his power to deliver, but he would direct their attention to a subject which had often impressed him, and would take for his text, "The Beauties of Nature at our very Door." He first compared the two existences, "city" and "rural," and in depreciating the former he excelled himself.

'Towns, he said, were the works of man, but the country was the handiwork of God. From your bedroom window in the city you look out on smoke, smoke, eternal smoke. Rows of dirty stone or brown brick chimneys stretch away as far as the eye can reach and end in smoke. Sickly flowers from neglected window-boxes try to raise their heads to meet the struggling rays of God's own sunshine. Wee dirty sparrows chirp about the roofs and disappear guiltily below the slates on observing your gaze, as if ashamed of their smoke-begrimed feathers. The noise of the workshop, the clatter of cab and car, the whistle of the locomotive, and the never-ceasing hum of an eager, rushing, struggling humanity, all unite to deny to the longing heart that peacefulness and repose which is characteristic of the country.

'How different, he continued, is our life in this peaceful valley of ours. Roses and jasmine cluster on our walls, and nod their blossoms into our bedroom windows. The sun's untrammelled rays peep past our window curtain and fill our hearts with warmth and brightness. The hum of the bee, the music of the birds, the rustle of the leafy trees, and the gurgle of the burn, all blend together in harmonious unison. Nature all around sings the praises of Nature's God; no filthy smoke, no dirty sparrows, no soot-begrimed chimneys, no clashing, discordant noises, nothing save the glory and repose of a wondrous paradise.

'Such was the burden of James Shaw's sermon. He never faltered, nor did words fail him, and for long after the allotted time he kept his hearers spell-bound by his adulations of the lovely locality in which their lot was cast. Nature to him was an open book whose leaves were well thumb-marked, and he never wearied of singing her praises.'

The Rev. David Couper made the following touching pulpit reference to the sudden and lamented death of our author—reprinted from the *Dumfries Courier and Herald*.

PULPIT REFERENCE

Taking as his subject Heb. xi, 13—'And confessed that they were strangers and pilgrims on the earth,' he said—'Since last we met together in this place it hath pleased Almighty God, in His inscrutable Providence, to remove from our midst a dearly-beloved and much-honoured member and officer-bearer of our church, whose death we all most deeply deplore. And, though the pulpit is not the place for pronouncing panegyrics or funeral eulogiums, yet his was a personality and a character so outstanding and unique that we cannot refrain from a passing reference on this occasion to one who was ever brought so prominently before us, and who was so closely identified with all that concerned our parochial life and history. The late James Shaw was a man of singularly gifted character. As to his literary gifts and scientific attainments, it is here unnecessary in this cursory sketch to refer. Suffice it to say, that he was a man of wide culture and varied attainments—a discriminating and painstaking investigator, always possessed of a high ideal, and loving truth for truth's sake. He was an ardent lover of Nature, and a keen observer of phenomena and events. He knew something of everything—history and poetry, archæology and philology, botany and natural history. He culled flowers from every field of science, and he delighted to impart to others the varied stores of information which he had acquired.* He was a

* Shaw's friend, James Rigg, writes *In Memoriam* of him :

*   *   *   *   *   *   *

'O, thou did'st love all beauteous things—
  Could'st read fair Nature's page
With poet's eye, by rippling springs,
  Or where loud torrents rage
Down mountain scars. And every flower
  For thee had message sweet ;
And bird and beast in field and bower
  Were thy companions meet !

Gone ! Best and wisest I have known—
  Earth gives me not another ;
A pall o'er Nature's face is thrown,
  Since thou hast passed, my brother !—
Hope says—Beyond Death's doleful dale,
  Where fairest flowers fade never,
With joy we may each other hail,
  Along the crystal river.'

While on the subject of In Memoriam, the lines by Shaw on the

hearty hater of all shams, and the idea of revolutionary
changes in Church or State was abhorrent to him. In
the social circle he was a universal favourite. His kindly
voice and cheerful manner made him welcome to every
home and heart. He was gifted with a most retentive
memory, and often in the hours of social and friendly
intercourse and enjoyment it has been a pleasure to listen
to the long poetical pieces which—a poet himself—he
declaimed with the enthusiasm and fervour born of
genius, and to mark the delight with which he flung himself into and caught up the spirit of the poet. He
had a ready power of analysis, and was at least a philosophical—if not always an exact—thinker. We can
testify to the uniform zeal, fidelity, and assiduity with
which he discharged the duties of his most honourable
and useful profession; and many who received the rudiments of their education from him, and who have since
attained to positions of distinction in our own and in
foreign lands, have reason to acknowledge the inspiration
and stimulus which they received from him, and to revere
and bless the memory of such a teacher. With all his
literary and scientific attainments—and these were neither
few nor small—he bore his weight of learning lightly, and

death of John Stevens, M.A., Rector of Wallace Hall Academy,
are worthy of reproduction. In some respects they are equally
appropriate to himself.

> ' Thy life was at its noon when clouds drew nigh,
> Slow gathering round it, ebon, black as night;
> Nearer they came, while thou in eager fight
> Smot'st them defiant, till we thought the die
> Was cast for triumph, not that we should sigh
> At a long last eclipse. Thy scholars stand
> Dazed, for they touch no more the leading hand
> That led them through the maze, nor hear the cry
> Of thee their forest guide. Nor these alone
> Hast thou left troubled, for thy words were sweet
> With honey from things hoped for and things known
> To all who listened. Rounder, more complete,
> May thy unresting spirit now repose,
> In that dear land that owns no human woes.'

—*Wallace Hall Academy Magazine*, May 1896.

was simple as a little child. It was this guileless simplicity
and transparent honesty that to me, at least, constituted
the great charm of his character. The name and fame
of such a man "we would not willingly let die." Long
and sorely will he be missed in our little parish. His
removal creates a blank in our community which can
never be filled up.

> "He was a man, take him for all in all,
> We shall not look upon his like again."

'By myself, and I am sure I may speak for my brethren
of the Session, his removal is deplored as a great personal
loss. We all loved him and honoured him as worthy of
the highest respect and the warmest affection. For the
long period of thirty-four years he continued with marked
success to instruct the youth of the upper portion of the
parish, by whom he was looked up to as a father, and
towards whom he ever exhibited the kindliest parental
affection. He was an attached member and a devoted
elder of the Church of Scotland, whose ordinances he
loved and valued. He defended his Church with might
and main, and both spoke and wrote in vindication of her
national position. But while holding tenaciously to his
own principles, he was of broad and liberal sympathies.
He was neither bigoted nor intolerant, but was perfectly
ready to recognise good in those who might differ from
him. Never have I heard him utter a harsh or an angry
word against anyone who may have treated him with
injustice; and all who have been privileged to enjoy his
friendship can bear the same testimony. As a private
Christian, he held fast by the fundamental principles of
the Christian faith, and ever manifested that large-hearted
charity which is characteristic of the true Christian gentleman. He sleeps his last sleep in our quiet old churchyard
in the beautiful valley, every inch of which was so familiar
to him, and which he loved with an almost passionate

fondness. There we leave him—his quiet tomb, beside "The Martyr's Stone," reminding us that while we are yet but "strangers and pilgrims on the earth," he is an honoured inmate of the Father's House.

> " Thy God hath said. 'Tis good for thee,
> To walk by faith and not by sight;
> Take it on trust a little while;
> Soon shall you read the mystery right
> In the full sunshine of His smile."   —*Keble.*'

So much for the testimony of our author's friends, who are unanimous in their high appreciation of his worth and work. Let us now see what sidelights are thrown upon himself and his surroundings by a reference to a few of the fragments of his earlier writings that chance to have been preserved.

In his reminiscences of Barrhead and Neilston (pp. 146 to 160 inclusive), and in 'Recollections of Beith and the Surrounding District,' introduced below, will be found many interesting references to his early life and business experiences, and to the characteristics of the people among whom his budding manhood was spent. He says :—

PERSONAL AND LOCAL REFERENCES BY SHAW

' Half way between Beith and Lochwinnoch may be seen, at the present day, the forsaken walls of a little temple of industry, named Roebank. They occupy a spot where Ayrshire and Renfrewshire meet. For ourselves, long stewed up in the great factories of Glasgow, it was quite romantic to lodge in Beith, for instance; get up in the summer mornings and walk for nearly two miles, betwixt rows of hedges in June's milk-white bloom, with singing larks ahead, and a fresh breeze from the Misty Law, untainted with smoke, blowing down our throats, and then to enter a public work without gate or wall or any prison-like accompaniment. For the first time the morning bell became melodious in our ears, like that of the bell of a rustic chapel, or of a Canadian horse bounding forward with its sleigh. At evening, too, you issued from the door of your workshop, and felt as you looked at the "Bicham" hill above it, purple with heather, or at the dam of the works in which golden and white blossoms of water-lilies floated tremulously, how much truth there was in the adage that "God made the country and man made the town."

'Winter was the most dreadful period to me, who had known the immunities of Glasgow. It was then that one felt the want of books, of lectures, and of classes. But in winter the works were oftenest most busy, so that those who were so inclined could console themselves by laying up money for longer days.

'Yet one winter day stands out clear and distinct in the writer's memory. It was the day of the grand curling match between the North and South, the Forth being the line of boundary. The whole of Barr meadow near Lochwinnoch loch was artificially flooded about a foot deep. This froze over and became slightly powdered with snow. Here some hundreds of curlers, headed by the late Earl of Eglinton, with brushes and channel-stones, set to work in earnest. The blue gleaming squares of cleared ice, upon which the merry stones roared, the thunderous shouting and pantomimic positions of the combatants, and the snow-white walks upon which the well-muffled spectators of both sexes sauntered, together with the bracing air and clear, blue sky, made one almost realise that sort of hereafter, or fields of Elysium, of which it is said some tribes in tropical countries dream. Never, except perhaps in Glasgow Exchange, did we see such fine specimens of our countrymen—lithe, brawny, red-cheeked, all of them the picture of comfort, and strength, and social welfare. As for the poor Earl, the vulgar crowded round his rink as round the gorilla at a show, so that the pressure of the throng sank him latterly in two inches of water. He was a tall, middle-aged man, with white whiskers and plain attire. Several of his tenants who were present on that day were after-wards recognised among that remarkable deputation which walked in procession to his residence in Dublin when he was Lord-Lieutenant of Ireland.

'We had a peep at another remarkable man, whose duties brought him to visit Roebank Printwork. This was no other that Stuart of Dunearn, who, in a duel, shot Sir Alexander Boswell of Auchinleck. Just previous to Stuart's visit we had discussed the whole story with Dr Spiers of Beith, a medical gentleman of profound botani-cal attainments. When Stuart, in his official capacity, examined the works, no mental eye but our own saw that day the yellow sands of Auchtertool, in Fifeshire, where the author of those celebrated Jennys—the Jenny who "dang the weaver," and the Jenny whose "bawbee" was of such consequence—received his death-warrant in the shape of a pistol shot. How many Scotch songs that bullet took with it to oblivion, along with the poet's life, it were hard to guess. Poor Stuart was a thin, old man, but his ques-tions exhibited great conciseness and intelligence, and he was interested in the operations of our works.

'At a green, straggling hamlet—we forget its name—between Roebank and Lochwinnoch, overlooking the fine scenery of Castle Semple, a dancing-master came to enliven the gloom of winter, and we resolved to attend. It was a curious, big, rambling hall, that in which we were taught, and smelled terribly of turnips. The dancing-master had a great many jokes—some humorous, but all gross—as if humour were a flower that could with

him be only reared in a dunghill.   Heavy country
bumpkins heaved up and down in these dances with
elephantine sobriety, and seemed to take as much
pleasure in them as a river-horse gambolling in the
Upper Nile. We from the printfield were much lighter
craft, and came into haven with less symptoms of distress. We recollect one farmer's son who was so anxious
to learn that he almost cast over his exertions an air of
piety.   No dervish could have been more in earnest.
He advanced and retired with the precision of a spinning-
jenny.   When the master cried *posit*, he and his partner
revolved around each other like the two balls which
govern a steam-engine. "Single gentlemen, advance,"
and Samuel came forward as if he were moving on that
bridge of one hair which the Mussulman has to tread
when passing over the gulf on the way to bliss; and
when told to look cheerful, he gathered about his lips a
few wrinkles, seriously meant for fun, but which was
such a thin, icy smile, that you rubbed your hands to see
it, not knowing whether to laugh or weep—for smiling
and blushing, save by imps or artists, can't yet be well
executed to order.   This dancing was of some use at
Roebank, when a newly-erected printshop had to be
opened.   On such an occasion, the hospitality of the
masters was unbounded.   Strangers were invited from a
distance.   The noise of bottles uncorking met you in
every house, and for a whole week at a stretch each
partner vied with the other in transforming his rooms
into apartments palatial, where, in good old Chaucer's
phrase,
        'It snowed of meat and drink,'
and in which the masters and the masters' wives were
"gracious as kings upon their coronation day."

'The little colony at Roebank, as we intimated, has
been quite broken up.   Some of its representatives

pursue business successfully in other localities; but at
present the appearance of the former busy workshops,
all silent, of the houses of the workmen empty, where
labour and amusement, anxiety and joy were concen-
trated, reminds us of the Persian poem, uttered by
Mahomet the Second, in the Church of St Sophia—"The
spider has woven his web in the imperial palace; and
the owl has sung her watch-song on the towers of
Afrasiab."'

Something of the energy of the man and his capacity
for turning every situation to account, even when apparently unfortunate at the moment, in the search for
knowledge, may be gathered from an incident related of
Neilston Printworks, in which he was employed, when,
after an accident, no more work was done that day, and
the opportunity was taken to visit for the first time the
Hunterian Museum in Glasgow, and a fillip given to his
love of Antiquarian research, which developed so con-
spicuously in later years. The living picture of the
'Labour Captain' and his army of busy workers portrayed in the sketch of Neilston, will, as time goes on,
prove a treasure to the student of the early history of the
Scottish labouring population, and provide an interesting
glimpse into the working qualities of the people and the
conditions which have so happily combined to secure for
Scotland that position of industrial prosperity of which
we have every reason to be proud.

If readers who had the privilege of Shaw's personal
acquaintance can accurately picture the coarseness
of thought and manners and the vulgarity in speech
and action of the lower types of workers with whom
circumstances compelled him for a time to associate,
they will all the more appreciate the sterling worth of his
character which emerged untainted from such a trying

ordeal; for it was a fact worthy of remark that he was
never known to use, even in trying circumstances, any
of those terms of imprecation in which some of our
countrymen still at times claim for themselves the
privilege of indulgence.   How the mind was employed,
and how the moral citadel was defended and occupied in
those early days with worthy reflections, aspirations, and
ambitions, may to some extent be understood by a perusal of the subjoined obituary notice of Alexander Smith,
the poet,* which refers the reader back to the time when
he was 26 years of age, before he thought of literary
pursuits other than as a recreation.   He writes :—

MEETING WITH ALEXANDER SMITH

'We well recollect the evening of our first introduction
to Alexander Smith, about fifteen years ago [probably
in 1852]. We at that time were lads, I may almost say,
pursuing the same avocation of pattern drawing, the
curiosities and vicissitudes of which profession Smith has
attempted to unfold in his tale of *Alfred Hagart's Household*. The scene of our introduction was Paisley, prosy
Paisley—which externally has the fewest picturesque
views of any town of its size in Scotland, with the doubtful exception of Dundee. But as the difference of the sky
to Newton and to his dog Diamond was tremendous, so the
difference of Paisley to travellers and to the eyes of its own
poets is great. Paisley is rich in poets—little ones, to be
sure, of the sparrow and mosscheeper quality—no nightingale or blackbirds—only one little Jenny Wren, yclept
Tannahill. Such as they are, Smith in his *Summer in Skye*
records his meeting with some eighty of these sons of song

* Alexander Smith, 1830 to 1867, author of *Dream Thorp*, was appointed in 1854 Secretary to the Senatus of Edinburgh University—
a position which he occupied with conspicuous credit till his death.

at a literary evening party! At the period of our meeting both Smith and myself were in what is called the
Byronic era, or perhaps somewhat more advanced. He
was meditating that poem of his, the *Life-Drama*
[published 1853], upon which he was afterwards to rise
as on a rocket. A humble amateur painter had brought
us together, and to his humble parlour some half-dozen
youths fast approximating to the greatness of genius,
and some quarter dozen admirers of genius, were assembled. In our debating societies we had attempted to
settle whether the painter, the poet, or the sculptor were
the greatest, or most deserving of fame; and each of us
was by either of these means on the highway to an
immortal goal. We had had our MS. Magazine illustrated by pen and ink sketches from both the painter
and the poet, and intended, you may be sure, to combine instruction with amusement—the best features of
Punch with those of, let us say, the *North British Review.*
Smith's fame had by this time waxed wider than any of
ours; he had come in upon us at an angle, and we had
somewhat of the schoolboy's feeling of "counting his
buttons." Macdonald, author of *Rambles round Glasgow,*
had spoken of Smith as a new wonder; and it was already
known that George Gilfillan, in his grand generous way,
had written words of encouragement. Macdonald was
not present at this sederunt, though he was the occasion
of it. To us literary young men in the pattern-drawing
and print-cutting line, on whom the dismal years of
1847-48 and following seasons had impressed hard marks
—hope was seen beaming, but beaming through a mist of
tears, and the six points of the "People's Charter," which
if gained would have made the lion lie down with the
lamb, were less likely to be gained than ever.

'We had not yet pondered that significant saying of
Goethe, "Here or nowhere is America," but looked

on emigration as the only door of escape from that effete
Great Britain where the bloated aristocrat, etc.—in short,
we were Fenians before Fenianism, and talked treason
like the present Reform League. Yes, we talked treason,
I remember; and those inclined to go an octave higher
introduced genteel blasphemy—an article which, either
in nice decanters or old pewter stoups, either with or
without a volley of oaths, is extremely marketable in
Paisley. Some of the older members had imbibed from
Robert Owen, the philanthropist, the consoling doctrine
that man had no free will, and that the most infamous of
wretches deserved a place under the wing of the Angel
of Pity rather than a noose made by Calcraft. Smith
was young then—probably twenty—very thin, with a
squint. He was quiet and reserved in manner, and had
no second party along with him to exhibit him. In short,
he was the lion without the lion's growl or keeper. After
such a fearful host of moss-cheepers and poets of that
species which we had encountered in Paisley, it was a
relief to find one who was so quiet, and who
exhibited no desire to spout his own verses. Of
course, it could not but come to pass that in such
company Shelley, Byron, and Leigh Hunt, not to speak of
Burns, were the first turned up; but they were turned up
with better chosen words than usual, and the tragedy of
" Cain " was discussed with less rapture than would have
pleased a Paisley weaving shop. The subject veered to
Shakespeare, and here Smith disclosed his strength. His
criticisms, I recollect, were very just; he knew as by
instinct the passages of wisdom and wit, and the salient
points of the notable characters.

'Gossip, criticism, and time getting exhausted, we
sallied out into the street without touching our lips with
anything more tangible than the wind of words. Smith
took my arm. We began upon that attractive but danger-

ous style of writing called "word-painting." We gave instances mutually from the *Ancient Mariner.* I admired the 'quiet tune' of Coleridge's midsummer brook, and Smith, the two lines contributed to that poem by Wordsworth, and so on the bare hard street, shining here and there with winter's rain, we shook hands, and the poet went on his way, and I saw him no more. "He may get very high," I said, "but he'll never be so great as Shakespeare." "Why?" said my companion. "Because he wants the physical constitution—he is not, to use a Shakespearian word, 'robustious' enough."

'Shortly after this period came the great events of Smith's life—his favourable notices from writers such as Lewes, then editing the *Leader,* and his personal introduction to men of such mark as the Duke of Argyll and the Lord Provost of Edinburgh. Aytoun's splendid dramatic poem of *Firmilian*—a parody partly on the *Life-Drama*—the ill-natured criticism in the *Athenæum,* so ill-natured that *Punch* had to come to the rescue, and other such events mingled, as usual, their gall with the wine of fame. His old father was proud of his son, and, of course, formed a higher idea of his fame than what Smith—who seems to have been always a modest man—would have formed himself. I shall never forget the sneer with which he disposed of a sensible criticism of his son's works in *Blackwood*—" Yes! damned him with faint praise!" Poor man! To us still standing in the vale with our MSS. weighing heavily on our chests, and pattern-drawers and print-cutters not in demand in the market, this young man seemed to ascend and leave us in a sort of Elijah chariot, and some who had grudges at his success then have before this gone, we hope, to that quarter in which, says Mahomet, all grudges are taken out of their hearts. Others again who survive the poet have also survived all envy of him, and have learned that duty and not fame is what ennobles life. Meantime the fine sayings of the deceased writer, the orient gems of his early youth, and the chaster and wiser productions of his riper years, these are with us in their beauty, and will be long after the grief over him is past. In his delightful book *A Summer in Skye,* though he is chiefly a poet and painter of landscapes like his brother-in-law Horatio M'Culloch, Smith sometimes, in plainest English, writes truest philosophy.'

Many years after the time when he met and entered into an ethical blood-brotherhood with Alexander Smith, the appearance of a short essay on *Thoughts from Thinkers* was evidence of the continuance of that elevated current of ideas which occupied Shaw's mind throughout, and raised him above the level of his rural surroundings,— thoughts which at one time inspired him with awe of the inscrutable working of the Unseen, rousing him to a sense of our insignificance, and which, at another, stirred his indignation against the brutal cruelties perpetrated by degenerate humanity. He writes:—

Thoughts from Thinkers

'In the eighth chapter of *Sartor Resartus,* Carlyle gives a noble reminiscence of a sentiment expressed in the eighth psalm, and occurring in the writings of the philosophers and fathers. It inculcates the lesson of humility taught every time we look at the stars, or contemplate the work of time; so that when we read the titles of certain pretentious books, such as, *The System of Nature,* we very much distrust whether the author sees greatly farther into hidden things than our own poor ignorant selves. "To the minnow," says Carlyle, "every cranny and pebble, quality and accident, of its little native creek may have become familiar; but does the minnow understand the ocean tides and periodic currents, the trade-winds, and monsoons, and moon's eclipses; by all which the condition of its little creek is regulated, and may, from time to time, be quite overset and reversed? Such a minnow is man; his creek this planet Earth; his ocean the immeasurable All; his monsoons and periodic currents the mysterious course of Providence."

'Few writers have obtained for themselves such a high reputation from a single sonnet, as Blanco White. In this wonderful little composition, which is entitled *Night*, we are required to take our place by the side of our first parent on the first day of his existence, and to try to realise the awe, akin to fear, which was likely to arise in his mind as the glorious orb of day set and left him. It would appear to him almost as if creation itself had been blotted out. But, as the clouds of night began to scatter, lo! the evening star and the innumerable host of stars and constellations which began the firmament would appear. Who could have thought such glories lay concealed within the beams of the sun? Who could have believed that the light which revealed to him every leaf and every insect should have made him blind to such countless orbs?

> "Weak man! why to shun Death this anxious strife?
> If Light can thus deceive, wherefore not Life?"

'The transient nature of man's life compared to a flower or a shadow, or like water spilt upon the ground which cannot be gathered up again, is expressed in a vivid manner by one whose heart vibrated to religious emotion, while his intellect brought the message of despair. Shelley in his *Elegy on the Death of Keats* thus gives utterance to the idea of the littleness of man's life in the presence of the enduring grandeur of creation—

> "The One remains, the many change and pass ;
> Heaven's light for ever shines, Earth's shadows fly,
> Life, like a dome of many-coloured glass,
> Stains the white radiance of Eternity."

d

'The grand imagery employed by the prophet Isaiah, Chapter xiv, where Babylon, personified, enters Hades or the shadowy underworld, and is met and upbraided by the dead kings stirred up from their thrones, has nowhere been more effectively employed than by the poet Cowper, whose heart was stirred within him against the cold-blooded cruelty, greedy cunning, and trickery of the Spaniards to the Peruvians. He refers with indignation to the shaven priest who sentenced the Peruvian monarch to death. He depicts the mean and beggared condition of Spain, the result of its overreaching greed in the New World, where neither age nor infancy was spared if these stood in the way of gold.

'Oh, could their ancient monarchs rise again and gaze, not on the proud Spain of the days of Philip, but on Spain ruined by the crimes it had wrought, how would these old Peruvian princes have taken up the strain of fallen Israel!

> " Do we see
> The robber and the murderer weak as we ?
> Thou that hast wasted earth, and dared despise
> Alike the wrath and mercy of the skies,
> Thy pomp is in the grave, thy glory laid
> Low in the pits thine avarice has made."

'Cowper was right. No reader of history can come to any other conclusion than that the sins of the parents are, in some mysterious way, connected with the sufferings of their children. National degradation is fruit, the seed of which has been sown, it may be, centuries before.'

Another combination of unique ideas, though of a somewhat melancholy aspect, found expression in verses written in 1868.

DEATH'S TRIUMPHS

> ' The world looks young, and fresh, and fair,
> The social cattle graze along,
> The lark's wild lay is in the air,
> The thickets hear the blackbird's song.

Yes, still I list the murmuring bee—
  The bleating of the mountain sheep ;
The skipping lambs I yearly see,
  And yet amid my joy I weep.

Where are the little wrens whose nests
  I peeped in thirty years ago ?
Where are my doves, that then had breasts
  I loved to stroke, and plumes of snow ?

Where are the deer that used to bound
  Behind our cot when moons were bright ?
Where is the old warm-hearted hound
  That kept my side by day and night ?

Ah ! not a horse that ploughs the field,
  Or on the highway drags its wain,
Nor milky mother, glad to yield
  Her foaming draughts to milkmaid's strain ;

Nor favourite dog, whose wise old head
  Watched o'er its master's weal or woe,
Nor priceless fowl nor pigeon bred
  With utmost care for grandest show ;

Nor not a lion caged, nor bear,
  And scarce a beast was wont to thrive,
Some forty years ago, so fair,
  And strong, and swift, is now alive.

For, swimming down the stream of time,
  Man strikes with stronger stroke than these ;
Compared to these holds up sublime,
  With greater art and steadier knees.

But ah ! the gain is dashed with loss,
  To think, though buoyant on the wave,
The brutes, whose path he used to cross,
  Are all before him in the grave.

Howe'er the grove, with vital tones,
  Resounds in early summer's morn,
Howe'er the bee or beetle drones,
  Or corncraik cries amid the corn ;

Howe'er the spring, with lavish hand,
  Brightens the iris on the dove,
Or paints, as with a fairy wand,
  Beauty on birds that mate and love.

No plumage bright, no pleasant tone,
  Belongs to those we first might know ;
Gone ! like the last year's rainbows—gone !
  They've reached the bourne where all must go.'

We turn next to the history of the inception and
development of that love of science which, as Shaw
advanced in years, more or less eclipsed his first love
—the love of literature.

The following Notes on Evolution, including unpublished letters of Charles Darwin—prepared by our author
for a contemplated autobiography—explain how he was
induced to study science, and show what encouragement
he received to develop a belief in the Darwinian theories.

AUTOBIOGRAPHICAL

G. H. Lewes and the Vestiges of Creation

'After much painful groping and thinking concerning
the mystery of existence, in the year 1852 I alighted on
a book which was none other than the *Vestiges of the
Natural History of Creation.** I perused it with eagerness
and astonishment. It opened up to me long vistas in the
obscurity of the Past. It marshalled, for my benefit,
thousands of facts which had hitherto refused to cohere,
and seemed like the key in Milton's *Comus,* which admitted the possessor into the palaces of eternity.

* The *Vestiges* first appeared anonymously in 1844, but its authorship was acknowledged by Robert Chambers in the 12th and last
edition, published in 1884. Although it was severely criticised by
leading scientific men, including Darwin and Huxley, for the
numerous inaccuracies which marred the early editions, and for
the scope given to speculations not based on scientific experiment
or authenticated observation, it was a work which took the public
fancy, and it exercised a powerful influence in popularising science
and in creating a wider and more general interest in the objects of
Nature than formerly existed.

'In 1853, the *Leader* weekly newspaper [established by Leigh Hunt in 1850] was being edited with great ability by G. H. Lewes, * and in its pages appeared a criticism of a new edition of the *Vestiges*. Lewes, as the most prominent Englishman of letters at that time, who espoused the doctrines of Comte and the positive philosophy, criticised the *Vestiges* from the standpoint of that philosophy, and instead of becoming enthusiastic over my favourite author, rather wet-blanketted him. Such, at least, was my impression, and anxious to break a lance to maintain the authority of my cherished text-book, I penned the following letter, which was published in the *Leader* of 24th September 1853, under the heading of *Literature*.

'The editor's brief comments upon it introduce it to the reader.

'"Our wish, at all times, to give both sides a hearing, no less than the suggestiveness of the communication itself, induces us to print the following criticism :

'"I confess myself much interested by the articles on the *Vestiges*. You are extremely happy in your remarks upon 'Time,' to consider which as a *positive* condition of change is absurd. Nevertheless, you have marked some passages from the *Vestiges* in italics as being erroneous, which I find escape the very objections you urge. For instance, the author of the *Vestiges* says, 'We might almost regard the progression (of animal life) as the result of *an aspiration towards new and superior fields of existence.*' Now, instead of this remark about aspiration being connected with *progress* seeming fanciful, I find it profoundly true. First from my own consciousness, the unrest within my brain, the love to be something better than I am, is at the root of my every advance in culture.

* George Henry Lewes (1817 to 1878), the confidant and literary guardian of Mary Ann Evans or Cross, ' George Eliot.'

'" Again, from observation, the naked savage's aspiration
to be independent of fierce extremes of heat and cold
causes him to use clothes, and the reaction of clothes on
his body changes the nature of his skin. Descending the
scale of animal life, there is not a single animal, however
dull, but manifestly prefers a certain quality of food, or
a certain habitat, which shall add to its comforts and
preserve its life and the life of its young ; and this continued inborn tendency always gives the new generation
a benefit, however small, which reacts on its physical and
mental nature, producing some kind of change. In
Chambers's Paper on *Animal Instincts and Intelligence,*
which you once called truly philosophical, the writer
observes that 'in studying the influences at work among
the sociable tribes it is impossible not to recognise the
probability, if not the certainty, of something approaching to civilisation, or the striking out of valuable devices
by the good heads which occasionally start up, which
devices are spread and continued by imitation. We find
that "necessity, the mother of invention," sometimes
operates in enlarging the sphere of action of a species,' and
Chambers then gives an instance of rooks adding turnips
to their articles of diet. Whenever this was done the new
food, etc., must necessarily react on their system, change
in some respects its nature,* and the change be transmitted to posterity ; yet this could never have occurred
without a desire, aspiration, or tendency for comfort and
longevity in the animal.—J. SHAW.''

* A striking instance of change of this kind was noticed by
Service in 1893—during the time of the great plague of voles, by
which much injury was done to the mountain pastures of Dumfriesshire and adjoining counties, through an exceptional and extraordinary increase of these usually inconspicuous rodents. Common
rooks, among hosts of other enemies, preyed on the young voles,
and he observed that a considerable number of them assumed the
beak and surrounding feathering which are characteristic of the
carrion crow, owing, it was believed, to the increase of flesh in their
diet. (*Cf.,* Report on Plague of Voles, 1893, pp. xiii, 45, pl. 4.)

'Upon this letter the editor, G. H. Lewes, as I assume, remarked :

'"Our objection to the phrase, 'Aspiration towards new and superior fields of existence,' was its metaphysical character, implying *consciousness* of superior existence, 'denoting a foregone conclusion,' and thus aiding and abetting the author's primary error of a 'plan.' The *fact* of progress is undeniable ; undeniable the effect of new *wants* in producing new forms of existence ; but

his diet, he may have

' or

In

it is

than

that

The letters of Charles Darwin trans-

with the

we

his son and

Lyell,

ddress

1864.

. . . I demur to the Duke's objection that the brilliant plumage of the male humming bird could not have been acquired through selection, at the same time entirely ignoring my discussion (page 93, third edition[*]) on beautiful plumage being acquired through sexual selection."—*Vide Life of Darwin.*

'The Duke of Argyll, like myself, had very likely never read the short paragraph on sexual selection in the third edition of the *Origin.* When His Grace's views

[*] *Origin of Species.*

were published in *Good Words* early in 1865, I felt puzzled at the statement of the case regarding the existence of beauty in animals. It seemed as if it were inexplicable by natural selection, and it began to dawn upon me, both from experiments and from observation, that some kinds of birds, pursuing the gratification of their tastes, had assisted to make their own species beautiful. I ventured at last to write to Darwin on the subject, and received from him, in reply, the following letter :—

    ' " Down, Bromley, 30th Nov. 1865.

' " Dear Sir,—Illness has prevented me sooner thanking you for your letter on the *Origin*, written with so much fervour and kindness. I am much gratified to hear that you have been defending my views, and in your country (Scotland), those who are bold enough to take this side of the question are few and far between. I am so weak, I must write briefly. I have reflected much on the question of beauty. It is a very complicated one. I quite agree with what you say on the beauty of birds, and the same view may be extended to butterflies and some other beings. I think I can show that the beauty of flowers and of many kinds of fruit is solely to attract, in the former case, insects for their intercrossing, and in the latter case, to attract birds for the dissemination of the seed.   Ch. Darwin."

' Early in 1866 I submitted my views on sexual selection to the Dumfries Antiquarian and Natural History Society, sending Darwin a newspaper report of the evening's proceedings, which drew from him the following reply :—

    ' " Down, Bromley, 11th Feb.

' " Dear Sir,—I am much obliged to you for your kindness in sending me an abstract of your paper on beauty. In my opinion, you take quite a correct view of the subject. It is clear that Dr Dickson has either never seen my book, or overlooked the discussion on sexual selection. If you have any precise facts on birds' 'courtesy towards their own image in mirror or picture' I should very much like to hear them. Butterflies offer an excellent instance of beauty being displayed in conspicuous parts; for those kinds which habitually display the under side of the wing have this side gaudily coloured, and this is not so in the reverse case. I daresay you will know that the males of many foreign butterflies are much more brilliantly coloured than the females, as in the case of birds. I can adduce good evidence from two large classes of facts (too large to specify), that flowers have become beautiful to make them conspicuous to insects. With my best thanks for your kindness and clear exposition of my views, I remain, etc., CH. DARWIN."

'Having acquainted Darwin with the facts upon which my paper was founded, he replied to me in April 1866.

'"Dear Sir,—I am much obliged for your kind letter and all the great trouble which you have taken in sending on all the various and interesting facts on birds admiring themselves. I am very glad to hear of these facts. I have just finished writing and adding to a new edition of the *Origin*, and in this I have given, without going into details (so that I shall not be able to use your facts), some remarks on the subject of beauty."

'This letter concludes with a promise to send me a copy of the new edition (the fourth), which was duly fulfilled.

'In the winter following I wrote a letter, which appeared in the London *Athenæum*, 24th November 1866.

FEELING OF BEAUTY AMONG ANIMALS

'"From the ancient references in Eastern literature to

the serpent charmers down to modern times, the facts showing that certain animals are gratified by music have been accumulating. He would be a bold man who would say that birds have no delight in their own songs.

' " I have been led to conclude from experiments which I have made, and from other observations, that certain animals, especially birds, have not only an ear for fine sounds, but also a preference for the things they see out of respect to fine colours or other pleasing external features. To begin with ourselves, the pleasure which we derive from a certain class of objects is universal and well-marked ; even when man becomes animalised, this instinct is never lost, but only undergoes modification. Christian babes and cannibals are equally vain of fine clothes, and have a similar passion for beads and glittering toys. Carlyle suggests that the love of ornament, rather than the desire of comfort, was at the origin of clothes. It is chiefly among birds, when we consider the case of animals, that a taste for ornament and for glittering objects, often very startling and human-like, is to be found. The habits of the pheasant, peacock, turkey, bird of paradise, several birds of the pigeon and of the crow kind, and certain singing birds, afford evidence of this. The Australian satin bower-bird is the most remarkable of that class which exhibits taste for beauty or for glittering objects not of themselves ; collecting, in fact, little museums of shells, gaudy feathers, shining glass, or bits of coloured cloth or pottery. It will be found with many birds that fine plumes, a mirror, and an admirer, are not altogether objects devoid of interest.

' " Another consideration leading me to the same conclusion is the fact that beauty in animals is placed on prominent parts, or on parts which by erection or expansion are easily, and at the pairing season, frequently, rendered prominent, such as the crest or tail. A spangle

of ruby or emerald does not exist, for instance, on the
under side of the wing, which is seldom raised, of our
domestic poultry. Such jewels are hung where man himself wears his, on the face and forehead, to court attention, like our own crowns, trains, shoulder-knots,
breast-knots, painted cheeks, or jewelled ears. I cannot
account for the existence of these gaudy ornaments to
please man, for nowhere are they more gorgeous than in
birds which live in the depth of the tropical forests, where
man is rarely a visitor ; I cannot account for them on the
principle that they do good to their possessors in the
battle for life, because they rather render them conspicuous to their enemies, or coveted by man. But
when I consider that the beauty of these beings glows
most brightly at the season of their love-making, and
that most observers agree that the female is won partly
by strength, partly by gesture, and partly by voice, and
that the male, whose interest it is to be most attractive,
is often in his wedding-suit the most gaily decorated ;
it seems to me that beauty, through a wider range than
has yet been generally acknowledged, is accessory to
love.

 ' " Butterflies, it is true, have gay patterns on the under
wing, but this rather strengthens than diminishes the
force of my argument, for with them, in a state of rest,
the wings are folded erect, whereas, others of that class,
as moths and hawk-moths, whose wings, when at rest,
are either inclined horizontally, or wrapped round the
body, have only the upper side of the wings beautiful.
It is to be noticed also that these creatures, out of the
three states in which they exist, are only remarkable for
beauty in that in which they seek their mates, and
whoever compares many of their males (as that of the
orangetips) to the females will find that gaudy colouring
also favours the former. These delicate and ephemeral

creatures are often to be observed flying lazily, as if aware of their splendour, and as if giving time that it might be seen.

' " Among fishes, it is amusing to watch the combats of male sticklebacks for the females, which can be witnessed in an aquarium, and to note how the victor waxes brilliant in hue, and the vanquished, if he survive, wanes greatly in splendour. Fishes, and more especially insects, are often destroyed through the strange attraction which light has for them.

' " Birds are caught, especially in France, through the same allurement; and those very fire-flies, whose luminosity is so pretty to us, I have no doubt find it attractive to themselves. They are caught by means of their eagerness for light by those West Indian ladies, who use them as jewels for their head-dress at a dance.

' " I am much strengthened in the conclusions at which I have arrived on this subject, by the reference made to it by Darwin in the fourth edition of his work on *Species*, a copy of which has just now reached me. The selection of beauty in their mates is there made to follow from their appreciation of it, so that effect and cause mutually throw light on each other. Some profound and interesting remarks are also added by the author, explanatory, on scientific grounds, of the origin of flowers, which strike me, although the remarks are very brief, as being the first likely solution of what has been for ages an inscrutable problem.   J. SHAW."

'On the 26th November Darwin wrote to me expressing the highest gratification at its perusal.

'Subsequently my contribution was referred to in a footnote, *Descent of Man*, Vol. II., page 382. The subject being new at the time, the letter was much quoted in newspapers both at home and abroad. I do not recollect any comments on it either in the journal in which it was originally published or in the periodicals which gave space to it.

'In the *Athenæum*, previous to this, I had called attention to the subject of Right-handedness in connection with Evolution, and I afterwards wrote on the subject in several other periodicals. Anxious to know what our great naturalist had to say on this subject, I ventured to bring it under his notice, and received from him the following candid note :—

' " Dear Sir,—I am obliged to you for your note. The subject of Right-handedness is a very curious one, but I have never attended to it, and can give you no additional facts.

' " 20th Feb. 1868.   CH. DARWIN."

' Having succeeded in obtaining a good photograph of a donkey, in which the animal had been under a surprise, I sent it to Darwin, explaining, and remarking he had given the long-eared one no place in his *Expression of Emotions in Man and Animals*. I received "many thanks for the excellent photo. The whole group, with the pretty children, is quite charming."

' It will be seen that in these letters, as in all others proceeding from the pen of our great naturalist, the exposition of truth was a main desire with him. No correspondent, however humble, was repelled by him if he thought he could profit by the correspondence. I have refrained from printing the letter 26th November 1866 verbatim, because—'

Here the manuscript prepared by Shaw ends, and the knowledge of the reason why the letters were not published verbatim died with him.

FEATURES OF SHAW'S PROSE WRITINGS

Shaw's style as an essayist is racy and endowed with the distinctive features of a strong literary individuality,

which maintains in the reader an unflagging interest.
Facts are marshalled, and appropriate quotations in prose
and verse are liberally introduced in support of his line of
argument; facility and tact in making apposite references
to side issues are conspicuous features. His writings
show him to have been a true lover of Nature, and an
astute and accurate observer of her every detail.

His locality sketches (the most of them written soon
after he came to Tynron) are replete with valuable
historical allusions and accurate and vivid imagery of
local surroundings, but our author is not slavishly bound
to his text, as he indulges in delightful flights of imagination to all the ends of the earth, to the realms of classic
and historic prose literature and of poetic fancy, carrying
his spellbound readers along with him. As a piece of
portrait-painting in words, the description of the 'eight-
and-eighty'-year-old crofter-woman in Arran, page 123,
is worthy of more than a passing notice. We venture to
predict that as she stands out in that page, with a
vividness which the striking figure of the original could
not have excelled, she will live for years in the memory
of many a sympathetic reader who peruses the paragraph
devoted to her. In the description of Lochmaben, page
115, one cannot fail to recognise the versatility of the
writer's mind, the vein of scathing but good-humoured
sarcasm which he flings at the uninterested and uninteresting residents and their pigsties, aroused by the
neglect of those things which antiquarians hold sacred,
the lamentable ignorance of the sleepy and easy-going
villagers, of the doughty deeds to which they owe their
liberties, if not their very existence as entities in the
Scottish population of to-day, and the literary and
historical allusions which come to his pen as it opens
vistas to the reader's imagination that flit before him
with kaleidoscopic variety of interest.

The humorous sketch relating to the common, prosaic, and uninteresting donkey here inserted may be taken as a typical illustration of the way Shaw sometimes dealt with a subject which attracted his attention away from the main current of thought pervading an article—a dangerous and even fatal practice in a writer, unless the diversion be made with conspicuous ability. The paragraph was taken from an account of Ardrossan, for which space could not be found in this volume.

'Old as Damascus or Egypt, the ass is somewhat sacred in our eyes. Covered with crimson and gold, kings and judges bestrode it from the grey dawn of Time. The self-sufficient prophet, awful and oracular to princes, heard as much from its lips as made his starry theories fall in a moment around him, like the sparks of a rocket, for thou, poor pariah, wert more awful and oracular than he! Pleased with a thistle, bearing thy black cross with saintly patience, is there a lady in the land who has scalded her cheeks over *Uncle Tom's Cabin*, and yet has never subscribed a penny to emancipate thee? Who that has read *Don Quixote* will not thrash once in a lifetime one of thy many tyrants? Not alone every man with a sense of humour or of awe, but every angry man who has talked figurative language is thy debtor. Call your enemy a liar, he chuckles; lying and swindling are intellectual rope-dancing or sword-fence: but hurl at him the name of ass, and you have delivered a blow that flattens his skull. Sons of Eve, full of original sin and actual transgression, prating of "drunken beasts," "stupid asses," "cold-hearted reptiles!" well did Humboldt remark that the apes become more melancholy the nearer they approach in shape to man!' (*Vide* also page 280).

To realise how the righteous indignation of the man could be raised to white heat and smiting attitude by the ill-advised criticism of a superficial and 'obliquitous'

observer, the reader should turn to Shaw's defence of
Mauchline, page 131, and there he cannot fail to trace
the scores which well-directed ridicule leaves on what
remains of the offender. To touch upon other phases,
the description of Moniaive, page 39, is prophetic as well
as poetical. Since the time that he wrote that 'This
pretty rustic village seems to have been built entirely to
please the painters,' the beauty of the district has been
discovered by James Paterson, the artist, who has succeeded in adding to its local- a European- reputation.*

Shaw's remarks on the courtesies of debate not only
speak for themselves and claim a befitting eulogium, but
they accurately describe the methods he employed in
dealing with an opponent of his views on debatable
points in science and literature.

The Courtesies of Debate

'Like fruit with dinner, courtesy in a writer is grateful,
if it is not necessary. A man may write plain truths without being surly. Respect towards those who agree with
you, civility to those who disagree, is not inconsistent
with self-respect. There is a feeling abroad, that when
a person is zealously engaged to a certain sect or doctrine,
his most consistent policy is to meet his opponents with
strong language. If some writers do not believe that " a
cry is as good as a lift," they at least seem to believe it.
They are fond of a little stamping and hallooing. But
strong language is not always convincing language, and
it is a great matter to be able to instruct and convince.
I have an instinctive apprehension that there is something wrong when a man's letter to me becomes sonorous

* Suffice it to mention three of the well-known pictures alluded
to—'Borderland' (a free rendering of Glencairn), in the Glasgow
Corporation Gallery ; 'Spring's Delay' (in the Dalwhat Valley), at
the Weimar Gallery ; and 'Glencairn,' in the Gallery of Auck-
land, N.Z.

with closely-packed adjectives of praise or blame. A still greater vice of writers holding conflicting views is that of peering into the consciences and brains of their antagonists, and discerning all sorts of turpitude and dullness. Their opponents are set down as having some sinister purpose to serve, not quite apparent from their writing, but all the more dangerous because folded in mist. Against one having occasion to illustrate his theme by frequent Scripture reference, it is urged that he is a "pietist," who wishes to stand well with the old ladies of both sexes. Of another, speaking with paternal reverence of a wise man or book, whose value he has proved on manifold occasions, it is hinted that he is a hero-worshipper. Your reformer of church music is set on to it by Cardinal Wiseman. You use the word *liberty*, and it is translated *licence*. You speak of progress, and find to your astonishment that you are an infidel. This hasty classification will by no means convince an opponent, and neither affects the truth nor falsity of the argument.

'When my antagonist discovers that I ingeniously pervert arguments, that I am dishonest, that I invent facts for the sake of theories, that the old serpent is at my ear, I have my own opinion as to his second sight. "O my friend," I say, "you are full of virtue, you seem to have bought the article up entirely." Often, too, with such a person there is an assumption of your mental as well as moral frailty, and an exultation in his own strength. So a debater, admiring his own paragraphs, wonders that his opponents are so wilful as not to be straightway convinced, and soon finds ways and means to reduce the miracle which are anything but complimentary. Such blows are, however, but so much beating of the air. If your opponent is worth arguing with, he is acute to a degree, and it is not his character but his reasoning that is the question. It would be more be-

e

coming to assume his good intentions in every dubious
point than to provide him gratuitously with bad ones.
Vituperation is cheap, and to be met with at every street
corner. Error needs light rather than heat. That
orator was manly who blamed his own prolixity and
confusion for the drowsiness and misapprehension of his
audience. I would often prefer snarling cynicism to
French gallantry, but true courtesy holds the mean
between these, it looks not for angels and imps, not for
nabobs and gypsies, but for gentlemen and well-disposed
citizens. I should like to see more of this sort
of gallantry imported into debate, and less anxiety
to have every charge met, and to get as much talking
time as your neighbour. Sow your seed in trust,
if truth, not triumph, be your object. If the material
which composes your light be gathered with your utmost
painstaking, then, to borrow a metaphor, your spark may
be of guidance "when the dance is over, when the tallow-
dips and wax-candles are burnt out, and the brawl of the
night has gone to bed." Should accuracy, frankness,
and clearness of statement fail to secure the approbation
of an antagonist at the time, it may win his conviction by-
and-by. Discussion is an opportunity for explaining
principles; do not waste the occasion by imputing motives.
It is pleasant to see how often the houses of Parliament
are exemplary in this respect, whereas at the other end
of the social scale, the " yill-cup commentators," with
their unworthy insinuations and slanderous home-thrusts,
contrast unfavourably the speech of man with the utterance or the dumbness of animals.'—[1864.]

In the character sketch of the Duke of Argyll—one
of the 'celebrities we have seen,' our author strikes a
happy vein in individual portraiture. A thorough appreciation is shown of the central subject of the sketch,

and a sympathetic unison with the methods adopted by
His Grace in discussing the profundities of science and
religion in relation to each other. He is, in short, depicted as the beau-ideal of a public man who instinctively
understands and practises the courtesies of debate. A
very different opinion is expressed of the aggressive
individual who represents the counterpart of a social
medallion in the following pronouncement on 'how we
ride our hobbies.' In it some of the harmless or non-
vicious weaknesses of humanity are appropriately exposed.

How we Ride our Hobbies

'I take it that most men have a hobby, or, to use a
milder word, a predilection (which is a hobby in germ)
for some particular doctrine, scheme, or pursuit, that they
believe is for the public good. For the realisation of
such a theory lurking in their hearts, they would sacrifice
more than ever they have yet done. With some, who by
no means lack enthusiasm, there is combined a tact
which rounds their angles and reveals their motive-power
in a gentle manner. Others, again, rock to and fro,
jingling their small wares amazingly—often altogether
tumbling, hobby uppermost. When you thoroughly
understand a man's predilections, he is either much at
your service or at your mercy; at your service if his aims
be lofty and his means select, but somewhat at your
mercy if his vision be narrow and his object trifling.

'Waters, for instance, has been a most consistent teetotaller for very many years. He believes in the Pledge.
He is well-versed in the statistics of his subject, and views
it from different points. He has proved his earnestness
both by his purse and by his works, and has had the
reward dearest to his heart, in being instrumental in re-

deeming many from prodigality and misery. As a cook
can salt meat without betraying the presence of brine, so
this man's zeal for temperance warms, but never scalds.
Even Porter, who does not share such enthusiasm, rather
likes it in his friend, and, what is more, takes kindly to
the good man's society. When the two gentlemen meet,
they can dismount from their different horses to try the
paces of each other's. Though the one deals in liquids,
the other in solids, they can both give and receive. Their
very difference of pursuit causes piquancy and freshness
in the interchange of their thoughts. Or, perhaps,
setting aside what is nearest their hearts, they can talk of
other subjects dear to them both, and the sober hours
steal past in mutual improvement. For friendship can
shed a dew softer than that which makes roses burst into
bloom. Wisdom can inspire us so that we are forgetful
of wine. Sympathy soothes better than opiates.

'That is one way of preaching sobriety; that is the
quiet way of using the hobby. There is another preacher
and a different way. Words with this preacher are more
prominent than conduct. There is a lecturer and an
audience betimes that seem to think that the divine laws
which tend to rectify the ever-erring human will, which
punish and reward, and cause the coward to respect the
hero, the thief to look sideways from an honest face, the
sot to envy the sober and steady, have been only recently
discovered and applied. These are they to whom the
Temperance Movement is a Morrison's pill, a panacea
for educating the stupid, humbling the proud, melting
hard hearts, and improving constitutions, down to the
constitution of wooden legs, as Dickens puts it in *Pickwick*.
This lecturer, when seen on the street, makes you feel
as if the Maine Law were passing, and the era of temperance hymns about to supersede that of national songs;
and you hasten out of his way. By riding his hobby too

violently in all seasons, and without respect to the predilections of any one else, he has succeeded in making the
advocacy of his cause disagreeable. The Temperance
Movement, like all of us, has occasion to cry, "Save me
from my friends!" The old wife was sore urged to it
when she exclaimed, "That fallow's aye in a stew: he's
left off drinking, and noo he's taen to flyting."
Blatant denunciation of one party and its habits implies,
of course, commendation as loud of the morals of
another. When a papal bull is launched, the Church of
Rome says to its heretics, "Orthodoxy is my doxy, as sure
as heterodoxy is yours." The members of the League
become too amiable and enviable by reason of this their
servant. The public winces also, not liking always to be
abused, and getting rather overdosed, at length, of a
newly-washed sot giving an account of his sottishness,
even though his moral should be conspicuous as a tavern-
sign, or as an Egyptian skull at a banquet.

'Grant takes the direct road to Richmond, careless
of expense or blood; Napoleon achieves a crown by
a *coup d'état;* but there are other gains than cities
or crowns, and other methods than the hop-step-and-
leap or steeplechase method. The latter plan, however,
is popular with novices. Society is to be reformed by
the passing of some bill. Knowledge is to be made
easy and universal by new systems, by an entirely
different kind of newspaper, by new buildings, by
bursaries, by making books suitable or sufficiently
entertaining, so that Young England shall laugh and
grow fat and wise. It is by degrees that we learn
to distrust the forcing method. Poor old Society must
reform considerably at its own time and expense.
Knowledge, worthy of the name, we find never to be an
easy acquisition. No hot-house system can raise us a
gigantic plant like Newton, nor discover a law of gravi-

tation. The direct method of fighting a vice is to paint
those who indulge in it as monsters, those who abstain
from it as models, like the wearisome blackguards
and insipid but perfect beings of temperance prize-
novels. I have found bad boys rather glorying in
being called bad names. Vice, black and naked, is not
so formidable as vice mossed over with tender associations, evil with good closely interwoven, "thoughts
accusing or else excusing one another." I grant that
the steeplechase plan, the plan of fierce invective, of
strong light and shade, of stringent watching of persons,
or making every new offence a peg to hang a moral on,
or a call for legislating, may have a temporary success.
Oftener, however, it drives the disease from the surface
to the heart, thence to be rooted out, if rooted out at all,
by the "still, small voice," and the silent eloquence of
worthy and generous lives.

'I prefer the indirect way of combating evils, which so
often manifest themselves indirectly. I like the old-
fashioned parable better than the revival sermon. I am
more likely to strengthen my morals by reading of
drunkards and knaves as truthfully painted by Shakespeare and Burns, Thackeray and Dickens, than as
drawn by writers and lecturers whose imaginations are
not sober. Give me the quiet way of riding a hobby, and
let me take the roundabout road whenever I think it
the nearest or the best.'

POLITICS AND RECREATIONS

In politics Shaw was a Conservative, and in the latter
years of his life he frequently took part in political
meetings, and sent contributions to the local newspapers
on the subject of natural politics, but he did not appear to
advantage in this sphere. His pronouncements were

often very severe, and their tone was not characteristic of the man, if judged by his own standard in any other connection. The most interesting point about our author's politics is the fact—as he has already told us when discussing the tone of political feeling among the community of the young men with whom he associated in youth—that he and his companions 'were Fenians before Fenianism, and talked treason like the Reform Leaguers.' To end by becoming a thorough-going constitutionalist after holding views such as these, was truly a remarkable reversal of opinion, but, after all, the change—shall we say for the better?—in the man, was probably no greater than the change which had been brought about by wise legislation in the political and social condition of the country during the half century which has elapsed since he first took an interest in the subject.

Shaw's participation in games of recreation was confined to indoors. Whist, carpet bowls, chess, and at times draughts, were his favourite sources of amusement in this connection, and he happily contrived in the intervals of play to charm his associates with an interesting résumé of the subject-matter of the books he was reading, with the outline of some important scientific invention, or the leading features of some soul-absorbing theory, or some archæological discovery.

LETTERS BY SHAW TO FRIENDS

Shaw maintained an extensive correspondence with a wide circle of congenial spirits with whom he was able only at rare intervals to meet in the flesh. A perusal of a number of excerpts which have been culled from letters to a few of his most intimate correspondents will serve to illustrate interesting phases of character which do not appear in their genuine simplicity in his studied literary pro-

ductions. They also show how fully and profitably the
time was spent when he was thrown upon his own resources
in leisure hours. The extractions have been separately
grouped under the names of the different correspondents,
and as far as possible arranged in chronological order.

To the Reverend David Morrison—latterly of the
Tron Church, Edinburgh, and formerly of Durisdeer
Parish Church, in the Presbytery of Penpont, Dumfriesshire—the first group of four was addressed by our
author as his 'Dear friend,' a form of beginning which
was a favourite with him. (*Vide* Appendix D on *Hebrews.*)

To the Reverend David Morrison

'October 15, 1870.

'Have you seen the *Earthly Paradise*? Somewhere I fell
on the remark that when completed it would be the
longest poem in existence. Well, it would require to be
good, for evermore one's leisure is getting scarcer in
these days, when so many demands are made upon it.

'I read Ruskin's *Queen of the Air* during vacation—but
the war prevented me from getting much more done—
and it strikes me as being about as fine a little thing as
Ruskin has done, more popular and less technical than
many of his other works. I had the key of Barrhead
Library when I was up, and sat one whole day among their
books. Grote's *Plato*, Ruskin's *Stones of Venice*, Mill's
Logic, Froude's *Essays and History*, *Crab Robinson Diary*,
etc., etc. Scott never painted "Dominie Samson" half so
well to my satisfaction, as I felt after my day's surfeit—
sometimes with one foot on the ladder swallowing half a
chapter—stolen waters are sweet.

'I took none of them home with me but *Westward Ho!*,
which I only got half through when I left. I have
purchased Buckle's *Civilisation* for winter.

'John Laurie and I had a raid into the regions of

Virgil and Ovid last winter. This winter we have braced
up our sinews for a mighty attack on old Horace.

'Yestreen Anderson sent me the April No. of the
Fortnightly with Swinburne's Critique on Morris. As
you say, here's a pretty orchestra of them praising one
another. Such criticism gives fine chance for a snarling
article. Apart from the usual blasphemy of Swinburne,
there are passages in his criticism as poetic to me as in
Rossetti's *Sonnets*.

'I will give an explanation of my vacation occupation
when I see you.'

'Undated.

'I have not read all Rossetti yet, but when I read
Eden's Bower, I circulated round the table for a while as
if I had got a glass of champagne on an empty stomach.
I think it is very passionate, weird, and original. "Sister
Helen" is a very finished ballad, but I don't like the
chorus. Hell and Heaven are names by far too awful
and hallowed to be turning up continually as they do in
this chorus—as a matter of taste I would have it out.
Regarding "Jenny" I have some queer speculations.
Carlyle's essay on "Diderot" sternly forbids literary
treatment of such a subject, but nobody will deny that
it contains poetry.'

'June 16th, 1872.

'Since I last shook hands with you on that dripping
wet day I have made one new acquaintance. He is a
gentleman partner in a factory in Glasgow, where hair
for wigs, mattresses, etc., is manufactured or prepared,
but the chief interest appertaining to him in my eyes is
that he is the author of *Carmina Vitæ, and Other Poems*,
(London, Chapman & Hall), and that he has a splendid
library filled with modern books, which he has kindly
placed at my disposal. I did not like to be too greedy,
but the first thing I flew to was Morris's *Earthly Paradise*,

despite R. B.'s article on the Fleshly School, which I have
this day read for the first time in the Contemporary.
The original charm which presented itself to me in *Jason*
has continued in all its potency, and I am only glad that
I have some of the stories still to read. The charming
simplicity and rich poetic diction of the "Man Born to be
a King," "The Proud King," "The Writing on the
Image," enchanted me, and the story of the doomed
Acrisius seemed to me all excellently told; and as for the
charge of warmth, I suppose no great poet can exist
without having heat as well as light—witness Goethe,
Burns, Shakespeare, and David. I can't find Morris a bit
warmer or more luscious than Tennyson.'

'October 31st, 1893.

'I beg to send to you the three volumes of George
Meredith, and Geddes and Thompson on the *Evolution of
Sex*, which I have had in my possession too long. The
Egoist and *Diana of the Crossways* are most original, far-
seeing, poetical and interesting. Henry Richmond is
just a little too "jumpy," and, of course, has the drawback to an English reader of being a little foreign,
although this very drawback may be converted into a
push in the German market; moreover, it has a more
appreciable vein of humour, with its etherialised Micawber,
its "Salvation Army Captain," and its "gipsy girl and
school-life."

'With regard to *Evolution of Sex*, the poet thereof has
not yet arrived, but the book is well and learnedly
written, and the chapters on the ethical side have general
interest. Have you noticed how Professor H. Drummond
is gaining for himself notoriety by writing Evolution down
to the general reader? . . . I have purchased Sir George
Douglas's book on *Scotch Fairy Tales*, which will do for
my Halloween. If you have a complete set of Meredith,
I should like to see *Richard Feverel* or *Rhoda Fleming*. I

have sold a résumé of my Letter on "Sexual Selection"—
which appeared in the *Athenæum*, 1866, and which called
forth a note of admiration from Darwin—to *Chambers's
Journal*, and shall have great pleasure in forwarding you
a copy of the number in which the sketch appears.'

To James Rigg, of 18 Wilton Drive, Glasgow, his
holiday companion, correspondent and confidential friend
of many years' standing, the next six extracts from
lengthy epistles were addressed.

To James Rigg

· May 1869.

' I received yours, and took a look at the passage which
has puzzled you. There are two ways of dealing with it, I
think. First, call it simple nonsense, and allow Carlyle
to be one of those wisest men who make slips or write
with the pen and not with the mind betimes ; or, second,
taken with context, it may mean that a portion at least
of our very compound and complicated nature is always
obedient to our hero. Even a sinner, as long as he sins
with compunction, is so far worshipping a higher ideal than
his own vile action, and, as long as he sins on the sly,
worships the same, for "hypocrisy is the tribute vice pays
to virtue." You know that the latest theory of a human
being is—that it is a bundle of cells, each having an individual life, some of them having a plant-life, others an
animal life. The whole are bound together like the
individuals forming a nation. The brain cells are the
oligarchy which adjudicate and direct the others, and
hearken to their reports carried to them along the nerves
of sensation, and issue out orders along the nerves of
motion. When these brain cells are excised, as has
been done with a frog, then the next cells in rank,
namely, those of the spinal cord, take the lead. But not

being used to govern they do it in a very unbusiness-like way. For instance, touch a headed frog, and the cells touched communicate their sensations along the nerves of sensation to the brain cells, which in turn order through the nerves of motion that the muscles be contracted, and the frog leaps out of the way. Do the same with a pin point to a beheaded frog's leg and it no longer leaps—all that the cells of the spinal cord know about the matter is to order the leg to move.

'To carry out our ideas of duty is what we ought to do, and our ideas of duty are in the cells of highest rank. But other cells call loudly to have their wishes gratified, and like spoiled children get more tyrannous the more they get their own way—so that the sensations of taste, etc., marshal out the poor drunkard at their will. Nevertheless, he is not so bad as he would be, because what is called the higher nature is continually putting on the drag and does often rein him in altogether. Here is a new subject for you.

' Were the Lord to make this globe and the whole solar system, and yourself and everything you see, one-hundredth less than it really is, would you know any change in size ? All persons of whom I have asked this, think not. If, then, suddenly everything became one-tenth of what it is, so that you wakened next morning with your body and eyes and the hills, etc., one-tenth less in size—would you know ? I think not.

'Extend the idea. Say that the Lord suddenly made everything 1,000,000,000,000,000,000,000,000,000 less, so that one foot would no longer be a foot, but a foot divided by the given denominator, and the earth and solar system no bigger than a grain of sand, would you know that any change had taken place, and that you were less than an ant, if the same relative sizes of everything were kept? I think not.

'*Ergo*, space is only a mode of thought—an idea of the mind.'

'Tynron, Wednesday.

'My dear 1,000,000 of Cells—Yours is to hand, from which I was glad to sympathise in your views about Carlyle and Space, and glad to hear that the latter subject had presented itself to your mind, and that you are persuaded that the Lord is greater than space, but that the latter is merely an illusion, or symbol, or outward clothing of the Invisible Omnipotence. You put questions about the cells which I am right glad to answer.

'Why are vegetables less intelligent than animals ?

'Because in plants, each single cell surrounds itself directly with a membrane of the so-called cellulose, the substance which we have before us in cotton, in wood, and in paper. The cells are by means of this individually shut up ; they can, it is true, influence one another to a certain degree, in that they can transmit material to one another ; but they cannot influence one another to an unlimited extent, etc., etc.

'I find the following in John Stuart Mill's address to the students of St Andrews—

'"To know the truth is already a great way towards disposing us to act upon it. What we see clearly and apprehend keenly, we have a natural desire to act out.

'"To see the best and yet the worst pursue, is a possible but not a common state of mind. Those who follow the wrong have first, generally, taken care to be voluntarily ignorant of the right. They have silenced their conscience, but they are not knowingly disobeying it."

'Further to encourage you to take up the *cells*, here is another extract :—

'"Physiology is the first science in which we recognise the influence of habit, and get a clear notion of what is meant by development and evolution. The growth of a plant or animal from a simple cell-germ is the typical specimen of a phenomenon which rules through the whole course of the history of man and society, increase of function through expansion, and multiplication of different organs doing different work, for one general harmonious end."'

' October 23rd, 1894.

'I think you are improving your versification. The "Staghorn" is first-rate, so is "Dandelion Seed," and the "Pansy" is as instructive as the "Mistletoe." The nutting season has often been painted, but you have a word or two more to say of it.* Was there ever before such weather in September and October? I only enjoyed my cistern for a week after I came home. Now we cross Shinnel to Glover's Well, but even pure Shinnel Water is not to be sneezed at. . . . If you purchase or get a look at the *Agnostic Journal* for Saturday last, you will see a reply to my "Lazarus." I guess it to be from the pen of the minister of Rothesay. I have forwarded an answer. . . . Just what an advanced Christian may write. . . . I have purchased Atkinson's *Forty Years in a Moorland Parish* (second-hand copy). It is very good. I am reading Dean Milman's *History of Christianity*. There is a deal of information in it. The Dean is often on the verge of being heterodox, but skates well within the boundary. . . . I shall entrust you with a commission. Purchase for me a bound volume of *Good Words* for 1881, in which my "Article for Boys and Girls" appears. I am pretty sure it is 1881, but make yourself certain before you buy it, and I shall send you a postal order. I gave it away some years ago—I mean the volume which I had, —as a marriage present to a lady friend who admired the article.'

---

* Rigg's *Wild Flower Lyrics* (A. Gardner, Paisley) was very favourably reviewed.

'October 17, 1895.

'I had a night with Professor R. Wallace. He has travelled some thousand miles in South Africa, and had many photos. Some of those of bushmen naked suggest our poor cousins. Have you seen a little shilling book, Clodd's *Primitive Man*, well illustrated? What a striking pair are the two restorations of the Ancestors of Man in the frontispiece!

'I had a call from Tom Brown.* He is still an observer. He says that he observed a strange case of *Commensalism*. It was a nest formed by a chaffinch in the fork of a thorn tree, in which a hedge sparrow came and laid its eggs as well as the chaffinch. He was watching with great interest whether the one would eject the other, or whether they would relieve each other at incubation, when by came a jay and ate and destroyed the eggs. He tells me that in Hertfordshire jays harry nests far more than mischievous boys do. Nightingale, redbreast, skylark's eggs are all the prey of the monster.'

'March 11th, 1896.

'Yours was duly received, and I was not a little surprised that you were still clinging to Wilton Drive. Nevertheless, if you have no garden of your own, you have the Botanical Garden at your feet, so go boldly forth and feast at Flora's banquet; thou art the called—the rest admitted with thee.

'I have been looking over R. S. Mutch's poems,† and find that my first criticism addressed to you was really a little too hard. There are a few short lyrical pieces addressed to children, which are really very pretty.

'Anderson, poet, seems to have been highly pleased by my comparison of his lays on children to Swinburne's,

* Farm manager to The Marquis of Salisbury at Hatfield.
† *Ballads and Poems*, by Robert Mutch, once schoolmaster at Woodside, Penpont, and then near Portree, in Skye.

because he wrote a short poem to me at the New Year, humorous and lively, which I have not yet answered.

'I had a letter from John Lindsay a few days ago. Alas! for us all, "We and ours are bound to death." His hand, never good, is now almost unreadable, but his mind is cheery, and he says Sir W. Scott would have eagerly interested himself in my collection of "Folk Riddles."

'About eight days ago I was in a new capacity. I appeared as a performer in both Part I and Part II of a programme. It was a concert at Wallace Hall Academy, Closeburn. We had a strong band, and a toy symphony, and quartettes. I gave them my story in the *Bailie* with new flourishes, "The Gowk's Errand." In the programme it was printed thus :—

Recital by Mr Shaw, " The Gowk's Errand,"   *Shaw.*
" Whistle and I'll come to you," Song, Mrs Robson,   *Burns.*

My delivery brought down the 600 feet to the floor with awful thuds. " Nae fools like auld fools."

'My great annual carpet bowl party comes off on Friday evening. I wish you could come. The Misses Reid [who at one time lived at Shinnelwood] made me some beautiful presents when they left—highest style of painting and needlework.'

'May 11th, 1896.

'That was an interesting trip you had with the Naturalists to Calder Glen, Lochwinnoch, which I was once in long before my mind had been wakened up to many of Flora's mysteries and beauties. Of your late effusions perhaps the one on the "Scarlet Pimpernell" pleased me best; of course the "Nursery Rhymes" were written to fill up an idle hour. I had a fifteen-mile constitutional with J. Shanks and J. Bell on 2nd May.

'Did I tell you I was lecturing to the Dumfries Branch of the Educational Institute of Scotland, on 18th April, on "Delusions, Popular and Fatal." I had the best meeting that has hitherto been held in Annan, and gave them fifty minutes with great unction. The majority afterwards dined in the Queensberry Arms, I being guest on the right of the chair.

'Surely this is Egyptian weather. Yesterday and Saturday skies Italian. I am happy to say that 29th is suitable. But what do you mean by 5.20? The train arrives on Friday evening at Thornhill at 6.21. You could perhaps be at the trouble of bringing me two small pots with ferns in them from a house at the foot of Buchanan Street — the Osmunda and Holly or Green Spleenwort preferred, as they do not grow here. I shall plan a fine circular, and we shall all pray for a fine day.'

This communication, dated November 11th, 1894, was sent to Robert Service, who, like the next correspondent, Paterson, is already known to the reader.

To Robert Service

'James Hewison, minister of Bute, made me believe that an adder-bead was exceeding rare. He said he would give £1 for one; so that he ought to be a good customer to Smith of Townhead. I did not purchase mine, however, at so high a figure, although I gave the old lady a few shillings for it, which she was much in need of. James Paterson and I went to Craigdarroch on Saturday [to examine the tumuli]. We got a fine day. I should say that the mounds are about two miles above Craigdarroch, almost on the watershed, between that glen and Dalwhat. Captain Robt. Archibald and Miss Dormer with the gamekeeper, made a party of six, but blackcock shooting was one-half of it. To me, leaving Tynron, it was rather fatiguing, and I can see it would need a day when the sun is much longer above the horizon to do

f

some work. We saw about a dozen mounds at no great distance. They were like cairns of stones. In some places the weight of the stones had rather sunk the ground, and they were flat, but mostly rather circular and a little raised above the surface. I believe there would be between twenty and thirty of them. The stones were mostly angular, and about two feet took you to the bottom. I think they must be artificial, but I have little experience of such things.

'You recollect a Dr Callander reading a paper on a Roman camp at Dunscore, so the past is represented. Some of the flat mounds or sunken circles looked very like those once pointed out to me at the base of Cairnkinna, parish of Penpont.

'In Brand's *Popular Antiquities*, Vol. III., is a good deal of information about adder-beads, and the story about them is much the same as that given out by the octogenarian lady here. (*Vide* Appendix B.)

'I thought the Marquis of Salisbury's speech at Edinburgh read well. I had an antiquarian pointing me out the old wall and other curiosities in Edinburgh in September.'

James Paterson has also been good enough to supply the following evidences of Shaw's attention to his friends at a distance :—

To James Paterson

'Dec. 20th, 1893.

'I cannot too much thank you for the beautiful volume, which, I am sure, I neither expected nor deserved. It was safely delivered by the post to-day, which must be a lucky day, since it gave me the present of *Peel* in the English Statesman Series from our clergyman, together with oranges for the school children from Mrs C. . . . Have you seen Sir John Lubbock's delightful little book on the *Beauties of Nature?* It betrays poetic appreciation, and at the same time is packed with information like an egg with meat. I see Rev. J. H. Hewison's *History of Bute* favourably reviewed in the *Scotsman*.'

'Nov. 11th, 1894.

'I have read with much pleasure the answer to his own question given by Professor Jebb. If I could have gathered together words and illustrations such as he has done, my verdict would have been similar. Truth first, and very likely the moral suggestion is contained in the picture. The decadence of serious belief in the mythology of Greece in the days of Pericles is well brought out. George Eliot in the *Spanish Gypsy* accentuates the similar waning away of darker and harsher views after the fall of Constantinople, when the children of the Renaissance sprung up, when the sculptured heads of the ivy-crowned Bacchus confronted the pale image with the crown of thorns (*vide* pp. 12, 13.)

'While we are at the gates of theology, and while Mrs Paterson is adding to her religious library, I beg to send you an excerpt starting, so far as I am aware, an entirely new difficulty, of which we are likely to hear more, as I understand more than one clever young clergyman are brooding over an answer which, should any one of them be published, I shall be happy to supply you with—*the Raising of Lazarus*. It is a quarter of a century since I read W. H. Lecky's extremely clever book on the *Rise and Influence of Rationalism in Europe*, written when he was twenty-six. I intend to have a look at it again, because I recollect his stating that earliest Christian Art represented Our Lord as very ugly. "More marred than any man," etc. You know the passage thus too literally represented. I have not since seen the subject alluded to. Almost I was afraid to feel how glad I was getting over these hills with Luna and Mars for comrades last evening.

I feel a little tired to-day, so have played truant, and am
working up a lot of correspondence.'

'Dec. 12th, 1895.

'Your letter received. I read last night "Raleigh on
Stevenson," and also the drama "Admiral Guinea."
Raleigh's criticism of it is excellent. I have hardly so
keen a nose for *style* as many of Stevenson's *critics*. I am
not aware that any novel of Sir Walter's was the less
fascinating to me on account of the fustian. The
imagery, the romance, and the delineation of character
with pithy or humorous turns of expression suffice.
Dickens has an extraordinary originality as a humorist.
But as a sentimental writer I never liked him, not even at
the death of poor Nell. My reading of Stevenson is
Tunstall Abbey, Treasure Island, Kidnapped, Catriona. I
liked the two middle ones, but have not read the *Master of
Ballantrae*, which I must try. Raleigh's remarks are
fraught with insight, and very interesting. Yes, I have
read the strange story of *Dr Jekyll and Mr Hyde*, which I
think your friend hardly values at its true price.

'I have finished the *Men of the Moss Hags*—Crockett. I
cannot say whether it is better than the *Raiders*, but there
is more history in it. Of course he sings to a popular
tune when he takes up the Covenanters, and some of his
scenes in both novels are sensational enough. We must
pardon a most melodramatic ending of *Moss Hags* as one
of the necessities of the novelist. It helped up the sale of
Adam Bede, and caused it to be read by thousands who
would not read it for what we read it for.

'I read *Marriage*, by Miss Ferrier, lately. She is buried
with De Quincey in St Cuthbert's Churchyard, Edinburgh.
Both Austin and Ferrier drag after the modern gingery
ones. But both are worth reading. Do you know anything of *Pater* or of *Coventry Patmore*? I confess here I
am dull.'

Of a large number of letters which the present Writer
received from Shaw, only the three annexed fragments are
now to be found. The first of these is of special interest
owing to the information it gives of the different forms
assumed by his contribution on 'The Mental Progress of
the Devil.'

'Dec. 27th, 1894.

'I am afraid some catastrophe must overtake you. Two
of your schoolmasters* writing in the *Agnostic Journal!*
Therefore would advise you strongly to get married and
leave these handsome sums at your decease to a nice
widow, whose relations will rejoice that you have cut up
well. That means a young one, of course, so as to make
the probabilities of the enjoyment of your funeral pyre all
the greater!

'Curious history that of my "Satan." First announced
to the world in humorous verse in the *Bailie*, then begged
by Service that I would allow him to put these verses into
a character's mouth in his novel of *Novantia* † in *Good
Words*. Thoughtlessly I gave away my money without
asking for a receipt, and I have no doubt some carping
critic will discover that the prose article which Anderson
[The Surfaceman] and you enjoyed is cribbed from
Service!

'Strange in one house where my leaflet happened to
arrive, Miss Macleod, daughter of the great Norman,
heard it read and was immensely interested in it. I
should never like to be rude, which the article isn't.
"Saladin" writes like an ogre.

'I sent a newspaper with Dumfries news to the Egyptians,‡ but have heard nought. . . . I fear, I fear that

* The schoolmaster other than Shaw referred to here is William
Stewart Ross, editor of the *Agnostic Journal*, who writes as
'Saladin.'
† *Novantia* appeared in 1874: republished as *Lady Hetty* in 1875.
‡ Members of the family resident in Egypt.

the pleasing anxious being of Stevenson has "left the
warm precincts of the cheerful day."'

                                      'Nov. 29th, 1895.

'I received from you a copy of the *Times* of 14th curt.,
with a letter of yours of some length on a subject of much
importance.   I shall try to find out to what extent
farmers like S. Brown [Bennan] and W. Tyre [Ma-
queston], sympathise with your views, and shall be happy
if your letter be generally accepted by farmers and vets
as a valuable contribution to the subject of tuber-
culosis.

'A hedgehog came into my school nearly a month ago.
I fed it on milk, egg, porridge, loaf-bread in milk, and had
a box for it to lie in.   It took food occasionally at night,
and slept in the box through the day.   Sometimes we got
it lying in the ash-pit, which it coveted evidently for the
heat.   All at once, this morning, one of the boys poking
into the box discovered it was dead, and I was rather surprised and annoyed.

'Miss Gladstone of Lannhall was here to-day trying the
children's religious instruction and giving them some con-
fections and nuts.   We are to have a Christmas tree and
tea for them on the 19th.'

                                      'Jan. 6th, 1896.

'Many thanks for your present of Joseph Laing
Waugh's little book [*And a Little Child Shall Lead Them*],
which is charmingly got up.   It is far from being an
inferior first story, and in the sketch of old Hastie there
is room for our supposing that he may develop a fund of
humour of which we have got a very small foretaste.
Frank Murray Dacre is sometimes too much of a saint for
my liking, and how typhus fever came with such a leap in
a healthy country home, except for the exigencies of a
novel writer, I cannot quite understand.   In return I beg
to send you a sketch for which I received payment in the

People's Friend. You will find it at p. 830 with my name attached.

'Hoping 1896 has begun graciously with you, etc.'

Shaw was not only a voluminous writer, but, as may be gathered from the specimens of his work which have been reproduced in this volume, he wrote on a great variety of subjects.   Indeed, in these days of specialists the fact will, no doubt, be regarded by some as a weak point in our author's position as a scientist.   Some subjects, such as Evolution, Right- and Left-handedness, The Beauty of Birds, The Mental Progress of the Devil, he took special interest in, and after considerable intervals of time, issued new editions of his papers on them.   The method of treating the subject last mentioned is unique and interesting, and as it was specially referred to in his correspondence (*vide* page lxxxv), and as the prose version could not be found until too late for incorporation in the main body of the letterpress, it is introduced here at length.

Mental Progress of the Devil

'One of the earliest theologians I have fallen in with who applied the great law of mental progress to the Devil was the pious Samuel Rutherfurd, minister of Anwoth, whose tall monument, half-a-mile from the church, is the pride of a poor but picturesque locality in Galloway.   In the seventeenth century the idea appeared to be in the air, and Buckle, in his *History of Civilisation*, Vol. III., has collated quotations from sermons and other sources bearing on this subject.   The gist of these quotations is that the Devil is an advancing student and still learning, there being no traces of senility in him, although so old. It is averred by several old Scotch divines that he is exceedingly knowing, partly by the quickness of his nature, and partly by the length of his experience. Six thousand years have not passed over him in vain. Compared to man, he has many advantages in the way of education. "He is more subtile, as being of greater experience, and more ancient. He is an ingenious and experimented spirit, of an excellent substance, of great natural parts, long experience, and deep understanding."

'We agree with these worthy old Scottish divines. If Sir John Lubbock's wasp, if Hengler's horses, if the late G. J. Romanes' monkey, if the last chimpanzee at the Zoo, not to speak of fallen man, be amenable to education, it would be highly illogical to deny that the teaching of experience did not help to brighten up the parts of an archangel whose excess of glory had suffered eclipse. Admitting a personal devil, we must admit also of a devil making mental progress.' *

> "Old Samuel Rutherfurd used to say
>   That the devil got cleverer every day;
>   Six thousand years had come and gane,
>   And left their impress on his brain.
>   At first he could but grope his way,
>   And wi' awkward plans get at his prey;
>   But now he steps softly as a cat,
>   And watches warily as a rat,
>   And can make a cover like a fox.
>
>   His head that at first got many knocks,
>   And his wings that flaffed too loud by far
>   Are improved—now his head's as clear's a star,
>   And his wings are as noiseless as a bat,
>   And he hides his horns wi' a satin hat;
>   And has sorted, they tell me, his ain club-foot,
>   And can dance a waltz in a patent boot,
>   For an auld deil canna be like a young,
>   And is bound to wag a wilier tongue.
>   King Robert Bruce and Fred the Great
>   Improved in war at a rapid rate;
>   And Gladstone, Diz, and Bobby Lowe,
>   Have improved in tongue-fence, sure but slow;
>   And the deil, wi' mair capacious brain,
>   Has left behind the tricks o' a wean,

* The following lines (referred to on page lxxxv) appeared as 'A New Idea for Theologians.'

Has heard new sermons, read new books—
Got better bait and line and hooks—
Kens what a mitrailleuse can do,
And has seen our telegraph wires bran new,
And's owre auld a cat to jump at a strae,
And owre auld a wean to scream at a flae.

O reader, just think what you'd be yoursel',
Were your years as many—your pow as bel',—
Your baffled schemes sae oft renewed
Wi' perseverance so great pursued,
Wi' 'prenticeship o' some thousand years,
And a pair o' average eyes and ears,
And wits, made quick wi' many a thwart,
You'd be king o' the black, or any art;
And be sic a journeyman, now, 'tis clear,
As never the like did on earth appear.

Ergo, the deil's far 'cuter now
Than when he kicked up the foremost row.

Sae I hope when we've got our scores to pay,
At the end of the game, at the end of the day,
Account will be ta'en wi' whom we've played;
For now-a-days it may well be said,
That our wiliest carle's a green young chiel,
When matched wi' the auld experienced deil."

'This idea of an immortal enemy of mortal man is exceedingly uncomfortable. Indeed, it might well smite the timid Christian with despair. Grote, the historian, thinks that the influence of Alexander the Great was inimical to the good of humanity, and that it was well he died in Babylon prematurely. Had he continued his career of conquest and destruction, and turned his arms to the West after laying the East at his feet, he might have strangled in its cradle that Rome and that Italy to which Europe is so much indebted. But no death after a debauch ever awaits Satan. There is no interruption to his diabolical tactics or to his nefarious conquests. No doubt humanity, both as an individual and as a series of generations, profits also by experience, and in this respect may become more sagacious and wary, and more ready to see through the wiles and anticipate the movements

of its mightiest foe. But the progress of the two con-
tending parties is not at the same speed, nor is that of
humanity so uniform as that of its antagonist. Human
life is short, devil life is long. The slow gains of
generations are frequently swept away by famines,
diseases, earthquakes, or, more deadly still, by hordes of
barbarians. Civilisation has thus too often to begin
anew. In the face of this we have the arch enemy of
mankind possessed of the transcendent gift of unlimited
time in which to mature his plans, mend his nets,
quicken his allurements, conceal his traps, sugar his
poison, disguise himself more and more artistically as an
angel of light. Truly, when he looks back on his former
self he must bewail many a lost opportunity for black-
guardism; he must grin at his initial cobwebs as but
poorly spun, and despise his old elf-arrows. If he takes
a minute's respite from concocting mischief, doubtless it
is to mourn over game that could have been bagged and
souls that could have been netted in the days of his
apprenticeship to his infernal trade.

'The importance of this factor of time lends itself by
illustration when we consider what might have happened
had less of it been granted to beings more happily constituted than Satan. Had Shakespeare died young, he
would have been famous for some erotic verses and a few
second-class plays. The mighty productions of his
riper years, "Hamlet," "Macbeth," "The Tempest," and
some of his most delightful comedies, would have
been lost to the world. Had Sir Walter Scott died
prematurely, he would have left us some spirited poetry
and an unfinished MS. of *Waverley* lying in a desk
beside some fishing-tackle; in short, he would have been a
star and not a sun. Suppose the Greek Plato had lived on
into the nineteenth century, no oracle of Delphi would now
be more earnestly and reverently consulted. He would be

a Colossus of such learning and genius as to sway our destinies as Gulliver swayed those of Lulliput. Mommsen gives us the impression that the daggers plunged into Julius Cæsar were daggers which made humanity stagger backwards some furlongs into chaos. Carlyle thinks the horrors of the French Revolution might have been toned down had Mirabeau survived.

'Every year we sigh over graves that close upon learning and wisdom, until we are ready to exclaim over our lost one, as King Lear did over his strangled Cordelia :—

> " Why should a dog, a cat, a rat, have life,
> And thou no breath at all?"

Nations fare no better. Not to speak of the dry rot or foreign irruption which ruined empires from Assyria downwards, consult Lecky's *Rise and Influence of Rationalism* for nascent, promising civilisations quenched by persecution. He pricks a hole in the old proverb that the blood of the martyrs was the seed of the Church. Bagehot's *Physics and Politics* makes us believe that the victory of Marathon was but a fluke, and had Marathon been lost, Europe to-day would have been another China.

'These instances may show how precarious and interrupted are the triumphs of that which is good, beautiful, true, interesting, and humane, compared with the steady gains of Lucifer, and not of him alone, but of his legions of angels which he has in leash, ready for consultation or devastation ; for, as iron sharpeneth iron, the fiend's wit is sharpened by the fiends. Industrious beings all of them, as old Hugh Latimer preached ; and their master early up and late a-bed, never a day but either between the stilts of his plough, or sowing, or reaping, or thrashing ; curious thrashing, too, preserving the husks and injuring the grain.

'Two thousand years ago the conflicts between the Devil
and Humanity were as equally poised as that between
Hannibal and Scipio; to-day we may calculate they are as
one-sided as that between Pizarro and Atahualpa. The
Peruvians melted away before the Europeans, because
they had not experience enough in the battle of life,
either hereditary or immediate, to enable them to cope
with their destroyers. It was like the case of carnivorous
quadrupeds introduced into islands that contained wing-
less birds. A few ounces more of astuteness, a little
better organisation of arts and arms, and these children
of the Sun might have held their own. In Satan's
simpler boyhood many a man who has succumbed
to him in London would have got off with barely a
scratch in Mesopotamia. It was well for father Abraham
to live when the great tempter's arrows had more misses
and fewer hits.

'What is to be done in our distress when the progressive development of humanity cannot keep pace
with the mental progress of the Devil ? Shall he be
allowed to accumulate his captives, and to go on building
new wings to his intolerable gaols? One would have
liked to have heard his after-dinner speech when he got
(*pace* Professor Beesly) Tiberius made the master of
the world. Even then he had his crosses, for neither his
Bible-reading, his logic, his miraculous power of showing
two sides of a sphere at once, nor, above all, his amazing
capacity of crushing a month's work into a moment of time,
could avail him against one who proclaimed and proved
himself greater than Solomon. But the conflict was so
arduous that the Victor was in danger of succumbing when
angels arrived and assisted him to recover (Matt. iv. 11).
In our great need, then, let us plead from every pulpit in
the land, that Michael, Gabriel, and every available
angel and archangel, cherub and seraph, be sent to hold

this Satan, ever increasing in cunning, and his tributary fiends at bay. Angel and ministers of grace defend us in the unequal strife, otherwise the torch of truth and the flame of piety may be blown out by the accursed breath of those immortal enemies who cannot help their brains growing at a quicker pace than those with whom they are at strife.

'On another occasion, when the Church had handed over to Satan nearly the whole population of the new world, and when, if he had been anything but the inexorable Prince of Darkness that he is and *no* gentleman (for he has not a spark of gallantry in his nature, witness Eve, Mary Magdalen, children unbaptised), he would have set these simple Peruvians, after being brutally used on earth, to 'some hill apart' in hell, where they could have hummed in ghostlier tones their artless songs sung to the motion of their sickles. But we dare not trust him thus far. His unexpected elation was shortly afterwards abated. Luther vanquished him with an inkstand. Next to angels, let us pray for inkstands. They have done a great deal of good work in paring his claws.

'Our last remedy must be to appeal to Rhadamanthus when our good and evil deeds are weighed in his balance. A heavy percentage must be deducted from these last, on the day of reckoning, to us moderns, from the fact of our playing out the game against a cleverer antagonist than either patriarchs or fathers played with. Under severe scrutiny and disentangling of motives many a seeming goat may be turned into a sheep. The difference of doom is so tremendous that no stone should be left unturned to prevent us from falling either into Dante's or the Devil's hell.'—*The Agnostic Journal*, 24th Nov. 1894.

On 11th January 1895, the copy of the foregoing

article sent to the present writer was followed by this characteristic post-card :—

'To take away the taint left by the article on the Adversary, look at *Chambers's*, 29th December 1894, for my discourse on " Beauty." Do you know I think a good history of the Devil would pay if one could get a proper artist. There is a head of prehistoric man in *Good Words* for January which could act as model for the Tempter of the earlier races. We could have Dante's, Shakespeare's, Milton's, Peden's, Burns', D's. In Paisley Exhibition this year, I saw a clever picture of him up a tree fishing, a bag of coins at the end of his line.—J. SHAW.'

SHAW AS A POET

A short and evidently hastily prepared biographical notice of Shaw appeared in Murdoch's *Scottish Poets* in 1883.

It must be admitted that the quality of his poetical work is lacking in uniformity, but his effusions are delightfully human, and in many there are passages of striking poetic beauty, while in others, touches of real life, of humour, and of refined feeling are abundantly conspicuous. What could be more original, yet true to Nature, than his 'Sonnets on Animals'; what more majestically solemn than 'Deep Solitude' and 'Winter'; what more heroic than 'Scotland's Name and Scotland's Fame'; what more light and airy than 'We're a' Mismarrowed Thegether'; what filled more with pawky humour than his metrical version of 'The Biter Bit'; what more patriotic than 'Bannockburn'; and what more tenderly romantic than 'The Beloved'?

BANNOCKBURN

And this is Bannock, down whose side
Fair autumn pours her golden tide !
The reapers ply their ardent toil,
And store in peace the precious spoil ;

While, rising from the gentle rill,
A thriving village clothes the hill,
Whence, as we pause, in cheerful hum
The sounds of toil and pleasure come,
From buoyant youth, from sober age,
From maiden fair and matron sage,
All mindless that the turf they tread
Blooms o'er the ashes of the dead,
That where *they* ply the busy loom
Their fathers found a glorious tomb,
And Scotland's blood-bought freedom rose
From the loved vale where Bannock flows.

Yes, gazing here we fondly turn
To that bright page of Scottish story
That links for aye with Bannockburn
The memory of her ancient glory.
Here still we view the earth-fast rook
Which Bruce to fix his standard chose,
Round which, in fierce protracted shook
The eddying conflict sunk and rose,
Till England quailed, and Edward proved
How weak are numbers, valour, birth,
Opposed to patriot Scotsman moved
To strike for country, home, and hearth.

Those times are gone : five hundred years
Have swept that scene of blood and tears ;
Southron and Scot, no longer foes,
Have blent the thistle with the rose,
And on the fields of ancient strife
Mix in the toils of peaceful life.
Yet, gentle stream, the spirit lives
Which to thy name its lustre gives ;
And should an envious foe profane
The humble turf that crowns thy shore,
Thy patriot sons would rise again
Strong as their sires in days of yore ;
And nerved by freedom, virtue, right,
Rush to the field, nor thence return,
Till, victors in the glorious fight,
They stood once more on Bannockburn.

THE BELOVED

In the depth of burning kisses,
  Nought except your eyes for light,
Bosom gleaming through your tresses,
  As through silken threads of night.

Night the while so calm and lonely,
  Deep amid the amorous grove,
One bird singing snatches only,
  And those snatches dreams of love.

In that hour of deep confiding
  Tears and blushes, hopes and fears,
Hands that trembled when dividing,
  Moments that were felt like years.

In that hour of sweet emotion,
  For which one might live and die,
When the heart in fond devotion,
  Sigh'd to smile, and smiled to sigh.

When the moonbeams, over zealous,
  Burst through clouds to kiss your cheek,
And the flowers around so jealous,
  Bend their little heads so meek.

While such perfumed air as rises,
  From the violet's purple breast,
Wildly other lips entices,
  On your own to seek their rest.

Could you blame me if with gladness,
  I could only overflow,
Till my love grew almost madness,
  And my transport bent to woe.

Night and day I had been doating,
  Night and day my soul been torn,
You were ever o'er me floating,
  On the rosy clouds of morn.

Now the shadow of my dreaming,
  Clasped me with all human charms,
And the angel coldly gleaming,
  Blushed a maiden in my arms.

True it is, that I may never
  With you either meet or part,
But forgive me if forever
  I must hold you in my heart.

LITERARY EXTRACTS

CHAPTER I

TYNRON

THE case of an individual who had been transplanted from the city to a house in Tynron became known to us. 'I am placed here,' he said, 'in a glen so beautiful, that, if a weak poet came to visit it, he would gush into verse, while a strong one would acknowledge that words cannot express the loveliness of Nature.' We thought our acquaintance a wag, as we had never heard of Tynron before, and dreamt that he was writing us from Ireland, and had misspelt the word 'Tyrone.' Since then we have got better posted-up in Dumfriesshire, and endorse the same opinion. Iris, flying through the sky, left the rainbow as a vestige of her track: so one fine day which we spent in Tynron, whose hours were indicated by the shadows of hills and trees, instead of by the ringing of

A

bells and the clatter of commerce, has left, after it has gone, a bright image on the mind.

The sheltered position of the glen of the Shinnel makes the larch trees straight, and adds another month to the length of summer. Tynron abounds both in much natural wood and in larch plantations. The trees follow the roads and streams, and so in autumn and early winter, Nature, like a rich and fashionable housewife, is enabled to throw down a new carpet of coloured leaves on the highway, or lay a fresh delicate border on the margins of the streams, every succeeding week, as the frost nips successively the plane tree and beech, then the oak, the ash, and the larch. The woods of Tynron are not large undefinable masses, but are pleasantly sprinkled amid green pastures, on the slopes of hills, and are gay in spring with the blossoms of the wild cherry, in autumn with the berries of the rowan. Then there are circular clumps in the meadows, which, when highly coloured as they were a month ago, contrasted strongly with the verdant sea of turnips around. On the parish road by the dykeside, sturdy patriarchs shake hands overhead, while others confer together in semicircles on some rising knoll midway up the park; perhaps marking out the old site of cot or farm-steading, for the sheep-farmer is here yearly diminishing both the population and the arable land.

We have traversed the glen of the Yarrow, and noted what the Ettrick holds out to the wanderer. We have read the old ballads and much modern poetry concerning these two glens; but Tynron, we have found, in all but its traditions, not a whit behind them. Wordsworth's poems on Yarrow are inimitable, but they suit Tynron nearly as well:

> ' Fair scenes for childhood's opening bloom,
>   For sportive youth to stray in;
> For manhood to enjoy his strength,
>   And age to wear away in.'

In the one glen as in the other, you may wish for a minstrel's harp

> 'To utter notes of gladness,
> And chase this silence from the air
> That fills my heart with sadness.'

In the parish of Tynron are two hamlets, one clustered around the pretty parochial church. The church, and the bridge beside it, are new; and, since the recent improvements by John Kennedy,* the laird [who died in 1866], the village is innocent of a single thatched house. The turnpike and parish roads here cross each other at right angles. The fine houses of Kirkland, Land Hall, Dalmakerran, and Stonehouse lie smiling around. The manse is cawed over by clouds of 'crows' (rooks), the glebe containing a cluster of lofty trees black with their nests. Further down the Shinnel, the Milton glows with hollyhocks and roses, and listens to the music of Aird's Linn—another Habbie's Howe. On a stupendous crag, overlooking the parish church, the farm-house of Auchengibbert is perched

> ' Like an eagle's nest, upon the crest
> Of the purple Apennine.'

The churchyard is in a breezy situation, and towers above the chimneys of the hamlet. The Celtic names of places on the tombstones would warm a highlander's heart like the sight of the tartan. Two miles farther up the glen, where the rough old drove-road from Sanquhar to Moniaive crosses the parish road near the schoolhouse, the capacious houses of Bennan and Maqueston peep at each other across the strath, lively with 'crows,' geese,

---

* This is the laird of whom it was related, at the time it was proposed to introduce a heating apparatus into the parish church, that he waggishly retorted, ' The glow of the gospel has done the heating in the past, and is ample alike for the present and the future.'

turkeys, and such like. Tall Killiwarren, with walls of enormous thickness, after long remaining a roofless ruin, has left off doing the picturesque, and is now a comfortable farm-house. The parish school is so completely beyond the reach of bells, that we hope its inmate will not commit Robinson Crusoe's mistake of losing a day. Near Strathmilligan, the last otter of Glenshinnel was espied, as lonely at midnight as a waning moon. From Auchenbrack to Appin, and all around the schoolhouse, the scene is Arcadian in the highest degree.

> 'Bleateth the sheep—the horns of Elfland blow:
> Smelleth the fir—the axe of the woodman ringeth:
> Ebbeth and floweth the water's sound—boundeth the deer.'

Knockelly, the other parish hamlet, would have done Sir Walter Scott's heart good. The mighty minstrel has been known to make a circuit to have the pleasure of crossing a ford rather than a bridge. To this day his grave is approached by a ford. Knockelly is also separated from the world by one, although it is nearly as stirring and has as many shops as the village of Tynron-Kirk.

Near Knockelly is Hogg's farm of Laight. The Ettrick Shepherd made a bad job of his farm. The messenger of woe arrived six times in one day while James was fiddling to himself in the farm-house. 'Maister, there's anither sheep got deed.' 'Skin't,' was the laconic reply; and then a neater set of the bow, and a fiercer attempt to master some coy sweetness. The Duke of Queensberry was very kind to Hogg, as was the Duchess of Buccleuch, who obtained for him on her deathbed the farm of Altrive rent-free. Around Knockelly and Laight is scenery from which he may have painted in his singularly weird poem of 'Kilmeny,' especially in the description of Kilmeny's coming back, Lazarus-like, from another world, after her mysterious disappearance, her speech an echo of its celestial harmony, and her face and forehead a faint reflection of its unspeakable purity and calm.

> ' Late, late in a gloamin' when a' was still,
> When the fringe was red on the western hill,
> The wood was sere, the moon i' the wane,
> The reek o' the cot hung over the plain
> Like a little wee cloud in the world its lane ;
> When seven lang years had come and fled,
> When grief was calm and hope was dead,
> When scarce was remembered Kilmeny's name,
> Late, late in the gloamin' Kilmeny cam' hame.'

Could Noël Paton not paint us that?

More interesting, however, than any other local object, is the celebrated Tynron Doon or hill, which forms a feature in the landscape of the west to the traveller between Sanquhar and Dumfries. It is about a mile from the junction of the Shinnel and the Skarr—a green conical hill, with distinct traces of a moat and the foundations of a castle on its brow. 'By what method did the builders get up their materials?' you naturally ask, wheezing and perspiring as you find yourself on its top. Scotch perseverance and the Kirkpatrick capacity of 'makin' siccar,' must be the reply; for to the Kirkpatricks it belonged, and was a sanctuary to Bruce immediately after he stabbed Comyn in the church of the Minorite friars. Darker than the dark woods which then swept up the Doon must have been the Bruce's forebodings as he threaded up the narrow avenue to the castle. Tradition says that he got his boots mended by the cobbler of Cairnycroft,* who was a botch, and so far bungled his work that the royal heel suffered from a nail—said Cairnycroft being near the base of the Doon. The 'cloud-capt towers' are included in a celebrated enumeration of striking objects that shall pass like dreams. The tower on

---

* In a marginal note in pencil the author records the fact that Dalwhat is also accredited with the possession of the unskilled cobbler.

Tynron Doon well deserved the epithet 'cloud-capt.' It must have been nearer the sky than most. How time changes all things! We met the other month carriages with lunatics from Crichton Institution, bound for an airing or picnic on this same hill. 'Love,' says the great dramatist, 'is merely a madness, and deserves as much a whip and a dark-house as madmen do.' Since Shakespeare's days the feudal castles have mouldered into ruins, and, instead of whips and dark-houses, the madmen have got palaces to live in, and the best-skilled physicians for servants.

The principal tributary of the Shinnel is Cormilligan burn. Far up in a side-strath of that name lives a shepherd-theologian, William M°Caw,* whose little work on the *Evidences* has reached a new edition. His house, the house of his birth, is lonely as a Pharos, and all around is as destitute of smoke and of cock-crowing as prophetic Peden once declared the half of Scotland would be. The shepherd sees his 'hirsel,' but no house save his own throws a shadow upon it. Here, from amidst heather, rushes, and 'spret,' he has gathered a garland for the temple of truth. We can bear witness that the portrait and landscape in the frontispiece of his little work are correct likenesses; and, like most others, we have wondered at the circumstances in which the book was produced. As if to indemnify the shepherd for the plain, cheerless prospect from his door, there is a view from his hill which is almost unsurpassed in Scotland. Cormilligan Bale, or Baal, is the name of several hills overlooking his house. Whether the word Baal is connected with worship of fire, is in this case uncertain. Cormilligan Bale, being of a ridge-shape at the top, and in the vicinity of other high hills, is not conspicuous at a distance; but standing in the front of a range, it commands a prospect vastly more extensive than

* *Vide* page 11.

any of its neighbours. We have the testimony of the shepherd, that on a clear day, the whole extent of the Stewartry of Kirkcudbright from Southerness to the hills of Carsphairn, including Criffel, Screel, Cairnsmuir-of-Fleet, and Cairnsmuir-of-Carsphairn, can be seen from its top. To the north-east, Nithsdale, from the Cumnock Hills to the Solway Frith, is within gaze, and far beyond the Solway, Skiddaw in Cumberland rises distinctly to view; while in favourable states of the atmosphere, St Bees Head can be seen. Moffat lies hid behind Queensberry Hills, but Lower Annandale, and the green potato-pit-like Burnswark Hill, are distinctly visible. The lofty summits of Ayr, Lanark, and Peebles, such as Cairntable, Tinto, and Hartfell, bound the view towards the north. Beneath your feet, the villages of Moniaive, Dunscore, and Durisdeer are perceptible, and with the aid of a glass, on a clear day, part of the Queen of the South * herself can be traced.

That unsatisfactory character, Mr Facing-both-ways, is an ubiquitous personage. A great living author lately heard him saying 'Yea and Nay at once.' We met him in Dante's *Inferno* :

> ' Hateful to Satan and to the angels of light.'

In Simpson's *Traditions,* we catch him again as Wilson of Croglin, Tynron, with a fair face for persecutors and Covenanters alike. He reveals not the secrets of the former to flesh and blood (for is not his word of honour plighted ?), but only to the chimney crook, taking care to have a Covenanter stowed within ear-shot. Not to this amiable half-and-half, but to Margaret Gracie and others who gave their energies and lives for the cause with true Joan-of-Arc enthusiasm, has a monument been lately erected on a desolate spot where the parishes of Penpont and

* Dumfries.

Tynron meet.   The monument contains an inscription as
follows :

> ' Ye ministering spirits who are hovering over,
> Guarding the dust 'neath its mossy cover,
> We raise not this stone to relieve you from care,
> Or discharge you from keeping your vigil here.
> Watch till the trumpet is pealing aloud,
> Watch till the Judge shall appear with the cloud :
> Then guide your charge to the gathering throng,
> When the judgment is set to avenge the wrong.'

The kelpies and other bogles haunting Scottish waters
are represented as exceedingly wicked.   This may arise
from the fact that a playful burn like the Shinnel can
rise in its wrath like a lion hastening to its prey.   On
Wednesday, 16th October last, twelve hours of continuous
rain sent this mountain-stream from its lowest to its
highest water-mark, causing the usual devastation of
water-gates torn from their moorings, bridges shaken,
trees uprooted, and highways rendered impassable.   Last
year, on 20th April 1863, a shepherd, James Edgar, aged
22, fell through a rotten plank-bridge a few hundred
yards above Appin Linn, near the Shinnel's head-waters,
and was borne down for miles by the remorseless stream,
which tossed out his cap here and his plaid there.   His
dog had given the alarm, but night set in, and uncertainty
prevailed for twelve long hours, till by daybreak the body
was found washed over a projecting rock, cut, but not
defaced.   Solemn fell the remarks of the preacher on the
circle gathered round Stenhouse cottage at the funeral.
The sun of manhood had set in an eclipse.   Truly there
had been but a step between life and death.

It would be an interesting question to discuss why
mountaineers are so fond of their native parishes ; but it
is owing, we think, in a great measure to their intimate
connection with the soil.   In highland parishes it is
difficult to establish manufactures, while in flat regions

the facilities of river and rail, and the more frequent occurrence of minerals, give occasion for the building of all manner of factories. Thither population swarms, attracted from one centre of handicraft to another by the rate of wages and the fluctuations of trade. Hence the lowlands contain a nomadic population, while the rural districts supply conditions of existence more favourable to permanence. The rocks and streams, all the features of the landscape which pleased the sensitive eye and ear of childhood, remain like old friends to the man of mature years. More than these, the families living around him while he was in his cradle are also the families who visit him throughout the greater term of his life. Tynron, Penpont, and Glencairn, being hilly, although not in the southern highlands, have some characteristics in common with the highlands of the north. Emigrants are almost unknown—no holy water, no godmothers, no special saints assist the unhappy youths born among these wilds. The Roman Catholic Church sends missions to many lands, but has no mission here.

The love borne by the parishioners of Tynron to their mother-glen is made evident by many bequests. A farm, Upper and Lower Cairnycroft,* has been left to its industrious poor, and a school has been twice endowed to improve its educational facilities; so that if direct means ever lessen the sum of poverty and ignorance, they have obtained a trial here. Among indirect means to mitigate these great evils, we would place wholesome amusements. Moniaive, the centre of the district, has no bowling-green [a defect which has been remedied for many years]; but both in Glencairn and Tynron nature and art combine in

* Lower Cairnycroft is the farm which, tradition says, Bruce gave to the old woman Brownrig, the compact being that she should become owner of all the land she could walk round, while the king ate the brose which she had made for the Royal fugitive from English oppression—a tale also told about the sproats of Urr.

winter to bestow the best of all bowling-plains—namely,
an ample dam, or loch, where curlers may practice the
roaring game. The curling pond of this parish is in a
romantic situation, and the traditional repute of the
curlers is great—a hundred and eighty bolls of meal for
the poor having been played for and won during one
season by the knights of stone and broom. A more
questionable reputation was that which the glen once
enjoyed for the excellence of its whisky ; yet, paradoxical
as it may appear, there is not a public-house or drinking-
room in the parish, nor, as far as we could scent out, any
sly nook for drinking the dew

> ' That's brewed in the starlicht whaur kings dinna ken.'

A tipsy soldier once coming up the glen in cork-screw
fashion, struck its timid urchins with dismay. 'Oh,
mither,' said the little messenger announcing the phenomenon, 'there's a big bleezing man taking twa steps
back and ane forrit every time he gangs.' Nevertheless,
Glenshinnel is not always a sleeping beauty. On suitable
occasions, its Doon blazes with a beacon, its barns resound
with the fiddle, and its street has had the audacity to
bestride itself with arches and festoons. [1864.]

> Give me but health and sunshine for a day,
>   I shall not envy kings their state and throne,
>   But wander, flower-crowned, through thy woods so lone,
> Or plunge where Aird's Linn upward sends its spray,
>   Or like a bee seek Milton's roses blown.
> In Tynron one grows young—the crab-tree throws
>   Wind-shaken apples at you ; and the nuts,
> The berries of the juniper, the sloes,
>   Invite you where the smoke of shepherds' huts
> Curls faint and far between. Night spreads her wing ;
>   Through eastern trees the moon begins to beam,
> Whereat the owls of Auchengibbert sing,
>   And the pale tombstones, church, and churchyard gleam,
> Surrounded by the hamlet like a ring.

A Visit to William McCaw

Author of *Truth frae 'mang the Heather.*

A lovely afternoon was last Tuesday, inviting birds to
sing, flowers to hold up their heads, and sedentary men
to walk. The sunshine was beating redly and fiercely on
the hills; not a breath of wind disturbed the air, and the
thin blue smoke of cottages went up by spiral wreaths
direct to heaven. The 'mansions of the great' had lost
their summer veil of foliage, and were getting exposed to
vulgar eyes. The larch was shedding its thin leaves,
making our roadsides brown. In well-protected dells a
few trees were still holding out their green banners. The
guelder-rose, the dog-rose, the hawthorn, and the sloe
were retaining firm possession of their scarlet or black
berries; the red rowans were withering on their stems,
and the 'bramble' berries hanging bitter and soaked with
October's showers. But all these ornaments of Nature we
had to leave behind, after passing through Aird's wood,
after passing the hamlet of Tynron-Kirk, after leaving
Bennan, and Strathmilligan, and Kirkconnel with its site
of an old Catholic chapel, behind us. Yet the trees were
loathe to bid us good-bye, and in sturdy rows, from
Strathmilligan to Kirkconnel, kept up a goodly show on
the left. At the latter place we observed a change.
The woodman's axe had been busy. The great ash in
which we first espied an owl's nest was still there, and the
warlock-haunted dwelling lay in ruins further on, but the
beautiful bosky glen, where darkness and coolness were
more attractive than July's fiercest beams, was gone.
Major Walker,* we were told, had had men employed
for nearly half-a-year cutting down larch trees, oak, beech,

---

* The late Sir George Walker, for many years M.P. for Dumfriesshire, and Colonel of the ' Scottish Borderer ' Militia.

and birch, and we could see from the ruts in the highway that the waggons had borne off many a ponderous load.

At a gate, locally called the *liggat*, we entered on the
moor. Fitful patches of heather darkened it — fitful
patches of russet ferns embrowned it—and here and
there its winding streamlet reflected the light of day, but
otherwise it was wide, and silent, and desolate, like a
shipless sea. No, not quite desolate, for the bark of
collies is upon our ears, and now four of them, various in
colour and size, are running round us—not at us—just
as they do with sheep. The secret of so great and unexpected a population lies in the fact that the shepherds
are busy close at hand marking the sheep before the
taking away of the tups. In these uplands, where no
yellow corn waves, where no mower whets his scythe,
save at the short harvest of bog hay, the seasons of the
year are marked, not by the various stages of grain, but
of sheep. Spring is the lambing season; May the month
for marking lambs; July for sheep-shearing; August for
weaning the lambs; October for dipping the sheep previous to winter; and early November for keeling them.
Thus every season brings its burden to the back, for at
extra times there is hay to cut, potatoes to raise, peats to
cart, and bridges to repair. At all great occasions the
shepherd's neighbours assist him, and hence the sheep
gathered on last Tuesday into the folds were superin-
tended by several shepherds busy with the rouge pot.
The sheep belonging to each respective *hirsel* are marked
so as to distinguish them from those of another. Some
get a streak on the back, some on the far side, some on
the near side, etc. The regular, or cart-road, if so it can
be called, to McCaw's house now proceeds from the gate
referred to before, along the side of the streamlet. We
choose, however, to take a pathway, which is a near
cut, and keeps much higher. The trail is quite easily

distinguished by day, but it would be impossible to
follow it at night, except with the aid of a lantern.
Blackcock, grouse, partridges, and 'crows,' on the
principle of tit-for-tat, startled us by their whirr or cry as
they rose near our path, just because we startled them,
evincing the truth of the remark, that our larger birds
are all shyer on account of the persecution which they
receive at the hands of man. Their scarcity this year
may depend on their natural enemies being too much
thinned. This appears paradoxical; but hawks, falcons,
etc., always prey most severely on the weaker birds and
those slowest to rise, and thus before the breeding season
they stamp out the diseased ones as we do with rinderpest, whereby disease is prevented from spreading.

Dr Grierson of Thornhill read a paper at the British
Association proving that the destruction of weasels had
caused the meadow mouse so to multiply that it was
barking the plantations at Drumlanrig. Considerations
of this sort show how much scientific education is needed
even for gamekeepers. Could not some more of it be
given, instead of wasting a year on boys learning a little
Latin which they never turn to much account? But we
are digressing, for now we have arrived at the shepherds'
post-office. The post-office consists of a recess under a
large stone whose prickly point, along with those of half-
a-dozen companions also with sharp noses, mark the
summit of a knoll. The neighbouring shepherd, when
he gets a letter from the post-runner, hoists a tall pole
among the rocks, and deposits the letter or packet
beneath the stone. McCaw is thus apprised of news, as
he can see the upraised pole from his doorstep.

The shepherd's house is a one-storied, slated, white-
washed range, with a porch. It consists of a but-and-ben,
a byre, a henhouse, etc. A stack of brackens was piled
beside the swine-houses. Around the house, on the ad-

joining fields, were very clear traces of the waving furrows
produced in the old-fashioned days when ploughing was
done with the two horses in a line.   The garden was
surrounded by a strong dyke, and one could easily trace
the parentage of it to the slaty trap of the district, as
the lines of cleavage which are seen vertically as it crops
from the beds of streams were seen horizontally in the
garden wall. A few trees, mostly Scotch firs, having a
blasted appearance like the trees in the scenic represen-
tation of the blasted heath of Macbeth, hung out their
misshapen arms and were bent to leeward.   The old
Scotch black rat, like a persecuted covenanter, has still got
himself stowed about Cormilligan, but his awful rival has
found him out, and will likely give a good account of him
in a few years. A small stream, called Jock's burn, runs
near the house—for it is necessary, for the purpose of
knowing where to direct little messengers for sheep, that
every burn should be christened. The site of the house
is a thousand feet above sea-level. The shepherd being
out 'marking,' we amused and instructed ourselves with
his library.   It is like the library of none of his class that
ever we took stock of.   A handsome copy of Locke's
Essay on the Understanding, a present from the late
Sheriff Trotter ; other presents for Sabbath-school labours
and from friends, and a large percentage of theological
works rewarded our gaze.   While we looked at the books,
his hospitable better-half piled on the fuel, and many a
dark-eyed little cherub was quizzing us from every conceivable cranny and opening, for in this respect M's quiver
is full of arrows. A stout lass, with a fine round Scotch
face and regular features, helped to pile on the table the
material for such a tea as promised to tax all the active
and latent powers of our digestive organs. It was what
is called a 'rough tea' : lots of everything, flesh of all sorts,
scones of all sorts and shapes, jellies, etc. The hospi-

tality of shepherds is proverbial. When taking the
census in Upper Penpont, a friend of ours encountered
three breakfasts, four dinners, and two teas. After the
shepherd entered we conversed on a great variety of
topics, from the papers read in the Ethnological section
of the British Association in Dundee to the late Dog
Show at Thornhill. Our host displayed neither fanaticism
nor indifference, but made moderate, well-balanced,
cautious remarks. We coincided in the question of the
Dog Show. It was a questionable affair, though well
meant. It is all right to judge by appearance, a cow,
horse, or sheep, for appearance indicates qualities of
strength, fleetness, fatness, or wooliness, for which these
animals are prized ; but the qualities which go to make
a valuable dog are more intangible, more mental, so to
speak. How can a show measure a dog's wit ? It is not
easy to see how the breed of collies can be improved,
unless by the unconscious selection by every shepherd
of the most suitable dog, which is the best guarantee
of improvement of breed, as past experience has
proved. (We could not understand why prizes were
given for castrated dogs.) The dog which got the
first prize at last show, I know, is not highly thought
of by its owner, although it is a beautiful dog,

> ' His gaucie tail, wi' upward curl,
> Hung o'er its hurdies wi' a swirl.'

Next morning we were up early to have a view from
Cormilligan Bale. Can this word ' Bale ' * come from the
same root as Beltein, and have any reference to savage
fire-worship and sacrifices on this hill of men and animals ?
We could not have had a finer morning. A bank of
clouds lay like furrowed sand on the eastern sky, and
glowed with ruby light, shading off to purple. From
Tinto to Criffel a sea of magnificent peaks loomed out

* Beal was the Celtic god of light.

clothed with every shade of blue. The distant world
broke the silence first by the throbbing of a railway
train, and then by the sound of thrashing with the flail.
The Stewartry, from north to south, seemed stretching
away from our feet. The Connerik, Benbuie, and Glen-
jaun were lighting their kitchen fires beneath us. A
white smoke was rising from Moniaive, and white columns
were gathering about the Nith. Little glimpses of lochs,
as Loch Æ, Loch Urr, etc., like half-opened eyes, were
afforded us. Tantalising promises were held out that the
Solway itself might be seen. Then came the gathering
of the sheep for 'marking,' in which the wonderful use and
sagacity of a well-trained dog displayed itself. The sun
broke out warm and brisk, shining on the western slopes,
making streams and their pebbly channels glisten, and making the very faces of the white sheep shine with a deeper
innocence as the soft whisk of their feet o'er green knolls
or through brown ferns came home to our ear, mingled with
the echoing call of the masters to their dogs. As we stooped
down to drink from the prodigal cup of the crystal burn,
we almost broke the Tenth Commandment from secret
envy of a shepherd's life, but the feeling was drowned by
one far deeper, and we heard ourselves murmuring :—

> ' Thy works still shine with splendour bright,
>   As on Creation's earliest day ;
> Angels are gladdened with the sight,
>   Though fathom it no angel may.'

Our visit to the shepherd will live long in memory,
and once more we bid him ' good-bye.'

NOTES ON TYNRON PARISH—1862 to 1895

The parish of Tynron is hardly so pleasant to the eye
of an artist as it was more than thirty years ago. At
that period we had several fords crossing the highway,

whose effect seemed so much more romantic than that
of the environment of a bridge. We had some of the
finest larch trees in the county. The wind, more
than the woodman's axe, levelled them to the ground.
The terrible storms of 1883-4 have left us only their un-
sightly roots, and the late storm—22nd December 1894—
uprooted or broke several thousand trees, some of them
the finest in the district. With the loss of the trees there
has been a diminution of owls, so that the long nights are
quieter with less of their screeching. On a few farms
when I came to the parish the cattle were black Gallo-
ways. These have disappeared, and Ayrshires alone are
seen. Cheviot sheep are giving way to the black-faced
mountain breed. Instead of vehicles going to markets
at neighbouring villages, cadgers' carts came to the farm
houses. Since the new Ground Game Act rabbits are
scarce, and hares are nearly extirpated. The squirrels
are fitful visitors. A great wave of them appears; then,
as at present, there is an ebb. The curious flat stones
which roofed the houses have disappeared in favour of
slates. The number of inhabited houses has decreased,
and their ruins are not always picturesque. Tinkers with
their donkeys do not now visit us. Umbrella-menders,
knife-grinders, sellers with baskets are scarce, but tramps
asking alms have noways decreased. The river Shinnel
runs as of yore, arched over for many miles with a beautiful canopy of natural wood. Illegitimate methods of
securing trout, with which it was well stocked, have
been put down, but the system of surface or sheep-
draining, by suddenly flushing the water and carrying away the spawning beds, is an angler's complaint.
The heritors having mansions in the parish are not now
resident. They spend only a few summer months with
us, or let their houses; so the work of smith, coachman,
and domestic servants is far less in demand. On the

B

other hand, houses that have been built or repaired within my recollection are much more comfortable for the inmates.

When I arrived in Tynron, and for years afterwards, water was obtained almost universally from open wells; chimneys were swept by setting fire to them; messages were conveyed across straths by shrilly whistling on fingers; towns were reached by bridle paths. The mountain tracks then used for driving sheep to the great stock markets, such as Sanquhar, not being much employed for this purpose now, are falling into decay. The people around me to a greater extent than at present knitted their own stockings, plaited their own creels, carved their own crooks, made their own curling brooms or 'cows,' bored their own 'bod-and-lamb' boards, squared their own draught-boards. A very few women smoked tobacco like men, and many men had chins like women. Broom was boiled, the juice mixed with hellebore and tobacco, and used as a sheep-dip. The sheep, in fact, were not dipped at all, but their wool was shed into ridges, and the composition carefully poured on the skin from an old teapot. There were no wooden frames for bees, only the cosy-looking straw 'skeps.' The Shinnel drove several mill-wheels, now it drives only one. As we have seen, there was a method of announcing the arrival of letters, by depositing them in a water-tight chamber of a cairn on an eminence a mile perhaps from the shepherd's house, and then erecting a huge pole or semaphore, which soon attracted a messenger. The limbs and backs of boys were stronger, and carried for you heavy carpet bags at 1^d per mile. Watches were worn in trousers' pockets. The school children were fitted out with stronger leather bags like soldiers' haversacks, containing their dinner as well as their books. Their books were much more carefully covered with cloth, and

in some instances with white leather. Their food was
more thriftily cared for, and there was no *débris*, as at
present, of leaves of books and crumbs of scone left on
the roadside near the schoolhouse. The plaid was a much
more common article of dress. It is now giving way to
the great-coat or waterproof, which is more convenient to
a shepherd, affording him pockets to hold milk for the
weak lambs, and covering his body better.

When I found myself in the interior of shepherds' and
dairymen's houses, the old eight-day clock, with wooden
door and painted dial, was common. It kept company
with the meal-ark, a huge chest divided into two com-
partments—one for oatmeal, one for wheaten flour.
Bacon, hams, and flitches, then as now, wrapped in newspapers, hung from kitchen rafters. Puddings were
wreathed round suspended poles. Fireplaces are gradually contracting—the older ones are the widest. The fire
in winter, eked out by peats and cleft-wood, is often very
violent in its hospitality. Seated in the cushioned arm-
chair, I have for a while maintained conversation by
holding up my extended palm for a firescreen, but was
generally obliged to push back my chair at the risk of
overturning a cradle or turning the charmed circle into
an ellipse. An inner ladder was stationed in the porch
or between the but-and-ben, up which the children or
serving men mounted to their obscure attic shakedowns.
On great nails, here and there in the walls, hung, and
still hang, crooks, shears for clipping sheep, lanterns for
moonless nights, mice traps with holes, rat traps with
strong iron teeth and springs. There were no carpets on
the rooms, but the floor was mottled with home-tanned
sheep-skins in their wool, and the mat before the room
fire was home-made, with all sorts of dark rags stitched
together, having a fluffy, cosy look. On the chest of high
drawers might be observed a family Bible, a field-glass,

a stuffed blackcock and pair of large ram's horns, or a
basket with curious abnormal eggs and with shells from
the seashore. A black cat, a brindled cat, and a 'muscovy,'
were generally crossing each other or demanding a seat
on your knee. You would feel something cold touching
your hand, and presently observe it was the nose of a
collie dog, generally named after a Scotch river, such as
Yarrow, Tweed, or Clyde. At the door of the poultry-
house was a little hole or 'lunky,' which admitted the
cats when shut out from the family domicile. On
Sundays, waggon loads of children, carefully packed in
straw, presided over by the maternal or paternal owner,
or both, would pass my house on the road to church ;
wives and maidens who could not command such a con-
veyance walked past, their shoes and stockings in a
napkin, ready to be put on at the rivulet's side nearest
the church. At that time the greater portion of the
families in my district were Cameronian or Reformed
Presbyterian. At the present time the Parish Church
has the greater number of adherents, and it being a
much nearer place of worship, these modes of travelling
are wearing out.

Ever since I came to Tynron, the child has entered the
Christian Church on a secular day. Neighbours are
invited, and the table groans with every kind of food.
Butter (salt, fresh, or powdered), bacon and eggs, sweet
milk and skimmed milk cheese, potato scones, soda scones,
'droppet' scones, treacle scones, tea, and a 'dram' are
part of the fare. The shepherds have a very restricted
number of baptismal names. At one time the fourth of
my boys were ' Williams.'

Weddings are celebrated in the same hospitable and
jovial style. I have sat in a barn or cheese-room, the
walls of which were lined with sheeting to protect our
clothes, and the floor sawdusted for dancing. The built-in

boiler was transposed into a platform for the fiddlers. The
tea was taken in relays; the minister, schoolmaster, and
small gentry occupied seats at the first table, which, as well
as the forms for sitting on, was improvised from slabs for
the occasion. The commoner folk and young herds were
next regaled at a second spread, while the elders smoked
tobacco outside. The dances did not consist of walking,
simpering, and circling round each other with planetary
regularity, but were like those that took place in Alloway
Kirk, as far as noise, life, and motion were concerned.
Towards morning came that awful ordeal, the pillow dance,
or 'Bab at the bowster,' an ingenious method of picking
out the 'bonny and weel-liked,' and placing the less distinguished at the bottom of the class. The best man having
picked out the bride, it next became her turn to throw the
handkerchief to whomsoever she chose. The happy swain
knelt as she stooped. The fiddlers shrieked a minuendo,
and the last kiss that ever alien lips should secure was
wrested from the bride.

Funerals were well attended, and the custom of having
a service prevailed, and only began to thin out after I
entered the parish. I was told by a well-wisher to get
acquainted with the people, and to attend all the sheep
shearings and funerals to which I was invited. The
attendance at funerals is diminishing, and generally a few
gigs now pick up all the mourners. The exodus of young
men and daughters into the large towns reacts on provin-
cial simplicity. I witnessed wreaths of flowers heaped on
the coffin of an old Cameronian, whose opinion, I am
certain, had never been taken on the matter. The humblest
family must have a memorial stone.

I shall pass over gatherings connected with sheep, killing pigs, etc., and remark that the 'kirn,' or harvest home,
is no longer celebrated. St Valentine's Day is forgotten,
and a Christmas present has superseded the Candlemas

bleeze.* Even the Hallowe'en described by Burns—the
turnip lantern and the pulling of kail stocks—is away, the
only survival being that, on Hallowe'en, mummers with
false faces enter your kitchen expecting an obolus, and
are highly gratified when you are puzzled and unable to
guess their names or even their sex. The gradual decrease
in our rural population, consequent on the abolition of the
Corn Laws, and the turning of Britain into a manufacturing
centre for the whole world, is evident in Tynron.

In 1801 the population was			563	In 1871 the population was			381
,, 1831	,,	,,	493	,, 1881	,,	,,	416
,, 1841	,,	,,	474	,, 1891	,,	,,	359
,, 1861	,,	,,	446				

That is, at last census, the reduction in population
compared to 1801 was 204 persons. The former considerable population has gone from our hills and dales
leaving some traces of itself in a few stones of
former 'bourocks' overgrown with nettles, and here and
there a few wild gooseberries and some plants, such as
monks' rhubarb and masterwort, of no value now, but
formerly used in poor people's broth. On the hills also,
200 feet above any arable ground, there are at present to
be noticed furrows once formed by the ploughshare.
Dividing the results of the last four decennial estimates by
four, we find the average population for 30 years is 400.

Our deaths from 1861 to 1891, both included, are 183,
or 6 deaths per annum to 400 population, which gives us
a death rate of 15 per 1000. By the same mode we have
a marriage rate of 6 per 1000, and a birth rate of 27
per 1000.

* At Candlemas the schoolmaster was presented with a small
sum of money by each of his scholars, and, at one time, a bonfire
was kindled in the playground, the boy and girl who gave the
largest donation being elected King and Queen for the festive day.
The teacher in return provided bread and cheese and oranges.
The recent custom was for the children to combine to present a
cake or other small gift.

This birth rate is less than that for the whole of
Scotland taken for the same period—namely, 27 against
33. The marriage rate is slightly less, and the death
rate is considerably less. In the 31 years over which I have
gone the death rate for Scotland is nearly 21 per 1000,
while that of Tynron is 15 per 1000. When we consider
that many of our young men and women emigrate to the
towns, leaving the older people remaining, our health
record stands out well.

As I have dealt separately with folklore, I shall
mention only one curious custom. A woman about
thirty or forty years ago caused her children to wash
their feet every Saturday evening. As soon as the
ablutions were performed, a live peat or coal was thrown
into the tub, the person doing so walking three times
around it. After this the contents were thrown out.

On Thursday, after the terrible snowstorm of 6th
February, a shepherd told me he could have predicted a
change, because on Tuesday evening 'Hurlbausie' was
far too near the moon. This strange word was the old
people's name for the planet Jupiter.

Art has decidedly improved. We have two large
memorial windows in the Parish Church, one of them as
fine as any window of the kind in the county. In sewed
samplers you have Pharoah's daughter rescuing the babe
Moses, and others of that sort. On the mantelpieces are
crockery hens sitting on delf baskets, brooding over
crockery eggs. But cabinet photos are superseding the
high-coloured prints of the happy pair courting, or going
to church to be 'kirked.' Red carts, red petticoats, red
cravats, red calico napkins still prevail, but the young
women coming back for holiday from domestic service in
towns are toning down the enthusiasm for primary
colours. The 'rack' above the 'dresser' with the dishes,
knives, forks, and spoons is sometimes a picture in itself.

The stone floor of the kitchen and the threshold are made gay with curious scroll patterns, white or red, by rubbing with caumstone (claystone). The taste for garden and potted flowers has increased, and at Yule, Christmas trees are in bloom with us. Concertinas and melodeons have multiplied. Queer old songs in which the heroine mourns over her highwayman executed, or in which disappointed love vows vengeance, or in which Bacchus is blest, are hiding their heads. There was a low suppressed murmur of disapprobation at the introduction of instrumental music in church.

Proverbs, some of them having an aroma of the sheep-walks, abound. I give a few not inserted in Hislop's *Collection of Scotch Proverbs*, although that collection professes to be complete.

The richt wrangs naebody.

He's a man among sheep, but a sheep among men.

There's nocht sae crouse as a new scoured louse.

She would mak' a gude poor man's wife; get him poor and keep him poor.

Ye're aff your eggs and on the strae (applied to one who reasons incorrectly).

Auld soles mak' bad uppers (that is, old servants make hard masters).

Hae as much o' th' deil in you as keep the deil aff you.

Gif ye winna hae walkers, riders may pass by (applied to girls who are too saucy).

He that lies down wi' the dogs rises up wi' the fleas.

He would mak' a gude poor man's pig—(*e.g.*, eats weel at every meal).

Tak' tent o' the hizzie that's saucy and proud,

Tho' her e'e's like the gowan and the gowan like gowd.

Whittlegair was the hero of a melancholy story. A

lady had given birth to a child by a previous sweetheart, and concealed the fact from the grim earl who had led her to the marriage altar. The child grew to manhood, and was in great poverty. His mother was wont to meet Whittlegair secretly and relieve his wants. A tell-tale aroused the earl's jealousy. Whittlegair was beset by the earl's minions, overpowered, beheaded, and his head brought home to his unhappy mother on a pike as the reward of her supposed infidelity. The Countess, on seeing her son's head, swooned and shortly after expired. I am sorry that, having received this story at second-hand from a daughter, I cannot repeat any of the verses.

The following child's rhyme was more common in Renfrewshire. I only heard it once in Dumfriesshire. It was sung to a young child previous to its learning to walk.

> 'Wag a fit, wag a fit, whan wilt thou gang?
> Lantern days, when they grow lang,
> Harrows will hap and ploughs will bang,
>   And ilka auld wife tak' the ither by the tap,
>   And worry, worry, worry, till her head fa' in her lap.'

'Lantern days' mean the days of Lent. In this winter of unwonted severity ploughs have not begun with Lent, though they stopped about Christmas.

About six years after my first residence in Tynron, my father and I listened to the sound of an aurora. It was a very bright aurora, sending streamers and luminous mist across the zenith. It was like the sound of rustling silk, falling and rising. It is a very rare thing to hear this; but I wrote of it to *Nature*, and discovered I was not entirely alone in my experience. Tom Brown, a member of the Dumfries Antiquarian Society, when early up at lambing time, saw at Auchenhessnane the spectre of the Brocken—that is, opposite to him, reflected on a bank of clouds about sunrise, he saw a magnified image

of himself, whose motions corresponded with his own.   My
neighbour schoolmaster observed 'Will-o'-the-wisp' one
summer night in a marshy spot between Shinnel and
Skarr.   In the store at Tynron Kirk is to be seen a shop
account-book made by a former grocer, bound in calf
skin, the hairs still adhering to it.   In that book entries
are made of sales of tow, showing that the spinning wheel
went round.   There are also entries of sales of barley meal.
Now, only a few rigs of barley are grown by one farmer.
Sermons are shorter, but there is more psalmody.   Thanks-
giving Monday has become secular.   Grace before meat
has nearly reached vanishing point.   Grace after meat is
most frequently taken for granted.   I fear Burns' *Cottar's
Saturday Night* is following Burns' *Hallowe'en* into the halls
of memory.

Before closing, let me say a good word in favour of the
scrupulous honesty of the great mass of the parishioners.
I have had, during a whole night, linen spread to bleach
or my blankets hung out to dry.   I have forgotten to
lock my door.   I have left the school door wide open for
a night without loss.   A cow might swallow half a shirt,
but no fingers ever pilfered one.   I lost a legging on the
hills, but the lost legging hopped back to me.   Carrying
my coat on my arm on a bridle path one sultry day I
dropped my spectacles, but my spectacles gravitated
towards my eyes again.   A friend of mine had a spill, but
a schoolboy carefully gathered up the larger 'spelks' of the
tram of the broken vehicle, and made me a present of
them, as he said, for my museum.   My bad debts in the
long period of my residence might all be paid with that
current coin of the realm upon which is engraved the
figure of the war-like saint vanquishing the dragon.

FOLKLORE OF TYNRON*

An old farmer who died three years ago in Tynron related
to me his experience with a witch in Closeburn, when he
was a boy. He was carting freestones from a neighbouring quarry, when his horse came to a standstill opposite
the witch's door. Two other carters passed him, and
only jeered both at the witch and the boy, when the
former, to whom he had always been civil, came forward
and with a slight push adjusted the ponderous stone
which had slipped and was stopping the wheel. 'Now,
go,' she said, 'thou wilt find them at the gate below
Gilchristland.' At that very spot he found the per-
plexed carters standing, both horses trembling and
sweating, so that he easily went past them and got to his
goal first. The same individual could name a person at
whose glance the milk being drawn from the udders of
the cows became blood while his sister was milking them.
I have observed horse-shoes nailed up against his stable
wall to scare away uncanny influences. A dairywoman
who resided beside me about fifteen years ago, informed
me that when young she had resided in Kirkconnel, and
that the house was haunted. At night strange faces
peered in at the window, and eldritch laughter was
heard. Her father once saw a red figure at dusk on the
ledge of the bridge, near the house, which appeared of
human shape, but disappeared as he approached. He
also, on one occasion, saw my informant's sweetheart
on the road coming to see her, although at the time
he was several miles off. A housekeeper I had,
who died a few years ago, assured me that, while
she was a servant to a medical man in Moniaive,
strange foot-falls were frequently heard in an upper room.

* A paper read by Shaw at a meeting of the Dumfriesshire
and Galloway Natural History and Antiquarian Society.

The doctor, after a while, suddenly took ill, lay down on a sofa and died, over the very spot on the floor where these alarming foot-falls had been most frequently heard. A young man, who had been attending classes in Edinburgh, came home, and one evening that I was in his father's house, set off a balloon after sunset. The candle in it set the whole tissue on fire while it was soaring above our heads. A shepherd, whom I knew, seeing a light from a distance, rushed in a state of great agitation into a neighbouring cottage, which happened to be near, and brought out the good man of the house. Both thought that it must have been *the light which is seen before death;* but the mistress of the house rather soothed them by remarking that such a light could not be seen by two at once. An old woman informed me that she had witnessed this premonitory light, which lighted up the interior of the byre while she was engaged in milking her cows, and she learned that her mother, residing some miles distant, had expired that same evening. Readers will recollect the fateful light in Sir Walter Scott's ballad of lovely Rosabelle. James Hogg, the Ettrick Shepherd, refers to an omen called the 'death bell,' a tingling in the ears, which is believed to announce a friend's death. As the 'light before death' could not be seen by two at once, so the death-bell could only be heard by one person at a time. The relations of a gentleman residing in Tynron have been warned of death by the sound of wheels upon the gravel walk leading to the door, when no wheels were there; and to a family in Durisdeer the warning came like a switch against the panes of the window. The old precentor of Glencairn, who died six or seven years ago, told me that while walking one moonlit evening in the garden in meditative mood, he heard a sound, as if a cart containing pieces of metal had been tilted up and the materials discharged. His belief was

that a murdered infant had been buried in that garden.
These murdered innocents were frequently heard wailing
about forty years ago in the corn and in the thickets
around Maqueston in Tynron. A gentleman of suspected
morality had occupied this house early in the century.
So troublesome were these sounds that the new tenant
had for a while great difficulty in retaining servants. In
Bennett's *Tales of Nithsdale* mention is made of the
custom of placing a wooden platter with salt, or more
correctly, salt and earth—for a turf was cut and put
above the platter—on the breast of a corpse. There is a
reminiscence of this in our parish, and the reason given
for the custom was, that it prevented the corpse swelling. In Thiselton Dyer's *Folklore*, and Napier's *Folklore of the West of Scotland*, the custom is referred to.
The plate of salt was intended for the sin-eaters who
came and devoured the contents with incantations, and
thus relieved the spirits clogged with earthy frailties, and
kept them from hovering too closely near their friends
and relatives. Pennant mentions the custom, suggesting
that the salt was an emblem of the incorruptible spirit,
and the earth of the body. When the sin-eater arrived
Napier mentions two plates—one of salt and one of bread,
which required to be devoured. A shepherd in Tynron
told me that he recollected seeing perforated stones, or
stones nearly perforated, from the channel of the stream,
attached to a rowan tree near a house at the head of the
Kinnel, and that he understood both stones and rowan
trees were looked upon as likely to scare away evil influences. At or near Fleuchlarg, in the adjoining parish
of Glencairn, might have been seen a hole in the wall
of the byre, letting out a rope, so that if the evil spirits
got in they could get out more readily by the hole. I
understand that when I was carried to church for baptism,
the young woman who carried me bore a piece of bread and

cheese in her pocket, to present it to the first person she
met, who was expected to bless me. Baptism being
private in Tynron, I have nothing of this kind to record.
The blessing of a beggar, however, was of such esteem in the
eyes of an old woman in Tynron that it secured a night's
lodging for many a tramp. Silver is lucky. A father
gave a lucky shilling to his daughter at her marriage.
Crooked sixpences are worn at the watch chain, so you
shall have silver when you first see the new moon. Turn
your apron three times and look at the new moon, wishing for a present, and a present shall arrive to you ere it
wane. One person, trying the experiment, received in a
present a pair of curtains, a dozen of eggs, and a hen. If
you see the plough coming towards you for the first time
of the new year, it augurs well, but if you observe it going
away, it is unlucky. It bodes ill to turn when you are
setting out on a journey. It is better for you should the
day be a wet one. Great care should be taken not to
burn hair or nails. It is unlucky to pare your nails on
Sunday, but if you pare them on Saturday, expect to see
your sweetheart the next day. Tuesday and Friday
evenings are the orthodox evenings for courting, but it is
not well to marry either on Thursday or Saturday, while
most Scotch marriages are performed on Friday. Wm.
McCaw, our shepherd-author, told me that when he was
young, many persons in contributing to a raffle wrote
against their subscription the word 'Friday,' expecting
thereby better luck from the dice. It is not well to
change situations on Saturday. 'Saturday's enter is a
short residenter.' I was astonished to find, on the other
hand, that she would be a bold bride in the North of
England who should elect to be married on a Friday.
When I was at Manchester last vacation, the mistress of
the house in which I slept was awkwardly placed because
her new servant would not come on Friday, the unlucky,

but would wait till Saturday, and her old servant departed
on Thursday.   How shall we account for such contra-
dictory views of the caprices of fortune?   As an instance
of a similar contradiction I give the rhyme about the
magpie :—

> 'One's joy, two's grief,
> Three's a marriage, four's death.'

Such is the rhyme I had, but I find in the North of
England a different version.

> 'One's sorrow, two's mirth,
> Three's a wedding, four's a birth,
> Five's a funeral, six is snaw,
> Seven draws the dead awa.'

In Dr Thiselton Dyer's *Folklore of Shakespeare*, occurs
the following variant :—

> 'One is sorrow, two mirth,
> Three a wedding, four a birth,
> Five heaven, six hell,
> Seven the deil's ain sel'.'

Shakespeare calls the magpie 'magit,' and attributes to it
uncanny influences.   I quote the following rhyme from a
native of the district :—

> '*Gang* and see the swallow flee,
>   *Sit* and hear the gowk,*   * cuckoo.
> The foal before it's minnie's e'e,
> And all that year ye've luck.'

If a hare cross your path to the left it is of evil omen,
but not if it cross to the right.   If a person eat the brains
of a hare he will be ill-tempered afterwards.   This
Tynron saying is somewhat like La Fontaine's estimate of
the hare, whose flesh produced melancholy.   In Swift's
Polite Conversation hare-flesh is called 'melancholy meat.'

> 'The robin and the wren are at God's right hand.
> The yeldrock and the sparrow are the devil's bow and arrow.'

> 'The robin and the wren made their porridge in a pan,
> Ere the robin got a spoon, the wren had them all done.'

A dairyman once asked me for the scientific name of the
'worm that first breaks through the coffin lid.' He also
informed me that the bat, and dormouse, and the hedge-
hog were three of the 'seven sleepers.' To rub shoulders
with a bride or bridegroom augurs a speedy marriage.
If a girl eat a herring before going to bed she has a
chance to dream of her sweetheart. A rainy wedding-
day goes with a 'greetin'' bride. It is the correct thing
to dance in stocking soles at the marriage of a sister or
brother younger than yourself—the sister at the sister's,
the brother at the brother's. It bodes not well to make
a present to your sweetheart of a knife or other sharp
article, lest it should cut love. It was a custom at
Hallowe'en to wind a clue in a kiln-pot with the expectation that your future partner in life might be seen
holding the other end of it. Should a girl scoop a hole
where three or more roads meet and apply her ear to it,
she may hear a whisper telling her the trade of her
future lover. If your palm tickle it is a sign that you
shall soon shake hands with the rich or obtain money.
Sitting down to meat causes the invited guests to arrive.
The tongs falling head foremost into the ash-pit is a sign
that a stranger is coming. An itching palm is a sign of
change of weather. If your right ear be warm or tingle
it is a sign that somebody is praising, but if the left you
are being reviled. A curly head is the sign of a quiet
temper. The hair of the eyebrows meeting above the
nose signifies unsteadiness and love of change. The
howling of a dog at night is indicative of death. The
burning of withered grass on the moors in spring 'cankers
the air and brings on rain.' The clothes of dead men
don't last long. A whistling woman and a crowing hen
are uncanny. An excellent cure for warts is to rub them
in the morning with your fasting spittle. It is unlucky
to turn either horse or vehicle 'widdershins'—that is,

against the sun. It is dangerous for future welfare to pour out any liquid turning your hand backwards. When a candle * runs—that is, when a 'shaving' descends down its stalk—look soon for the coffin of a friend. If a window-blind fall of its own accord, it is unlucky. Bees leaving a hive full of honey is a bad omen. Bees are encouraged to settle when swarming by loud noises and rattling of instruments. It is unlucky to spill salt at table or to help another to it. Cast some salt over your left shoulder and your mistake may be rectified. To drop your umbrella or walking-stick shows that your

---

* The superstition about the spark in the candle is very common in the north-eastern counties of England, but the details only bear a partial resemblance to those that are understood in Dumfriesshire. The belief is pretty general that the lustrous spot or spark, which shows itself when any portion of an untrimmed wick protrudes through the flame, indicates the arrival of a letter. A charming illustration of this is to be found in the verse from the old Border song entitled, *The Ship Boy's Letter*—

> ' Here's a letter from Robin, father—
>   A letter from over the sea;
> I was sure that the spark in the wick last night
>   Meant there was one for me.
> And I loved to see the postman's face
>   Look in at the dairy park,
> Because you said 'twas so woman-like
>   To put my trust in a spark.'

An English antiquarian journal, alluding to this superstition, says if the glowing spark should drop on the first shock it is an indication that the letter has already been posted. Another mode of devination is practised by means of a pin and a candle. The anxious lover, while the candle is burning, sticks a pin through the wax, taking care that it pierces the wick, and repeating the words :—

> ' It isn't this candle alone I stick,
> But Johnny's heart I mean to prick ;
> Whether he be asleep or awake,
> I'd have him come to me and speak.'

It seems as if the final word ought to be pronounced 'spake,' and if so, the superstition might be voted Irish. However, the maid who has appealed to the candle patiently watches for the result. If the pin remains in the wick after the flame has passed the spot where it was inserted, 'Johnny' (or whoever he may be) is sure to appear ; but if the pin drops out, then the young man is faithless.— *Dumfries Herald.*

C

mind is likely to give way. The cuckoo remains until it gets an awn of barley in its throat. Thirteen at table is unlucky. He who rises first runs most risk. Better, in such a dilemma, for all to rise at once. To dream of a wedding signifies a corpse. The grandfather of a lady in Tynron dreamed he was at a ball with his sister, who appeared in a white dress. She left the ballroom, saying to him, 'You will not be long in following me.' She died in a short time, and he died soon afterwards. If you dream on Sunday morning, you shall have a letter within a week. One instance has reached me of a person seeing another sitting in a chair when the person thus seen was not at all in the room. Brewster accounts for similar visions by diseased condition of the retina. Swallows building in your eaves is lucky. Crickets leaving the house is a sign of death. The 'calm' which accumulates on the bars of a grate foretells a visitor. The bright spark often seen on a candle declares, if it falls, a letter is posted to you; but if it sticks to the side of the candle, it denotes that it is only on the way to be posted.

Such are the greater part of my gleanings of folk-lore in Tynron and the neighbourhood. I fear there is not much new in it; but it may give you an idea of the residuum of belief which still lingers on from the time which some people have named 'the Ages of Faith.'

GHOSTS

'Oh! there are spirits in the air,
  And genii in the evening breeze,
And gentle ghosts, with eyes as fair
  As star-beams among twilight trees.'

So sings a modern poet, who can hardly be accused of superstition. I was struck by the resemblance between the Kirkbean ghost story of the man supposed to have been murdered by the brother of his lady-love and Boccaccio's story of *Isabella* and the *Pot of Basil* so admirably versified by Keats. In the latter, two brothers engaged in the tragedy, the motive being the same; and in both the body is disinterred. Isabella secured the head of her lover, and Miss Craik of Kirkbean, the skeleton. Isabella put the head in a large garden flower-pot and grew basil over it, watering it with her tears. Miss Craik, it is to be supposed, would keep her skeleton in a closet. Can the Kirkbean story be the Scotch variant of a far-travelled tale? Omniscient Andrew Lang could have a word to say on this.

The belief in ghosts is so widely spread, and the details are often related so circumstantially, as to demand a large quantity of evidence to prove a negative. A quarter of a mile from where I write a 'white lady' hovers by moonlight over a pretty little cascade (Paul's Pool), overhung by hazel and alder trees. True, it was only visible to the eyes of a former generation; but may not the eye only see what it has the power of seeing? The poet Shelley says—

> 'While yet a boy I sought for ghosts, and sped
>   Through many a listening chamber, cave, and ruin,
>   And starlight wood, with fearful steps pursuing
> Hopes of high talk with the departed dead—
>   I was not heard; I saw them not.'

Our experience has served us no better. It is well known that Kirkconnel, in Tynron, was a haunted house. Weird faces, with grinning teeth and fiery eyes, were wont to peep in at the windows on winter evenings. Eldritch sounds and low moanings proceeded in the darkness from the copse around. Indeed, had there not been a considerable use made of cast horse shoes, of rowan branches cut when no eye saw the cutter, of 'fow' (house-leek) growing on the thatch, and a careful observance paid to certain new moon and other duties, life would hardly have been worth living in that lonely shieling. Satan himself was once seen sitting on the ledge of the bridge which crosses the dark defile near it, but, scared, he fled beneath the starlight noiselessly down into the deep recess. Certainly a haunted house has a few advantages. Sometimes the 'wraith' of a person approaching disclosed itself, although the visitor was yet miles away, and so the house could be made tidy and the bacon fried in time. When arguing on this subject with a true believer, I was told to read, if incredulous of ghosts and wraiths, Matthew xxvii. 52-53, and were I not convinced I should get a 'gliff' before shuffling off the mortal coil.

The Greeks saw ghosts. Their appearance in the classic tragedies is startling. In the poems of Ossian one reads of them as flitting about, the stars dim twinkling through their forms, as Arcturus twinkled through the great comet of 1859. Thin and unsubstantial must be their texture. One old philosopher calculated that their bodies were a thousand times thinner than the atmosphere at the level of the sea. If all stories be correct, there are not only ghosts of human beings, but of clothes; not only ghosts of horses, but of harness. Shakespeare would be duller reading but for ghosts. We are told that usurpers are haunted by the ghosts of the kings they have deposed. The great tragedies of *Hamlet* and *Macbeth* have each its ghost. The elder Kean always brought down the house when he, personifying 'Hamlet,' addressed the murdered father's ghost. Precious jewels are many of our old ballads in which the ghost appears. Peden and the Covenanters were apter to behold black bedevilled dogs than ghosts, but the Laird of Cole and the haunted house at Rerrick remind us that the ghost mingled with less acceptable apparitions. In Simpson's *History of Sanquhar* credit is given to 'a venerable minister of the name of

Hunter' of Penpont, for laying the ghost [of Abraham Crichton, Provost, 1733] that haunted the churchyard. Still, it was thought Hunter did it at the expense of some years of his life.

In that strange book, *Sartor Resartus*, in the chapter, 'Natural Supernaturalism,' Carlyle extends the domain of the miraculous. He thinks it was loss of time in Dr Johnson tapping on coffins in vaults, visiting Cock-lane, and otherwise making journeys after spirits. Did Dr Johnson not know that he was himself a ghost? He was an appearance coming out of thick darkness which no man can penetrate, glittering for a few moments as on a shining bridge, and then disappearing into darkness as thick as that from which he issued.

There is a tendency in these degenerate days, when Herbert Spencer's heavy volumes are replacing *Dwight's Theology*, even in some quiet country houses, to send ghosts and devils back to the chambers from which they first emanated, and to find that they are but part and parcel of that wondrous being called man.—*Dumfries and Galloway Herald and Courier*, 21st November 1894.

MONIAIVE *

Tea was at one time sold only by the apothecary, and many of our modern articles of diet commenced their career as medicines. So change of scene—change of air—a month at the coast—formerly the exclusive privilege of the rich man with a diseased liver, have now become luxuries not to be dispensed with by middle-class society. Jolly husbands require to transport their buxom wives to the coast, and buxom wives move thither in crowds, with lots of great, clean, thriving children walloping around them. Excuses are easily coined to

* The ancient spelling 'Minnyhive,' being obsolete, has been discarded.

obtain a pastime so diverting, and fashion compels many
a one to our watering-places whom thrift would restrain.
Mr So-and-so finds he must take a house for the holidays
to prevent any whisper of his coming down in the world,
or that his business is not paying so well, or that his credit
is not what it used to be.

But wherefore do people always flock to the coast?
For my part, I don't at all care for that great hungry
sea, so monotonous and so barren. The ocean is a cruel,
cunning monster, valuable only because it is a highway
between land and land. How many precious ones, too,
have its billows clasped and held for ever in their cold
embrace! The worthless acres of Neptune are owned by
no proprietor, bought and sold in no market. Occasionally
the surly waves yield you a breakfast, but they are always
quite as ready to make a breakfast of you. A bee-master
told me that he had a bad chance with his bees on the
shore, for they had only a semicircle for pasture-ground,
whereas the bees of landward towns had the whole round
of the compass at their disposal. I envy the bees of the
landward towns. They ought to buzz more melodiously
for that. I neither like the sea nor the crowds that
frequent the shore. The latter straggle along the beach
outvapouring with the vaguest of motives. I doubt the
genuineness of their admiration of scenery, and other
kinds of admiration. But give me some rustic beauty of
an inland town, whose charms have not been too frequently exposed to the stranger's view, whose aborigines
are unsophisticated, to whose coasts strangers do not
come in shoals like herrings in their season, whose shopkeepers and groceries are not precisely exported down
from Glasgow for the summer—some sober, sweet rural
spot, with liberty to roam around on every side, no great
dull sea to stop me. There let me saunter away my
vacation.

Surely of all towns Moniaive has a claim upon me, for
it suits my purpose entirely. Reader, did you ever see
this little village? If not, hire and pay it a visit. It
lies at the meeting of three straths, which at that point
merge into a wider and warmer glen. Three sweet
waters murmur round the little town, and then fall into
each other's arms, forming thenceforth but one. Delicious
little streams are these, in keeping with the fairy groves
and tangled wilds through which they bicker. The streams
near the commercial centres flow through groves of
beauty also, but then you have to hold your nose when
you get near them.

Witness the Kelvin at the West End Park of Glasgow.
No Narcissus can fall in love with his reflection in it, for
the chemical works on its banks have dyed it until it is
as shadowless as your soup. Not so the burns of Moniaive. There you can court your shadow, and are likely
to fall in love with everything on which your shadow falls;
and, having once got in love with the locality, there are
a thousand ways of rendering the attachment permanent.
There are opportunities of viewing the town from a
thousand different points, for this pretty rustic village
seems to have been built entirely to please the painters.
No town, not even Edinburgh, is commanded by so many
mountain summits in various directions. Chiefly from Dun-
reggan hill can you see to advantage all the glens unfolded, all the streams glittering, every little street, every
house and its garden, the churches, schools, inns, and
shops, until you get acquainted with them as if they were
members of your father's family. Neither is the prospect
an Oriental illusion. You are not charmed with the
distant view and disgusted when you pace the streets.
The houses of Moniaive are tidy, white-washed, or
painted. Flowers are wreathed round the porches, or
grow, profusely trained, against the sunny walls. One is

surprised to find how considerate the boys of the village
are. The pigeons hop fearlessly along the streets, the
daw is everybody's pet, and the solemn old gled squints
at you from the nearest chimney. The gardens, clustered
together, send the bee and butterfly on various errands
over the street. The 'cushat croodles amorously' from its
native woods. At many an angle a blackbird quacks
from among the currants; while scoured jelly-pans glisten
in every other kitchen. Evening comes, and the owl
flits in the suburbs or whoops from an adjoining thicket.
At sunset ducks are dozing or gobbling in the quiet pools
of the burns—at moonrise the same pools are wrinkled,
like a laughing face, by the circles of the jumping trout.
At morning the 'gudewives' get breakfast ready, and the
first cloud of thick, blue smoke is charming by reason of
its Highland odour—a sweet and varied composition,
arising from the mixture of wood, peats, and coal for fuel.
Very unlike is this smoke to the dark masses overwhelm-
ing the inhabitants of the coal and iron districts, and
pouring down in the form of sooty rain on all shirts and
linens bleaching within its reach.

Happy shirts of Moniaive, watered on your bleaching-
greens by beads from no polluted Lethe! Fortunate cats,
converted into no mince-pies by London speculators!
Lucky damsels, not yet sophisticated, whose crinolines are
not too wide, and who are not yet converted into coquettes
by too many snobs, swells, idlers, and loungers from our
great cities! May the years of your lovely solitude be
multiplied, and your green hills screen you from invasion,
from railway accidents, and from factory smoke!

I like, too, the large proportion of one-storied houses in
this little town. Since the building of Babel to the
present time the erection of tall houses meant for many
different families has been a curse. Build tall houses, and
the closely packed families cannot all have gardens. Build

tall houses, and you establish a sort of spirit-rapping over
each other's heads, and knock against each other's faces at
evening on the stairs; while the sewerage, never good in a
rural town, becomes abominable—instead of the flower-pot
a rank 'jawbox' at the stairhead. Is the bosom of our
mother earth so narrow that we must make our nest
among the stars? Is the breath of our mother earth so
tainted that we must get away from it to smoke long
pipes on a third or fourth flat? The heads of our fellow-
citizens are not made of wood, surely, that we should
expose them to a shower of chimney-cans, slates, tiles
and lodging notices, with every hurricane which blows. A
stair is a masonic curiosity; when well-drawn it looks fine
in a picture; but it is a sad bore in reality to people
without ample leisure and servants; and it will be so
while Newton's law of gravitation is in force. Moniaive,
I am happy to state, is wonderfully free from the nuisance
of stairs. Birds have nests, one family per house; bees have
hives, one apartment per family; Tartars have tents, and
Indians possess wigwams. All these, guided by simple
primitive instincts, are innocent of stairs. Wretched
authors of books, soured old maids with parrot-cages,
astronomers with 'elbows out their coats,' creep voluntarily,
step by step, to their garrets.

In Moniaive, too, the place of the dead is sacred. The
churchyard is two miles from the village. This is wholesome and well arranged. It is ugly to see a Golgotha in
the very midst of a town, crowded with graves, while
dirty ragged boys swarm round the sexton every time he
digs, peering with undevout eyes on the bones of their
forefathers, which pious relatives once thought safe from
mortal ken. The town maintains a handsome hearse,
which is in attendance at every funeral.

Strangers settling here would find bank, post-office, gas,
street-lamps, and a public hall. Botanists and anglers

would be quite at home in the vicinity.   Noble trees
encircle the old mansions of Craigdarroch, Caitloch, and
Maxwelton, all within short distances of the village.
The new princely house of Major Walker,* not finished,
towers like a giant in the distance, commanding three-
fourths of the little town from its topmost turret. The
trees at Craigdarroch are very noticeable.   The thin
white-stalked birks tremble like orphans beneath the
massive protection of spruces, larches, oaks, and beeches,
so well-grown and with such brawny arms, that 'night
seems all day to sleep in their branches'; while waves of
odour circulate among their boles.

  Thoughtful students, lovers of Nature, who hate sea-
sickness and that noisy, brawling sea, and prefer hills
swelling with heather and thyme, where, on fresh pastures
screened by larch-woods, the sheep are bleating—persons
who pray to be delivered from the vain crowds which
jostle at fashionable watering-places, bringing the organ-
grinder and all sorts of tobacco and bad puns along with
them—would do well, in company with the corncrake, the
cuckoo, and the swallow, to visit this interesting locality.
Renwick's simple monument is here, built about half a
mile from the old market-cross; while the descendants
of the Scottish Convenanters and martyrs, having somewhat of their creed and habits, still linger, like rare
native plants, in hamlet, glen, and mountain - furrow.
[1864.]

> At Moniaive I sit as on a throne,
>   Surrounded by the threefold sound of streams,
>   And there, in summer twilight, through my dreams
> Flit fair-haired rustic children, and the tone
> Of silvery laughter which I call my own ;
>   While roses festooned on the cottage rows
> (Sweet nests ! they wrong you when they call you streets),
>   Give me their incense, while around me flows
> White smoke made slightly odorous with peats.

        * The late Sir George Walker, *vide* page 11.

What guant old houses with old trees around,
Tis mine to see! Craigdarroch in the North,
And in the South, where speckled kine abound
On holms of Cairn, the parish church looks forth
O'er bristling tombstones to the old, old mound.

DUNSCORE

The bailies and councillors of Dumfries had risen early, and with undaunted breasts had buckled on their best in presence of the snows of March, for that day they must walk in procession, and eat goodly meat, and utter bland discourses, and roar out lusty cheers. With the magistrates the people also arose on the tiptoe of expectation, for Saint Crispin's Day was to be revived, the Volunteers were to give salutes, and the fair town was to be decorated. Arches, processions, illuminations, bonfires, *feux-de-joie,* dinners, and after-dinner speeches, all came off as arranged, and the carnival which swept over the land in honour of the marriage of our Prince was coming to a close, when a countryman who had missed the train went wearily plodding on his way to a town sixteen miles north of Dumfries. For a while the lurid light reflected by the clouds denoted where the great bonfires were burning, and what the great centres of population were busy with; but soon the way became solitary and dark. The traveller, who trod the road for the first time, and who had to wait long at the parting of the ways till some chance passer-by would inform him of his proper path, might well have envied the 'English Opium-eater,' who in similar circumstances could have lain quietly down behind a hedge, and awakened when the sky was blue and the earth musical and gay. Not having the constitution of De Quincey, it was as well not to try the plan which a pair of wearied limbs were suggesting, but bear right on for the first available inn. By-and-by a loyal house, all flaming with 'tallow-dips,' hove in sight, and soon 'mine hostess' made all right for the night. The only thing odd about the accommodation was the extraordinary height of the bed, making the sleeping-couch of the traveller resemble somewhat the tree-cradles of the Indians of the Orinoco. Next morning, while waiting for hot water to scald his razor, the stranger raised the window and looked out, and—there was Dunscore!

Making use of the traveller's note-book, the present writer would aver that Dunscore is a little village built entirely without any prearrangement on the part of the builders. In fact, the houses seem to have been engaged in a reel, and to have stopped dancing in the middle of it. To this day, every 'Jock has his Jenny' thereabouts. Two inns, two churches, two schools, and several other worthy pairs of houses and of persons, make up the hamlet of Corlack, or, in common parlance, Dunscore, whose inhabitants thrive by the banks of the river Cairn, and receive their newspapers once a week by the Dumfries and Moniaive omnibus. In good sooth, except on the weekly market-days when the whirl of gigs sends clouds of dust over the heads of the admiring children, this place is quiet and sleepy, the very acme of dullness and drowsiness. The moor is quiet, the green rising knolls around are quiet, the trees are quiet, or, when the wind is high, sing drowsy hymns, and the Cairn is too far away to be noisy. The lotus-eaters of Homer or of Tennyson would find this locality very much to their mind. One could vegetate here like a garden-edible, and grow fat like an apricot on the sunny side of a wall. A friend of ours last winter favoured this district with a lecture on the Millennium. The silence of Dunscore hills and glens, the slowly-curling smoke, and the murmuring streams and trees, the far-off rattle of the cart laden with wood, or the appearance of a flock of sheep on the distant highway, are suggestive of peace, and of the fraternity of the lion

and the lamb. Probably the parishioners have private
squalls and heart-burnings enough within-doors, but these,
we should think, they would drop at the threshold. An
angry man would be a paradox where Nature is so tranquil.
The singing birds would make a rude oath appear
impertinent.

Yet the parish of Dunscore has heard groans, and fiery
hearts have chosen it for a home. Ask for the old tower
of Lag. The last inhabitant of that square, narrow,
massive ruin, Sir Robert Grierson, was swift to shed the
blood and augment the privations of the Covenanters;
and many a time in these sequestered glens and dales
the conventicle has dispersed itself when the dragoons
were in the distance. But the Covenanters had friends as
well as enemies in the parish. John Kirk, the proprietor
of the square tower of Sundaywell in Glenesslin, often
opened his gates to screen the fugitives, and protected
to the utmost the ejected ministers.

The vicinity of Dumfries has been adorned by the
generosity of an inhabitant of this parish, namely, Dr
Crichton of Friars Carse, whose munificent donation of
£100,000 laid the foundation, built the walls, and otherwise endowed the noble lunatic asylum of the county.
On the property of Friars Carse is the farm of Ellisland,
in which our national poet resided during some of the
most important and fruitful years of his brief life.

No great proprietor holds the parish of Dunscore under
thumb. It is portioned out pretty equally, and possessed
by what are called 'bonnet-lairds.' One of these lairds
gets credit with a large party for 'having a very big
bee in his bonnet.' Thomas Carlyle,* our modern
Jeremiah, full of hero-worship, German learning and
history, happens to be one of the heritors of Dunscore.

* The reader will note that this sketch was written while 'the
sage of Chelsea' was alive.

Carlyle married a Miss Jane Welsh, a lineal descendant of the son-in-law of John Knox, by which marriage he became possessed of the farm of Craigenputtock,* in Glenesslin, towards the west or Galloway side of the parish. About 1825, Carlyle formed the singular resolution of locking himself up in this dreary moorland farm, far from the amenities of towns or the common sources of social enjoyment, 'solely,' he says, 'with the design to simplify my way of life, and to secure the independence through which I could be enabled to remain true to myself.' Here for several years Carlyle revolved in his own peculiar way the social and philosophical problems, and here he wrote *Sartor Resartus*, a book which has been variously reviewed—some critics placing it only second to the book of Job, and others consigning it to the limbo of nonsense! So little Dunscore contains two shrines. Apollo has visited the parish twice in the garb of a farmer, and to the simple inhabitants only passed for such. It would have been well for Burns had he exercised somewhat of the strong will evinced by Carlyle, and separated himself from company unworthy of him and degrading to his genius. Dumfriesshire did not improve poor Robert. He did not live, even at Ellisland, a life at all in keeping with the grandeur of his sentiments and the aspirations of his better nature. As original and as great as Carlyle, he was neither so moderate nor so wise.

Our traveller, who first viewed Dunscore parish from the window of an inn, arose one lovely May morning, a morning when heaven's light was falling on the mountains like pearls from the bosom of Juno or the Queen of Love, and passing the stately parish church of Glencairn, crossed the Cairn at Crawfordton bridge.

* Carlyle left this property to Edinburgh University, and the income is spent in providing the funds for the Jane Welsh bursaries.

Blackbirds, fat with the generosity of spring, were piping in every shady bush.

The scenery in the lower part of Glenesslin was sylvan and beautiful; but as the stranger proceeded upwards, the hills on either side grew black and steep, and the country heathy and full of dreary peat-bogs. At last he 're-connoitred' Craigenputtock, and was at first mistaken for a London bookmaker. After an excellent tea, however, matters began to improve. The stranger fancied that the plain two-storied building might with all its homeliness be a snug, convenient dwelling. Some excellent old trees shielded it from the storm. As for the garden, it was plain that, as Emerson, writing of his own, says, 'he who looks at it must discover that the owner has some other garden.' We have heard of Carlyle being a smoker, but not a florist. He has tried his hand at weeding out 'shams,' and whether he have the art or not, no one can deny that he has the industry necessary for success.

Twice during a goodly term of years the landlord has cantered on pony-back from Dumfries to look after his property. Being bantered about the hairiness of his face by one of his old neighbours, he declared (taking the pipe from his mouth, and talking in plainest Doric) that he had not time to shave. Those who know the laborious life which Carlyle leads, will take this saying for more than jest. Very captivating are the novels of Edward Bulwer Lytton, but the reader of *Sartor* will remember the vow contained therein, never to read them after getting through *Pelham*. There is a reasonable excuse for not reading novels and for not shaving for a man who works hard, but for that dreadful class of human beings who talk of *ennui* and 'killing time,' such amusements might be medicinal.

Our traveller was afterwards located in a cathedral

city of England, whence he sent us an angry and amusing
letter.   He had purchased a ticket for a course of lectures
under some Christian or scientific association.   As he took
his seat one evening in the hall, a pompous-looking man
in holy orders marched up through the audience to the
rostrum with the air of a country schoolmaster, whose
creaking shoes frighten the nut-cracking boys into
silence.   This *pastor fidelis* had got the subject of modern
infidelity to handle, but instead of treating it in a satisfactory manner, he took out of his intellectual pocket
a wax doll of the Dunscore heritor, the puppet strings of
which he made to go, explaining the motive-power after
a theory of his own.   He then fell to cuffing and kicking
the image, and latterly exposed it to thunder and lightning
of his own getting up.   At last, when the place of its
eyes was scarcely discernible, when its stumps were
broken like that of Dagon of old, and its nose was considerably awry, he bestowed on it a few repentant kisses,
gave it a smart cuddle or two, and finished with an important recipe: ' Beware, my audience, of making Carlyle
an idol—there is no harm, however, in treating him as
a doll.'

In contrast to this estimate, we will close by giving a
few words on the author of *Sartor* by a modern professor
in Glasgow :

' Carlyle loves the lyre, but it is the lyre that builds
the walls of cities. . . . He does not rest in truth, paint,
sing, or prove it, but breathes, moves, fights, and dies
for it.   Like Luther's, his words are battles.   There is
nothing grander in literature than some of his litanies of
labour.   They have the roll of music which makes armies
march.   His *French Revolution* is prose, but it is such
prose as the world never saw before. . . . As a historian,
he is notably exact, and his descriptions of places and
events are as fresh as Homer's.'

Carlyle is 69 years of age. I wonder if he'll ever see
Dunscore again.

> In churchless graveyard lies a wolf of mine,
>   His grave, 'tis said, lacks greenness, and his name
>   Is as a black fly in thine amber fame—
> Grierson of Lag ; now where he quaffed his wine
> Is a gaunt, roofless tower where screech-owls dine.
>   My Ellisland—well, 'twas in tipsy mood
>   Burns cursed it—like a fair face in a hood
>   It smiles from bowers of green ; but bare and high,
>   Where over quaking bogs the cold winds sigh,
> And where the May-flower hardly blooms in June,
>   And late, late comes the swallow or cuckoo,
>   Stands Craigenputtock, where our Carlyle drew
> Sour milk from my thin breast—his every rune
>   Bitter as smoke of burning heath—but true.

A VISIT TO CARLYLE'S FARM OF CRAIGENPUTTOCK

This is a Dumfriesshire shrine not easily reached. It
is high in Glenesslin, in the Parish of Dunscore,
on the borders of Kirkcudbrightshire. Carlyle describes it well in that letter of his to Goethe, which is
quoted in most biographical articles, professing to give a
sketch of the sage of Chelsea. From far over the
Atlantic the wise man of the West — Emerson —
found him out in this secluded nook. In the late
biography of Professor Wilson, transmitted to us by an
affectionate pen, we have an account of a tryst between
Carlyle and Wilson to meet each other at Craigenputtock
Wilson proposes to get by a stage coach to Thornhill,
where Carlyle will meet him with a pony—for beyond a
disposable barrow, wheeled vehicles were scarce in that
part of Dunscore—and Wilson has some dream of romantic villages between Thornhill and Carlyle's farm. The
farmer undertakes that his wife shall wear her Goethe
brooch, and that they will have a holiday — much
philosophising, and much climbing among the heather.

D

It would seem that Christopher, however, allowed
Craigenputtock to be unvisited. It was here that Carlyle wrote that solid and beautiful essay on Burns, which
struck the keynote of much subsequent writing on the
same subject. Here also he composed that book which
reads like no other, *Sartor Resartus*—'written in star-
fire and immortal tears.' It is strange that little
Dunscore should contain two shrines, sacred to the
memory of at least two of our three greatest literary
Scotchmen — Craigenputtock and Ellisland — though
the first is yet scarcely far enough away in time to
get that enchanting blue colour around it with which
distance invests the mountain. About this time next
century there will be a much greater anxiety as to what
sort of farmhouse that is, or shall we say *was* (for we
are going at a rapid pace now), which contained and
nurtured the author of the *French Revolution* and of
Frederick, when the youthful giant was accomplishing
his earlier labours.

But to our recent visit. Lately, when poring over
the tombstones in a local churchyard, we espied the
magic word 'Craigenputtock' on one of them, and coming
to learn that it represented the genuine article, we thought,
'Well, if from there to here they can transport their dead,
the journey thence cannot be very serious for one quite
alive.' Serious it by no means was, except finding that
the pilgrimage must be performed alone, for what boy of
sense would go far out of his way to see a nest from which
the birds had flown, even though it should have been
an owl's, which was the goddess of wisdom's own bird?
One had but to lie down with the lamb and rise with
the lark, taking the advice literally, and not going into
quibbles and metaphysics about it, as doth charming Elia
in his essays. The sun had not advanced very high in the
heavens when we found ourselves several miles on our

way, walking in the latter days of May, by the side of the
river Cairn, which was bubbling the softest of stories,
and wooed by the most odorous of winds. There also
burst on our sight, what the pervading greenness of pastoral districts often forbids, whole acres of broom in
bloom—that plant which Linnæus is said to have so much
envied our country for possessing, and which, if we recollect the story aright, almost took his breath away the
first time he gazed on its splendour. Broom, furze, sloe,
'hagberry,' were in blossom, and the ferns had unrolled
themselves and were not frost-blighted—though they are,
like potatoes, very tender when holding up their fans of
rarest green. We entered at once into the feelings of
Ruskin when he exclaims that it tends to make us
morose that so much of our holiday-time and converse
with Nature is withheld till autumn. After the protracted indoor life of winter, it is most cheering and
refreshing to witness every leaf in a freshness which
whispers of no decay, and the variety of the tints of green
are quite as beautiful for a landscape painter as the more
highly-coloured foliage of autumn. Life in early summer
is oozing out of every pore. It is then that blossom,
fragrance, the song and beauty of birds, and the various
sounds, habits, and colours of insects, are all most interesting. Add to this the greater length of day in June
than in September, and we think our case a very strong
one either for transferring our usual holiday-time, or com-
promising matters by taking the one fortnight say in early
June, and the other as before. With such thoughts we
turned away from the valley of the Cairn and ascended
Glenesslin. Every step we took now caused matters to
alter for the worse. The trees grew stunted, the wayside
flowers paler and smaller, we exchanged the thrush and
blackbird for the curlew, the glen got narrow, and the un-
covered bones of the hills jutted out. Dreary undulations

of heath, and, last of all, swampy peat-bogs, put us in mind
of that bleak Caledonia which—together with its naked
population, bringing down the deer for present food by
sheer speed of foot—disgusted the Roman soldiers from
the orange-groves of the Po and Arno—at least, so says
the ponderous author of the *Decline and Fall*, whom it is
not easy to trip up. More than once Carlyle uses the
goose for a simile, and more than once did we meet with
flocks of geese grazing near the farmhouses on the way
to his former residence. It was a great relief when
we got so high that we could overlook the wild rough
hills on either side, and see the purple mountains of
Galloway soaring up into the white clouds of the blue
sky.

Fortunately, when we called at the veritable door of
the house we wanted, we found the tenant-farmer at
home. Our host was—what we had hardly bargained
for—an admirer of his landlord, and possessed cartes
and letters sent him from the latter, which were
interesting to look at. The house itself was a plain
two-storied building, homely, but convenient. It was
not directly on the public road, but commanded it.

Stories that had reached us of Carlyle's smoking pro-
pensities were confirmed by the experience which his
tenant had of him during two visits a goodly term of years
apart. It appeared also that in these visits he not only
indulged in easy clothes and smart riding, but also spoke
the plainest Doric. His tobacco reached him through
that shortest of clay pipes called a 'cutty,' and, at his
second visit, his beard was independent of the razor. His
letters about business matters, cutting and flaying trees,
crops, sheep, etc., were in a small neat hand, the punctua-
tion well attended to, and the matter right in the writer's
eye.

It would appear that we were only the second visitors

who had arrived out of sheer respect for the former occupant in the time of the present tenant. The first one
was in connection with the London press. Our host gave
us a long convoy down the glen, and we purposed to go
home the same night, but the sky getting black, we preferred nestling in a primitive house in which the schoolmaster of the district lodged, and into whose bed we
tumbled—the said personage being abroad. Next morning
we completed the circle, and after getting home, heard
a good deal about eccentricity and a wild goose
chase.

Since writing the above, we have learned that a new
tenant, a Carlyle, and a relative of the great author,
has obtained a lease of Carlyle's little Dumfriesshire
estate. This bit of news will be interesting to many of
the admirers of the Dunscore laird.

It should not be inferred that Carlyle never left his moorland
retreat, as he and Mrs Carlyle paid many pleasant visits to their
intimate friends, Dr and Mrs James Russell, at their beautiful
little residence, Holm Hill, charmingly situated on a knoll near to
Nith Bridge, overlooking the river, and within half-a-mile of
Thornhill village. The house is the property of His Grace the
Duke of Buccleuch, and is now occupied by the Misses Wallace,
the sisters of the present Writer. The wooden seat to which
Carlyle retired for work and reflection is yet to be seen under the
shade of some large trees in the gloomiest part of the grounds,
where no sun can penetrate. It still bears the name of 'Carlyle's
seat,' and it faces a dreary, uninteresting stone wall, overgrown
with moss and ivy, separating the arbour from the main road to
Dumfries—any distant view being completely shut out by the wood
and the steep bank on the other side of the road. The encircling
gloom would have depressed the feelings of anyone but Carlyle,
but there he spent many solitary hours in preference to the gay
and sunny surroundings which were left behind him. On these
visits he has been known to refuse, rather unceremoniously, the
proffered acquaintance of local dignitaries, who, while calling on
Mrs Russell, had learned of his presence, and asked to be introduced to him. He, probably without considering Mrs Russell's
feelings in the matter, too readily imputed the motives of his would-
be visitants to vain curiosity rather than to a desire to show respect
to his age and philosophic distinction.

PENPONT AND SKARR-GLEN *

Situated between the larger towns of Thornhill and
Moniaive, Penpont seems to have sucked out from its
two neighbours a considerable quantity of vitality. It is
a progressive, thriving town, where new houses and old
houses are jostling against each other for room, while its
two neighbours are reverend veterans reposing on their
laurels, having got their wisdom-teeth and every preroga-
tive and faculty of manhood. Nay, it is whispered (but
we believe it not) that these two are getting gray-haired
and rheumatic, that they are not so bulky as they once
were, that both their work and wages have decreased
considerably, and that their most promising children are
in the habit of forsaking them, to seek their fortunes in
Glasgow, in Liverpool, or in the Colonies. It is amusing
to see how the new and the old houses commingle at
Penpont. Here an ancient aboriginal structure, with
thatched roof, bearing a goodly crop of weeds, and with
windows no larger than a kitten's face, is pressed on both
sides by handsome two-storied buildings constructed of
the red freestone of the vicinity. Our sympathies are
with the oppressed: we do not like to see these
old houses overshadowed, deprived of proper draught
for their chimneys, and rendered shabby by these
new, impudent dandies. Better to be entombed than
exposed to such dishonour. Modern architecture has
done little as yet for the church of the parish. Of
course, we are not comparing it with a high ideal. All
that we would say is: Step into the neighbouring
parish of Tynron, and you will see a church fitted for a
rural congregation which might teach the heritors of
Penpont better things.†

* ' Scaur ' is the modern, if not the more correct spelling.
† The present beautiful and capacious building here desiderated,

From Thornhill, across the Nith to Penpont, the walk is delightful. Drumlanrig Castle, its widespread parks, and the blue Lowthers forming a screen, are on the right. A fine bridge spans the Nith at a considerable altitude above the stream—so considerable, that what De Quincey calls My Lady Tenebræ, who lurks in dark waters, inviting the disconsolate to her arms, converted Nith Bridge once on a time into a 'Bridge of Sighs'—a poor, unfortunate creature having leapt from its ledge; and for a sign there was found, when daylight broke, a single slipper. The brewer of the district, M‹Kaig, has here established a garden, which, despite all that teetotalism may say on the degradation which attends the brewing of malt, is a garden so trim and fertile that any teetotaler of taste might wish to have one like it. Of the curious old sculptured stones of Scotland, which we believe have been photographed most extensively by the members of a great book-club, one is enclosed by a railing in a park adjoining. Having passed through a fine avenue of old trees, the road becomes gay with churches and manses; while the Keir hills on the left, and the turreted and brown house of Capenoch, one of the seats of the Dumfries-shire branch of the Gladstone family, lurking amid the dense foliage, overlook the traveller. Entering Penpont, you find a pretty street, Pringleton, with square patches of flowers and shrubs before each door. Having got through the village, the gate and porter's-lodge of Capenoch, and the curved white walls meeting at the wide entrance, enliven the scene. You next come upon the Reformed Presbyterian

was erected at a cost of over £3000. The foundation was laid in 1867, and it was opened in 1869. The organ, of excellent tone and quality, by Forster & Andrews, Hull, which cost £350, was introduced in 1875, being the first in the county located in a county parish—that in Greyfriars Church, Dumfries, alone preceding it.

church and manse, most pleasant, clean, elegant buildings, not at all in keeping with the gloomy Calvinism with which their accusers are apt to taunt the members. It is a pity that this well-placed, well-attended kirk, whose pew-holders are drawn from a circle of 30 miles in diameter, should so lately have suffered disruption. Somewhat of the feeling which fills us with emotion when surveying an ivy'd tower seizes on us when we think of the descendants and representatives of the 'Hillmen,' or 'Cameronians.' They have their roots far down in the dead kingdoms of the past. They are peculiarly Scotch, and more than that, Lowland Scotch. They are descended spiritually from John Knox himself, and we question whether they are not the eldest born of his children; and yet to see the small remnant wrangling and separating in these latter-days, after remaining united against all the frowns and seductions of the world for centuries, is, to say the least, painful to contemplate. Leaving their church, to which so many wearied pilgrims repair every Sabbath day, where the Skarr murmurs so gently, and taking a last fond look of the glorious valley of Nith winding away in the far distance, we pursue our course into the highland and pastoral portion of the parish. The turnpike-road is high above the roaring stream and its curtain of wood. The heathery hills tower up on every side, almost threatening to meet, while through the dark and narrow gorge the burn dashes, adorned by a few smiling haughs and comfortable-looking farm-steadings. After four miles delightful rusticating, during which we had the honour to meet 600 head of Highland cattle—large-horned, tousy tykes, mostly two-year-olds, direct from Falkirk Tryst—we arrived at the house of the parish teacher of the locality, whose habitat is truly denominated Woodside. He received us with mountaineer hospitality, and promised to be our guide, not only to the sloe, bramble-berry, and hazel covers, but to the dreaded Glenquhargen Craig, in whose inaccessible cliffs the eagle is famed to have its nest. For, as the traveller who arrives at Alexandria and ascends the Nile to Cairo pauses not, but by depth of purse and suppleness of limbs moves right on, and keeps his face directly towards the Pyramids ; so he who would become acquainted with Penpont will not rest until, far above Chanlockfoot, far beyond the hum of a busy world, where railway-whistle never was heard, he stands face to face with this precipitous mass whose brow is lifted 1000 feet above sea-level. From the schoolhouse at Woodside to Glenquhargen, on each side, but especially on the right, tower up tremendous hills—green to the summit, it is true, but scarred by winter-streams, whose whinstone beds, dark-blue in the distance, stretch from the top, in shape like attenuated fans. Vast boulders, rolled down by the storms of ages—

> 'Crags, knolls, and mounds confusedly hurl'd,
> The fragments of an earlier world'—

obstruct the course of the river Skarr. Lovely side-straths branch off occasionally from the main glen ; but everything betokens gradually the approach of the desert. The trees are limited to the birch and hazel, and these are stunted—Glenquhargen having got sad poverty-stricken specimens clinging to its base. Little mounds, russet with fern, variegate the uniform green. Here on its south and south-west side is the notable craig, challenging the boldest grog-fortified tar to ascend it. Cleopatra's Needle has been subjected to the soles of British feet; the members of the Alpine Club have written volumes which make us fear the eagle's nest would not be safe; but we confess to our shame that we three visitors utterly failed to mount Glenquhargen. The weathering of the whinstone has spread out large

sheets of rotten marl, and before the climber gets midway, the beetling of the rocks above is so extremely
favourable to giddiness that a retreat to the Skarr has
to be sounded. One good thing is gained by attempting
to climb; you are possessed of a far livelier idea of the
real height. In this lonely quarter of the world, it is
strange to observe how certain sounds apprise you of the
depth of the silence. Don Quixote's inamorata had a
voice—not like Cordelia's, which was 'soft and low, an
excellent thing in woman,' but one which, said Sancho
Panza, 'I could hear at a league distant.' Perhaps
it was not so stentorian after all, for we heard Chanti-
cleer's notes of love or defiance nearly as far away.
When we tossed our stones with giant arm down the
abysses, Echo startled from its cave as if the tricky Pan
had alarmed it. It is worth noticing, that Pan's trick of
screaming, startling to Echo and to the lonely traveller,
is the origin of our word 'panic'; for Pan, though a
shepherd's deity, had a good deal of roguish fun in his
nature.

A Winter Walk in Penpont and Tynron

In the midst of these short days of darkness, hurricane,
frost, snow, and flood, the sun broke from his swaddling
clothes one morning and sent his level rays across the
Sanquhar moors, and painted the eastern clouds with
such splendour that it was an easy matter to imagine
that you saw his car whereon he used to mount when
Greece was young—his car and his swift willing horses
neighing with eagerness to start, and shaking the lingering darkness of the dawn from their manes. Great
clouds of rooks circled between us and the sun, and the
hedge-sparrow, with short, fitful warble, invited us to
trust for once to the weather, and take our ticket at

the station. Compared to leafy summer, there was a
wondrous change on the banks of the Nith, but the dark
green of its numerous spruce trees still preserved many a
fairy nook from intruding eyes. At other points, houses
that we had never seen before, were exposed. At Thornhill, a courteous driver of an omnibus, and a boy decked
in grey costume, and with a trumpet like a miniature
volunteer, invited us to a seat. An old gentleman, with
a very wide nose, and a pair of glasses a-straddle it, kept
poking us with his elbow, and supplying us with snuff, of
which he took enormous quantities. The fine old race of
snuffers is on the decay, and getting as rare as otters in
some parts of Nithsdale. What an air of comfort these large
ornamented powder mulls throw around one. You are sure
the owner is well with his creditors; and when calmly
solving some problem connected with church or state, he
brings out his sneezing-box, opens it on creaking hinges
merry as a cricket's chirp, taps it on the back, and with
a snort like a grampus, discusses the contents; then you
may be sure the next score of sentences will shed a flood
of light on the vexed question, or perhaps set it at rest
for ever. Pleasantly did the old man chat of the Capenoch,
which we saw to our left, and of the old Kirkpatrick family,
dead and gone—of Sir Thomas's enthusiasm for curling—
how he loved the roaring game—of the *mésalliance* of his
son—how his young soul became all on flame with the
tailor's daughter. These, and kindred topics of the Kirkpatricks being discussed, our friend took to the Nith—
pointed out Dalgarno churchyard, in which, he said, the
present Emperor and Empress of the French had each a
great-grandfather lying entombed. 'Thornhill,' quoth
he, 'is just Burns' Dalgarno.'

> 'I gaed to the tryste o' Dalgarnock,
> And wha but my fine fickle wooer was there?
> I glowr'd as I'd seen a warlock.'

We clapped the old man on the shoulder with such
violence as to make his spectacles quiver. 'Thank you.'
Sure we've got up almost all the localities of Burns' songs.
Hair of Feuchlarg but the other day pointed us out from
an eminence on his farm the very house in Glencairn
where 'Willie brew'd a peck o' mat, and Rob and Allan
cam' to see.' A quiet house it was, lying in the fold of
the hills, with its blue smoke floating jagged and lazy
above it, far away from Forbes M'Kenzie, and very fit to
be a palace for drunken kings, for there at all events they
would not quarrel with their neighbours.

Our snuff-taker next discoursed to us upon the unknown stone with its sculpturing at Nith Bridge; how it
had at one time been the stone to which boats were
fixed in the days of ferries, but that on one occasion
nineteen persons having taken seats in the ferry-boat
were joined by a twentieth, who smelt of sulphur. The
consequence was that the boat was upset, and all save the
very questionable stranger and the oarsman perished—
the stranger never having been seen again. This gratuitous mischief on the part of Diabolus set people anxious,
and the first bridge at Thornhill was built. A very
curious interjectional sound was made by the speaker
when in a hurry, which I have often noticed in Dumfriesshire—namely, a sound like 'whoa.' You ask a question,
and 'whoa' begins the answer. It is used as a kind of
stepping-stone whereon to steady before taking the
spring, or as a sort of sandbank to the shooter behind
which he takes aim, for no sooner is 'whoa' uttered than
the usual sounds which constitute words flow freely into
sentences.

The fine new parish church of Penpont, now nearly
finished, next became a topic; and, bidding goodbye to
our friend who was on the way to Moniaive or Minnyhive
(the latter being the form which preserves the original

Celtic meaning, as in Minnybole now called Maybole, ought to get the preference), we dropped down, a little after passing the church of the Rev. William Milroy, and got into the highland part of Penpont *en route* to Glenmannow and Glenquhargen.

A fine day in winter! It is like an apple of gold in a picture of silver—it is a gem made glorious by its setting. Consider how little light there is in winter—how lazy suns get up at nine o'clock and haste to bed at four—how many days the sun is never seen—and then you will realise what a pleasure such a day brings. The temperature, always lower than on a fine day in summer, allows you to get over the ground at a quicker rate. The roads, slightly hard with frost, keep your shoes light and clean, and the rarity of the atmosphere enlivens. Not only the hedge-sparrow warbles and talks to his friends, but every wandering vagabond who has been hewing wood and drawing water for the last fortnight gets out of his prison and takes the highway leading to new possibilities of existence. The farmer who has been confined to the fire-nook, wearing his nightcap and getting ill-natured with the fatigues of the nursery, is airing himself and his horse. The old crone is creeping along the hedges to have a chat with her older cousin half-a-mile off. The village maiden with shining morning face has bade adieu to her mirror, and ventures with basket of butter to market to see and be seen. The dog lying opposite the hearth and snapping and hunting in dreams is on the scent of hare or rabbit. The poultry confined to monotonous artificial feeding are scattered picturesquely across the knolls of 'yonder green field after worms and slugs. The mole digging long time laboriously and deeply for worms, as we poor Britons will shortly need to do for coal, is raising enormous brown heaps across the lawn, and partly doing the ploughman's work by turning up the soil near the surface. So furious have been the recent floods that here in a ditch we have the little hillocks first-covered with water and then the water slightly frozen at the edges. The glen of the Skarr has a magnificent opening—narrow, with high heathery hills on either side, and a tumbling river thickly shaded with trees on the right hand, while several streams leap across the highway, and have rustic wooden logs laid across them for foot passengers, while forded by gig and cart. The old stocking-weaver had a primitive house among the trees, near to where the Skarr plays fantastic tricks with the rocks, and has scooped them out into every form of pot, caldron, or rocking-stone. But, alas! the little man with the bald head and large eyes, and thin locks of hair nicely spread over his crown like tufts of yarn drying on a boulder,

> 'Sleeps at last that long, quiet sleep,
> Never more to wake or weep,'

beside his martyred covenanting ancestors in the adjoining kirkyard. Small were the stocking-weaver's demands and supplies while in life—a house with one room, one window, and one closet, without a bit of garden, or any poultry or pig; but dead, no grandee in the parish gets any more accommodation.

> 'Napoleon, whom the world did dread,
> Now that his wars are o'er,
> Sleeps like a beggar on a bed,
> Measuring six feet by four.'

Gradually we approach Laight—a farm once held by the Ettrick Shepherd, who used to ask down the rent to a price at which he could 'fen'.' He was inquired at by the Duke of Queensberry, if he made it nothing, would he have a profit? 'Yes,' quoth James, 'provided your Grace would stan' between me and the rot and the Februar' snaw-wreaths.' The road becomes higher, until

looking round us at Auchenhessnane, we see the river,
dwindled by distance, twining like a silver thread among
the chocolate-coloured branches of 'birk' and alder. It
is a mistake to think that there is no variety of colouring
in winter among trees because they want foliage. The
brown larch; the white-branched ash; the oak, grey or
green with lichen and moss; the almost red twigs of the
birch, with its white trunk speckled with black; the
spruce, almost blue; the red berries of the guelder-rose
still unplucked, and in sheltered places the hawthorn's;
the sheep, newly keeled, and the russet tufts of withered
ferns—these make up a variety nearly equal in tints to that
of autumn. Add to this, in soils where there is iron, the
rich brown of the newly-upturned furrow, gladdening
one's heart with the idea of future seed-time and harvest.
Sounds too occur. The torrent roars more hoarsely.
The startled black-cock screams, the thrush pipes a rusty
song on a tall tree-top at noon, and at rare intervals a
puff of smoke and crack reveals that a bullet is winged
against some hare or rabbit. Three roebucks bounded
past, like skiffs swaying up and down across billows with
their sterns painted white, and the blue-winged heron,
with its webless feet and long legs, rose from the pool at
our feet.

Now we are at Knockelly—sweet pastoral hamlet!
Knockelly, the second town in Tynron for size. Alas!
why has it no gardens? Never, since we read a poem in
Dr Grierson's museum at Thornhill, to the effect that man
having lost Eden tries to realise it still by keeping a small
patch of it, like a domestic pet, behind his door, with a
bower for courting at the further end, can we forgive the
landlord who grows his corn or other crops close up to the
peasants' window, dooming the country broth-pot to far
more starvation than that of the beggar's of Bethnal
Green. That at Knockelly—where land is cheap, and

there is no London market, where there is a trouting
stream in which the inhabitants may bathe every morning—there should be no opportunity to mitigate the
hardships of life by cultivating flowers or vegetables or
bees, seems to doom the inhabitants to drink the cup of
Tantalus daily.

What revels our fancy played at the rustic school of
Woodside—to the urchins of which we were about as
interesting as Wombell's Menagerie drawn by camels or
elephants would be to the youthful sciolists of Dumfries
Academy. How much we admired Chanlockfoot, and
only wished we were there in the nutting season. With
what a shudder we saw the trees beginning to grow
dwarfish for want of soil, and the bones of the bare hills
sticking out beaten by everlasting storms. We sat
down on the very spot where the Duke and a party
from Drumlanrig had a picnic a few years before, and
thought that after all a pair of good eyes were wonderful democrats, and gave us possession of the Duke's
property nearly to the same extent as it is enjoyed by
the excellent owner of seven-eights of the parish :—

> Great boulders in the roaring Skarr,
>   Or quietly spread athwart its holms ;
> Green slopes, wood-clothed, that rise and war
>   With every blast and cloud that roams.
>
> Manse-like farm-houses, large and white,
>   Dead leaves that make the roadside brown,
> Odd gipsies begging for a mite,
>   Gigs pulsing up, carts rumbling down.
>
> Turning, we bid you all goodbye ;
>   And patting on the curly head
> One rustic child, say, with a sigh,
>   ' You'll be a man when we are dead.'

A LOCAL SAMSON

High are the hills of Penpont, broad are their shoulders,
tough is the whinstone which composes them. Broad

also are the shoulders of many of its parishioners. The quantity of cubic inches of air which their lungs can contain is enormous, and the muscular development of their limbs is a thing for which we well may be thankful. The raw material of the soldier abounds in the glen of the Skarr, in the straths overlooked by Glenquhargen Craig, in the soft undulating valleys which roll away from the base of Cairnkinna. Thin-blooded tailors are reared in towns on the sweating system in ill-ventilated garrets; shopkeepers, light and wiry, with swift wagging tongues, leap the counters like kangaroos, or ascend little ladders among soft goods with the agility of squirrels. Pale mechanics, pale preachers and teachers, with sour looks and sourer stomachs, fed on sago and arrowroot, tea and tobacco, to whom the 'haggis' immortalised by Robert Burns, eaten before going to bed, would be all night upon their groaning breasts, heavy as a nightmare or night-mastodon—these be your civilians. He whom Burns celebrates as the 'laird of the Cairn and the Scaur,' and who won the world-renowned whistle, would, for strength of digestive faculty, tested by John Barleycorn, have drunk blind a whole suburb of weavers.

But the mightiest production of Penpont parish was a local Samson, John M'Call of Glenmannow,* which is a farm not far from Glenquhargen. Although only six feet high, his shoulders were broad as a barn-door, and his limbs were moulded of iron. His clothes of hodden-gray were loosely fitted as if to allow for still greater growth, his bonnet lay softly and kindly on his head. (Oh, what headaches, what neuralgia, what tic-douloureux can the chimney-can hat be accused of!) His huge oaken staff was like a weaver's beam (how these weavers are slighted!), and the grasp of his hand was like the

* 'Glenmanna,' modern spelling, and 'Glenmanno' in the *Ordnance Gazetteer of Scotland.*

E

embrace given you by the coming together of upper and
nether millstones. The young clergyman newly inducted
into Penpont felt to his cost the warmth and pressure of
Glenmannow's squeeze. He had finished his sermon, and
was much 'blown' by exertion; he was thin and emaciated,
and looked remarkably like a subject for delicate ladies
to revive by means of cakes and wine when he came
tripping forward to respond to that mark of respect
usual on such occasions—namely, the shaking of hands.
Folk of all ranks and both sexes thronged forward for the
salutation. There was a rustling and a hustling. The
fragrance of musk and the smell of boiled turnips mingled
around the preacher's head, shedding a curious kind of
incense on the ceremony, and the squeezing to get forward
was quite exciting. Among the first, by main strength, was
Glenmannow. He was gallant enough, however, to give
way to a lady, whose jewelled fingers were a strong contrast
to the hand of the Samson-like shepherd. The preacher
had scarcely time to mark the 'new suit of hodden-gray,
the red and blue striped plaid, the black wool 'rig and
fur' galligaskins on the legs, each formed with a long
stripe to cover the upper part of the foot, and linked by
two holes over his third and great toes,' when his hand
was in that of Glenmannow. Now, M'Call, though strong
as Goliath, was innocent as a dove, and almost unconscious of his own firmness of muscle. The preacher, too,
had struck him as being a gun of very wide bore, so he
heartily rocked to and fro the pulpy fingers, assuring their
owner that he wished him the best of luck; that to sit
under him would likely be a pleasure, and that he 'maun
gie him a ca' sune, or they would be owre head and ears
wi' the clippin.' Meantime the minister felt as if his
mouth were filled with Cayenne pepper, or as if a horse-
power fly-blister were on his back. 'Tears starting from
his eyes, the preacher gazed on his fingers after the fierce

encounter, and found blood oozing from beneath every nail. He crammed the whole four into his mouth, and hurried out of the churchyard without any more shaking of hands.' As for Glenmannow, he had the proud consciousness of doing his duty, and had mingled with the crowd, quite unaware of the torture he had administered. So have we seen some poor compliant imbecile drink glass about with a 'seasoned cask,' and next morning the seasoned cask congratulating the imbecile, all smiles; while the latter, though he tried to smile, had a head splitting and throbbing. Take care of unequal matches. Take care of a *mésalliance.* No wonder, when people usually met honest John of Upper Penpont, they 'thrust only their forefinger, cocked like a pistol, into his palm extended to salute them.'

On one occasion Glenmannow was returning from Edinburgh, when a stranger, struck by his appearance, inquired if he had a taste for wrestling. 'Some, but no very meikle,' replied Glenmannow. 'I'll tie my horse to this alder tree,' said the stranger, who was a well-knit fellow, with something genteel in his appearance, 'and let us try a throw or two on this soft meadow.' Glenmannow gave a half-willing assent. They were equal in height, but the stranger was the slimmer, though, what he wanted in bone, appeared to be compensated by activity. The stranger, in shorter time than we take to tell it, was placed in that position in which

> 'The tip of the toes and the point of the nose
> Look up to the sky like the daisies.'

'My opinion of Scotland has risen with my fall,' quoth the stranger; 'and, in reply to your question, I say, no; I want no more wrestling, but I want to know your name.' 'Ye wud wunner what's in Scotland,' said Glenmannow; 'but I, Jock M'Call, reside at Glenmannow, a tenant of the Duke of Queensberry.'

The stranger, on the other hand, announced himself as
Viscount Kenmure. Glenmannow at once ducked and
unbonneted, begging pardon for his impudence in
'warsling wi' sic a great man, but that it was an acci-
dental sin.' Ever after Kenmure and the rustic shepherd
had a warm feeling towards each other, and met like
friends on equal terms, for the noble Viscount practised
and admired the manly art of self-defence.

James, Duke of Queensberry, resolved to astonish the
Cockneys with the strength of his shepherd. So, amid a
number of trained men, proud of their prowess, he announced that he could bring up a raw recruit—a shepherd
from his Scotch estates—who would turn out more than a
match for the nerve and sinew of London. The test-
game chosen was that of putting or throwing the stone.
Soon large bets were staked, chiefly against the Duke, who
lost no time in writing to John M'Call, to whom his
request was that of an Emperor, brooking no refusal.
The material to be thrown was a large ball of lead, and
the place was a bowling-green or cricket-field in the
Metropolis, surrounded by a high wall. Out strutted the
English champion with the bluster of the turkey and the
peacock's pride, looking as sprightly as possible, and
suggesting ideas connected with Glenmannow's bonnet,
galligaskins, stiff appearance, and uncombed hair, which
caused the spectators to titter much at the shepherd, and
to look on him as some clown or clumsy follower of the
Duke, brought forward in jest. Glenmannow heard not
the laughter of the Philistines, for his whole soul was
directed towards the champion and towards his own mission for which he had travelled so far.

Thud came his opponent's quoit or ball right up against
the wall amid a perfect explosion of applause. But, while
hats were tossing and the welkin ringing, Glenmannow,
urged on by a whisper from the Duke, was screwing up

every muscle to its proper pitch, though affecting the
greatest ease in his manner. 'Will you throw off your
coat? it will give you greater freedom,' said His Grace.
'Coat for *that*,' replied Glenmannow, 'I guessed it was to
be some great sky-rocket o' a throw that I was brocht a'
the way to London to see—something that I could hae
thocht on a' the way gain' hame. Na! na! nae coats aff
for that; ye micht hae done't yoursel'.' Then poising the
ball a short while in his hand, and repeating as by way
of incantation over it,—

> 'Auld man o' Maybole,
> Can ye shoe a wee foal?
> Yes indeed, and that I can,
> Just as weel as any man,'

he suddenly let it fly. 'There,' he cried, 'and he that
likes may gang and fetch it back.' The ball curved forward as if from the mouth of a cannon, cleared the wall
by a few inches, and alighted on the tile roof of a house
beyond. Crash it went through the tiles, penetrated the
somewhat rotten garret-floor, and rolled upon the second.
The people of the house rushed out in confusion, thinking
the French had landed, or that the man of the moon had
lost his balance and fallen down. His Grace won the
bets, paid all damages, and sent Glenmannow home to
his wife Mally with a year's rent in his pocket.

The Duke of Buccleuch, at that time colonel of a
regiment of fencibles, happened to be passing between
Dumfries and Sanquhar, and having made Thornhill his
station for the night, he billeted himself on the Duke
of Queensberry at Drumlanrig Castle. The latter having
enlightened his guest on the characteristics of Glenmannow, it was resolved to break a practical joke upon
the Shepherd-Hercules. Six of the stoutest grenadiers
were dispatched, with a formal billet, and with orders to
beat up Glenmannow's quarters, cross him, find fault with
everything, quarrel with him, and, if possible, overpower

and bind him, without injuring either his person or his effects. Those were the days (it being towards the end of the 17th century) when roads in Upper Penpont were little better than sheep-tracks; so through moors and mosses, 'mang winding bogs and leaping burns, the red-coats went forward provoking the curlew and lapwing, who, to mislead them from their nests, wheeled in airy circlets round them, as they defiled past the base of the mighty Cairnkinnow. From the top of Glenquhargen they first espied the low thatched-roof dwelling of Glen-mannow, the peat-stack leaning against the gable, and a hut—which contrived to pay a double debt, being barn, byre, and stable—attached to the other end of the moor-land shieling. At a short distance was a round 'bucht' in which the shepherd was wont to pen his flock. The party of military men arrived at the door-step a little before noon. Wife Mally was churning, and had a meal in preparation for her husband, who had not yet returned from 'looking his hill.' Soldiers were such rare visitors, that had Glenquhargen itself exhibited signs of coming to see them, Mally could scarcely have been more sur-prised. An uneasy feeling possessed her, as when an 'un-canny' bull entering your garden begins to look narrowly at your flower border when you are at the opposite side of the same. Trying to conceal her uneasiness made her only more awkward, and the soldiers, who perceived how timorously she asked them to be seated, began to work upon her fears.

'That bayonet of mine won't clear,' said one of the visitors, 'since it got soiled with the blood of that con-founded old herd who dared to refuse us the best he had.' 'Mally,' says the historian of this incident, 'was at this moment dishing the porridge in two "goans"* for her-

* Strong wooden vessels bound with hoop iron to hold the staves forming the sides in position.

self and John, when she made a dead pause, and letting
go the foot of the pot, suffered it to fall with a force which
jerked the "cleps" out of her hand,' and thus pot, porridge, and all were dashed upon the floor.

'I'll wipe mine from the old mole's blood before it
dries,' said the other fellow, 'and then it will not rust as
yours has done.' By this time Mally had reached the
threshold.

The porridge goan first dished was smoking beside
those spilt, when one of the soldiers exclaimed, 'Hand me
over these porridge.' 'Oh, no,' retorted Mally, 'if there's
ae thing on yirth our gudeman Jock would go through
fire and water for—it's his porridge cog. Gif he met his
best friend in the middle of his porridge, he wouldna let
on he kenned him,' said she, making a desperate attempt
to take the humorous view of the case. 'But, gude
friends, I assure you, he'll brain you if you do that,' she
again exclaimed, as the stranger clutched the dish sacred
to her lord, while at the same time she swept a cupboard
of its bread and butter with a view to serve them; but
nothing would satisfy her remorseless guests save a spoon
to each from a wicker creel in the corner. Enter Glenmannow: 'What's a' this; and wha's a' this?' 'Well,
sir, we've got a billet upon you from the Duke of Queensberry, with whom our Colonel, the Duke of Buccleuch, just
now is stopping.' 'Ye're making mair free than welcome,
I doot. A nicht's lodging ye'll get since sent frae the
Duke, but did the Duke say ye were to yoke on my
porridge like a wheen collies?' 'Like what? Hold your
peace, you clodpole, we are the king's servants, and ought
to be served without a grumble.' 'Go,' interposed the
leader, 'put a bullet through that fine fat calf and let's be
somewhat jolly with a roast on the moors, if old clod-
hopper's wife can cook it. Come, Mrs Braxy, take your
mouth from your master's ear, and attend,' for Mally was

whispering to Glenmannow her impressions and what
conversation she had heard, with intent to mollify him,
but had quite a different effect, to the joy of the
soldiers, who saw the tempest rising. 'Ye'll roast my
calf; I'll roast you,' exclaimed the shepherd. 'Down
with him, down with him,' roared the soldiers. Glenmannow had only time to toss his plaid on the bed and
relinquish his staff, too long for close quarters, and
turning round like a stag at bay he seized the first fellow
by the collar and the thigh, and using him both as his
sword and shield, with such fury and force, that, glad to
find the road to the door, the opposing party reached the
'bent' more terrified than injured; but he who was
trussed in Glenmannow's embrace had his skin stained
black and blue like that of his savage warrior forefathers.
Feeling himself fast becoming of the consistency of a
jelly, he howled most piteously for mercy. Glenmannow, deaf to his cries, rushed with him out-
of-doors, but chancing to spy one of his own carts
placed on end, he tore from it a shaft, first tossing the
soldier from him on the grass as the remorseless billow
heaves its wreck upon the strand, and with the huge
limb upon his shoulder, started off in the track of his
enemies.

And now occurred a chase with none to match it in the
annals of Penpont or Durrisdeer. The soldiers were the
most speedy, their pursuer had the longest wind. The
heels of the soldiers were spurred with fear, those of
Glenmannow were winged with rage. At the top of
Glenquhargen, the five, somewhat scattered, looked back,
but they seemed not to have gained a rood. At Cairnkinnow, favoured by his knowledge of the ground, the
shepherd was no farther from the last one than the length
of his evening shadow. At Gowkthorn they durst not
look round—they heard the 'thud' of the strong man's

footsteps, the wheezing of his throat. At this latter
place, fortunately for them, Glenmannow fell. He was
up in a minute, but as the ground slopes towards Drumlanrig the soldiers gained so much that henceforward
hope became a motive for their further speed. Staggering
like men overcome with drink they reached the western
staircase which leads into the court of the castle. Informed by the servants of their approach, the two Dukes
were waiting to receive them behind the balustrade.
The poor fellows had to be wiped of dust and sweat, and
restored by stimulants. Glenmannow rushed up only
three minutes behind. The cart shaft was on his shoulder.
His lips were foam-covered like the winner of the Derby.
His bonnet was lying among the heather where the last
covey of partridges had risen screaming in terror. The
Duke of Queensberry, though used to turn the helm of Glenmannow whichever way he pleased, lacked heart to meet
him in this mood, and left the first brunt of the encounter
to the Duke of Buccleuch, who, however, failed to stop
him, for Glenmannow rushed past upstairs into the court
of the castle; but doors were many, and getting confused,
he made for the kitchen, the road to which he best knew.
Here, a cook, fat and good-natured as Falstaff, and
various servants with fine faces and soft words, one offering
him spirits and water, another putting forward a chair, and
the cook herself taking the cart shaft as a handy bit of
future fuel, acted as modifying circumstances, and restored
the shepherd's long lost equanimity. 'Hang it,' he exclaimed, after a deep pause, 'its been a trick o' the Duke's
after a'; I see through it; I see it, I see it a'. Dangerous though, richt dangerous; I micht hae choked aff the
first ane like a "whitterock," or mauled the neist ane like a
rat.' A feast explanatory and conciliatory followed, and
all got back to headquarters well. Mally, with a
woman's forgiveness, had cared for the bruised soldier

left on the grass; and when Glenmannow got home, the
king's servant, well-wrapt round with blankets, was able
to be placed on horseback behind a guide, and conducted
to Drumlanrig, where a few guineas plastered the broken
bones.

Glenmannow died in 1705. It is sad to think that over-
exertion in lifting an immense stone, about four miles
above Drumlanrig, with a view to turn the current of the
Nith, was the proximate cause of death, though he lived
to a pretty long age. His curling-stone, proportionate to
his mighty arm, is in Dr Grierson's garden, Thornhill.

THORNHILL AND DRUMLANRIG

In some respects it is a misfortune for a small town to be
too near a large one. The poets would never have sung
of Venus if she had always shone at the edge of the
moon like some despised scintillation of the greater luminary, some Norfolk Island or other penal colony ready to
receive the refuse of its greater neighbour. London or
Glasgow spread out their huge wings, and the surrounding villages disappear under them like chickens in a
shower. Maxwelltown, though in a different county, is
swallowed by Dumfries. A stranger, not intent on careful distinctions, gives to the latter all the credit due to
the former. Who ever makes the plain, truthful statement, that to Kirkcudbrightshire belongs the glory of a
museum and an observatory, with a camera of such
transcendent power that Dumfries has to conceal its whims
under all manner of Venetian and other blinds? The
lesser town lying too near the greater, suffers by this in
many ways. Its shopkeepers listen to the unmusical
jingle of money in the pockets of those who hurry
onwards attracted by the great bargains over the bridge.

The restless, the gay, the frolicsome, hasten by omnibus, rail, or by other and cheaper methods, to mingle themselves with the glare, the stare, and the pressure of the Babylon of the locality, just as all rivers leap, trot, or crawl towards the ocean, which has plenty of water of its own already.

But when a town stands, like Thornhill, fourteen miles apart from one much larger than itself, and seven miles from any rival, it has a chance of educating its own talent and developing its native traits after a fashion which is fresh, singular, and striking. As in landlocked seas and huge isolated lakes we look for species of fish and molluscs distinct from that in the Atlantic or Pacific, so a certain definite manhood, such as the parish of Morton has peculiar conditions for rearing, ought to be expected in Thornhill.

For instance, when Thornhill suffuses with loyalty over some royal marriage or the like, it sets up its own arches instead of paying trains to see those of others. It even ventures on its own roar of applause, without either desiring or listening to the lion-roar of Dumfries. When some Burns' Anniversary is in the wind, does Thornhill rush abroad to sit at the feet of the great Professor Gifts-and-graces, and thump the floor of the City Hall? I warrant not: Thornhill has its chairman and its dinner, and a report about itself like the best of them. When in this town beards get troublesome, or when the brains of eight-day clocks get unsettled, the facts are announced to a barber and a clockmaker all its own. Native talent feathers the nests of those whom love, or comfort, or necessity call to live in each other's eyes. Indigenous merchants aid at house-heating. Aborginal tailors encompass with tape many a brawny chest. Its own doctors bring home at regular or irregular intervals the interesting fairies said to be found squatting in the bosom of its

cabbages. Nature and art have conspired to make
Thornhill what it is—an independent little member of
a great community, a solid shining star—not a demi-
nebulous cloud, merely feeding some more potent neighbour.

When you arrive at Thornhill Railway-station, you are
often slightly reminded of the fatness of the land (if you
have not been using your eyes while traversing the line),
by perceiving a sprinkling of the carriages of the local
nobility and gentry waiting for their owners. But the
ignobile vulgus has a noble chance as well. Two omnibuses
contend for the possession of your person, and as the fares
are moderate and the passengers limited, you have an
excellent opportunity of driving a bargain, and getting
ten times your weight in luggage slipped in beside you.
The first object of attraction to the traveller will be the
very excellent parish church towering on an eminence
near the town. The church visible has few better representatives than this strong and graceful structure. Having
entered the town, the old Market-cross, the spacious and
beautiful Buccleuch Hotel, the wide streets, the flag roofs,
and the carefully protected young trees rustling before
every other door, will convey peculiar impressions. Should
our traveller, however, think the town slow, let him visit
it on a ' hiring' day, cattle and dog show day, or great
bowling tournament time. If he is a linguist, he will hear
the dialect, from the calm, well-balanced remark up to
the shout of admiration; while his vision will be gratified
beholding the healthy rural faces of Upper Nithsdale.
Twice ten hundred upturned wondering eyes, inclusive of
the eyes of spectacles—all those eyes which at other times
survey the baking, brewing, sawing, shoemaking, and
general upholstery and clothes departments of horse and
man in the vicinity—will be zealously engaged, some
viewing Cheap John, some Cheap John's dupes, others

poring into the mysteries of Nature from the curve of a
Dahlia to the shape of a pigeon's beak.

Again, if our tourist had rather don the sporting-jacket,
let him to the bowling-green, and he will face antagonists
who have learned a goodly trick or two; or should Sir
Stranger be disposed to try a rifle-range either with
volunteers or on the adjoining moors, or to fill a basket
from the Nith, he will discover in Thornhill some who are
'to the manner born.' Yet in a short time an uneasy
feeling, making itself known like gentlest ripples at first,
will heave in his heart like a billow. From the moment
the omnibus set him down at the Cross, through all his
bowling, shooting, and fishing, a great quadrangular castle,
with turrets at the angles, and with windows past counting, has been courting his attention. It would be to see
Hamlet without the part of Hamlet, to be at Thornhill and
not visit Drumlanrig. My view-hunting friend, be on the
alert. From woods of green and deepest blue comes
the great limpid Nith, murmuring in a fairy dome, or
anon falling into a dark pool with a water-kelpy at its
bottom, taking its lunch of pike and eel. Near the sweet
hamlet of Carronbridge is the ford or steps by which you
cross the Nith, right opposite Tibbers Castle. Here the
river neither foams and roars like a bully, nor frets like a
child, but sweeps on in translucent majesty, full of wide
shallows and pleasant songs, and quiet spaces beloved by
the trout, over which the midnight moon might doze,
thinking it saw its mate, and the swarming stars wink
down on an underworld paved with golden images of
themselves. Tibbers Castle, whose resurrection just now
is going on, we shall leave to the consideration of the
Antiquarian Society. Let us pause, however, before the
favourite residence of His Grace the Duke of Buccleuch.
Does the name sound prosily? Call it then the residence
of the Graces and the Muses. Be its gardens as the

gardens of Bagdad, as the sunny terraces of Eden. To
live a week in Drumlanrig—to call those flowery parterres
one's own—to be lord of those voluptuous roses—of those
strange greenhouse plants, whose leaves vie with the
rainbow in colour—to be driven by a pair of high-curving
intelligent horses round such walks, in presence of such
beeches and elms, were suitable, Sabbath or holiday, for
a stormy hero, fighting, fair day and foul, amid the dust
and sin of a stupid wilful world. Let us be grateful.
Drumlanrig Castle is ours while we view it and enjoy it.
Look at it well. Open your nostrils to its perfumes. Be
curious about its trees and flowers. When you sit
down to con the poet's books, you will find the fire of
them brighter since you have seen what they try to
describe. The poet enters with a lantern into a photo-
graphic gallery collected by yourself.

Drumlanrig Castle, which occupied ten years in building,
was finished in 1689. There is a tradition that William,
first Duke of Queensberry, who built it regardless of
expense, and who was unpopular in the district from his
anti-covenanting zeal, resided only one night in the
palace it had cost him so much to erect. During that
very night he was seized with a temporary fit of illness,
and was exasperated at the inaccessibility of medical
advice. He abandoned the castle in disgust, and wrote
upon the bills of the artificers who had been engaged in
building it, 'The deil pike out his e'en that looks herein.'
Drumlanrig is in the parish of Durrisdeer, and at the
present parish church stands the grand mausoleum of the
Nithsdale Douglases. An aisle surmounts the sepulchral
vault. Within, there is a marble monument by Roubaillac,
representing James, second Duke of Queensberry, and
his Duchess. Here the much-disputed question of what is
the proper costume for historical figures cut in stone may
be studied, for the sculptor seems to have been pre-

Raphaelite in his tastes. The Duke is rendered immortal, and so is his enormous wig. His figure, his attitude, and his trappings did not move us to tears. The simple face of the Duchess seemed perfect in execution. Why should not costume as well as features be idealised ? The actors of the Grecian tragedies appeared before the audience in masks, yet history and sentiment were not deprived of reality by that. The difference between a brave man and a coward, between a philanthropist and a sensualist, may be made manifest by the artist, and our proper emotions be awakened, without being too curious as to whether a swallow-tail or a toga were the ancient wrappage of the man. Character, strong enough to affect our character, is what ought to be read of in books of history, in oil pictures, or in stone statues. It is thus that music may in effect represent either life in Arcadia or death on the field of fight, since it arouses in us such emotions as the originals were likely to do. De Quincey heard a street-boy whistle 'The Battle of Waterloo' better than he saw it acted at Astley's. We are digressing. To return to Drumlanrig : at the bottom of the staircase there is a painting of King William of Orange on a white charger after the battle of the Boyne (1690), by Sir Godfrey Kneller. There is a curious portrait in the gallery. It is one of William III, and bears on its face ugly marks—records that in the '45 the castle was in possession of the clansmen. In the year 1777, Drumlanrig, on the death without male issue of Charles, third Duke of Queensberry, passed to William, Earl of March. In 1810 it went by entail to the Duke of Buccleuch. Up to 1827, when the present proprietor * arrived at his majority, it was greatly defaced and neglected. Lord Palmerston, in his last speech at Tiverton, amused his audience, and took credit to himself for having more than doubled the grass-blades on his

* The late Walter Francis, 5th Duke.

property, since he had covered many acres of shifting sand with pasturage. 'Those who saw the Highland roads before they were made, have highly appreciated General Wade.' So those who have visited Drumlanrig to-day will be lost in admiration at the change produced by care and cost in less than half a century. The noble proprietor is liberal in allowing the poor sons of toil a day's holiday in his policies. A few weeks ago, the Freemasons of the west and south took advantage of this liberality, and quiet Thornhill was dazzled and bewildered with processions, music, and banners, while the Freemasons, one and all, behaved themselves as handsomely as if Solomon had led them to examine and admire his Eastern temple.

In Thornhill there is an opportunity for the 'intelligent boy' to test the strength of his capabilities. We refer here to the very excellent private museum of Dr Grierson.* The collection is so noteworthy and so varied as both to attract and distract the powers of memory. A fine opportunity was given to the children in the village on one occasion. They were required to enter the museum in successive bodies, each group spending half-an-hour or so in the room, and each individual making the best possible use of his eyes. A competitive examination in writing was afterwards instituted, and it was amusing to observe the various papers written under these circumstances. Small prizes were promised to those who should write out the best and most intelligent account of the various objects, or who distinctly named or otherwise indicated the various articles composing the collection. The animal-loving boy—the boy who had the largest organ of wonder—the boy who recollected distinct things, but piled them all in inorganic masses—the boy who had a talent for classification and a sense of order, and he whose cranium was too thick-skinned for the darts of ridicule to pierce

* *Vide* page 309.

through, were all represented in these little catalogues.
It was surprising to perceive how much had been recollected. A few boys and girls had more than a hundred
articles distinctly enumerated. The monstrosities sailed
in the full tide of every description. The common names
of some familiar objects were sometimes forgotten, and
periphrastic expressions, little better than masks,
indicated what was meant. The 'cast' of the skull of
Burns seems to have passed current in many cases for the
genuine article. The following is a specimen of the pell-
mell style :—'In Dr Grierson's museum are a Caledonian
bull's head with five shots, a cat-o'-nine tails, and the
signs of the zodiac painted on the roof.' A clever guess
as to the coin of a certain reign was introduced, but upon
the whole there was a general faithfulness of narration.
The result was encouraging, and has tended, we hope, to cul-
tivate a taste for natural history and antiquities, where otherwise there existed few motives for such interesting pursuits.

A lady deeply read in modern romances laid bare to us
a cheap mode of travelling. ' Have you been at the Lake
district this season ?' 'Oh yes! Wordsworth took me
there.' Stokers and drivers, whistle and keep up your
steam ; managers of railway companies, project your lines
and make comfortable your carriages, for I don't at all
believe this kind of competition will hurt you. This spirit
of ours has a wonderful liking for its old mate, the body,
and soon drags the latter to wherever Scott or Wordsworth are in the habit of taking its airy self. Nevertheless, we recollect that our first introduction to the parish
of Morton was that unconsciously supplied by Horatio
M'Culloch. It was a glorious painting of old Morton
Castle—Morton Castle, about two miles from Thornhill,
its day's work all done, and now reposing dismantled and
asleep. Instead of tapestry, the weed upon the wall ;
instead of dance and song and banquets, and spectacles of

F

hanging on the 'dule tree,' winged ants, biting fiercely
at tourists, and rare ferns, inviting the white little hands
of ladies to cull them. Horatio, we are thankful for your
introduction. We, too, have seen Morton Castle under
far other, perhaps under more genial, auspices. We have
mingled with the members of the Antiquarian Society in
its court, and, if we mistake not, a friend of ours, having
one weak point, namely, that of rhyming, has written a
ballad about it.* Morton Castle, Drumlanrig, Durrisdeer,
Thornhill, the best of friends must part; therefore, for
the present, adieu!

THE BUCCLEUCH FAMILY

While Alexander III was engaged in the serious task
of rendering his kingdom free of Norwegian influence—
while the flower of his chivalry was mustered round his
banner in that arduous struggle which terminated successfully in the great battle of Largs—one of the knights
summoned to do service under him was Richard de Scott
(1249-1285); and from him the present family of Buccleuch can trace their descent. Richard's descendants
acquired extensive possessions in Ettrick Forest and in
Teviotdale, and in the reign of James I we find Sir William
Scott of Buccleuch exchanging an estate in Lanarkshire
for one half of the barony of Branksome upon Teviot,
then belonging to Sir Thomas Inglis. Most likely, Sir
William was desirous of obtaining an estate which lay so
near to his Roxburgh and Selkirkshire possessions, and so
he persuaded the mild and peaceably-disposed Inglis that
his Lanarkshire castle was a quiet, out-of-the-way dwelling; although, after the bargain was concluded, he
boasted that the cattle in Cumberland were as good
as those of Teviotdale; and so he proceeded to initiate
or continue a system of raids and forays into Eng-

* See page 93.

land, the art of which was well learned and practised by his successors. So far did the Scotts
hold their own in this debatable land of alternate
Scotch and English plundering and skirmishing, that
James II granted to Sir Walter Scott of Branksome, and
to David his son, the other half of the barony of that
name; the feu-duty being the payment of a red rose.
This charter is dated February 1443, and in the same
month part of the barony of Langholm, with lands in
Lanarkshire, was conferred on Sir Walter and his son, in
return for the needful assistance which they had given
the king in his dubious and hazardous contest with the
house of Douglas. Buccleuch, from which at a remote
date the family obtained its title, is a lonely district—
once a parish—in the wild, mountainous, and moorland
country through which flows the Rankle burn, and is included at present in the parish of Ettrick, Selkirkshire.
Songs and traditions from a very early period point out
the place as being named from a doughty deed of valour
in hunting accomplished there by a member of the
family.

> 'In Scotland no Buccleuch was then
> Before the buck in the cleuch was slain.'

The splendour of the ancient barons of Buccleuch in
their castle of Branksome on the Teviot is alluded to in
The Lay of the Last Minstrel. A number of gentlemen of
their own name held lands from the chiefs in tenure for
guarding the castle :

> 'They watch, against Southern force and guile,
>   Lest Scroop, or Howard, or Percy's powers,
>   Threaten Branksome's lordly towers,
>   From Warkworth, or Naworth, or merry Carlisle.'

Sir Walter Scott of Buccleuch, who flourished in
the reign of James V, distinguished himself by deeds
of arms in the disastrous battle of Pinkie. This was
he who, after the death of James IV at Flodden,

took part in the game of king-stealing, then being played by the queen-mother against the wily Earl of Angus. Through the connivance of the Queen and Buccleuch, a disturbance was raised on the Border formidable enough to justify Angus proceeding thither with the boy-king for the purpose of quelling it. It was when leaving Melrose on his return home, and immediately after having parted with his allies the Homes and Kers, that Angus espied a thousand horsemen placed on an eminence. The Earl exclaimed: 'Yonder comes Buccleuch with the Border thieves of Teviotdale and Liddesdale;' and placing the King with a few guards on a rising knoll, instantly advanced to the charge. The King secretly wished that Buccleuch, who now rushed forward with his Borderers shouting their usual war-cry of 'Bellenden,' should win. The Homes and Kers were too near the scene of action, and, returning, decided the fate of the day against the Scotts, who were driven through the small village of Darnick. The vanquished, however, made a good retreat, and one of Buccleuch's retainers, an Elliot by name, struck Ker of Cessford dead with a lance. His death occasioned the mortal feud which raged long and violently between the Scotts and Kers. Eight Scotts perished in this skirmish, which was fought in July 1526. Buccleuch and many of his clan were declared guilty of high-treason, but, owing to the royal intercession with the parliament, after the King had shaken off the yoke of the Douglases, Sir Walter was restored to his lands and honours. In certain evidence afforded by the King, we obtain a glimpse of the aforesaid Walter as he appeared to the bodily eye in that distant period. The monarch, who wished to make out that Buccleuch had not met Angus with a hostile intention, averred that Sir Walter was not armed, but only dressed in a leathern

coat, with a black bonnet on his head. Sir Walter
at a later period paid dearly for this encounter,
being murdered by the Kers in the streets of Edinburgh in revenge for their leader killed at Darnick.
This famous and valiant baron was warden of the West
Marches of Scotland, and succeeded to his grandfather in
1492. He was slain in the encounter with Sir Walter
Ker, 1552.   His grandson, of Kinmont Willie celebrity,
succeeded to the lands and titles of Buccleuch. This
knight bore a good repute for wisdom and daring. Kinmont Willie was an Armstrong, and a retainer of Scott.
Being a notorious reaver, he was kidnapped by the
English, who pursued him into Scottish ground, and
thence transferred him to Carlisle Castle. Buccleuch, as
warder or keeper of Liddesdale, complained that the
English authorities had violated treaties, and sent a challenge to Lord Scrope, the governor of the castle, which
the latter prudently declined. Buccleuch next secretly
collected about three hundred men, and marched by
night to Carlisle. The night was as black as a wolf's
mouth, while rain poured in torrents. After incessant
labour, it was found that the scaling-ladders were too
short, but Scottish perseverance and forethought were
triumphant. By means of mining, a postern-door was
burst open—the few guards taken by surprise were easily
driven back—Kinmont Willie was snatched from his
dungeon, and had the pleasure of shouting good-night to
Lord Scrope, and bawling out a request for news for Scotland. Queen Elizabeth was so enraged when she heard the
report of this exploit, that she demanded that Buccleuch
should be sent a prisoner to England. The matter was
taken up by the Scottish Parliament, and King James VI
tamely and servilely advocated that the wishes of the
English Queen should be gratified. The Parliament stoutly
opposed him, and the Scottish chief settled the quarrel

by offering to visit Elizabeth personally at the King's
request. 'How did you dare,' quoth the Queen, 'to
commit such an aggression on my territory?' 'I know
not the thing,' replied Sir Walter—for he bore his
brave grandfather's name—'I know not the thing a
man dare not to do.' The Queen, who could add
inspiration to her people in front of the Spanish armada,
knew bravery too well and appreciated it too highly
to make the knight the object of her spite, and he
returned to Scotland not only scathless, but with honour.
The adventure of Kinmont Willie belongs to the year
1596. It is but just to add that, although the character
of this member of the Buccleuch family stands high, it is
to be feared that in 1570 he was privy, along with many
others, to the scheme, which succeeded too well, of
the murder of the Regent by Hamilton of Bothwellhaugh.
On the very night after the accomplishment of this vile
deed, the Scotts and Kers made a foray into England
with more than usual violence, and when one of the injured party attempted to awe them by threatening to
bring upon the plunderers the attention of the Regent,
the chief of one of those powerful Border clans replied
that the Regent was as cold as his bridle-bit. As those
were not the days of post-horses or quick transmission of
intelligence, it must be inferred that the plan of as-
sassination was in the keeping of a number of Queen
Mary's adherents.

This Sir Walter's star, however, continued to ascend.
In 1606 he was raised to the peerage for his services to
the State. Civilisation was extending its empire, and the
Borders were getting too narrow and too hot to hold
their numerous marauders. Sir Walter carried away
large numbers of them to foreign wars; and, chiefly
in reward for this service, he received the title of
Lord. He enjoyed his new honour only five years, and

in 1611 was succeeded by Walter, his only son, who added
to the family titles those of Lord Whitchester and
Eskdale, and Earl of Buccleuch. Francis Scott, the
second Earl, obtained the extensive but secluded and
wild district of Liddesdale, once the possession of the
proud house of Bothwell. He bought, likewise, large
estates in Eskdaill and the barony of Dalkeith (1642), a
barony which also belonged to a famous Scotch family—
namely, that of Morton. The hereditary jurisdiction of
Liddesdale remained with the Buccleuch family till 1747,
when the then Duke received £600 as a compensation for
its abolition. Earl Francis seems to have been a wary
and successful member of the family, with a good eye to
the main chance; for he is one of those of whom
history says little, and yet, by means of his purchases, the power and influence of his family were
extended greatly. He left only two daughters, the
eldest of whom died childless, the second inheriting
the titles and estates. This was Anne, whose good
luck seemed to culminate by her marriage in 1663 with
the son of a king. This scion of royalty was the James
Crofts of the Restoration period, whose mother, Lucy
Walters, is described by Evelyn as 'browne, beautiful,
bold, but insipid.' Crofts had not completed his sixteenth
year on the evening of his wedding. He was created
Duke of Monmouth, and in 1679 was appointed com-
mander of the army sent northward to crush the rising
of the Covenanters, which he accomplished successfully
at Bothwell Bridge. Lauderdale, and King Charles the
father of Monmouth, loudly complained of their general's
mercy to the recusants in Scotland, which caused Monmouth to become a great favourite in turn with the Non-
conformists of England, among whom he made an almost
royal progress in the western counties. In 1685, he
headed a rebellion against his Uncle James, and was

miserably defeated at Sedgemoor, and shortly after
executed at Tower Hill, having been married twenty-two
years. His widow retained the title of Duchess, as well as
that of Countess of Dalkeith, of which Monmouth was Earl.

Anne, Duchess of Buccleuch and Countess of Dalkeith,
is she who is represented in *The Lay of the Last Minstrel*
as receiving the aged Harper at Newark Castle, on the
Yarrow, and of whom it is said :

> ' In pride of youth, in beauty's bloom,
>   Had wept o'er Monmouth's bloody tomb.'

The Duke left a family of four sons and two daughters.
His lady afterwards married Lord Cornwallis, by whom
she had children, and continued to live in great splendour
at Dalkeith House, where she died in 1732, at the age of
81. Francis, grandson of Monmouth, succeeded to the
title of Duke of Buccleuch. Of him it might be remarked, as it was of Queen Mary,

> ' The blood that flowed through Bruce's veins
>   Again went, glowing, through that cheek.'

However, the family still retained the surname of
Scott. Duke Francis obtained a restoration of his grandfather's earldom of Doncaster and barony of Tynedale,
and so became a peer of Great Britain. In 1720 he
married the daughter of James, second Duke of Queensberry. This was a fortunate connection, for, in the
long-run, it brought coronets and coats-of-arms, castles,
parks—numberless acres, game preserves, battle-fields,
whole villages, into the family of Scott. Not that this
family needed such, in any great measure, to advance
its influence and dignity; for from the days that lands
were gained by

> ' Cracking crouns o' Border louns,
>   Or harrying nowte frae Southron louts.'

until those, when the humbler but far subtler weapons of

tongue and pen succeeded sword and shield, the Buccleuch
family has cleared a space around it equal in magnitude and
importance to that claimed by any of its rivals.   The third
Duke of Buccleuch was born in the same year that witnessed the battle of Culloden, and in him there seemed to
unite much of what had made both Scotts and Douglases
powerful and respected—namely, common-sense and practical sagacity.   We find but scant historical notices of his
immediate predecessors in the stirring years of 1715 and
1745, and must conclude that they acted a cautious part
in politics.

If one wished to apologise for the diverting of a great
man's energies from a public into a private channel, he
should have a case in point in the biography of Dr Adam
Smith, whose influence was so beneficial to the young Duke,
and, through him, to Scotland generally.   It was in 1763,
after Smith had occupied the chairs of Logic and Rhetoric
in succession in Glasgow University, and after his lectures
on the Theory of the Moral Sentiments had been the
chief topic of literary Scotland, that his career of public
usefulness was brought to a close by Townshend, who had
married the Countess of Dalkeith, and who engaged him
to be tutor to the young Duke.   The liberality of the
terms was great, considering the value of money at that
period.   An annuity of £300 was settled on the philosopher for life, and Smith, resigning his professorship,
set out with his noble pupil to Paris.   Charles Townshend,
second son of the third Viscount Townshend, had married
the Countess-Dowager in 1754.   He had opposed, from
his seat in parliament, the marriage bill of 1753, intended
to put shackles on imprudent early marriages.   In his
speech, which was full of wit, he scrupled not to make
himself an illustration of his own argument, and asked if
the abler younger sons were to suffer further impediments
than that of birth to prevent them rising in the world.

He further stated that his own whimsical father had already debarred him from an advantageous match, and that therefore he would do his utmost to oppose the bill. His marriage with the wealthy heiress in the following year was a practical commentary on his own speech. Nevertheless, the wisdom of his choice of Smith for a tutor to his step-son has been fully justified.

Having letters of introduction from the great Scotch philosopher and historian, David Hume, Smith and his youthful charge became acquainted with some members of that galaxy of encyclopædists whose writings had so much influence on the destinies of their own country. Smith accompanied his pupil through a part of the Continent, and returned, after a sojourn of two years, to Scotland, where the philosopher retired into obscurity, living with his mother, and writing *The Wealth of Nations*, while the Duke became a resident on his own estates, which he greatly improved. His Grace always retained feelings of gratitude towards his distinguished tutor, and appointed him in 1780 to a lucrative situation in Edinburgh, where his income was such that he wished to dispense with his annuity, a proposal which the Duke would not entertain.

Meanwhile, this truly noble proprietor devoted his life to agricultural improvements, and to the amelioration of the condition of his tenantry. Dr Carlyle of Inveresk, Jupiter Carlyle, whose interesting autobiography but lately (1860) saw the light, lent his assistance and counsel to the Duke, whose estates in Mid-Lothian and in the south of Scotland began to blossom after centuries of comparative neglect. Grasses and grains, hedges and ditches, were introduced, a new plough was adopted, manure was driven from the large towns, and every means which science and capital could dispose of were employed to enrich barren soils. The example was infectious—as all example in high places is—for we have known a

stingy squire or a public-spirited baron alter the character of a whole neighbourhood. The present high
state of agriculture in Mid-Lothian dates, in its rapid progress, from the period to which we refer. The construction of roads, the breeding of sheep, and the building of
more comfortable and scientifically-planned houses for his
tenantry, were the uniform business of the good Duke's
life. Not a loud man this, pouring out volumes in St
Stephen's or elsewhere, but one distilling blessings like
the summer rain-clouds. A warrior storming bogs, and
rendering waste and wild obedient to the plough, is not a
favourite with Fame, who keeps her trumpet for a select
class.

> ' The forest murmurs rood on rood,
>   Melodious with the leaves of trees :
> Unknown, unseen, though quite as good,
>   In quietness grow the roots of these.'

The world's real concern about any man should be, we
think, not how he stands in the temple of Fame, but how
he has acquitted himself in the circle of duty. This
Henry, third Duke of Buccleuch, died in 1812, and was
succeeded by his eldest son, Charles, who enjoyed the
title only two years. Harriet, the lovely young Countess
of Dalkeith, afterwards Duchess, was a favourite with Sir
Walter Scott, and suggested to him the legend or goblin
story incorporated in *The Lay of the Last Minstrel.* The
sale of this poem was unprecedented, and it was the first
publication stamped with the genius of its author.

Walter Francis (father of the present Duke), who was
born 1806, and succeeded 1814, is said to have walked
much in the steps of his grandfather, and to have been popular with his tenantry. Not to mention many churches and
schools which he has built, we will only refer here to his
enormous expenditure connected with that great under-
taking of public benefit, the harbour and port of Granton, on
the Firth of Forth, which was cited in Parliament as having

already cost upwards of £300,000. The Duke has estates
in seven Scotch counties south of the Forth, is sole heritor
of whole parishes, possesses the island of Inchkeith, and
is patron to more than thirty churches. He is Marquis,
Earl, Viscount, and Baron in Scotland, and is a British
peer, besides which he holds many honourable local
offices. Two of the most notable circumstances of his
life have been the famous entertainment given to him by
his tenantry in 1839, at his ancient seat of Branksome on
the Teviot, and the Queen's visit to Dalkeith Palace.
The first of these events came off with a kind of feudal
magnificence. A pavilion, in the style of an ancient
baronial hall, with all that upholstery and candelabra
could do for it, was fitted to seat upwards of a thousand
persons. Representatives arrived from Lanarkshire, Mid-
Lothian, and Dumfries—even from the fishermen of New-
haven. Liddesdale men also were present, sons of the
Elliots and Armstrongs who entered Kelso on the day of
the false alarm of invasion (1804), playing—

> 'O wha daur meddle wi' me?
> And wha daur meddle wi' me?
> My name is little Jock Elliot,
> And wha daur meddle wi' me?'

The mixed assembly feasted and cheered to their hearts'
content, gazed on the buck's head and antlers above the
chair of honour, and saw—painted amid the stars of the roof
—'Bellenden,' the ancient battle-cry of the clan of Scott,
and near it, in letters of gold, His Grace's maxim of 'Live,
and let live.' Teviot felt for a day as if the tent of a
Scythian monarch had been pitched upon its banks, and
the revels and rough hospitality of a court were transacted.
There sleeps in Dryburgh Abbey he who has sung best
of Teviot—sweet Teviot! with its beacon-fires extin-
guished, its mailed warriors dead, its waters murmuring
gently as if they had only heard the pipe of the shepherd—

never the bugle of the warrior.   But oh! how the heart of
Sir Walter Scott would have thrilled had he been present,
how his cheers would have mounted, how his pen
would have described what Branksome presented on that
auspicious day!   For the great novelist was always foremost to cast a stone upon the cairn commemorative of his
distant kinsman, the bold Buccleuch.

Reviewing this great historical family, it seems to have
had a valuable inheritance of shrewd caution and practical
sagacity.   We have found that there is nothing of martyr-
dom and metaphysics, and little of law or literature to
record about it.   Its undeniable energy has poured itself
out on facts rather than on ideas, and for whole generations flowed noiselessly on.   Perhaps it is better that it was
so.   We will cheerfully recognise diversity of gifts, and
continue to trust that many different sorts of families and
of individuals, well-known, obscure, and unknown, as well
as heroes, martyrs, and public speakers, have been of
incalculable service to our dear old country.

Ballad of Morton Castle

Tradition says that Lady Morton was guilty of a
criminal passion towards Edward, a vassal of Lord
Morton, who, being already betrothed to Agnes of Carron,
Durrisdeer, respectfully repelled the advances of the
lady, whereupon the latter represented the case entirely
the reverse of what it was to her lord, making Edward
the aggressor, who had vainly attempted to seduce her.
Earl Morton immediately called Walter and Gilmour, his
vassals, and ordered them to chain Edward in a little
dungeon, and allow him to perish of famine.

Lady Morton now adopted new tactics.   She dropped
provisions into Edward's miserable cell, and tempted him
with the Elysian prospect of freedom ; but, fortified by the

Holy Virgin and by the image of Agnes, he continued to repel all temptation. Relenting at last, when her victim threatened not to survive the cruel treatment, the lady sent a trusty page to Agnes, instructing her to set out on a pilgrimage to Morton Castle, and to implore the Earl on her bended knees for the restoration of her lover. Instead of softening the Earl's heart, this plan only roused up his fiercest jealousy. He could not understand why Edward was still alive. Gilmour was immediately hung on an oak tree for neglect of duty, while Walter, being pardoned, was ordered to procure from Knockingshaw two wild colts, which were soon caught, their heads loosely bound together, and Edward stretched behind them on the ground. The cords were firmly bound to his feet, and then entwined round each colt:

> 'And on each hind-foot of the pair
> Was fixed a spur of steel,
> That Edward, as along they flew,
> Their furious kicks might feel.'

The horses being frightened into speed, rushed forward to Durrisdeer, and stood by Carron's stream, and there a shepherd found them with Edward's head separated from the body. The remains were buried where they were found, and into the same grave Agnes soon followed, the place being marked with a stone. The spot is at a short distance from the road leading to Durrisdeer church, on a small eminence, which bears the appropriate appellation of the 'Heads.'

Such, at least, is the wild story, though there are great difficulties in the way of its authentication.

[The following story was versified from the oral tradition narrated to the Dumfries Natural History and Antiquarian Society, while the party was assembled round the venerable ruin on the occasion of their late excursion, 7th July 1868.]

> My lady's gown wi' gowd is fair,
> My lady's hawks fu' swiftly flee,
> Wi' kame o' gowd she straiks her hair,
> But whaur is a' my lady's glee ?

Her sparkin' een they never tire
  To look on ane o' laich degree;
Her snaw-white bosom hauds a fire
  She daurna let her maidens see.

My lord has gaen to fecht his faes,
  But there's a fiercer fae at hame.
Fause thochts hae made the lofty base,
  Fause words will bring the proud to shame.

That serving-man o' laich degree,
  He thinks it luckiest to be true :
' St Mary keep me pure and free,
  Though Norman een should pierce me through.

' The blude-red wine I mauna taste,
  For blude-red lips I daurna grene,
I mauna touch that jimpy waist,
  I daurna please thae winsome een.'

My lady's evil spirit's gane,
  But rest that spirit canna find,
And back it comes nae mare alane ;
  Wi' fraud, wi' murder noo it's joined.

My lord's come back, he' faught his faes,
  But here's a fiercer fae at hame ;
Nae English reaver noo sae base,
  Nae Paynim half sae void o' shame.

Quoth he : ' What briar has torn thy skin,
  Thy skin o' daisies bleached in rain ?'
Quoth he : ' What cat has scratched thy chin ?'
  And aff he kissed the fause blude-stain.

Quoth she : ' The briar, the cat ye seek,
  Wi' lustfu' arms he left sic sted ;
The dungeon door I've made them steek
  On ane wha would hae forced thy bed.

' For if your lady hadna cried '—
  ' Fause fiend !' broke out that lord sae grim,
' Let him be on twa horses tied,
  And tear him piecemeal lith and limb.'

Frae Morton Castle forth they glare,
  Frae Morton court keen-spurred they rear ;
When shrieks and sighs were heard nae mair,
  The horses lowsed at Durrisdeer.

The body eastways fell i' the wood,
  The head fell to the west its lane ;
But whaur the head rowed down in blude,
  Maid Marian's han' put up a stane.

That serving-man o' laich degree,
    He thocht it luckiest to be true ;
He rests frae rage, frae evil free :
    My lady, is there rest wi' you?

CLOSEBURN AND CREEHOPE * LINN

Closeburn is a word derived, says the antiquary, from
Kilosburn or Kelosbern, and these from *Cella Osburni*, as
if the parish had been first of small extent, and the
church only intended for the old aristocratic family and
its dependents.   There is a strong unconscious tendency
to twist names derived from a foreign tongue into intelligible vocables of our own language.   The Celtic *alt maen*,
or high rock, has been transformed into Old Man (of
Coniston), Old Man (of Hoy), etc.   Dun-y-coed, a ' wooded
hill,' in Devonshire, is now called Dunagoat.   Cape
Hvarf, literally, in the Norse, Cape Turnagain, has
received the appellation of Cape Wrath.   Château Vert
has been. converted into Shotover Hill ; Beau chef, into
Beachy Head ; Burgh Walter, the castle of Walter of Douay,
who came over with the Conqueror, into Bridgewater ; and
Beau lieu, into Bewley.   It is thus that language, which
is a more permanent possession than landmarks, charters,
costume, or even race, is subject also to its own laws of
change, and is ready betimes to utter uncertain sounds.
The Indians of North America have been almost exterminated, yet the great geographical features of the
continent are stamped with their seal.   The Mississippi and the Rappahannock, the Alleghany and the
Winnipeg, are likely to wear on their foreheads the names
bequeathed by extinct races.

Standing one day in Kilmalcolm churchyard, above the

* ' Crichope,' the spelling adopted in Geikie's *Survey of Scotland*
accords with the modern local pronunciation.

ashes of James, Earl of Glencairn, a clerical friend remarked that newspaper and magazine poetry was generally
worthy of the oblivion to which it was consigned; yet as
in our cold Scotch waters, in the upper Tay and Spey,
pearl fisheries are established, so some *Song of a Shirt* or
precious lyric might be fished up from the vast ocean of
printed matter, of which so much was foam. 'Fancy,'
said he, 'such lines as these meeting one's eye in a
newspaper : '

> 'Gorgeous are thy woods, October,
>   Clad in glowing mantle sear,
> Every tint of beauty blending,
> Like the West when Day's descending,
>   Thou'rt the sunset of the year.' *Hugh MacDonald.*

Now, if a person in Dumfriesshire were willing to realise
the picture, we should invite him with us to Creehope
or Crichope Linn, in the parish of Closeburn. Through
the sandstone rocks, the water, idling away its energies
during long ages, has wrought for itself a bed as fan-
tastical and whimsical as any that could have been
framed in a feverish dream. Dream-grottoes there are,
and sunless abysses for all manner of eyeless monsters.
Here, the rock is rifted above, not much wider than
the slit in the shopman's counter; yet you dare scarcely
step across, lest the hungry boiling stream beneath
catch at you and fulfil the threats it thunders in
your ears. There, the boulder is chafed forever by the
foam and spray, and you fancy it a proper throne for elves
and kelpies to sit on, with their elbows resting on their
knees, complaining of the bluntness of their teeth, and
sighing, like the ogres in the story-book, for more human
flesh. Yet over all this fury there looks a magnificence
of foliage like that which surrounded Alastor in Shelley's
Spirit of Solitude. At every turn, too, you have glimpses
of beautiful glades inviting you to explore some more
lovely mystery. There is the saffron ash, the rowan tree

G

in full fruitage, with its lacelike twinkling leaves, the red
oak, the beech burning itself away. There also is the
hazel, with its nuts all too seductive for schoolboys, and
suggestive of another hazel, or of its neighbour the birch.
I wonder, by-the-by, if these instruments of punishment are as much in vogue as in my young days.
Hood says, those schoolmasters who in this life whip
boys excessively, are very properly, at the close, transferred to that pit which has no bottom to it. I think
they might safely be tumbled down one of those enormously deep-looking Creehope gullies. It was among
these thundering cascades that Walter Scott placed the
closing scenes of his half-historical, half-imaginary Balfour
of Burleigh. Scott's descriptions of religious enthusiasts
are always wanting in depth. His genial pencil painted
no gloomy Rembrandt-like interior, simply because his
own soul was deficient in fire and gloom. He had not the
heart of a martyr, and so, when he represents one, we
have raging words and wire-drawn rhapsodies. But when
the great novelist treats of those who flourish after the
brunt of battle is past, of those who, instead of pushing
incessantly forward, chiefly occupy themselves in looking
back, who garnish the tombs of the prophets, and war
with rust and mould, and with the effacing finger of time,
he is more at home. What a charming portrait has he
drawn of the Antiquary! How he lingered over such a
character as Old Mortality! By reference to the notes
appended to that last-mentioned novel, it will be seen
that Paterson, the original of Old Mortality, whose person
and pony are cut in stone, and exhibited at Dumfries
Observatory, was a native of Closeburn parish.

The Elves' Chair, in Creehope Glen, has been transformed, in this iron age, into a quarry. The Soutar's Seat
is still intact, being, according to tradition, the lurking-
place of a covenanting shoemaker. The Grey-mare's

Tail is a spot where the water descends nearly 100 feet
perpendicularly. It is in the upper and bare part of the
glen, where the stream is small, and of course only sublime
during the time of ' spate.' The glen is exceedingly well
adapted for a visit, walks having been hewn, and ladders
fixed, in order to help the tourist through the most
inaccessible ravines. They will be fortunate who find
the linn and its beauties, like ourselves, without seeking
for it. We were led to believe that its chief interest was
geological, and so entered with the hope of catching sight
of a rare fossil in the naked rocks, or of noting the
disposition of the strata. Guess our surprise, when, instead of pocketing a new encrinite or madrepore—*new* to
us, but of an age altogether beyond thinking of—we met
with a panorama of wood and water such as we have endeavoured to indicate. It is an irksome thing to go
hunting for beauty. Deer-stalking is not half so dis-
appointing.

> ' Walk softly ; woods are musical,
>   And forest-fawns at play ;
>   Put Nature's beauty on the stage,
>   How quick it swoons away ! '

In this respect the luxury of travelling does not place
the poor man so far apart from the rich as might at first
sight be imagined. It is well to risk something to see
Creehope Glen, but it is not well to grumble because you
have no chance of seeing it, or find fault with it when
seen, as people sometimes do with the Falls of Niagara,
for not being sublime enough. Much depends on your
own eyes. There is truth in the sentence, ' He who has
seen the moon burst from a cloud, has been present like
an archangel at the creation of light and of the world.'
When we invite people to Creehope Glen, we cannot, of
course, forecast a single day in the calendar; neither
have we any remedy for a fit of dyspepsia, if the walk
from Closeburn railway-station is not suitable medicine.

There is a most remarkable educational institution in Closeburn. One of those prosperous Glasgow gentlemen who made his money by commerce, and who therefore may be included in that class who have no grandfathers, has made up for his want of a long genealogical tug-rope by casting out a stout cable behind him. In 1723, John Wallace mortified £1600 for the purpose of erecting the school, which, in his honour, has been called the School of Wallace Hall. Its managers are the Presbytery of Penpont and the laird of Closeburn. Five patrons were appointed to nominate the rector, being three brothers of the name of Wallace, the minister of Closeburn, and the town-clerk of Glasgow. £200 were used in building the houses and purchasing the rector's glebe. £1145 were appropriated to purchasing land in the adjoining parishes. The remainder was laid out in repairing and enlarging the buildings. The deed of mortification requires that the elementary branches, with Latin and Greek, be taught. A rash reasoner might infer that this great, beneficent John Wallace was but a crotchety, small-souled man after all : at least he has left instructions that, in choosing a candidate for the school, all other qualifications being equal, preference was to be given to one of the name of Wallace. If John were coming to life now, he would be astonished to behold what a large tree has grown from the seed which he planted. The money expended in purchasing farms has yielded, owing to the increased value of the land, an annual income which is now said to be something near the half of the whole sum originally bequeathed. Taking into account its comparatively thin, rural population, we question if there is in broad Scotland a parish so expensively educated as is Closeburn, and not only expensively but liberally. Education in Wallace Hall School is gratuitous to the natives of the parish in which the founder of the institution was born. Ye born dominies, who, after years of circuitous marching, expected to snatch the lawyer's wig or the minister's gown and bands, or perhaps mount up into respectability in the doctor's gig, but who at last have fallen from your lofty air-castle, and are lying prone, weltering in your learning—inclined, perhaps, to mope because there are no prizes in *your* profession—look up, for in Closeburn there is a prize. Only, the apple being one, and the needy, greedy candidates legion, you must not be too sanguine.

Dr R. of West-Hillside was a believer in phrenology, who had carefully measured a hundred heads of the people, and projected them in diagrams. From these he constructed a huge outline, which he called the parochial head. This head he was wont, by the method of super-position, to compare with that of Robert Burns, Walker, Scott, Dr Chalmers, Joseph Hume—the notables of the earth—and thus to discover what bumps in the parish were lying lea, what organs were well cultivated, and what lines of divergence or resemblance could be drawn between the parochial 'representative man' and the heroes of man-kind. Some were sanguine enough to infer that in this manner you could discover the intellectual wants of the parish, and also what sort of preachers, teachers, and leading men it contained. If phrenology be true, we would expect the Closeburn representative-head to give evidence of the cost of its culture. Whether the best of education, when offered gratuitously, deepens the desire and reverence for it, is a social question which we will not at present discuss.

The old Scotch family of Kirkpatrick, the creation of whose baronial title dates from 1685, possessed until lately lands in this parish. The Closeburn estate passed into the hands of Sir John Menteith, whose principal seat was in Ayrshire. More recently it has been pur-

chased by one of the Bairds, of Gartsherrie Ironworks.
Grose, the antiquarian, whose name has tickled the public
ear by reason of the humorous epistle addressed to him
by Burns, has given a drawing in his Antiquities of the
old Castle of Closeburn.   It is a very ancient fortalice,
about fifty feet high.   The village of Closeburn is two-
and-a-half miles south of Thornhill.   It is a cosy little
place, not far from the Nith.   The houses are one-
storied, with flag-roofs.   The gardens are trim, well-
sheltered spots.   The lime-kilns of the locality are conspicuous objects from the adjoining hills, filling the air
with their white smoke.   The bowling-green-looking
parks on Nithside are well stocked with cows and steers.
Queensberry hill, and other haughty eminences, are
dotted white with heavy sheep.

What says Horace, *Ode* 2, Book v.?

> How blessed the man who, free from care
>   Like mortals of an earlier day,
> Follows his plough through wholesome air,
>   Strides, with his kine, through fragrant hay :
>
> Who, thriving not by sword or sail,
>   Nor caring how his tongue shall wag,
> Fills to the brim his foaming pail,
>   Or stuffs his corn in many a bag :
>
> Who whets his pruning-knife betimes,
>   Cool-shaded by his poplar trees ;
> Who shears his sheep and croons his rhymes,
>   Who smokes his pipe or smokes his bees.
>
> The blythe winds pelt him with ripe pears,
>   He sauntering all his garden through ;
> Watching his gins, he nips his hares ;
>   Fondling his dogs, he feeds them too.
>
> His sun-burnt wife, with loving smile,
>   Piles on the logs and trims the hearth ;
> And rosy children, free from guile,
>   Once more make paradise on earth.

Paradise on earth ! neither easy to make nor to be had
ready-made.   Have you considered the condition of the

rural labourer, or of any white slave soever, with no hour his
own save the sleeping and eating ones ? In the cities a cheap
train draws into it the artisans, the men of coal and iron.
In the country, when the Glasgow and South-Western gave
its grand cheap excursion, it was with pain I witnessed
that scarcely a country labourer took advantage of it.
'But they are simple and thrifty,' you say, 'and content
with home amusements.' I have seen them at fairs simple
without thrift: and there is the dark spot of illegitimacy
on our south-western rural counties. Sons of Adam do
clutch at amusement, and if it come not to them out of
books, fiddles, and fire-arms, it will come rough as the
Russian bear, and dangerous as the hornet. Beautiful is
the country, but also taxable, and must pay for every
loose screw, for all the ignorance and all the boorishness
that it carries on its flowery bosom.

> Shut up and hid from every common eye,
> Like far-descended heir-loom, is thy linn.
> The common traveller heareth not its din,
> Whether it brawl o'er rocks or gently sigh,
> Margined with flowers, yet shrouded from the sky.
> Nor knoweth he the jewel hid within
> Thy casket, Closeburn, nor thy 'Soutar's' seat,
> Nor the great leap thy Crichope takes from high,
> Far up in that secluded green retreat.
> Here the lone Covenanter snatched his meal
> In perilous hour—sword hanging by his side ;
> Here like a water-kelpie did he feel
> His beard grow long—here, steel in hand, would glide,
> While down the open vale did Clavers' horses ride.

SANQUHAR AND KIRKCONNEL

In ancient times every town had its guardian deity,
to whom sacrifices were offered. In the deep recesses of
every grove, young and beautiful naiads murmured songs
to the murmuring springs. Pan, with his cherry cheeks,
his rosy mouth, his flat nose, and his goat-like horns, was

the god of shepherds; the winged Mercury took charge of merchandise : in short, there was a general division of labour among the upper ten thousand, and the various interests of the lower world were committed to their charge. I forget whether there was a guardian angel of old castles, but if not, we can easily suppose that there was one. This will be convenient for present purposes, for we have a message which we wish him to deliver. We would like that the spirit which haunts Sanquhar Castle would leave off sitting there, sad by moonlight, like Marius on the ruins of Carthage, and take a step up to Drumlanrig, in the garb of an old mouldy Douglas, or in whatever disguise may be most suitable, and present a petition in the interest of the old building to its noble proprietor. Poor old Sanquhar Castle, there it stands, like threadbare decayed gentility, in the highway. Every passenger by the Glasgow and Carlisle Railway can wag his head and point his finger at it. During the last thirty years it has suffered to an amazing extent by the ruthless hand of Time. Its stairs are all gone within the memory of the inhabitants of the burgh. In the spring-thaws, large portions of it tumble annually into the court. No iron band clasps its old bones together. No restoration or preservation of it is attempted. Yet, considering it merely as a picturesque object, and altogether apart from its traditions, it is surely worthy of kindly treatment. An old aristocrat being twitted with the fact that the cotton and iron lords were building palaces rivalling or surpassing those of the nobility, replied : 'I know what you say is true; but they cannot build such trees or avenues as ours.' The same remark is to be found elsewhere :

> 'They build their houses on our land,
> All up and down, where'er they please;
> But, Heaven be praised, they can't command
> Our glorious old ancestral trees.'

But if ancestral avenues point out how old a country
or a great ruling family is, how much more so does a
ruin. In America, from its Atlantic to its Pacific shore,
not one old feudal castle nods to the moon. Sanquhar
town itself owes a debt of gratitude to the antiquated
fortalice, for from this it obtained its name. The town
for centuries spelt 'Sanchar,' or 'Sancher,' which is the
Celtic *saen-caer*, an old fort. Cadets of the Earls of Ross,
the famous Lord of the Isles, are mentioned as the earliest
proprietors of the fort and surrounding lands. It belonged for some time to the English in the reign of
Edward I. It passed by marriage from the Rosses to the
Crichtons. In 1630, Sir William Douglas of Drumlanrig
purchased the whole property. The castle now became
the property of the Douglases of Nithsdale. Even after
the Duke of Queensberry had piled up the grand palace
of Drumlanrig, he is said to have slept there only one
night, and to have spent the remainder of his time at
Sanquhar. In the days of the second Duke of Queensberry, Sanquhar Castle, its gardens, its isleted fish-pond,
its moat, its spacious deer-parks, were abandoned to their
fate. Then came the Goths and Vandals, the greedy and
the needy, to prey upon the carcass. Its leaden roof was
carried off piecemeal. Its walls saved the trouble and
expense of making quarries. The noble and the illustrious,
somewhat of the power and beauty of which Nithsdale
was proud, used to assemble for counsel or for amusement
under these walls. The buildings had vibrated to the
music of the sweet musician and the dance of the neat
light foot. They had upheld tapestry woven with the
record of heroic deeds. Now the stones had to submit to
other uses. Pigs required to be fattened under their protection, and the uncouth sounds of hovel and sty were all
the harmony they were doomed to hear. Talk of a monument to Wallace and the brave men who fought for

Scotland's freedom. Well, here at Sanquhar is a monument of heroic deeds all but pulled to pieces.* Instead of
any local choral-union assembling around it to chant its
praises, we have cows 'routing' in its court; and yet,

'When Edward held down Scotland
  With iron arm of might,
He seized on Sanquhar Castle;
  It was guarded day and night.

Up rose a Scottish peasant,
  For his heart was boiling o'er:
"We'll yet get Sanquhar Castle,
  And we'll enter by the door."

The peasant came with fuel
  One morning to the fort;
They lowered down the drawbridge,
  And they taunted him in sport.

"Hew our wood and draw our water,
  Ye hungry Scottish crew,
For bread and kicks be thankful;
  They are good enough for you."

They had raised the huge portcullis;
  But the peasant fixed his cart
Right between it and the drawbridge;
  Like a man who knew his art.

They could not raise the drawbridge;
  The portcullis would not fall.
The carter drew his dagger;
  His friends were at his call.

In they rushed through hall and turrets,
  Put the English to the sword;
And once more its keys and banners
  Were those of its rightful lord.'

The town of Sanquhar, which is twenty-seven miles
north-west of Dumfries and thirteen of Thornhill, is nearly
wholly composed of one long street a quarter of a mile in
length, and about a quarter of a mile from the Nith. The

* This eloquent appeal on behalf of the ruins of Sanquhar Castle
is now being answered by the restoration work undertaken by the
Marquis of Bute, who in 1894 purchased the castle and upwards
of 100 acres of land from the Duke of Buccleuch.

southern portion is mean, but the northern part contains
some good, well-built houses. In this quarter is situated
the town-hall, a substantial, commodious, dark building,
with a heavy outside stone stair, and a town-clock. This
useful building was erected solely at the expense of the
last Duke of Queensberry. The parish church is a fine
edifice, to the north-east of the town. Sanquhar was a
Burgh of barony from a very ancient date. In 1598 it
was constituted a Royal Burgh. The population of the
town is under 2000, and is not increasing. Like the
last of a broken-up, decayed clan, a few weavers
and weaving-shops still linger here. The mineral resources of the parish are abundant. Entering the Nith,
near Sanquhar, are the streams of the Crawick and the
Euchan. On the latter there are a fine freestone
quarry and an excellent mineral spring; while the former,
for picturesque beauty and variety of woodland, is not
inferior to Creehope Linn. The Duchess of Buccleuch
has rendered access easy to its varied scenery by having
paths cut and rustic bridges erected. Dissenters muster
strong in Sanquhar. The learned and veteran Dr
Simpson still (1865) presides over an attached congregation here, and when we last heard him preach he displayed all the homely fire and frankness which he has so
often admired in those whose life he has attempted to
portray.

In June 1680, Richard Cameron, one of the extreme
party, who held by the perpetually binding obligations
of the Solemn League and Covenant, and who refused the
indulgence offered by Charles, owing to the Erastian and
galling conditions which clogged it, with about twenty
equally zealous persons, well-armed, entered the town of
Sanquhar, and stood around the market-cross. Here they
read the Sanquhar Declaration, and in the market-place
formally renounced their allegiance to Charles II, who

had so grossly abused his power. Moreover, they went farther: they declared war against the king and all his adherents. After this act they retired to the hills between Nithsdale and Ayrshire. Five thousand merks were set by government on Cameron's head, and three thousand merks on the heads of his companions. Nevertheless, they succeeded in evading capture for a month. Towards the end of July they were surprised at Aird's Moss, in the parish of Auchinleck, by dragoons under Bruce of Earlshall. A brave but desperate fight ensued. The odds were all against Cameron, who was killed on the spot, and his hands and head were hacked off, and fixed on the Netherbow Port of Edinburgh. To commemorate this episode in Scottish history, the inhabitants of Sanquhar last year (1864) erected a handsome obelisk on or near the spot where the Declaration was read.

The title of our sketch is 'Sanquhar and Kirkconnel'; but what of Kirkconnel? Shakespeare's grand tragedy of *Macbeth* opens with 'A blasted heath, thunder and lightning; enter three witches.' We advise the managers of the Metropolitan theatres to send down their painters to Kirkconnel, for a barer, more desolate-looking parish we never gazed at. Its nakedness is appalling. Not a bosky glen, not a mysterious corner, scarcely a clump of trees meets the eye. Shelley says:

> 'I love all waste
> And solitary places, where we taste
> The pleasure of believing what we see
> Is boundless as we wish our souls to be,'

so he would love Kirkconnel. One thing the flat moorland gives you which is denied in the straths: the sun getting low, before he hides his head, indulges you with magnificent, highly-coloured sunsets. The village of Kirkconnel is one which you cannot walk through without the inhabitants practising a strange ceremony. They all

flatten their noses against the window-panes. A stranger
likewise seems to affect the atmosphere in some peculiar
manner, for no sooner does he pass than they open all
their doors to admit a free current of air. 'Oh,' you
say, 'that is only common curiosity.' Perhaps so ; then
I shouldn't like to live where people were so curious
about you. Is there no pursuit in which they could en-
gage tending to improve themselves, and to keep them
from living, like parasites, the one upon the character
and doings of another? When a man fulfils his duty,
gossip glances from him like water from waxcloth. Yet
the inquisitive nature of rustics saves them sometimes from
paying for police. In the great ocean of a city the feeble
swimmer sinks unheeded—his cry is not heard in that
mighty roar *—

> As amid instruments of graver tone
>   The human voice urges its course in song,
>   At times unheard, at times heard clear and strong,
> So, after circling Sanquhar like a zone,
>   The Nith, in breezy autumn, 'neath its trees
> Murmurs and sings. October ne'er begins
>   But in the castle's courts must browse my horse,
> Thence trot Dumfries-ward, while I count the linns
>   And pools and rocks of Nith, and watch its course,
> O'erhung with the tall ash-tree's yellowest gold,
>   The Guelder-roses' vine-like leaves grown red,
> The birk with ghost-like stem, the row'n trees old,
>   Alders and hazels with their top leaves shed
> Above the happy trout that dream in that sweet bed.

WANLOCKHEAD AND LEADHILLS

To those who have been filled with a longing to see St
Kilda or some such island, 'placed far amid the melancholy

* Had this been written a few years later, it would undoubtedly
have made reference to Alexander Anderson, 'The Surfaceman,'
whose beautiful verses, written in this secluded spot, have elevated
Kirkconnel to a position of importance in the history of Scottish
literature.

main,' and who have neither time nor money to gratify
their wish, we recommend a trip to the above-named
places.   Until we saw them we did not think that Dumfriesshire presented anything so queer, so utterly dis-
similar to everything else we have yet witnessed in the
county.   Our omnibus gallantly dashed through Thornhill.
Drumlanrig, half veiled by foliage, exhibited now and
then its lordly front, and soon we arrived at a valley filled
up in its lowest recesses by the winding Nith, adorned by
trees, the seeds of which had been sown by winds and
wild birds.   All this we had seen, as has every traveller
by the Glasgow and South-Western Railway, but departing
from the Nith at a sharp angle at Mennock toll, we
began slowly to wind up an excellently macadamised road,
at every turn of which the glen became more contracted,
the trees scarcer, the hills higher, the stream narrower
and fiercer, and the vegetation more Alpine.   At last our
horses could drag us no longer, and each passenger had to
descend and begin to measure the earth with that pair of
compasses wherewith Nature had provided him.   Dark
mists, dark heath, dark-winged butterflies, grey whinstone,
and black-faced sheep were for ever turning up ; while
sometimes, far below us on the solitary road, the thin wail
of the much-diminished stream continued to be heard.
The hills were now fast becoming mountain masses, on
the right dark with heath, on the left verdant with the
freshest grass.   These mountains were variegated with
the parallel tracks of the sheep, or seamed from top to
bottom with the dry stony beds of winter torrents.   It
seemed as if we had rolled back the wheels of time for
eighteen centuries, and had fallen upon that Caledonia
which Gibbon, not, perhaps, without a touch of his solemn
sneer, has described, when he remarks that the Romans,
the lords of the fairest portions of the world, turned
sulkily away from bogs and hills saturated with cold mists,

over which the deer of the forest was hunted by a troop
of naked barbarians.

We can recollect how, after having suffered much
discomfort sailing through Kilbrannan Sound and viewing
the wild back of Arran, we admired the populous town
of Campbeltown, living—by means of its distilleries and the
untamable appetite which the sons of Adam have for its
whisky—as luxuriously as tyrant Cambyses did of old
when his soldiers, or rather his hordes of fighting slaves,
were falling by thousands in the Libyan desert.

For leagues around there was not soil to produce wild
fruit, not to mention cereals, and yet Campbeltown was
living grandly on the best of Europe and the East, had its
comfortable houses and posse of professional men.   Well,
at a corner of this wild Dumfriesshire glen, when the
region was becoming drearier than ever, our surprise at
seeing Wanlockhead, its rows of houses facing various
points of the compass, its churches, its school-room, its
managers' houses, its stunted trees, its blighted potatoes, its
sheep and cows all tethered by ropes, and grazing a circle
whose area could be calculated from the length of the said
rope—our surprise, we repeat, at thus espying lead-produc-
ing, hen-poisoning Wanlockhead (for a hen won't live in it
—it dies through picking lead), was great in the extreme.
The unmistakable one-storied long, low row of miners'
cottages, characteristic of these cottages in all localities,
was there, but it had peculiarities of its own besides, for
each row was thatched with heather as black as coal, and
looked all the blacker from contrast with the whitened
fronts.   The groups of children, too, were as curious to
us as we could be to them.   There they swarmed around
our slowly-moving omnibus, giving no cheer, making no
impudent remarks and mistaking them for smartness,
like the city children, but mute as a shoal of fishes when
gathering round the lights which are occasionally used to

attract and betray them. Neither fashion nor wretchedness had set its mark on their attire, and if they were
somewhat bare-legged, they had got such well-moulded
calves as argued a capability of resisting many noxious
influences of wind and weather. From a hasty glance we
should say that 'red hair,' as it is not very correctly
named, was fully more plentiful among them than in the
lowlands. When coppers, etc., were thrown to them, they
also evinced such eagerness to become possessors of the
coins that, though they may never have heard of King
Midas, it was plain the itch for gold was on their fingers.

Thirteen hundred feet above the level of the sea, in a
land of lead mines and mist, and stunted vegetables,
where the banners of frost and winter are first planted,
and where sleet showers love to powder the lap of May,
it is wonderful that no monument is to be found in a
public place commemorating the services of coal, candle,
and oil. Surely a universal chill must have crept through
both Wanlockhead and Leadhills when they read
John Stuart Mill's speech upon the exhaustion of coal.
Here, too, looking around, we found it explicable why
Sanquhar is noted for its curlers, for if men and ice are
needed for this sport in any parish, the latter necessary
may be relied on here for several months out of the twelve.
At Leadhills, having been received with great kindness
by Niven [Manager], three-fourths of our party resolved to
don the miners' dress, or whatever dress would not spoil
by soiling, and descend one of the shafts. Perhaps the
appearance of our party marching half-a-mile to the pit
mouth in our new attire was the most ludicrous incident
of the visit. How so many pairs of red trousers and caps
and blouses could be collected and placed at our service
was surprising; but how we all looked after our trans-
formation was far more marvellous. We had been lately
reading Carlyle's *Clothes Philosophy*, wherein it is set forth

that just as molluscs, including both sea and land snails,
are resolvable into species by the difference of their shells,
so the *genus homo* is divided into ranks—into nobility and
ignobile vulgus—by means of clothes.   The quaint author
then imagines a House of Lords, whose garments had all
blown off them, and what a poor House of Commons, or of
'equal' barbarians it would instantly become.   A better,
and we should say a much safer experiment was this change
of men of various callings into miners pure and simple.
Here Jove was shorn of his dignity ; Mars of his heroism ;
Apollo was no longer a dandy, but a distressed steel-pen
vendor ; it was impossible to distinguish the *Savant ;* the
judge was inexorable no longer ; the poet might roll his
eye in frenzy, he was only a digger of lead, and his eye as
leaden-looking as any other ; there was nothing about the
mien of the schoolmaster to inspire the urchin with dread,
nor about the manner of the clergyman to rouse a sleeping
conscience.

'A saint in crape is twice a saint in lawn,' but only a
poor miserable sinner like the rest of us in balloon
trousers and rusty blouse.   The very doctors too ; you
could see that when they shook their heads, the motion
was as insipid as the nod of a bulrush.   By pairs—as of
old the creatures went into Noah's ark—with small candles
stuck in clay candlesticks extemporised 'for the nonce,'
was this strange procession lowered in buckets two hundred feet sheer into the underground galleries where the
lead or galena is obtained.   In those dim regions, where
Lethe and other rivers of oblivion were rolling, many
things were interesting, but chiefly the ways and works
of man in thus extracting, from the rugged bosom of
the rocks, one of his instruments for conquering matter.

Allan Ramsay, second to Burns as a Scottish poet,
was born in Leadhills, his father being a manager
of the works ; and while some of the party were

H

eagerly inspecting and determining the house or site
where Allan was born, others were as eagerly poring
over what Allan never dreamed of, but which some
day may also have their poet—namely, the fossil
graptolites or zoophytes, which occur rarely in the
Silurian measures, and which existed in the dark mud of
the Silurian seas, and did not outlive the period. A few
of these, we believe, have been found in the shales of
these mines. Indeed, the immense antiquity and flickering
light which falls on these and other venerable creatures
places them on the realm of that land in which poesy delights. When we had once more ascended, the sun, whose
face had been veiled in fogs and thick clouds, rolled a
few lazy smiles across the moorland, and then betook
himself once more to his blankets. It was very distress-
ing. We were so elevated, and yet had such limited
views. A capital luncheon in Noble's, however, did much
to clear off the cobwebs, and we next hurried through the
works at Wanlockhead. The various methods of utilising
the ore, and converting all that would convert—the very
smoke, for instance—into lead, did more to realise to us
what the 'diggings' in Australia are than volumes of
newspaper accounts.

From of old these hills have gathered into their grim
folds miners looking for various metals, gold, silver, and
lead; and the history of the district, as collected by Dr
Watson, must be an interesting one indeed. Of the
two towns, we should prefer pitching our tent in Leadhills, which looks more cosy and regular than its near
neighbour, and in which a fine inn is a-building and
nearly finished. Strange that in these bleak wilds, high
up on the roadside between the two towns, that flower
beloved of poets and lovers, the violet, whose colour
Shakespeare says is sweeter than the lids of Juno's eyes,
and whose perfume he compares to Cytherea's breath,

should be growing on the 2nd of August in such profusion
and variety. Some one, too, whose cheek had been
reddened or whose lungs had been expanded by the thin
keen air of these his native hills, has looked back to
them with a longing, lingering gaze, and conferred on
their denizens a handsome stone monument, pouring out
its gallons of pure water, an excellent bequest where
poisonous lead streams and fumes abound. And now,
regretting our stay was so short, and that the 'place of
graves' was one we were obliged to leave unvisited, pouring with sweat, and panting to be in time for the omnibus,
whose driver was *not* sitting waiting 'like patience on a
monument,' but rather like impatience on a spike, we
dart a last fevered look at rarities worth pondering over,
and shaking hands with friends at the rate of forty per
minute, bid farewell to one of the most singular of all
the many places we have visited.

LOCHMABEN

Let us hold a wake over the dead that are not buried.
Let the pibroch from afar utter deep wailings of sorrow.
Be the drum muffled, and the step slow. Be the chorus
of our song, 'Woe to thee who spoilest!' The Rizpahs
are few in Israel who place themselves between the unclean birds and their prey. There is no such music now
as the chink of Old Mortality's chisel among our church-
yards, the jingle of the almighty dollar alone is dulcet and
harmonious. Ye utilitarians of Lochmaben—parish of
many waters—rich with the gifts of Ceres and of kings,
what account have ye to give of your own and your grandfathers' stewardship? Ye 'Scots wham Bruce has often
led,' how have ye suffered Lochmaben to do this? The
castle of the glorious Bruce was given to it as an heirloom.

It might have been a shrine like the vale of Delphi, like the holy city of Mecca; it might have been a temple to teach us and our children lessons not a few—lessons on the inner life of the feudal system, on military strategy, on masonry, and on other and higher subjects. Yet Lochmaben has suffered the crown to fall from its head, the bracelets to slip from its wrists. Lochmaben, like the parson in Fielding's *Joseph Andrews*, had an eye to the swine, knew the value of a crackling, distinguished itself in bacon and lard—kept up in its back-courts, kept up in its fore-courts, in castle and in town, a perfect file-firing of 'grumphs'; and all the while helped, as much as it could, to put the Bruce's Castle out of the way.

This is a serious, not a laughable subject. When Madeline Smith was tried in Edinburgh for a cold-blooded murder, people ran to get a stone from the noted one's house. Into condemned criminals' cells ladies have crept for a lock of the highwayman's hair. George IV, the fat Adonis, has some statues: trinkets of his, palaces included, have value for sightseers. Tom Sayer's autograph is saleable. Travelling showmen know the value of Burke and Hare, or the Gorilla done in wax. Bruce, on the other hand, who shortened his life for Scotland and made Scotland what it is, had his brothers killed, his wife imprisoned, and his manhood turned into premature old age for us. The Countess who crowned him was confined in an iron cage. The friends of his youth fell fast around him, leaving him lonely. Highland and Galloway kerns, bloodhounds and famine, had to be kept at bay by him. From the nursery upwards, we inoculate our thin, cowardly blood with his valour; and yet this nation, which has made conchology a study, and fills museums with the shells of extinct molluscs, has suffered Lochmaben Castle, the faithful warrior's home, to crumble into the heterogeneous ruin that it is! Verily, our idolaters and iconoclasts are blind!

We quite well remember what a miserable, wet, dreary day it was when we first entered Lochmaben. We looked in vain across the street for some one to direct us concerning the castle. A cough was heard—we darted through a close, and espied in red nightcap an oleaginous man with a belly like a hemisphere. He was leaning over the walls of his piggery, and with a walking-staff poking forward to the snout of the 'olid' animal some sweet, tender leaves of cabbage. His cough, which was from his stomach, formed a duet with the matins of the swine. He viewed me mildly, then resting his double chin on his double-bosomed waistcoat, gave a snort like a grampus, and putting in a miniature shovelful of black dust at either pigeon-hole, and handing us the silver casket, on which was an inscription signifying whom, to the extent of a sneezing-mill, Lochmaben delighted to honour, he entered upon conversation. Nature has imprisoned some of her best and mightiest spirits in uncouth forms. Mirabeau looked like a tiger that had had small-pox; Socrates was no dandy. Of an ugly Englishman it was said that he was only ten minutes behind the cleverest man in the realm—it took so long before his brilliant conversation cancelled the impression which his countenance created. Our drover was rather of this class. We soon found him genial, and full of rough, homely sense. 'So you have come to Lochmaben,' quoth he, 'not looking after bacon, but after baronial halls. You have no two-storied or otherwise suitable building for smoking hams with oak-chips or the like. You are a bone and a rag gatherer, valuing the bones and cast-clothes of departed fortresses, and hanging up diagrams of their skeletons in your closet. You fill your chests with coins that are rusty, and old genealogical lists. Well, sir, I can

tell you where you'll get something in *your* line. I know
a house in the burgh in which you will find two fine
jambs that once were lighted by the fires of the Bruce in
his own ancestral halls. If you step into our school-house,
you may catch an urchin drawing a caricature on—our
castle-walls. I am not dead-old yet, still I remember
being present at the sale by auction of the grand old
castle-key, found by an inhabitant of the Heck. The upset
price was 2s 6d, but no purchaser was found. Then was
it handed to Vulcan, who made out of it an excellent pair
of peat-moss spades.' Reader, I groaned. I remembered
the fine Moorish ballad, still said to be chanted around
Morocco, concerning the Alhambra of Granada. Its
burden was, that, though the Moors had been expelled
from the most glorious buildings in the world, still they
had a little consolation left them. The following is something like the echo of the strain :

> ' Where our forefathers bent their knees,
>   They've placed their Virgin and their Cross ;
> Yet still we keep the sacred keys,
>   Memorials of our grievous loss.
> Granada's seized—the Alhambra's gone ;
>   The swine may feed, if there he please,
> The owl may hoot above the throne ;
>   But still we'll keep the sacred keys.'

Comparing Scot with Moor, we were rather disheartened.
    The castle, which once overspread sixteen acres, and
which no feudal contrivance or war-engine could storm,
and which was by far the strongest castle of the Border, was
granted by David I to Robert de Brus along with the
lordship of Annandale. The Bruces came over with the
Conqueror. The grandfather of him who is represented
as crying—

> ' Welcome to your gory bed,
>   Or to victory ! '

died at Lochmaben. The 'Scots wha hae wi' Wallace
bled ' took, under their lion-leader, Lochmaben fortress.

Blind Harry furthermore avers as to Wallace's clem-
ency :—

> 'Then Wallace said : " Madam, your noise let be ;
>   To women yet we do but little ill ;
>   Nae young childer we like for to spill." '

This address being intended to soothe the hysterical
lady who was invoking saints and sinners with her inter-
jections.

Edward, who held possession of Lochmaben in 1298,
strengthened it, and Dumfries Castle as well, in 1300.
When Bruce was flying from London, he met, near the
Borders, a messenger from Comyn to Edward, advising
severe punishment for the fugitive.   Bruce seized the
letters, beheaded the bearer, and reached Lochmaben six
days after leaving London.   From Lochmaben he proceeded
to Dumfries, where that dark deed was transacted of which
we have all read.   When the monarch's crown was secure
upon his head he handed over his paternal inheritance
to Randolph, Earl of Moray.   Edward III of England laid
hold of it.   After suffering severely from its garrison,
David II stormed it and executed its governor; but his
triumph was short-lived, and forty years afterwards the
Douglases took it sword in hand.   When James II determined to overawe the haughty Douglases, he possessed
himself of their Eskdale and Annandale estates, and
attainted the Earl.   Lochmaben belonged, from that
time till the Union, to the Scottish Crown.   It was visited
by Queen Mary while it was under the custody of the
Maxwells, who subsequently lost their office for defying
'our most high and mighty prince,' James VI.   In later
years the governorship fell to the Johnstones, who had £300
per annum—the right of fishing in the lochs—a fat cow ;
also, for maintaining the garrison, thirty-nine geese and
'Fasten's-e'en hens,' from every parish in Annandale,
whenever they required it.   Upwards of a century ago,

Annandale rebelled against the exaction, and procured its abolition. Perhaps the unpopularity of this strange sinecure is one cause of the dilapidation of the castle, which commenced shortly after the Marquis of Annandale lost the plea, and abandoned the fortress as a place of dwelling.

The Lochmaben Harper was a knowing one. He accomplished the feat of stealing, through his accomplices, the high-spirited horse of the Lord Warden at Carlisle. He then pretended that while he was charming every-body in Carlisle Castle with his music, his own mare had gone astray, although he never had possessed one. So he obtained damages for the imaginary mare from the very man whose real horse he had stolen.

> ' " Alas, alas," quo' the cunning aul' Harper,
>   " And ever alas, that I cam' here !
> In Scotland I lost a braw cowt-foal ;
>   In England they've stown my gude gray mear."
>
> Then aye he harped, and aye he carped ;
>   Sae sweet were the harpings he let them hear,
> He was paid for the foal he had never lost,
>   And three times owre for his gude gray mear.'

Lochmaben parish should be interesting to the political economist and to those who are accumulating facts in connection with the law of entail. It is pretty much sub-divided, and in the hands of small proprietors, resembling the French system more than the Scotch. It lies in the midst of bonny Annandale, 'a land made blithe with plough and harrow.' Our drover told us he once saw an owl perched on the spire of the very handsome parish church. We should like to be perched there also, but to have better visual organs, for there is much of land, tower, town, and loch all around to be admired. But whether one have human eyes, eagle's eyes, or double-strong glasses, either of the telescopic or microscopic kind, it would tax him to discover what grace, beauty, or

interest, historical, sacred, or profane, belongs to the tall
stone of the public cross, for which we are told the burgh
bartered their mill and their mill-lands, property now
worth more than £100 per annum. This bargain was
unlike the Lochmaben Harper. Again and again we
circled round this cabalistic column sticking in its freestone socket. We viewed it from every angle, and submitted it to every available organ of sense. Either it was
a mere block, or our head was such.

But we confess that it would be as audacious for us to
attempt to crush Lochmaben into a single sketch as to
delineate Napoleon in the page of an encyclopædia. The
drover obliged us to promise him a second visit—the sky
to be like silver—our spirits like mercury—and not only
the weather-cocks, but every hill and every vale adorned
with gold.

KIRKMAHOE

Gathering its tributaries all around,
   Like children to its breast from far and near,
   The Nith does 'mong my clover holms appear,
And glides close to Dalswinton's storied ground,
   With plenteous salmon all our guests to cheer;
Yet not forgetful of the former days
   When two Scotch poets whipp'd its waves to hook
   Those finny ones' forbears; and in a nook
Like Ellisland there grew Apollo's bays,
Or, long ere Scotland's poet tuned his lays,
   Remembering with what face the Bruce did look,
A-burning Comyn's castle, while his sword
   Showed stains of Comyn's blood, seen by the blaze,
He pointing with it near the torch-lit ford.

CHAPTER II

Local Sketches—Arran, Ayr, and Renfrew.

Arran (1865)—Mauchline—Mauchline and Mossgiel—Barrhead—Neilston.

ARRAN

When we first set foot on Arran it had not been completely used up by tourists and summer visitors. There were some nooks and corners thereof which had not been profaned by the reconnoiterer or the opera-glass. The instincts of the greater portion of its inhabitants were not modified by commercial transactions, and roused into restlessness, when the Saxon stranger appeared. Gold studs and diamond rings, smart shooting jackets, sleek black coats, and, above all, the white choker, were not so grateful to the aboriginal mountaineers, as blood is to a leech, or heather to a bee. An acquaintance, who had married an Arran girl, met us at dusk at Brodick, and carted us right on to Currie. The roads were rough, and the pony was one of mettle, so we were churned, and tossed, and jerked. The queerest little pop-guns of screams, and the merriest chorus of laughter, was the dower of our stiff old cart. We recollect one fairy — with teeth as white as a negro's or a chimney-sweep's, cheeks 'like lilies dipt in wine,' and that sort of curls which are said to be nooses for lovers' souls—whose fate it always was to get a seat with a cushion, and though this cushion

was the fattest gentleman's knee, still the happy 'limb'
made no remonstrance, but went to sleep as quickly as a
purring cat. At last there blew upon our faces, over beds of
herring-entrails and exhumed shell-fish, and through dark
hedges of fishermen's nets drying in the moonlight, a
wind laden with odour which mingled with the smell of
peats, and which told us we had arrived at the centre of
Currie, in which hamlet we proposed to roost for the
night.

It was August, and yet the hamlet of Currie had not then
spread the net in the sight of the birds of passage. Irish
lime had not discovered the front walls of the cottages,
and odious comparisons, between the meanness and
liberality of lodgers, had not been made by the cottars.
We were taken into the parlour of a lady who had seen
the berry of the rowan ripen on the jagged rocks above
her own kail-yard for the last eight-and-eighty years. Yet
her eye was not dim. She could still crawl out (like a tortoise toward the sunny garden wall of autumn), and, seated
on her boulder or 'summer-seat,' drawn up between her
window and door, there knit, pare potatoes, gut herrings,
and talk Gaelic. Within doors she could smoke, dis-
charging little clouds of tobacco-reek and little peals of
Gaelic alternately. She had grandsons felling trees in
Canadian backwoods, and grandsires related to princes
and to kings. Her face was a marvellously old one, yet
strong and massive. Time had been working at these
wrinkles in the brow until they were deep and fixed, like
furrows in adamant. Almost as if in malice, Time had
been drawing up the chin nosewards, and heightening
the cheek-bones, and taking lustre out of the eye. After
she had discussed her 'lunt,' she would crouch with her
chin on her palms, looking into the brightest ember of
the kitchen fire. One could fancy the unseen spirit
within her was again animating a lithe body on some

antediluvian bleaching-green, or perhaps groaning over some scene which the cruel sea gives to a fisherman's wife. Or it might be she was listening afresh to the strains of the bagpipe as a last farewell was blown to one of the many groups of emigrants which Glen Sannox has poured out from its deep defiles. Yet it was pleasant to see no abrupt influence at work, cracking her heart-strings, ere her usefulness was half expended. Frost had not blighted the fruit, which was about to fall quiet and mellow on the bosom of the kind earth. Care had not scratched out her hair. Disease had not drawn a single tooth. She had never known dyspepsia. She had neither raved in fever nor shaken with ague. If her days had not been brief and delightful, like the heroine's of a sensational romance, she had through moons and seasons, without much hasting or pausing, gone through the dull duties of a common lot in a conscientious spirit for the most part. Dodging was not the rule of her life, nor great bargains the aim, and there was a peace written on her face which told you that she had her reward.

There is close to the hamlet of Currie, between it and Glen Sannox, a churchyard without a church—for the latter, dedicated to St Michael, has left no trace behind. This is the loneliest cemetery we know. For days it is visited by nought save the great shadows of those clouds which come rolling out, torn and trailing, from the profound abysses of the neighbouring glens, or slide from the shoulders of the gigantic hills. Few tears moisten these little mounds, for the eyes that should have wept for the sleepers beneath are gazing on Canadian fields, or drowsy perhaps at Virginian camp-fires. But when the east wind gathers up the spray of the Atlantic it sprinkles it here; and at dusk you can see the white sea birds, noiseless as snowflakes, gliding like ghosts among the old

headstones. What struck us most, on perusing the in-
scriptions, was the great age of many of those entombed
beneath. Compared to the number of suns granted
to our mercantile populations in the large cities, the
years of the octogenarians of Arran were a striking
proof of the wholesomeness of the conditions of their
existence.

But to return to our landlady. We had to wait a considerable time until one should arrive who could talk
English and keep us from wearying. During our wait we
indulged ourselves by keeking through the keyhole. The
august personage arrived and cut the loaf—each sheave as
thick as a rhinoceros hide. We slept in an apartment
whose window was so small that, had a kitten looked in,
there would have been an eclipse. The Sybarite who cried
when he found a ruffled rose leaf beneath his side would
have been shaved many times by the rough ' haimert-made '
blankets which encompassed us above and below. In the
grey of morning we had some doubts whether a small whale
had not been stranded in our bedroom, but these were
dissolved when we espied our two pairs of boots, well oiled
from stem to stern. Had we been Russian noblemen, to
whom oil is meat, drink, and ornament, we could not
have been treated more generously. Having got out of
doors, we plunged, with the enthusiasm of tyros, into the
first quiet pool whose waves were kissing the brown sand,
and after congratulating each other (for we were twain)
on the vast amount of vigour infused by sea-water bathing compared to immersion in fresh, we had a race, after
the fashion of Robinson Crusoe and his man Friday ; and
to our savage amazement discovered that we had but dipped
into a pool of the Sannox burn near to the meeting place
of salt and fresh. Our next lion was the mighty Goatfell,
on whose bare scalp we intended to set foot. Rain pre-
venting, we contented ourselves with a visit to the manu-

factory of barytes, a valuable vein of which crosses the
Sannox burn about a mile up the glen. The ore is washed,
ground to pulp, boiled with sulphuric acid, and then run
into troughs. It is then dried at a high temperature and
cut into solid pieces, which are dyed at the manufactory
or packed in barrels. Its use is to form the body of
many pigments. Landscape painters would pronounce
the whole works a sad blot on the beauty or sublimity of
Nature all around; but the same lapse of ages which
softens the angles of a feudal tower and makes bareness
flowery, destroys also the softly-rounded, mellow-coloured
cabins of wretched cottars, and gives us prosy angular
buildings, with more comfort to the rent-payers, let us
trust. And now let us trudge from Currie to Brodick.
The walk of fully five miles is as fine as any we have
attempted. The sea is broad enough and the mountains
high enough, and the streams which leap across your
path fierce enough, to give you a proper idea of the land
of Fingal and Ossian. Immense boulders are occasionally
met with between the highway and the shore. On one
called the Cat's Stone (Cath or Kath Stone = battle
stone), as large as a common-sized Presbyterian kirk,
an enormous rowan-tree had planted itself by way of
steeple. Would the field mouse be building its nest
in the crevices of this isolated rock when Alexander
was fighting the Persian King? If we were sufficiently well acquainted with the hieroglyphics, the autobiography which every object in Nature writes of its movements, we might answer. In the meantime we are glad
to escape from our own question, and admire those huge,
clumsy fish, not unlike the porpoise, which the natives have
christened 'pellocks.' Slowly they tumble up their
backs, like some boat, bottom uppermost, rising from its
grave. Here is a whole 'school' of them, as the fishermen say, taking successive draughts of the blood-renovat-

ing atmosphere. Lord Jeffrey stole a good simile and applied it to Tennants' *Anster Fair*, from the walloping of
these sea-dogs. Speaking of occasional fine sentiments
in vulgar description, he says that the author's best things
were 'porpoise-like, and showed themselves above the
element they live in.' But where is Goatfell all this while
—the great mountain that had sucked us towards Arran
as it draws towards it the wandering clouds? Alas! like
the old forgotten folk who jostled Shakespeare on the
street, and knew not whom they were beside, we were too
near the mountain to see it. No doubt our road was all
the grander to us with a consciousness that the cloud-
capt pyramid was standing 3000 feet nearer the sky than
we who were at its base, but it was not till we had
reached Invercloy that we had a proper view of the fair
proportions of its grey mottled sides.

Our second visit to Arran was modern. Once more
we arrived at Brodick—Brodick now no more. This fact
was a most singular one to us. So the long snug row of
houses, nearly level with the beach — the inn whose
garden glowed with fuchsias—the chained eagle which
screamed below the big ash tree—the old capital of the
island was no more. The mighty ducal arm, stronger
than the arms of the ancient mist-born giants, had lifted
up Brodick and swung it with all its inhabitants over the
bay to Invercloy. 'Presto! begone!' said the dexterous
magician, and presently the thatched row, with all its
flower-plots, glided over in some unimaginable way, and
became neat and modernised on the other side. The old
inn became His Grace's stables, and, in lieu thereof, is a
grand one, scaring commonplace mortals like ourselves,
as Royalty sweeping past a shop-boy makes him tremble.
As in days of yore, we tacked and veered round the
clergyman, so now we held our head awry from the new
hotel. It is easy for factors and architects to tell us

about the 'improvement' that has been transacted
here.

> ' I remember, I remember
> The house where I was born ;
> The little window, where the sun
> Came peeping in at morn.'

There are recollections which cannot be transposed. If,
as Wordsworth says, ' Heaven lies about us in our infancy,'
some most delightful associations must have been torn
away from the oldest inhabitants of Brodick.

From Invercloy to Lamlash the highway trends away
from the seashore, and scales a wide heathery moor.
After having saluted a doctor of divinity, we were next
arrested by a viper, lately killed by a carter's whip. Its
variegated coat glittered in the sunshine, and its
double-fanged tongue was ready for the scientific
man's microscope. Remembering that its being vivi-
parous has given it its name of viper, and shuddering
when we thought of what an ugly paragraph its kin
could still supply to the penny-a-liner—a paragraph quite
different from the smooth sentences of the aforesaid
doctor—we entered Lamlash through a very fine deep
shadow formed by trees embracing above our heads from
opposite sides of the highway. What mighty hulk is
yon, as black with human beings as exposed carrion with
mid-summer flies? An answer to our question was soon
given, for, when we arrived at the village, we found no
lodging-rooms, and had to take refuge in a house in a
neighbouring glen. Lamlash Bay is the well-known
citadel of the Firth, wherein, from King Haco of Norway's days till the hours of the last hurricane, vessels in
distress can ride free from every insult of Auster or
Boreas. It is a drunken little place, where, except a
villa or two picturesquely placed, nothing seems to thrive
so well as the inns. In winter the sailor, and in summer

the visitor, pays the landlord's taxes and license. The
church is a mean building, not much better looking than
the stables of the great Invercloy Hotel. Our cottage in
the glen was different from the one in Currie in this respect, that landlady and daughter ascended a ladder which
was scarcely fit for a fat hen, and reposed between the
rafters and the ceiling, where peats are generally stored.
The ceiling consisted of canvas nailed and stretched
across the joists, and wrinkled like wavelets above our
heads when subjected to its living cargo. The beams of
the morning sun lighted us on the road to Larg. We
ascended a high, mountainous path, and then descended
into an enormous gully, which widened towards Kilbrannan Sound. At Larg we dined in the stable, as the
new inn was only a-building, and the old one unfit for use.
Circling round a bleak, undulating country, we arrived
opposite the little island and lighthouse of Pladda. On
the way we had an opportunity of viewing the Arran
peasantry returning from church. They were not, certainly, 'bare-legged Hielandmen wanting the breeks,'
they were only bare-footed. The women took to scarlet,
blue, and gold dresses, as rustics generally do, and the
primitive colours were the fittest contrast to leaden skies
and primitive rocks. Skirting round by Kildonan, we
had eggs and whitings at Whiting Bay, and with difficulty got the loan of a 'machine' for Lamlash. On the
morrow we overcame the brow of Goatfell, descending
into Glen Sannox, each for himself, at the nearest (we
were still twain). While taking lunch at Glen Sannox
burn, and awaiting our comrade, we happened, by chance,
to descry a figure like a crow in the glittering granite
several hundred feet up. A strange feeling seized us.
Was my companion stuck in a crevice? After an
arduous ascent backwards, here was M. B.—not precisely
like the Arran woman who, while stepping across a narrow

I

chasm, far below which boiled the mountain torrent,
lost self-possession and remained astride, like Lot's wife
pillared in salt, till providentially rescued—but perhaps
placed as frightfully.   Two legs were dangling over an
enormous perpendicular rock, and the owner sitting un-
easily on the treacherous marl formed by the weathering
of the granite.   To turn or to attempt to move back was
the signal for the rotten stones all around to move downwards, carrying their burden with them.   The scene, at
its first look, brought the perspiration over our brow;
but, using all our caution and cunning, we brought
our stranded friend off safely, with a 'looped and win-
dowed' pair of inexpressibles.   The sheephead broth
and mountain dew of Currie Inn restored his equanimity;
but henceforth let no one thoughtlessly descend from
Goatfell into Glen Sannox.   My companion declares that
he felt, while sitting on his uneasy seat, as if he would
go mad, as he heard the grim wind rattling across the
loose shingle around him, like musketry on a field of
fight.

Of men who have made luminous dark Arran, with its
dark centuries, there is mythical Fingal and immortal
Bruce.   Arran has been often in good society, and before
royal academies, learned geologists, and such like; but it
has few men of mark among its own sons.   Sir Walter
Scott has described Loch Ranza in the *Lord of the Isles.*
In Kilmorie parish are huge caves near the coast—the
King's Cave, the King's Larder, etc., where Bruce hid in
the day of his distress.   In one of these, Fingal has left
the mark of his foot as it was on his natal day.   It is
twenty-four good inches in length.   Fingal must have
stalked twelve feet high (like a man in a mirage) when
his beard was grown.   Was it this enormous fellow who
hunted out all the badgers, foxes, and weasles?   His
larder would require to be good.   'His jaws (says an

unpublished MS.) were as the basalt of the Holy Isle,
his tongue like a sea-trout in Loch Jorsa; his voice was as
the Torlin in flood; he drank whisky from the skin of
the smuggler — whisky mixed with juniper and with
meal; the gathering of his brows was as the furrows on
the beach, and the gleam of his eye like the fire that con-
sumeth the heather.' [1865.]

MAUCHLINE

The Americans sometimes honour us with a visit, and
print books about us which it is possible, if not pleasant, to
read. They snarl in the face of the British lion, and when
they pat his mane they have some palpable purpose to
serve. A clever American, whose book on us went the
round of the newspapers, and whose death we have had
since to deplore, namely, Nathaniel Hawthorne, has told
us of our moral qualities, our intellectual characteristics,
and our physical bearing; has spoken frankly of our ladies,
our household gods, our great men, and our national
shrines. Poor Mauchline, he whisked through it on
Sunday, and some of the dust of its famous snuff-boxes
got into his eyes, which caused him to see mottled sunshine and sights altogether odious. It was when he
arrived at Mossgiel, however, that he screamed outright.
Here was a house, representative of its class, which was
a standing insult to the seventh commandment. The
mothers and wives reared from infancy in abodes like these
could never be such as brave men would ever set a lance
in rest for, seeing that they could have no reputation to
defend. 'Such a habitation,' he says, 'is calculated to
make beasts of men and women'; and then he goes on
to talk of dunghill odour, narrowness, and filth. He was
stared at, too, in Mauchline, so disagreeably and so un-
reasonably that the begging Italian contrasts favourable

with the rustic Scot. The long-winded sermons were so
many yards of wet blanket, and the farmers were about as
civil as their collies. It seems that in the eighteenth
century a great poet walked about Mauchline, when

> 'The rising sun o'er Galston muirs
>   Wi' glorious light was glintin'.'

In the nineteenth, the gifted author of the *House with the
Seven Gables* saw, in the same vicinity, 'nothing sylvan or
rural, as ugly a place,' etc. Well, we don't envy the
American spectacles, but prefer the honest old pair that
strode over our grandfather's nose. When Diogenes, the
uncomplaining cynic, curses not his tub, we may not think
more of the tub, but certainly we think none the less
of Diogenes. If the house was good enough for Burns
to write great and lofty thoughts in, homely proverbs,
shrewd allegories, even though the reek did spew out of
it, and the rats in the rigging were restless—so much the
more for Burns. If the folk about Mauchline are in
wretched, soul-destroying circumstances, and yet are found
to be industrious, moral, Christian—so much for the folk
of Mauchline, swimming strong, with breast thrown out
and head erect, above the billows of circumstances.
There was quite as much to disgust a sentimental
Jonathan, we guess, about Mossgiel and Mauchline in
Burns' time as now; nevertheless, heroines were found
there also, whose charms of mind and body are fit
to be sung of yet in the most fastidious drawing-room
of Boston. We Scotchmen don't quite despair of better
houses and sanitary improvements. We have made
some little way already in the right direction; and
if Americans are so astonished at our condition, are so
convinced that their morality would melt away under
similar surroundings, we will pity our cousins with such
slippery morals, and take as good care of our own as we

can. Did your readers ever think of America, with its
valley of the Mississippi capable of feeding millions of men
and horses, its beef at 1d per lb, 'its goose-sauce and
apple-dumpling for the poorest working man,' and not,
after sighing to get there, next sigh lest they should ever
need to go there? 'A fu' cup is ill to carry.' We hear
occasionally about getting fat and kicking, and certainly
material prosperity coming quickly—coming rather un-
expectedly, is not like the glass of whisky ordered by the
doctor, but like the gallon imported for the revels of the
night. It takes the strongest possible constitution to
get up next morning, wash regularly the face, and get
regularly and patiently through the duties of the day. It
may be questionable if beef at the minimum, a soil that,
'if you but tickle it, will laugh at you with a harvest,'
and apple-dumplings to the mast-head, is paradise after
all. Mahomet was sensual enough at times, but he never
rested in sensualism. Even he from whom our word of
evil omen, 'Mahoun,' is coined, had nobler in his eye
than goose sauce when he wrote, 'Paradise is under the
shadow of swords.' We in Scotland here have evils
enough to complain of, big enough motes and beams in
our own eyes to take out, from the aristocrat with gum-
flowers at Almack's to the wretched cottar with the steam
of sewers dripping from the ceiling of his house, but,
through all our vanities and wretchedness and meanness,
a few everlasting stars shine in upon us, whose light at
times brings us to our knees. We are proud of our old
families, of our old castles, of our old Presbyterian forms,
of our old songs, ballads, and traditions. We have not
yet formally established the worship of the almighty
dollar. Nay, we give some credit to a high-priest among
us here and there warning us of prosperity's enchanted
land. One of the wisest living Scotchmen has told us
that 'there is a payment which Nature rigorously exacts

of men and nations, in the shape of dooming them to possess money, to have their bloated vanities fostered into monstrosity by it, their foul passions blown into activity by it, their life and all its manful activities stunned into frenzy and comatose sleep by it.' America lacks neither cleverness, nor physical energy, nor painted houses, nor luxuries, equalling those possessed by old Tyre; but her denizens are lean with lack of patience, and restless with elasticity of conscience.*

The reader must pardon aforesaid digression for the sake of Mauchline, which is rather a venerable place in Scottish records, being mentioned as of value in the twelfth century. The monks of Melrose are celebrated in rhyme for the excellence of the kail which they made ' on Fridays when they fasted,' and their pot was helped to boil by a grant made to them in 1165 of the extensive forest on the upper branches of the Ayr river, which included the present parish. A colony from the head establishment in Melrose resided at Mauchline till the Reformation. A wild, rough population, of mingled Scotch and Irish descent, was thinly scattered over the district, and much improvement came of the monks settling therein. The colony possessed extensive jurisdiction over their estates of Mauchline, Kylesmure, and Barmure, and courts for transacting justice were held at Mauchline, which was created a free Burgh of barony by charter of James IV. St Cuthbertsholm, east of Catrine, is named from the chapel dedicated to St Cuthbert; and another chapel stood on the Greenock water, in the parish of Muirkirk. In 1606, an Act of Parliament transferred the whole district from the hands of the monks into those of Lord Loudoun—an act which, nowadays, from its anti-Papistical nature, seems like a step the right way; but it was really a great misfortune to Mauchline at the time,

* The events of 1898 happily changed this unsympathetic feeling.

for the reign of the Melrose monks was much more
equitable and popular than that of their successors. The
charter of the town as Burgh of barony was burnt in the
conflagration of the Register Office, and Mauchline has not
since been endowed with power to elect its own magistrates. The day on which we entered the town was one
on which the light was falling on mountain and moor like
pearls from the bosom of Juno—the Queen of Love.
The very locomotive which bore us from the north seemed
to hop as daintily along the line as the hares across the
furrows; and, truly, when we entered the town, we did
not think that it was inhabited by the grandchildren of
the 'Jolly Beggars,' but by steady, comfortable-looking
people, whatever might be their system of 'raising the
wind.' Snuff-boxes, cigar-cases, woollen blankets, and
plain and fancy weaving, we were told, could all be executed here.

> ' Who would have thought it,
> That snuff could have bought it?'

was once suggested as a heraldic motto for an English
family that had purchased estates from the profits of
snuff; and certainly many tidy houses in Mauchline—
houses of brick or stone, with clean windows and doors—
bespoke that the folks of the town had made a happy hit
with their staple branch of industry (box-making). The
capacious Gothic church—built of red sandstone, like
the public buildings of Dumfries—with its noble tower
nearly one hundred feet in height, commanded the village
somewhat in the manner of the feudal castle of the olden
time, which overlooked in grand style the humble feudal
village.

It was while residing in the mean but-and-ben cottage
of Mossgiel, near Mauchline, that Burns found a wife, and
inspiration for some of his most valued songs and poems.
In Mauchline churchyard the little daughters of the poet

are buried. In Mauchline he ate the haggis, and saw the
'Jolly Beggars' and the 'Holy Fair.' He was a Mauchline
parishioner when the first edition of his works was
published in Kilmarnock, then an inconsiderable town of
between three and four thousand inhabitants. His brother
recollects the exact spot where he first recited to him the
'Address to the Deil' while following the carts between
Mauchline and Mossgiel. The farm of Mossgiel is the
one on which the 'Mouse' was scared and the 'Daisy'
grown. Jean Armour was first espied by him on the
village green, 'churning' [or 'tramping,' with naked feet
and nether limbs], the clothes in a manner which would
frighten modern prudes, who are afraid to talk of the legs
of the table :—

> ' I see thee dancing on the green,
>   Thy waist sae jimp, thy limbs sae clean,
>   Thy tempting lips, thy roguish e'en—
>   By heaven and earth, I love thee.'

It was in Mossgiel that he wound up the eight-day
clock, made by Brown of Mauchline, which, after accompanying him in all his wanderings, ticked in the
ear of his widow for thirty-eight years after the Bard's
death, and at the auction of her goods was, after
a stout competition, knocked down for £28. O clock!
where'er thou art, be thou like the talking oak of
Tennyson some day, and tell us with what strange
feelings thine owner sometimes gazed at thy hands
sprawling abroad over thy face, when he scarcely knew
the short one from the long, and heard, after all the fun
and fury of the night, thy still small voice. One of the
queerest productions of the Poet's Mauchline pen is that
same 'Address to the Deil.' Old Persian theology
presents us with the idea of two mighty good and evil
spirits in continual war. In Hebrew literature towards
its later periods, the same thought becomes prominent.

Then throughout the Church of the Middle Ages the awful fiend, from being simply strong and malicious, acquires traits borrowed from many a Pagan deity with whom he was confounded, and in this composite character he was haunting the imagination of the Scottish peasantry when Burns intensified the popular conception of him, presenting us with some of the most graphic features. ('Sneck-drawin' dog' is an epithet borrowed from turpitude in cattle-dealing. He who obscured the rings marking age on the horns of cattle, to make the beasts sell for younger than they were, was called a sneck-drawer.) The portrait of the evil principle given in the poem suggests to us the experience or traditions of a rude state of society, when lawlessness lurked in the depths of the forest, when murder and robbery waited on the night-belated traveller, and even the last sanctuary of safety, the church, was not always safe—

> ' Whyles on the strong-winged tempest flying
> Tirling the kirks.'

At other times scaring the wanderer from that ' howff' of poacher, outlaw, gipsy, and other Ishmaelites—the ruined dwelling, or the ' grey castle nodding to the moon.' The time had gone past when Satan was at the zenith of his grandeur, when he formed compacts with his witches and his wizards, who were burned in thousands by Catholics and Protestants alike. The baleful comet was past its perihelion. It blazed no longer with terrific intensity in the sky at noon, but it still was bright enough to be seen by night. There is a story in Scott's *Rob Roy* of an escape, the swimmer allowing his bonnet and plaid to float on and get all the bullets, while he himself dived under and disappeared in the overhanging copse. We fear this is the method of the ' Deil.' He knows what use to make of kenspeckle clothes. Perhaps it is the half-consciousness on the part both of poet and public

that the 'Deil' thus addressed is only a scarecrow, which
once passed for a reality, that makes us think the conclusion (full of pity, and with a ray of hope and friendly
feeling as for some old acquaintance low sunk) to be a
conclusion both funny and Christian. He who would
study how immortal is Satan, and what an odious Proteus
he is, must catch him in Goethe's *Faust*. Mephis-
topheles has dropped the club-foot there, and, instead of
turning the milk within the churn into butterless whey,
uses the silver pill and the malicious whisper with effect
as fatal as the most spiteful could wish. Aquinas' prayer
for the Devil, Burns' benevolent sentiments towards him,
Aird's strange conceits about the motherless and sisterless
individual, we take to be wailings over folklore not entirely
creditable now ; but the sweat and agony of every honest
soldier in Life's battle bear witness to the vitality of an
unseen principle which is earthly, sensual, devilish.

A more powerful poem has ever seemed to us that on
the 'Holy Fair,' which Fair was transacted around the
Church occupying the site of the present Parish Kirk of
Mauchline. The eighteenth century has been pronounced
a godless one—not without truth. The *Autobiography
of Dr Carlyle*, of Inveresk, is exceedingly interesting, but,
to our thinking, an irreligious spirit pervades it far more
truly, because less conscious to its author, than Shelley's
Queen Mab or Hume's *Essays*. The poet, at an age
when one would have expected him to have been writing
sonnets to his mistress's eyebrow, exclaims on the very
threshold of his poem—

> 'How wonderful is Death—
> Death and his brother Sleep.'

To us there is more religion in these two lines than we
could find in all Jupiter Carlyle's recollections and impressions of his century. Strong convictions imply attempts
to proselytise ; but what missionary efforts worthy of the

name did the Churches of Scotland prosecute during that
period? We are afraid many of the ministers of that
century were Pagans, as thinly veiled as the Popes of the
Reformation. Thanks to Burns! His strong truth-loving
nature could no longer say, with solemn air, this sacrament
at Mauchline was worship. If worship at all, it was like
that of the Samaritans, who feared the Lord, and yet had
each his pet god. Bacchus was worshipped, and Venus
was worshipped. Fun and superstition and hypocrisy
were exceedingly amiable at the offerings thrown their way.
The preachers were not living epistles, but poured out sermons that had done their work and were pointless—poured
them out like day-drudges, sweating and groaning, not
like prophets, inspired, seeking the inmost depths of their
hearers' hearts by revealing to them what was in their
own. A shrewd audience ever knows the earnest words
of a brother man, and distinguishes them from play-acting
though it does not always say so. The bluebottle scents
dead carrion and buzzes thereabout. The 'yill-caup commentators' like rant, or cant, and are not much excited
about truth. Burns set an Egyptian skull on the table
when he penned these lines—a picture of what took place
in the very middle of a religious ordinance in the citadel
of the orthodoxy of the day—

> 'Now but and ben the change-house fills
>   Wi' yill-caup commentators:
> Here's crying out for bakes and gills,
>   And there the pint-stoup clatters;
> While thick and thrang, and loud and lang,
>   Wi' logic and wi' Scripture,
> They raise a din that in the end
> Is like to breed a rupture
>   O' wrath that day.'

*A Letter from a Blacksmith to the Ministers and Elders
of the Church of Scotland*, published in the year of the
Poet's birth, fully bears out the painting of this wonderful poem, and shows that the Popish mummeries and

religious frolics prevalent at the period previous to
Knox's Reformation were being again transacted in new
guise in Scotland. Burns struck at them, as the first
French patriots did at the Bastile, and the nuisance has
not been possible since.

The poem of the 'Jolly Beggars' gives us Venus and
Bacchus worship once more, but then there is no pre-
tence to anything else. Surely in this 'Cantata' is a
comment on the text about sunshine falling on the evil
and the good. Fate and inclination had made these
hewers of wood and drawers of water. Sumptuous people,
chatting comfortably in carriages, passed them in summer's
heat and winter's snow, balancing accounts with the other
world by occasionally dropping sixpences in their gaping
wounds, after getting sixpence worth of fun or service out
of the pariahs. But kind Nature, their mother, takes
these outcasts also by the hand, leads them, too, through
the mazes of her dance, till they grow weary and sink in
her arms. Without either claret or cognac,

> 'They ranted and they sang :
> Wi' jumping and thumping
> The verra girdle rang.'

The son of Mars sings a song showing that something
more than sugar-plums and pig-wash had been in his bill
of fare. When the fate of his country hung in the balance,
he had flung his arm and his limb into the scales ; and,
when patriotism should sound her drum, he was ready to
clatter on his stumps at the call. The 'Jolly Beggars'
are despicable ; but when I look at them through a
catholic poet's eyes they are not wholly despicable. They
are not so bad as Lord Dundreary. The stuff that goes
to making men is in them. The rough, wild tones of
Shakespeare are in the poem. It is not decorous or
genteel—when were rags ever so ?—but it is genuine, and

portrays, not sick wealth, but healthy poverty, and health is worth all the medicines.

Time fails us to speak of the Mauchline 'Mouse,' the Mauchline 'Louse,' and the Mossgiel 'Daisy,'—lessons now engraved on the rock, though first written out on a slate in Mossgiel garret, at the twal' hour, by a hand that had held the plough half a day previously. Mauchline may well be proud of the Bard. It is embalmed like Pharaoh; it is lighted up by visions; it is mossed over with tenderest associations. The sins of Burns were black and mournful; but the accusing angel will recollect that his great heart suffered and wrought much for truth, and taught us much of duty, and that he has strengthened many a pilgrim with self-reliance, and scorn of cruelty, cowardice, and wrong. [About 1865.]

Mauchline and Mossgiel

In April we took train from Thornhill to Mauchline Station. Although the wayside flowers are later by three weeks than usual, still the sloping railway banks were here and there gilded with the glowing gold 'of the star-like *Tussilago farfara,* popularly known as 'dishilago.' Proceeding in a four-wheeler, we drove along at a pretty pace from Mauchline to Catrine, obtaining fine glimpses of the forest glades of Ballochmyle. Excellent as our horse was, it was nothing compared to the winged Pegasus of a local dealer, who dashed past us in his spring-cart much in the same mood as Tam o' Shanter when he felt inspired and 'glorious.' When we entered Catrine we found ourselves in a level basin, screened in by hills. The streets were symmetrical, and through one broad street, facing the factory, purled a streamlet of pure water. It presented an appearance rather monotonous and quiet. This Catrine, which possesses, we are told, the largest water-wheel in Scotland, had but few points to regale either artist or antiquary, being wholly given to the manufacture of cotton cloth. After a refreshment in the 'Burns Hotel,' we proceeded to the hamlet of Sorn, beautifully placed on the river Ayr, with its long row of houses, its manse, and church, all built on the right bank of the river, with doors facing the south. The country around is extremely diversified and heavily timbered. Bird life was plentiful, and the air was filled with the notes of the lark, the blackbird, thrush, and other favourite songsters. The sun was bright, yet its brightness but served to reveal the extraordinary backwardness of the season—the trees without any flush of green, and the grass fields brown and bare. From Sorn Manse, with pilgrim's staff in hand, we made our pilgrimage next day to Mossgiel. The farmers were in the very midst of their sowing, and men, women, horses, and harrows lent a lively appearance to the russet furrows recently turned up by the plough. Passing through Mauchline, we got upon the Kilmarnock Road, and by traversing the very field in which Burns ploughed up the daisy, and having on our left hand the adjoining enclosure in which he turned up the mouse's nest, we arrived at the farmhouse of Mossgiel, which presents to view a building very unlike that in which the Poet resided. The only part of the house which remains the same is the walls of the under storey. The old garret, in which the Poet wrote some of his well-known poems, and the thatch roof over it have been removed, and the dwelling improved into a plain slated two-storeyed house with five windows and a door in front. Opposite the front is a high hedge, the thorns being, it is said, planted by the Poet's own hand. The tenant-farmer preserves in frames the MSS. of the song of the 'Lass of Ballochmyle' and the letter

written to Miss Alexander, and sent to her along with
the verses. We understand that there has been some
controversy as to the genuineness of these relics. To our
not very critical eyes they looked extremely like Burns'
handwriting, and, should they be authentic, must possess
a very high value, since the MS. of a not superior poem,
that of 'The Whistle,' was lately sold by a farmer in
Tynron to a Scottish nobleman for £150. Mossgiel farm is
situated on a basis of trap, on the water-shed between
the valleys of the Ayr and the Cessnock. The word
'Mossgiel' is of Gaelic origin, and is said to mean 'the waste
or fallow ridge.' A finer view it would be difficult to find
in the South of Scotland than that to be obtained from
the door of the house. Opposite, on the line of the
horizon, were the hills around Dalmellington, streaked
with snow. The land of moor and martyr around Muirkirk was visible across beautiful Ballochmyle, and the
finely-wooded banks of the Ayr ran like a curved fringe
throughout the plain in the foreground. Nevertheless,
there were changes undreamed of by the poet-farmer
obtruding themselves on our senses. The smell of guano
was modern, and the chimneys of the box factories and the
gaswork at Mauchline, as well as the high and massive square
tower of the parish church, were features in the landscape
unknown to last century. Burns refers in the song on
the lass of Ballochmyle to the mavis singing in every glen.
To our ears the blackbird was the main singer of this
early April day. The skylark and the yellowhammer and
redbreast came next, and only at rare intervals were we
startled with the loud piping of the thrush as he sat on
his perch far up on the bare high tree. We were unable
to form a nosegay of Mossgiel flowers, picking up, after
much search, a daisy or two, a sprig of whin, an early
veronica, a lamium, and the spring potentilla. When the
poet Wordsworth visited Mossgiel he was fortunate enough

to obtain a day so clear that the peaks of Arran vivified
the scene. Every landscape in Ayrshire that admits of a
view of those blue serrated granite walls gains by the
outline. It is strange that Burns, who must have seen
those romantic and towering mountains so frequently,
should have made no reference to them in his poetry.
But his life was a fast and passionate one, and his admiration of natural objects was generally interwoven with the
praises of the beauty who was uppermost in his fancy for
the time being.

Leaving Mossgiel, we came back again to Mauchline
in order to visit some of the houses enshrined in the Poet's
verses. Poosie Nancy's house, the scene of the revels of
the 'Jolly Beggars,' faces the church gate. It is a two-
storeyed thatch house, with windows of unequal size, two
of them very small. Nance Tinnock's house is also intact.
In the former you may sit at ease and refresh yourself
with a measure of Scotch whisky out of Burns' stirrup-
cup, a wooden dish, hooped with 'saugh,' which forms the
chief object of attraction in one of the oldest shrines of
Bacchus existing in Ayrshire. Walking in contemplative
mood through Mauchline Churchyard, one's heart is inclined to become sore at the poetical immortality of several
of its tenants. Their memories are not preserved in
amber, but in the brine of satire. Too much of Burns'
poetry breathes the spirit of the Ishmaelite. The great
satire which makes Mauchline Church and Churchyard so
celebrated sets up, in part, a bogle of its own to shoot at.
Lads and lasses were proud to see each other. Smiles
and jokes were interchanged. Weary pilgrims refreshed
Nature with homely bread and cheese and a modicum of
spirits. Sons of the earth talked of the weather and the
crops. Sons of the Church commented freely on the sermon. They thought of their sins and their clothes. Why
not? Christianity, the joy of the whole earth, the bearer

of good tidings, can surely tolerate smiles and laughter, as well as seriousness. People read the 'Holy Fair,' and are indignant at the religious farce, so they say, into which the celebration of the mysteries of our religion had declined. All this, it is remarked, was winked at by the Church of Scotland—a church planted by wrestling and prayer, and watered with martyrs' blood. Our own opinion is that things were not a bit blacker, but rather somewhat whiter, with our national religion in the time of Burns than now. In the large gatherings depicted there doubtless were excesses and individuals of tainted reputation, but we believe the average character of the peasantry there assembled was quite as good as that of the Poet whom Scotland admires. The theology satirised in the 'Holy Fair' was, it must be remembered, that same theology which had reared a man like Burns' father, and under whose shadow had grown up such scenes as are pictured in the 'Cottar's Saturday Night.' Suppose one were inclined to be as one-sided as Burns is in this poem, what could he say of the professors of Christianity in the present day? They are as mixed a lot as ever was then. Yet we rather care to look on the brighter side of the shield. It is not by debiting half the world with levity and hypocrisy, but by crediting it with honest intentions, with a sense of the infinite, with a conscience and a longing for the nobler life, that you can make proselytes to a better faith. 'Tidings of damnation' may be very rude tidings to deliver, but as long as the distance between right and wrong is infinite, we suspect they, too, must at times get to be heard.

Mauchline of to-day is much altered from that of last century. A new street has been driven through it, and the Cowgate, once the principal artery between north and south, is now like a side vennel. Part of the open space at the cross has been enclosed in the churchyard. The

K

priory or castle stands in a very dilapidated condition,
and there is a manorial and seignorial-looking gateway,
which has now become a beggar-lodge. Farming and
box-making are not at present money-making, and these
being what employ labour in this district, there is consequently a dullness visible throughout the town. Let us
hope for better times, when prosperity shall arise and
houses and human beings grow more plentiful in this delightful and interesting part of Ayrshire.—[A recent
production.]

BARRHEAD

We distinctly recollect the arches which spanned our
native town at the passing of the Reform Bill. The fresh
damp smell of the foliage of newly-cut wood—the large
showy garlands of flowers—the enthusiasm of the men
working and the women with children in their arms looking on—have obtained a permanent place in the photo-
graphic gallery of our brain. We recollect, too, that
having spent every farthing of admiration over our own
arch—the one fronting the Printers' Row of Crossmill,
and therefore suburban in character—we pressed grandfather into service to satiate our curiosity by leading us to
see the arches of our neighbours. By-and-by we got
elevated on his back, and we suppose no Roman General
to whom the Senate had decreed a triumph could have
experienced more delight.* To the grandchild the main
street of Barrhead seemed like a vista leading into a
millennium of sweetmeats, toys, jingling bells, cockle
shells, and merry maids all in a row, and to the good
old Radical giving him the ride we have no doubt it was—

'A path of glory opening in the west,
    To golden climes and islands of the blest.'

* At this time Shaw would be in his sixth year.

Each new arch seemed to revel in a splendour which the
other lacked. The dull air was no longer a substance
administering life to our lungs in common with dogs and
cats, but it vibrated with peals of music, and was filled
with banners of quaint device. Always when we look
back into the morning of existence we cannot well get
through these arches into the times before they were
spanned. Doubtless we remember previous events, but
as the planet Jupiter shines so bright that its moons,
though equal to stars of the sixth magnitude, cannot
be seen by the naked eye from their proximity to
the brightness of their primary, so this one great
event has considerably obscured contemporaneous occur-
rences.

The Printers' Row, to the east of Barrhead, on the
Glasgow Road, was a peculiar little hive. It contained
the domiciles of the printers, out-door labourers, and
other mechanics engaged in the calico printworks of
Crossmill * on the Levern, then held by Thomas Stenhouse & Co. It was a long two-storeyed row, with attics.
None of the dwellings consisted of more than a 'but' and
a 'ben'—or, in other words, of more than two apartments ;
but there was an ingenious mixture of single apartments
on both floors. Another one-storeyed row, which has
since been razed and the site built upon, was named 'The
wee thack row,' and was entirely composed of single
apartments. In this quarter, which represented the St
Giles of the community, the poorer workers were consigned in sad proximity to each other. For half a century
the printwork, without hurry and without pause, pursued
the even tenor of its way. There was neither flow of
trade nor depression. The day of toil rose and set with
the punctuality of an Australian sun. At six o'clock in

* It was at Crossmill that Shaw became a partner as a master
printer, as recorded in the introductory sketch of his life.

the morning, for eight months of the year, the bell rang regularly, and as regularly at six in the evening. In the winter the arrangement differed. There was no half-time nor over-time. From the water-wheel, which supplied the motive power, to the 'tearer' or 'tear-boy' who stirred the colour-sieve, up to his master the printer, all was motion for ten hours per day, all was relaxation afterwards.

The consequence of this peculiarly steady disposition of affairs was that the workers became like a tribe or clan. Everybody knew his neighbour in a sense which it is impossible to realise by the nomadic dwellers in great cities. The date of your birth was public property. The very hour was registered in some annoying memories. Jock had 'come home' just when the Irvine coach had passed—Jenny about the time the newspapers arrived. In connection with these important circumstances, the community depended generally on the services of a 'howdy,' or female doctor, a profession which has become obsolete, and there was a 'blythe-meat' which alone of all days in the year introduced us to a *terra incognita* of jams, jellies, and rum-punch. At the christenings or baptisms, which were done in the parish church of the Abbey, Paisley, three and a half miles distant, some favoured young woman was trysted beforehand to carry the child to the font — which meant to bear it in her arms all the way, and could not therefore be looked on as combining ease with honour. One of the party took charge of a large piece of cake and cheese; and the first person met, let it be the blind man with his dog, let it be the member of the county on horseback, was pressed to receive it and expected to turn with the procession a short way, and to give the child his blessing. With the exception of church attendance on such days, and on the occasion of the Sacrament, the community lived like heathens. A strange secular spirit crept over its members, who, in politics were, root and branch, Radicals. The weekly newspaper was read by rotation on the Saturday evenings in the different houses to crowded audiences, and went far to supply the place of the weekly sermon. The parish church being nearly four miles distant, and situated in a large town, which had little in common with the Crossmill community, contributed not a little to this state of things.

There was an amazing amount of self-dependence among the members, considered as a clan or body. Were any sick? They knew who had the gift of prayer. John Edmonstone, the clerk of the works, wrote nearly all the private letters. Pate M'Watty, who nowadays would have been confined in one of the wards of a lunatic asylum, killed all the pigs, which no one was allowed to keep unless so poor as to be an occupant of a single apartment. Jock Watson at night, after his day's work, mended all the shoes, of which far fewer were used then than now, for almost all schoolboys went barefooted.

It was a printer who supplied the excisable liquors, and one of the workers bought the monopoly of selling the damaged calicoes to the others. What the community as a whole excelled in was kitchen gardening. The onions, leeks, carrots, parsnips, and potatoes produced by each from his little plot generally carried all the prizes before them at the shows. In poultry they were nowhere, for an edict from high quarters disallowed the keeping of hens, for the sake of the keeping of peace. A few printers, led by the manager of the works, became florists, and the manager's tulips were things to be wondered at. They were all named, and had pedigrees. We recollect well our first introduction to them in full bloom beneath his canvas shed. It was like the intro-

duction to the music of Beethoven. It seemed to be
a glimpse of Eden—

> 'With these her holy offspring,
> Creations of the light,
> As though some gentle angel
> Commissioned love to bear,
> Had wandered o'er the green sward,
> And left her footprints there.'

And as Adam had named all the beasts, so we had tulips
rejoicing in martial and in philosophic names. A row
towering above most others, exquisitely marked and
symmetrically shaped, were Radical politicians, in accordance with the creed of their owner. His whole garden
otherwise was a model of trimness and good order, well-
stocked, but not over-stocked, with fruit trees, beneath
whose blossoms sang innumerable wrens, and at whose
ripe fruit there pecked legions of blackbirds and starlings.

In this little community the advent of the New Year
was very marked. Shortly after twelve o'clock of 'Hogmanay' night we were wakened by the arrival of the 'first-
foot.' In rolled, across the clay floor, a jar, containing a
gallon, more or less, entitled a grey-beard, and following
it a patriarch with his whole family. Everybody was thus
bound to visit everybody else in the row, and the drinking
of so many healths became a very serious affair before
evening fell. Nevertheless, there was a hilarity, a shouting, talking, leaping, dancing, and laughing about the
affair, which made it more noisy than dangerous.
There was much eating as well as drinking, and
some singing mixed with both, so that the percentage of inebriation was less than might have been expected. A wedding was another cometary derangement
of the system. Hackney coaches were then unknown,
and often an important part of the ceremony was the
marching to and from the manse to get tied. These

marches were generally announced to the outer world by the firing of guns on the line of procession, and by the formation of circles on the highway at regular stages, when luck was invoked over the blood of good John Barleycorn. Lads and lasses were in their best attire, and they laughed the bitterest sleet shower to scorn.

At funerals hearses were little used, and the coffin was borne on spokes covered with a mort-cloth, for the preserving and loaning out of which there was a society. It is almost superfluous to add that these were not conducted on teetotal principles. The printworks were situated four miles distant from any parish school, and generally some old weaver taught the elements in a worn-out weaving shop near at hand. If no weaver required to stoop so low, then a man with a pin leg or wanting an arm was sure to fill the gap. Many of the workers taught their own children, and perhaps those of a neighbour, to read. The national benefit of parish schools is a Scotch hobby much too violently ridden. Barrhead, with 6000 of a population for instance, has been destitute of a parish school ever since it was a town, and even now there is not one nearer than Neilston, with a bad road of two miles intervening; and the same could be said of many other villages whose intellectual progress has depended more on a desire to learn than any fostering from without. For a hundred years the parochial and endowed schools have been most unfairly distributed, and their distribution guided by no wise central plan. It must not be imagined that although the community was like a clan there was anything like equality in many respects. There was a well-marked scale of gentility. Into some parlours it was as great a favour to be admitted as it is, in higher circles, to be present at a Royal levée. The longest settled families and those enjoying the highest incomes were, other things equal, those which constituted the local nobility.

Barrhead Fair, with its horse-races up and down the open street, its hot pies in ale-houses, and its various gimcracks, was then well attended, but the regular holidays were in August at Paisley races. 'Days at the Coast,' except when disease required, and steamers and railways, were things unknown. The oil creuzie or 'long eights' threw a light in the nights of winter (when gloaming 'dauners' and work beginning with daybreak were the custom) on many a shrewd, honest face, while the news from London and the speeches of Earl Grey were the political capital of the hour.

About a quarter of a century ago the family of Stenhouse met with commercial disasters, and new methods of printing rendered the Crossmill ways old-fashioned. Trade left the district, and the community of more than fifty years' standing was broken up as completely as the trapper breaks up a community of beavers in the Hudson Bay territories. With melancholy feelings we gaze upon the empty workshops every time we look at them from the Barrhead and Glasgow Railway. The great beech hedges to screen the cloth when bleaching on the greens, so full of nests, are rooted up; the little canals are stopped with mud—once crystal streams from which water was laved on the linen; the big house of Stenhouse, on which we gazed of yore as on a palace, is a mouldy-looking building compared to many houses of less pretension; the Printers' Row is a shabby affair, full of broken panes and Irish; the splendid plane-tree is a stump; the old tower of Stuart's Raiss is waxing smaller in size; the big burn and the wee burn (for we named streams like Humboldt's South American savages by such simple generic terms) are defiled by unutterable abominations; the delightful gardens are waste and grown over with nettles; and the well-known men, women, and children, with their joys and sorrows, shall never in all time people that spot again.

Neilston

Although its younger sister, Barrhead, has become
by far the most populous town in the parish, yet
Neilston is a town dearer to the memory of its natives
in foreign parts, because its population is of a less shifting
character, and therefore there are far more bonds of kin
and more mutual knowledge of one another in the older
town than in the more recent. Observe a funeral *cortège*
passing through Barrhead—it is almost as if it passed
through Argyll Street. Nobody looks with an eye of
interest, and it is only a chance if the stranger can be
informed on the street concerning the departed. Whereas,
in Neilston, under the same circumstances, the houses are
all empty of children, eyes are at every window, and a
hush prevails along the street. The very surnames of the
people are witness of fixity—Carsewells, Youngs, Gilmours
and Andersons, for instance, prevailing in a kind of
Celtic fashion. And yet, compared to Barrhead, Neilston
has a forlorn and wearied look. It stands on high—
a mark for winds and storm. A treeless moor stretches
on three sides around, and a great hill, named ' Neilston
Pad,' quite impracticable to the argriculturist, looms
against the southern horizon. The streets are narrow
and crooked, and the houses very motley; a few
aristocrats, a few of the middle class, with ashler
fronts and green painted railings; but many a poor
plebeian with 'crow-step' gable and thatched roof, and
windows so small that the days of the glass-tax are
painfully obtruded. The church shares in the general
meanness, although there is a myth in connection with
it—namely, that its steeple is the highest in Scotland,
not as a steeple but owing to its site. In the glens
around Neilston, bleachfields have been an institution for

a century, and great supplies of cheap female labour from
the Highlands, and chiefly from Mull, have mixed much
Celtic blood with that of the original inhabitants.   These
poor, ignorant girls must have felt a mighty change from
the peat-reek and heather of their fatherland to the prison-
like incarceration of them in large central buildings of
the public works called 'women-houses,' there to toil with
unremitting regularity.   Their condition, however, has
been greatly ameliorated during the last dozen years,
partly by the progress in wealth and intelligence common
to the nation, and partly by legislative enactment.
On a summer Sunday morning it used to be rather a
picturesque scene to see numbers of them winding their
way by a bridle-path, in the gaudy dresses they much
affected, across Fereneze Braes, past Glenkilloch and the
Kissing Tree for several miles, to obtain Gaelic sermons
in Paisley.   The uplands which they traversed have
been made popular of late by being the battlefields
of the two last sham fights, and, although very bleak,
they afford from their summits such views as we
have not seen surpassed in the Scottish Lowlands, embracing the basin of that old shallow sea which a study of
the raised sea-beaches on the Clyde leads us to suspect
filled, at no very distant geological epoch, the plain
whereon Glasgow and Paisley now repose.   Instead of an
odd canoe (such as turned up at the Drygate, in London
Street, in St Enoch Square, and near the confluence of the
Clyde with the Kelvin) meeting the eye of the gazer as in
the prehistoric period, there are church spires of two brave
cities pointing to heaven, chimney stalks, colleges, and even
a grand palace for madmen, who so late as Shakespeare's
days 'deserved a dark house and a whip '—all these have
grown up as by the stroke of the enchanter's rod.

Our liveliest recollections of Neilston, however, are
not of its bleachfields, but of a delightfully situated little

printfield named Gateside, which occupies a spot about a
mile from the town in the vale of the Levern. A quarter
of a century ago more money used to be disbursed at its
monthly pay-day than at any other public work in the
parish. So quickly had its prosperity grown upon it that
there had not been time to form a village around it
necessary to accommodate the workers. These were
drained from a very wide area, embracing the whole extent
of the parish. The enterprising and hard-work-
ing gentleman who carried on the works was one of
those 'captains of industry' whom Thomas Carlyle
would have been delighted with. He was a pattern-
designer, with a Frenchman's taste and an Englishman's perseverance. Instinctively he ministered to the
whimsical wants of fancy—far more whimsical than those
of the most motley democratic mob when bent on
modifying or making constitutions. Like all true labour-
captains of whatever sex, like Cromwell or Queen Elizabeth for instance, he was happy in the choice of his
subordinates. Even in the faces of the meanest 'tear-
boy' who stirred a sieve in his works, he could tell whether
there was any promise written of successful manhood.
If there was dexterity enough about the boy to mark him
out as an incipient foreman, he was not lost sight of.

Our labour-captain's own toil was enormous. Chance
workers, roused occasionally by a crazed clock, and
brought to the works a couple of hours too soon, saw
a light burning at the master's window. His personal
influence was an atmosphere filling the vacant squares
outdoors, and the large printing and cutting shops
within.

In one huge attic forty designers, engravers, and
print-cutters used to tremble when they heard the
peculiar creak of his shoe-leather. All temporary
shams vanished; and sometimes, without the labour-

captain uttering a syllable, we had that silence which
is golden—the silence of the tongue, and our manhood was being moulded for a couple of hours at a
stretch by the hard incessant sweat of toil, and the busy
sounds and motions of its numerous tools. People called
him lucky. He knew the change of styles : he knew
what patterns of silk, of muslin, of wool suited the
market ; he knew what new colour would take, for the
merchants put him up to it. But such suggestions
remind one only of the spiteful books proving that
Wellington and Watt, Napoleon and Rowland Hill have
no real glory because they were advised to do what they
did. Newton says he made his discoveries by always
'fixing his mind,' and this mind of our labour-captain
was one subjected to anxiety and attention beyond most.

The 'Gospel according to Mammon' became, under his
teaching, twenty times more respectable than many a
half-discredited Gospel of higher name. Lord Dundreary
ought to have paid this man to be taken as an apprentice
into the works. That sad typical character would have
suffered here most pungent regeneration.

And so, because such an individuality had got possession
of a few worm-eaten weaving shops, these weaving shops
became latterly too small to hold the very tools of the
labourers ; and suddenly, as drawn by the music of
wisdom, cartloads of large stone columns, and beams of
stubborn wood, came in from neighbouring quarry and
woodyard, and building went on until there was no more
feued ground upon which to erect. It was a curious spot.
Nature had never meant it as a hive of industry, but art
conquered Nature.

Sloping right upward from the works were the primeval
hills, green and sheep-dotted. Directly on the boundary
line was a natural wood planted long ago by winds and
birds. How beautiful in early spring, as one crossed the

inner area upon some message of business, was it to pause
for a moment and look up at the wild cherry trees in full
blossom, and listen to the blackbird's song. O, happy
blackbirds, how careless, how free you were; or at least
seemed to be, for we had not then read and believed Sir
John Lubbock's curious statement about the comparatively
unhappy and anxious lives led by almost all wild quadrupeds and birds. How pleasant to ramble through this
wood at the meal-hour—its anemones, and primroses, and
wood-sorrel. We see them even now in bloom. In after
days, when botanical tastes were more developed, it
was a pleasure to pluck even the unsavoury plants,
provided they were such as had grown in this wood of
yore.

Even that necessary fluid—the life-blood of a public
work—water, was denied to the site. No matter. A
nineteenth century labour-captain could surely do what
dull Peruvians and old, dim Romans had done; and so an
aqueduct was constructed, and water brought nearly two
miles away from a feeder of the Levern, which had all
again to be conducted across arches, and poured faithfully
back into the Levern, lest ought be lost to the works
farther down. The water came from Tannahill's 'Glenkilloch's sunny braes,' a glen which, though inferior to
that of Campsie, is extremely sweet and pretty, and
possesses two series of singing cascades, which have worn
out punch-bowl-looking recesses, well known to young
Neilston in the bathing days of July.

But not only was the site a difficulty conquered, but
the artisans—drawn from such distances—were not always easy to manage. In dull times they readily slipped
away altogether; in brisk times they were apt to be caught
as in traps by the public-houses on the road. Every
apprentice in several departments required to pay half a
guinea of entry money, from which his health was drunk.

When several apprentices entered at once, a day was
appointed in which their money should all be melted in
a gorge of meat and drink. Some trifle of a 'recom-
pense' was exacted from each person attending. This
was in addition to the seven guineas required for trade
purposes. How the fellow tradesmen of the neophyte
scented afar off the coming joy as a condor scents
carrion on the plains ten thousand feet below! The
whole animal nature of forty persons confined together in one room, all sitting on stools for ten or more
hours close to each other, and necessarily either improving or degrading one another, seemed by turns to show
itself fiercer and at more frequent loopholes as the day of
revels approached. The repartee became grosser—the jest
more hideous, the laughter like a satyr's. Sometimes an
elder would issue a stern rebuke, and the cowards would
quail, but the general resource of the more delicate
natures was silence and work. On Monday morning
following the debauch many stools, like steeds without
riders, a dull, dogged, style of working, a heavy atmosphere of tobacco and drink, and an unusual quantity of
effervescent draughts, told that joy had fled and pain had
set in. To the credit of others, different phases of
development took place. On the wings of some sweet
tune, whistled with wonderful clearness and correctness,
amid the clattering of saws and punches, the better
nature of a musical brother proudly careered. By others
again, politics, social questions, and theological dogmas
were argued with a point and perspicuity which would
have done credit to the *Saturday Review*. Nay, so keen
was the war of wits, that Nemesis even here overtook the
doomed ones, and a day of judgment, in patterns and work
not fitting as they ought, told the philosophers that men
ought specially to know what they professed to know, and
do what they were paid to do.

One day, when we were all sitting as usual, an awful crash took place. To the imagination of more than one the roof was falling. Seven-eighths of the artisans rushed to the door, and the labour-captain was crushed in the passage with no more ceremony than his humblest servant. Well we recollect the optical delusion. We saw the roof falling piecemeal, but it was only the windows which were on the roof that were all driven in by brick-bats and darkened by a shower of tiles. A boiler had exploded and blown up the roof, and this was the blown-up roof coming down. Several men were killed, so the works were stopped from breakfast time. It says something for the brains of some of the workmen that the short holiday was the first introduction of the writer and a few others to the Hunterian Museum, Glasgow. On another occasion, an awful night of storm had flooded the roads on our way; rising before five every morning, we marched by the foot of the hills two miles (often with no other companion than the moon), hasting before old Isaac would ' shut the gate' five minutes after the bell. When we arrived, a white-headed seer, who never spoke but on great occasions, was relating the fearful story of the bursting of Glanderston dam, at the base of the Craig of Carnock, and the sad havoc and numerous deaths and narrow escapes caused by the unlooked-for flood.

Perhaps it may be thought from this sketch that the tradesmen of the time were rather gross; but it is justice to remark that the rural population of Neilston always seemed to us its rudest element. The most offensive scenes ever we saw enacted were in connection with agricultural revels; there was always some art exhibited in an artisan's debauch, but with farm labourers and small farmers, strength, sound, and fury mixed often in a perfect whirl of madness.

Scattered like autumn leaves are the faces to which we

refer, and Gateside Printworks of to-day perhaps does
not contain five persons who lived at the time alluded to.
There is something pathetic, yet delightful, in the idea
which has sprung up in recent times of the re-unions of
people who have hailed from the surrounding country into
such an absorbing centre as Glasgow. We can easily
fancy an old Neilston or Barrhead man uttering such
names as Neilston Pad, Shelfield Toll, and Bourock, at a
Glasgow soiree of the natives, and find that there was a
spell in them equal to that inspired by a poem or a song.

But persons cause us to thrill even more than landscapes. Neilston for nearly thirty years, and Barrhead
for little less, have been blessed with a clergyman and a
schoolmaster, around whom closer associations will be
twined in the minds of many of the rising generation.
The former has been a strong worker in the vineyard—a
man of keen logical faculty, full of detail, easy, plain, and
fluent as a preacher, and a gentleman in manners. The
latter might sit for the portrait of the father in the
'Cottar's Saturday Night'—one of those faces in which
our high abstractions of peace, goodwill and beneficence
are incarnated, which always finds us and leaves us
young. Many may rank higher in classical attainments,
but none know better how to get into children's hearts,
and the schoolmaster once there can soon get the
alphabet and the catechism to follow.

We should have liked to revert to another profession
—that of medicine; but alas! our dearest friend, after
forty years of usefulness—a man of shrewd, keen insight,
who knew a snob as an Indian knows an enemy by the
very trail—has fallen in with that misfortune which Dean
Swift dreaded when he looked at the tree whose decay
had begun at the top.

CHAPTER III

In Carlyle's Native District—British Association Meetings at
Birmingham, 1886, and at Aberdeen, 1885—The Dark Side of
Evolution—Sonnets on Natural Selection.

CARLYLE'S NATIVE DISTRICT *

On the first Saturday of August 1886, I set off from Dumfries to Kirkconnel churchyard, in company with a number
of members of the Dumfries and Galloway Antiquarian
Association. The morning was dark and lowering, but by
mid-day the sun broke out, and we had a lovely August
day. We went by rail to Lockerbie. At Lockerbie
Station there were two waggonettes in waiting, and ladies
and gentlemen, members of the Society, entered, and
then we drove off. Near Castlemilk we were joined by
Johnstone, forester to Sir Robert Jardine, M.P., who
pointed out to us on the left of the Lockerbie and Carlisle
Road, three peaks, known as the Three Brothers, which
had all the appearance of the craters of extinct volcanoes,
and the theory became stronger when he showed us some
of the stone of the district in the vicinity of the Three
Brothers metamorphosed into lava. He seems a most
ubiquitous fellow your volcano; a true citizen of the
world, manufacturing and advertising his fireworks, alike
in the Torrid and Arctic zones; or, perhaps one should
rather call him a denizen of the universe, for one of the

* A lecture delivered to young men at Moniaive, 1886.

L

few indubitable facts in connection with the moon is, that although there be no man in the moon at all, it must have had a terrible time of it once, when it reeled and staggered under the violence of these same volcanoes, whose tremendous craters, higher than the Himalayas, can be seen by the telescope. After we had passed the extinct volcanoes, Johnstone next directed our attention to a farm on the left, where Edward Irving was wont to address an audience gathered from a circle whose diameter was twenty miles. To the right he pointed out Mainhill, and especially a small window in the gable, at which Thomas Carlyle studied in the recess while he was enrolled as a student at Edinburgh University. About mid-day we arrived at Ecclefechan, the one town of importance in the parish of Hoddam, and important to us only because it contained the room in which Carlyle was born and the grave in which he lies buried.

> ' Such graves as his are pilgrim shrines,
>   Shrines to no code or creed confined—
> The Delphian vales, the Palestines,
>   The Meccas of the mind.
>
> Sages with wisdom's garland wreathed,
>   Crowned peers, and mitred priests of power,
> And warriors with their bright swords sheathed,
>   The mightiest of the hour ;
>
> And lowlier names, whose humbler homes
>   Are lit by Fortune's dimmer star,
> Are there, o'er wave and mountain come,
>   From countries near and far.'

So in 1822 sung the American Halleck of Robert Burns, and so may we now in 1886 apply his verses to Thomas Carlyle.

Everybody now knows or has heard of that plain two-storeyed house, that plain church, that quiet, unpretentious village, and that plain, unostentatious 'lair' girt round with an iron railing, and containing a dark oblong stone

carved over with the names of Thomas Carlyle and
his blood relations interred below.   Such a spot is
interesting to all who read and think, but especially to
those whose hands are made horny by labour, and whose
bodies have become lean by thought.

Here lies one to whom comforts and luxuries and repose
were as nothing compared to 'plain living and high thinking.' His motto was *Laborare est orare*. He, and he alone,
is honourable who does his day's task bravely, whether by
axe, or plough, or pen.   There is nothing grander in
literature than some of these 'litanies of labour.' They are
like trumpets arousing us to put forth new energies.
But enough of Carlyle at present.   The waggonettes are
waiting.   Soon they are filled, and on we drive towards a
long straggling village named Eaglesfield, and nicknamed
'Poverty Raw.'   I don't believe it is either.   It lies on a
fat hollow.   It has been a priest's field, and Ecclesfield,
or the land belonging to the church, has suffered phonetic
change.   It is the same word as 'Eccles' in Penpont, and
the first part of the word is also in Ecclefechan.

As for poverty, this village was signally free from its
signs—no squalor, but universal coziness and sweet cottages,
with their flower borders in front and kail- and potato-
plots behind, and a population of bees greatly in excess
of 'bodies.'   As we proceeded, we reached the house and
grounds of Sir John Maxwell of Springkell.   We found
that these were let to an English merchant, hard times
having visited our landed gentry.   Afterwards we walked
on foot in search of romance, and the very 'shores of
old romance' were reached when we got to the banks of
Kirtle.   There, embowered amongst noble beech trees and
conifers, was a beautiful wooden octagon house, named
Helen's Bower.   Around it was a musty floor of fir-tree
cones and decayed needles and pins.   That curious plant,
'Oneberry,' or 'Herb Paris,' or 'True Love,' was growing

profusely around. Perhaps it was planted there with
reference to the story of Helen of Kirconnell, of whose
true love we will talk anon. In Sweden it is called
'Trollberry' or 'Pucksberry.' In Perthshire it is known
as 'Devil in a Bush,' probably because the uncanny-
looking blackberry is surrounded by four leaves. Here
it was so luxurious that we counted five leaves on many
specimens. The name 'True Love,' it may be remarked,
comes from the Danish *Trolove* or *Troth-love*, to betroth, in
which word we find a reference to the old custom once
observed by the Danes as well as by Scotch and English,
of making a curious kind of knot as an emblem of
plighted fidelity. Now the leaves of 'Herb Paris' have
much the appearance of a true-love-knot, and from this
fact the plant has obtained its popular name.

There was an artificial pathway, umbrageous and high,
down which we strolled, having the limpid waters of the
Kirtle murmuring beneath us to the left. Rustic bridges
spanned the stream—one being the trunk of a single tree.
By one of those rustic bridges we crossed, and soon found
ourselves in Kirconnell kirkyard. The walls of the church
alone remained, but many of the headstones were extremely interesting, recording the last resting-places of
the Bells, Carlyles, Johnstones, Armstrongs, Irvings,
Maxwells, and other Border names. Some of these
stones had rude sculptures. One portrayed our first
parents and the serpent standing beside that 'tree whose
mortal taste brought death into the world and all our
woe.' Another represented a faithful pair walking their
pilgrim's progress, hand linked in hand. But the objects
of greatest curiosity were two 'thruch-stones,' more like
coffins in shape than tables. A sword and a cross were
rudely chiselled on one of these stones, with the inscription: *Hic jacet—Adamus Fleming.* [The name is now
obliterated.]

The story of Adam and Helen is first told in the first
edition of Sir John Sinclair's *Statistical Account of Scotland*.
In the burial-ground of Kirconnell are still to be seen the
tombstones of fair Helen and her favourite lover, Adam
Fleming. She was a daughter of the family of Kirconnell,
and fell a victim to the jealousy of a lover—being courted
at the same time by two young men, Fleming and Bell,
one of whom, thinking himself slighted, vowed to sacrifice
the other when he again discovered him in her company.
One afternoon, Helen, when walking with her lover
along the banks of the Kirtle, perceived him lurking
among the bushes, and noticing him point a carbine, rushed
between the gun and her lover, and received the wound,
sinking and expiring in her favourite's arms. Adam
Fleming gave immediate pursuit, overtook and hacked
Bell to pieces. Afterwards he went to the wars in Spain.
Nothing, however, could remove the melancholy cloud
which brooded over him from that dreadful day onwards.
He soon returned, and at last was found lying dead on
Helen's grave. Sir Walter Scott discovered a variant,
namely, that Fleming pursued his enemy to Spain, and
slew him in the streets of Madrid.

The following is the old ballad :—

> ' I wish I were where Helen lies !
> Night and day on me she cries ;
> Oh that I were where Helen lies,
>   On fair Kirconnell lea !
>
> Curst be the heart that thought the thought,
> And curst the hand that fired the shot,
> When in my arms burd Helen dropped,
>   And died to succour me !
>
> Oh think na ye my heart was sair,
> When my love dropt down and spak nae mair !
> There did she swoon wi' meikle care,
>   On fair Kirconnell lea.
>
> As I went down the water side
> None but my foe to be my guide,
> None but my foe to be my guide
>   On fair Kirconnell lea.

> I lighted down, my sword did draw,
> I hacked him in pieces sma',
> I hacked him in pieces sma',
>   For her sake that died for me.
>
> O Helen fair beyond compare!
> I'll make a garland of thy hair,
> Shall bind my heart for evermair
>   Until the day I dee.
>
> Oh that I were where Helen lies!
> Night and day on me she cries;
> Out of my bed she bids me rise,
>   Says "Haste, and come to me!"
>
> I wish my grave were growing green,
> A winding sheet drawn o'er my een,
> And I in Helen's arms lying
>   On fair Kirconnell lea.
>
> I wish I were where Helen lies!
> Night and day on me she cries;
> And I am weary of the skies,
>   For her sake that died for me!'

This is a picture by an old 'master,' name unknown. It is not easy for a modern to paint one like it. Wordsworth tried his hand at the theme. He begins, if I recollect aright, somewhat thus :—

> 'The fair bride Helen when she sat
>   Upon the braes of Kirtle,
> Was lovely as a Grecian maid
>   Adorned with wreaths of myrtle.'

Evidently this picture makes a bad beginning. We will turn its face to the wall.

I suppose all the old ballads have now been gathered. The race that could repeat them by rote is gone. I have not succeeded in adding one to our great National Collection. Professor Child of America has brought them all together in several magnificent volumes. His appeals through the Newspaper Press for any that might have escaped printing procured him next to nothing. Sir Walter Scott with his Border Minstrelsy was not a

day too soon in the gleaner's field. The old stone
crosses I believe will follow the old ballads. Soon
they will exist only in photographs. That day we
saw a beautiful stone cross in a field, only a few yards
from the public road, between Ecclefechan and Carlisle,
not far from Kirtle Water and Robsgill. My heart gave a
thump when I thought how it was at the mercy of any
rascal who happened to get on the spree, with a highly
developed bump of destructiveness. Witness the damage
done in a short time, this season, at old Cumnock, when
the roughs and keelies from Edinburgh came into that
village with a cheap excursion train. To such persons an
elegant stone cross beautifully carved out of a single
stone, and frail with the storms, frosts and thaws of
centuries, would be no more than a wooden Aunt Sally,
and would likely be used for the same purpose. One of
the finest boulders on Nithside was blown to pieces one
day with gunpowder, because the colliers about Sanquhar
wanted some fun. Monuments either of the Glacial Period
or of the Mediæval have a claim on the sympathy of
every lover of knowledge, of every Mutual Improvement
Society.

BRITISH ASSOCIATION MEETING—BIRMINGHAM

And now, with your leave we shall pull up another slide
of our lantern, and instead of accompanying me on the
first Saturday of August, you will please come along with
me on the 31st on a journey to Birmingham.

Starting at Thornhill for Carlisle in the forenoon, we
arrived there about noon. Two ladies in dark apparel
and of small dimensions began to chat with me after we
left Dumfries, and the lateness of the season was shown in
this, that we both for the first time observed the reaper

cutting the golden grain. In many fields that were uncut
a curious appearance presented itself, namely, patches of
oats were quite green, and patches quite ripe and yellow.
A farmer blamed the backward May and June for ar-
resting growth altogether on parts of the same field, and
the greenness was the suspended animation of the seeds
restored by genial July and August.

The two little Misses became eloquent in favour of
'Co-operative Stores,' which, they thought, if properly
patronised by the public, would restore our long-lost
comfort and prosperity, and entered into terrible com-
putations concerning these leeches, the retail dealers. I
said that to me bankruptcy, which seemed almost to be
courted by reckless dealers, was more dreadful than
ignorance of the Co-operative Stores' system; since it introduced goods into the market at rates so cheap as to
reduce the honest dealer to poverty in his attempt to
compete with the immense sacrifices of Pedlington & Co.,
who had secured the bankrupt stock of Trotter & Jumper,
and were selling it at their own money for the benefit of
their regular customers.

By the time I reached Carlisle I had a compartment to
myself. A tall fellow in the costume of a railway servant
seized hold of my Gladstone bag ere I was well on my
pins, and began putting queries as to my intended journey,
and making himself ever so obliging. He said I had
more than half-an-hour, and he would take charge of my
luggage. His breath smelled of some strong liquor, and
I said, 'But who are you?' 'My dress might reassure
you,' he said. 'But what's your number?' He gave me
to understand his number had been taken away from
him. 'There's a tip for your information, but I will
take care of my own luggage. I come from Scotland!'
With a heavy handful, but a light heart, bag in hand, I
struck out for Carlisle Cathedral, and, having seen it, got

back in time for my train, which took me on to Birmingham. I arrived at Birmingham about six o'clock. A swarm of boys solicited that same bag once more. The weather being sultry, these boys were all in shirt sleeves, but none of them had bare feet. I chose one who after seventy yards began to change hands, and at about a hundred was getting strangely contorted. I then flung him my greatcoat and umbrella, and took charge of that same bag for more than half a mile.

My kind host happened to be at the door, and, on seeing me give the boy a sixpenny bit, informed me, while shaking my hand with a pressure which almost flattened my fingers, that I was soft. I thought he meant my body was soft, judging from the specimen in his grasp, but it appeared he meant that my mind was soft. The municipality of Birmingham had enacted that a cabman's charge for less than a mile was not to exceed sixpence, so I could have got body and baggage brought to the door for the sum I had given to that weak-armed urchin. True, but how was I to know?

Now, how am I to describe Birmingham? I had an idea that it must be more sooty than Glasgow, and as full of narrow unpleasant streets as Manchester. It was far otherwise. Although many of its streets seemed built on a flat meadow, yet some of the most important had all the advantage of being built on undulating ground. As a rule, the streets were never very long, and abounded in circus-like turns which exposed the finely decorated fronts to advantage. The English custom of having narrow houses let from top to bottom to one tenant, prevented the erection of those enormous four and five storeyed houses, which in Glasgow spread, long before sunset, a dismal gloom across the narrow street. In hundreds of streets two storeys was the rule—higher houses the exception. The chimneys were remarkably high, which pushed up the smoke away from the streets. There were curious bits of old Birmingham with door steps or outside stairs on a higher elevation than the main street, with crow-step gables fronting the road, the roosting-places of pigeons that knew well where to go for the cab-stands. The houses were built of brick, but the elegant and substantial public buildings were of stone, and of some of these the stone was granite itself. There was no great river directing the run of the streets, and there never was a town in which it was easier to lose one's way. The munificence of its local magnates had provided several parks for public recreation, and the municipality had purchased others. Ponderous steam tramway cars of immense length ran, at a rate not exceeding eight miles per hour, through all the principal thoroughfares. The passengers on the top were secured in foul weather by an awning spread across. Birmingham boasts the largest railway station in the world, being the station of the United North-Western and Midland. There are bridges for passengers, tunnels for luggage, stands for cabs, stalls for books and papers, and an innumerable trampling as crowd after crowd disgorges. Bells are in no way mute, and whistles seldom rest, while the cabs rattling, and the heavy waggons getting under way, all impress you with the idea that Birmingham is catching the world by speed of foot.

I entered myself as an associate of the British Association, and on Wednesday evening, 1st September, I sat in Birmingham Town Hall, lighted up as it was with the electric light, so clear and yet so cool, and heard the president, Sir William Dawson from Montreal, discuss the whole question of 'how the seas began to flow and leave the solid land.' Nearly two thousand well-dressed ladies and gentlemen crowded the area and galleries, and listened intently as the president went on explaining how

this seemingly solid earth was once one great mass of
steaming hot treacly fluid which gradually cooled and
hardened at the surface!   Then he told us how a mass of
matter shrinks and occupies less space as it cools, so that
the interior of the earth began, as it were, to leave the
surface.   The surface, deprived of its support, cracked
and gave way, forming hollows along the lines of greatest
weakness, and these great hollows were the basins of
future seas.   Seas were formed by the precipitation and
condensation of the immense steam atmosphere as it
began to cool.   There were strong reasons for believing
that those great cracks in the basins of our oceans occupied
the very same areas as they had done since stratification
began.   One of these reasons was that, speaking generally, seas were always deeper in proportion as they re-
ceded from land.   Another reason was that the floor of the
ocean far out from land and at more than three miles
depth, exhibited, in the specimens brought up by the
dredge-net, no trace of sediment carried by rivers from
the land, but was made up of the decayed shells of
animals and of volcanic and meteoric dust, or of matter
carried out by floating icebergs.

Local changes there had been many.   The whole
North of America was more than once an archipelago,
and the Isthmus of Panama did not exist.   These British
Islands had been more than once joined to the Continent
and severed from it, and the disintegration of rocks by
rain and frost had carried out immense quantities of
pebbles, sand, and mud into the ocean, while the force of
the tides had worn away the coast line.   Still the great
continental masses and the great oceans were in much
the same relative positions as they occupied since the
dawn of life, in the deep mud of the old Silurian or older
Laurentian seas.

In honour of the British Association, an exhibition of

manufactured articles gathered from a radius of fifteen miles around Birmingham, was opened in the Bingley Hall, a great iron-and-glass two-storeyed building, capable of holding, so I was told, 15,000 persons. In the evening there was a conversazione. Sir William Dawson and the Mayor of Birmingham and their ladies received us. The hall was lighted up by the electric light. We had workmen engaged at their various vocations as in the International Exhibition, Edinburgh. We had a lighthouse whose electric light was intermittent, and it flashed at intervals with dazzling splendour along the whole breadth of the hall. We had first-class music and first-class microscopes. At one time your fancy was carried along by the splendid execution of the band; at another, your eye was engaged looking at the little blood cells chasing each other in the current disclosed by the microscope in the web of the frog's foot.

It would weary you, especially those of you who have been to Edinburgh, to continue this at greater length. My impression was, that although the Birmingham Exhition covered a smaller area, and had not the variety of the Edinburgh Exhibition, yet it was worthy of the vast emporium in which it stood, and contained within it perhaps as much wealth as its Scottish sister.

I was very fortunate in getting booked on Saturday, 5th September, for the excursion, which I had set my heart on, namely, that to Stratford-on-Avon—the birthplace and grave of Shakespeare. About eleven o'clock that morning, in the reading-room of the Midland Institute, there fell a darkness so thick and heavy that all writing and reading was suspended until the gas was lighted. Afterwards, in the Art Institute, while we were gazing on the quiet pictures, statues, and objects of antiquarian interest, a terrific thunderstorm raged; and, picking up a cab, I was glad, through deluges of

rain, to get to Snow Hill Station. After the train started
for Stratford matters improved. The fields on either side
of the railway were for the most part green with the
aftermath, and the country was moderately well wooded.
The fields were, on the whole, smaller than those enclosed
in Scotland. Neither wheat nor oats were grown in
any quantity. I saw beans and turnips, however—the
latter a heavy crop. When we arrived at Stratford-on-
Avon the Mayor received us. The party numbered two
hundred, and we were divided according as we had been
provided with return railway tickets, red, white, and blue,
sixty-five of each class being issued. Each sixty-five was
placed under a leader. My ticket was red, and it behoved
me to follow my leader, who took us right off to the house
in which Shakespeare was born. A second party began
at the Memorial Buildings, and a third at the grave of
Shakespeare in the Parish Church. The house in which
Shakespeare was born, after many vicissitudes, is now
under the charge of a public department with a curator.
It is an old wooden two-storeyed building. An elderly
lady took us from room to room of the house, which is
filled with articles of Shakespearian interest. In one
room hangs Shakespeare's will, with one of the few
signatures of Shakespeare. I understand that of all the
reams of paper which Shakespeare must have filled with
writing, nothing remains, not a single autograph letter
written by him, only his name attached to his will, and
other two signatures by him to important documents.
In a case, too, was his signet ring, which had been
accidentally discovered at the beginning of this century.
Many portraits of him adorned the walls, and many old-
fashioned articles, illustrative of his writings, filled the
glass cases. Of all Englishmen Shakespeare is the one
of whom we should like to know most, and of whose
biography we know least. How can we account for this?

Was it the fault of the masses or the fault of the classes? Carlyle says, 'Were it put to vote, whether should we give up our Indian Empire or our Shakespeare?' the majority would not give up Shakespeare. And yet, when the great genius travelled on his earthly pilgrimage his worth was not recognised. As Emerson says, 'They could not see the mountain near.'

We next went to the site of the house in which he lived for the longest period. The house was pulled down, but the garden and site form a small pleasant public park. Then we arrived at the Memorial Buildings, erected at an expense of £30,000, containing a museum, library, and theatre. The theatre is somewhat in the style of the Globe Theatre, London, and every year there is a week's acting of Shakespeare's most esteemed tragedies and comedies therein, by the best actors. Excursion trains are run, and the inns and private houses in Stratford are filled. I scaled the tower and had a pleasant view of the bricky town below, clean and quiet, but adorned with flags and flowers in honour of our visit. Our party next visited the church, and gazed on the hallowed place which contains the remains of this transcendent genius, and saw the bust sculptured and erected in his honour on the wall. This, to his credit and that of his admirers, was not placed there tardily, like an after-thought, but shortly after he was buried. The church itself is a beautiful Gothic building, well worthy of the town which gave the Poet birth. The Avon was a larger river than I had anticipated. It was flowing slowly, but its waters were unpolluted. A few light boats were on it. Its banks were lined with drooping willows and large masses of phragmites in purple blossom. The Mayor afterwards entertained us all together in the Town Hall, and presented every visitor with a copy of the *Graphic* newspaper containing some illustrations of Stratford.

Thunder and lightning were the accompaniments of our tea or coffee and sandwiches, and amidst blinding flashes of forked fire, we took seats in the train which conducted us back to Birmingham, which we reached by 9 P.M.

My next excursion, Wednesday 9th, took me to Warwick and Leamington. As my Association ticket gave me double journey for single fare, I did not want to take my chance of a ballot and go with a party, and be treated by a local magnate, but set out on my own hook, my luggage being light and my wants few. Bread or potatoes, and a chop, or a glass of the excellent milk which is much sold here, or a handful of the delightful plums, Victoria or greengage, of which you could have a saucer full for a penny, sufficed me. I sauntered through Warwick, through the very middle of England, and on the day of Warwick races, with feelings which even a cynic might have envied. Its church and its chapel filled me with admiration. The Earl of Leicester's Hospital was a poem carved in wood. When I entered Warwick Castle—the finest remains of a feudal castle extant in England—and was led from room to room, 333 feet in length in a direct line, each filled with art treasures, with trophies, with old armour, rare pictures, rare furniture, tapestry, china rose-enamelled—a lost art— oil pictures of worthies I had heard of since a schoolboy, I found myself on enchanted ground.

In the park attached to the castle is an antique vase, dug up from the bottom of an Italian lake, a vase of white marble, capacious enough to hold 163 gallons. A greenhouse has been built specially to cover this beautiful specimen of ancient art. In one of the rooms is a punch-bowl capable of holding a hogshead of toddy. An old woman could recollect of its having been twice emptied on two different days, celebrating the coming of age in the olden time.

Through the tallest cedars I had ever seen, I peeped
from a window down my River Avon once more.

> 'Happy is England! I could be content
> To see no other verdure than its own,
> To feel no other breezes than are blown
> Through its tall woods with high romances blent.'

This I found myself repeating, as I stood on the highest
point of Cæsar's Tower along with three Yankees, who
were watching the flight of a flock of carrier pigeons let
loose from their cotes. 'Do you see that upper portion of
the Tower of St Mary's Church,' I said, 'rather newer than
the rest?' 'Yes,' was the reply. 'Well, it cost £10,000
to take down the old lightning-struck part and put up the
new.' I was answered with the usual answer, 'Might not
the money raised have let the spire alone and ministered
to the poor?' Such a question cannot be answered by
logic. Our instincts, however, inform us that who builds
a church for God and not for fame, has a motive nobler
than many of the motives by which many of our American
cousins build up their fortunes of almighty dollars.

I shall not detain you with Leamington, a fashionable
watering-place, suburban to Warwick, save to say that it
was like finest cloth cut in most approved fashion. 'Upholstery,' as Carlyle would say, 'and the fine arts could not
do much more for any town than Leamington.'

Next day, Thursday, you must take train with me for
Coventry—Coventry of watches and ribbons—Coventry of
Peeping Tom—Coventry with the three famous spires, seen
by Tennyson while meditating his poem of Lady Godiva.
I wished to see a marvel—a public building with a highly
ornate wood front. My queries had not been properly
understood. I was sent on a false quest. The way was
long, the day was hot, and before respectability fairly
left the street, and before it was getting into tumbledown-
looking houses, I noticed a sign yclept the 'Blue Pig,

Thomas Atterburn.' True, Thomas, on being cross-ex-
amined, said I had been misunderstood, and had come a
long way off the goal, or perhaps somebody had done it
for a lark. Not feeling the least like a lark, but perspiring
more than the animal painted on Thomas's sign, and
damped a little by my disappointment, I asked for a 'half'
of spirits and water. 'Irish or Scotch, sir?' 'Do you
think I would drink Irish spirits?' I said, giving a sniff
which made Thomas, no doubt, think I was a Unionist,
for he immediately filled out Scotch. 'I prefer both your
whisky and your enterprise, you Scotch—it's superior, sir,
double X—you lead, but as for them Irish, why, if
people won't lead they must follow.'

Leaving Thomas, I got a Coventry weaver with blue
fingers and a great white apron, who conducted me to
another famous place, and assured me that 'although
watches was holding their own, ribbons was low. And do
you see that one?' he said, pointing with his blue finger to
a splendid bicycle a-passing down the street. 'Coventry
beats the world for them, and for making the three-wheelers
as well. There's more money comes in to us for them
than for ribbons nowadays.' 'What! for bicycles and
tricyles?' 'Yes, sir, you've got the names stuck on your
tongue. I s'pose you've learned elocution. They're too
new-fangled for me. I neither bother riding them nor
naming them. Little wheel may follow big wheel, or big
wheel little wheel for me. It's all the same, so as it gives
work to the poor man, but there's many o' them here as
had's to do with less beer, and as hasn't buttered their
bread so thick this last year or two. But there's St Mary's
and yon's St Michael's, said to be the largest parish church
in England. It just swallows up crowds of them, and
looks empty and hungry after all.' 'Why is it,' I said,
that when you wish to send a person into obscurity you
say, "Go to Coventry?"' 'Because Coventry means "Con-

M

vent Town," and it's just like as you would wish the
fellow that irritates you to be put into a convent.' I
made my bow and took farewell of blue-finger and white
apron, and set out for Kenilworth, about five miles distant,
and was much pleased with the clean town, redolent,
however, of the smell of tan-works. Soon I came to the
ponderous and extensive ruins of Kenilworth Castle, in
which for seventeen days, Robert Dudley, Earl of
Leicester, entertained Queen Elizabeth at the rate of
£1000 per day.

Kenilworth is one of those places which is lighted up
by 'the light that never was on sea or land, the consecra-
tion and the poet's dream.' Sir Walter Scott has done for
Kenilworth what he has done for the Trossachs and Melrose
Abbey, made it the goal of an interminable stream of
tourists.

After I had well rambled through its great empty
spaces, I wandered forth to the banks of a small stream
that runs through what was once the Castle Loch, and
looked at the majestic pile frowning above me on a small
eminence with the visitors on its turrets, and on the sill of
its empty windows looking scarce as large as beetles. It
was pleasant to learn from the most reliable recent
researches that that painful story of Amy Robsart existed
only in the brain of the great magician of the North.

It was thus I reflected, as I rested alone by the water-
course like a solitary mermaid, sitting by the shores
of old romance. I endeavoured to fish out from the
bottom of the stream a water plant I had never noticed
in the Dumfriesshire burns. I gathered a little bouquet
of flowers and wondered why Nature was 'so careful of
the type, so careless of the single life.' The old question
of whether novels were of any use at all, or whether,
having such short time here, and so much to learn, we
ought only to concern ourselves about realities—a question

much emphasised by Thomas Carlyle—came again to the front.   Of course such a question has its other side. Fairy tales, the beautiful myths of old religions, the pictures, music, and novels of the present day, duly selected, may be used as recreations to make our mortal labours light.

And now to you, my audience, for the third time, I have given a short account of my 'Holiday Rambles.'

> ' The stately homes of England,
> How beautiful they stand
> Amidst their tall ancestral trees,
> O'er all the pleasant land.'

British Association Meeting, Aberdeen 1885.*

On the 8th September I set out from Glasgow for Aberdeen.   After leaving the valley of the Tay the country was entirely new to me.   As I glided through Strathmore, obtaining glimpses of Cupar-Angus, Forfar, and Montrose, and passed over the South and North Esk, I was surprised at the fertility of the region.   As the railway drew near to the German Ocean the plain became less arable.   Stonehaven and Dunnottar Castle were for a few moments visible, and afterwards the land on each side of the railway seemed wind-swept and barren, with patches of heath intermixed ; whilst on the side of the sea many wild precipices and gorges reminded me of similar scenes witnessed while with the Society in its excursion to the coast of Kirkcudbright.   As I came in sight of the Granite City I recollected that the first occasion on which I heard the word ' Aberdeen' was in the child's rhyme—

> ' Prood skyte of Aberdeen !
> Selt your mither for a preen,
> Selt your father for a plack,
> Whatna prood skyte was that ? '

* Read before the Dumfriesshire and Galloway Natural History and Antiquarian Society.

Possibly such a rhyme pointed back to a period when
each county and almost every glen nursed a clannish
spirit, and was jealous or spiteful of its neighbours. Old
people tell me that it used to be almost dangerous for
a Tynron boy to appear in Moniaive owing to the indig-
nities he was likely to suffer merely because he was
not one of them, just as the dogs of a town gather
snarlingly round a strange dog. With some such thoughts
I entered Aberdeen, but these thoughts were pleasantly
dissipated when I perceived that instead of the *hostis*
being likely to meet with any hostility, a warm welcome
was accorded to the members and associates of the British
Association, who were arriving by degrees from all quarters
to spend a week within its precincts. With pride I paced
along the noble Union Street of this northern city, and
saw for the first time its houses and pavements of grey
granite. Somewhat plain and Doric seemed the architecture, and somewhat sombre when the sun was be-
clouded, but in the clear shining after rain the granite
sparkled beautifully. Another feeling which gratified me
was that I had found myself in a large town rich in its
association with the historic past, and containing many
memorials of its wisdom, its heroism, and its misfortunes
throughout the bygone centuries. On the evening of
the 10th, I listened to the address of Sir Lyon Playfair
[Emeritus Professor of Chemistry, Edinburgh University,
who died Lord Playfair 1898], the President of the Association, delivered to a brilliant audience of about
2000, which filled the Music Hall. The President
spoke for an hour and three-quarters, and his voice
throughout was distinct and agreeable, reaching the
farthest seats in the area and galleries. On Thursday,
stimulated by the earnest advice of our late lamented
President, I looked, first of all, into the Geological Section
and heard Professor Judd delivering his address as Pre-

sident of the section. Several years ago I had read with
care that delightful book of Professor A. Geikie, entitled
*The Scenery of Scotland viewed in connection with its Physical
Geology.* Under the teaching of Geikie and other masters
I had come to consider that the observed facts of geology
during these recent centuries could best explain the
changes that had occurred in the long vistas of the
geological past. We were taught not to emphasise
too much the work achieved by the volcano and the
earthquake. Denudation was considered to be the true
cause of the multiform appearances of mountain and
valley, long plain and sharp ravine. It was assumed
that at a height not greatly exceeding the average
height of the twenty or fifty highest mountains of Scotland, there existed in the far distant past an undulating
floor or bed of the ocean. By gradual subsidence of the
sea and elevation of the land this approximately level
ocean floor was slowly uplifted high and dry. From the
moment of its first elevation above the sea in the shape
of islets and islands its coasts were bitten by the waves,
and during its gradual elevation every inch of its surface
was incessantly attacked by the subaerial forces—rain,
snow, frost, floods and glaciers. Under these influences
the softer material had been washed away and deposited
in the surrounding ocean, thus leaving great river valleys;
whereas the harder materials had suffered comparatively
little, and still, to a great extent, remained with us in the
form of our mountains and hills. This was the teaching
of Lyell, partly founded on observation—partly a reaction
from that of the Catastrophe or Plutonic school. Professor
Judd mainly differed from this school in getting quit
of the fancy that Scotland, at any former period with
which we are acquainted, presented an approximately
level surface like that of an old ocean floor, as seen in
Texas, for instance. He did not deny the mighty influence

of denudation, but he called to his aid the volcano and the earthquake which raised up or toppled over immense mountain masses. The Scotland and the Scandinavia of to-day had at one time huge chains of mountains like the Alps or Andes. The mountains of the North Highlands and of Scandinavia were basal wrecks. Denudation and earthquake had worn them and toppled them, and now we are face to face with their venerable remains. For ages this geological area was the scene of active volcanoes, raising by eruption vast masses of matter, of great earthquakes rolling and dislocating mountains, of wide streams of lava, some of which have hidden, sealed up, and preserved pieces of stratified rocks which never were dreamed to have been represented in the geology of this area. All very lofty mountains, the Professor said, are young mountains. They have not had time to be denuded and rifted apart as the mountains of Northern Scotland and of Norway and Sweden have been. I can only refer those interested to the address itself, which has since been printed.

In the Biological Section, what interested me most were the newest discoveries in the osteology and embryology of the mammalia. Professor Struthers* read a paper on the Tay whale, and a discussion followed. I ought to state that the skeleton of this monster was exhibited in one of the courts of Marischal College. The remarks which Professor Flower made on it were extremely suggestive and interesting from the point of view of evolution. The Professor urged that we must give up the view held by the earlier evolutionists, who looked to a succession of animal life from the reptiles to the amphibia, from the amphibia to the oceanic mammals, and from those to land mammalia. The whale bore about on its body the distinct marks of its pedigree, and that pedigree pointed to it having been the descendant of an animal that spent its life in the marshes

* Afterwards Sir John Struthers, who died in 1899.

and along the shores of the ancient world. The whale-
bone whale, although more altered than any other mammal
to suit its oceanic life, still preserved certain rudimentary
characteristics. It had teeth in an early stage which
never cut the gums, hair on certain portions of the
fœtus, especially around the region of the mouth,
rudiments of pelvic and thigh bones, and traces
of an organ of smell, decidedly pointing to its being
the descendant of a four-footed, hairy, toothed land
animal.

In 1876 I read a paper before the British Association
entitled ' Mental Progress of Animals,' in which I advanced a number of general considerations, and especially
the very important consideration of man sooner or later
coming to reside among them, to show that an impulse
must have been given to the sagacity of animals, either to
maintain themselves against man, or to serve him. So I
was sorry that I was not present when Professor Cope read
his paper on ' The gradual increase in size and complexity
of the fossil mammalian brain,' because he arrived at the
same conclusion from observation as I had done deductively.
From another source I have been happy enough to become
acquainted with his views, namely, from a book recently
published on *Mammalia in their relation to primeval times*
in the *International Scientific Series*, written by Dr
Schmidt, Strasburg. According to the high authority
of Professor Cope, who has had opportunities of studying
the extraordinary exhumation of fossil mammals in the
western states of North America, as well as the European
collections, the earliest known hoofed animal, *Coryphodon*,
has a brain, whose circumference can be measured from
well-preserved specimens, which showed an inferior type
of organisation, owing to its insignificant size and the flat
surface of the greater part of it. It is, in fact, the lowest
and most reptile-like brain known to us. The diameter

of the larger portion scarcely exceeds that of the spinal
marrow. Altogether, the brain of this earliest known
hoofed animal has more the appearance of that of a lizard
than of any other existing mammal. The lowest strata to
the east of the Rocky Mountains contain the remains of
Brontotheridæ, gigantic animals, whose bodies exceeded
that of the elephant in bulk, but they had shorter limbs
with four toes on the front feet and three behind.
Compared with the skull in these extinct tapir-like or
rhinoceros-like creatures, the brain must have been extremely small. The contrast reminds us of the relative
proportions of the reptilian brain. I recollect that in
1883, I listened to Professor Boyd Dawkins delivering his
sectional address at Southport, when he illustrated the
semi-tropical valley of the Thames as it was likely to
appear in Tertiary times, with its warm marshes, and
its sub-tropical vegetation, all alive with mammalia, like,
and yet unlike, those of modern Europe and Asia. He
illustrated his remarks by means of diagrams. Some
of the figures he presented, such as those of the hairy
mammoth and rhinoceros, being enlarged from the
figures scratched on ivory by the ancient human inhabitants of caves. I listened and gazed with a feeling
of curiosity, not unmingled with awe.

The recent discoveries of Gaudry at Pikermi in Attica,
not far from the site of the celebrated field of Marathon,
were alluded to in one of the discussions at Aberdeen,
and I have been fortunate enough to be able to cite an
interesting passage from the works of that French
naturalist. He is referring to the extraordinary abundance
of large game met with in India and in Africa by travellers, to Dr Livingstone describing herds of four thousand
antelopes, and hundreds of zebras and buffaloes, and
numbers of elephants passing him betimes, and then he
says—' However splendid such pictures may be, Old Greece

could offer even grander scenes. In fact, while the whole
of Africa is the home of but one species of elephant,
Pikermi had two different forms—the mastodon and the
dinotherium, the principal giants among four-footed
animals. Africa has only one kind of giraffe ; Attica
possessed a giraffe surpassing all the living species in size,
as well as the *Helladotherium*, an animal with short
legs, it is true, but larger than the giraffe. Among the
living Ruminants there is none to compare to the
Helladotherium ; the camel is much inferior in size. Africa
has one species of rhinoceros, distinguished by its rudimentary incisors, whereas in Pikermi are found a
rhinoceros of the African type, another of the Asiatic
type, and, in the *Aceratherium*, probably also a genus
related to the rhinoceros. The huge thick-skinned animal,
the *Chalicotherium*, is unequalled by any of our day. The
skull of the ' Erymanthian' boar exceeds by one-third
that of the wild hog ; and among wild hogs are some that
exceed the wart-hog and the masked boar of South Africa.
The earth-hog, the largest of the Edentata in the old
world, is a miserable creature compared with the *Ancylo-
therium* of Attica. Lastly, the lion is surpassed by one of
the Carnivora of Attica, the panther by another. Without
doubt, in those Tertiary times, England was connected
with the Continent, and Greece was connected with Asia
by plains now covered by the sea ; and we must imagine
those plains to have been provided with a more luxurious
vegetation, for the marble hills of Pentelicus, Hymettus,
and Laurium produce now only small plants upon
which the bees find their food. I am glad to quote these
extracts as a specimen of that scientific imagination which
Professor Tyndal thought of so much importance in helping us to realise the world as it was in olden times, ages
before Troy's proud towers were built, or before Helen
had become the cause of wicked war. It is questionable

if the beings of Greece's varied, beautiful, and fertile
fables; if the Cyprian Venus, herself a wonder, a world's
delight, a passionate goddess, born, as the poets tell us,
of the flowers and the foam of the sea; it is questionable
if Minerva, leaping in full blown panoply from the
Thunderer's brow, are more interesting, more astonishing, than these discoveries turned up at Pikermi by the
spade and the pick-axe of the scientific investigator of
Nature.

In the Anthropological Section, which met in the Long
Hall, Union Street, I heard a curious paper read by J.
W. Crombie, Balgownie Lodge, Aberdeen, on the children's game of 'Beds,' or 'Hop-Scotch,' as he called
it. The theme was illustrated with large diagrams.
The name of the paper was 'a game with a history.'
Crombie had made drawings of the game of 'beds,' as
he had seen it marked out in several European countries,
and had come to the conclusion that it was a game
played in Pagan times, to which a religious character had been assigned, and upon which certain modifi-
cations had been made by the Church during the
Middle Ages, converting it into a kind of Pilgrim's
Progress from this world to the world to come. I
have had some communication on this subject since with
Crombie, and have been able not only to give him some
new facts, but even to discover, through the aid of an
elderly lady resident in South Ayrshire, a trace of
religious influence as shown by the old name given to
one of the courts. Dr Munro of Kilmarnock, who has
written a valuable work upon Lake Dwellings, read a
paper in the Anthropological Section, and amongst other
views he held that the Lake Dwellings of Southern
Scotland were built by a Celtic race. The only shade
of corroboration which I could give for this view was this,
that one of the excursions of this Society took me many

years ago to Sanquhar. Sir William Jardine was
then President, and under his guidance we examined a
building constructed of piles, which a singular circumstance, reducing the water below its usual level, had exposed in the Black Loch of Sanquhar. Now, I daresay
you all know that the great majority of the place-names
in Sanquhar are names given by a Celtic-speaking people.
I complained at Aberdeen, and I complain here, of the
neglect into which the valuable canoe has fallen, which
was obtained from the loch at the time the crannog was
exposed. We know that if wood be continually under
water, as that canoe and these piles must have been for
centuries, it will endure ; or if it be continually dry, as in
Egypt, or within doors, it will last ; but if this canoe is to
lie exposed to the weather, as it was lying the last time I
saw it in an obscure place, a back court of a house in
Sanquhar, exposed to wet and dry, it is not for its good.
That canoe is a priceless relic, and ought to find a place of
honour in one of our local museums.*—*Dumfries and
Galloway Courier and Herald.*

The Dark Side of Evolution

At the Aberdeen meeting of the British Association
this year, 1885, it was cheery to listen to the preachers
on Sunday—even to those of the stricter sects—and to
notice what a change had come over their sermons since
1859, when the Association sat there before. Evolution,
instead of being treated as a dream, or spoken of with
indignation mingled with awe, was bidding fair to become
a theological pet. In the forenoon discourses, a minister
of the ' Auld Kirk ' spoke of Christianity as containing
within itself the principle of evolution, which would

* The canoe was nevertheless permitted to lie neglected; a
portion of it still remains, 1899.

steadily lead up to the millenium, when the hewers of wood and drawers of water would be as comfortable and as cultured as most of their more favoured brethren. In one pulpit a quotation from a Presidential Address by Sir William Thomson [now Lord Kelvin], was read respecting the enormous antiquity of the earth and the sun, and hopeful views were inferred from it. It was not shown that we do not need to dip deeply into Sir W. Thomson's works before meeting with the awful doctrine of ' Dissipation of Energy,' which teaches us that this universe of motion, heat, light, life, and beauty, is slowly tending towards a congeries of motionless, cold, dark, lifeless, and colourless suns. It is said Carlyle once exclaimed, that after all, the stars were an ' awsome' sight.* If it be true that only the stars with bright white light are young, that the reddish stars are adults, whose glory has waned away from that of Vega or Capella, and that there are —who knows how many—black burned-out suns in the shoreless abyss, we must feel a shade of awe mingling with our wonder and our pleasure, as we gaze upon the starry heavens. Our own satellite, the moon, suggests thoughts anything but cheery. There it shines, but with reflected light, and no water, no air, no appearance of life has been detected on its surface. Although, when younger, it was evidently the centre of stupendous activity, in the present it has all the characteristics of a corpse. It may be said that the death of our own planet has begun at either pole, where an impenetrable shroud of snow and ice is laid down. Until some theory, more plausible than any that has as yet found favour with physicists, shall convince us that it is otherwise, we cannot, with any feeling of elation, contemplate the awful waste of light and heat evolved from every luminary into infinite space.

* Carlyle's words were, ' Eh, man, isn't it awsome !'

Coming to the animal and vegetable life on our own planet, whose age is so great, we have countless multitudes of the lower forms of life, simple protoplasmic specks and germs of which it is hard to conclude whether they are vegetables or animals. Professor Huxley devoted his address as President of the British Association at Liverpool, in 1870, to showing that the hypothesis of 'Spontaneous Generation' was a hypothesis that had been beaten along the whole line. If there be no spontaneous generation, these lowly forms must have gone on for millions of ages reproducing their lowly offspring, without evolution coming to their aid to make them different from what they are, for we find the same microscopic, dubious-looking, simple forms of life in strata of almost any age.

But a more cheerless doctrine still than that of permanency of type is that of degeneration, of loss sustained after gain achieved. At Aberdeen a great deal was said in the biological section about whales. The learned professors agreed that the anatomy of the whale suggested its descent from a hairy, toothed, four-footed, terrestrial mammal, so that what it had gained in order to thrive in its watery element it had more than lost by being incapable of existing on land. But the degradation suffered by leviathan in the course of its life-history is as nothing compared to that of the barnacle or of its neighbour the sea-squirt, as revealed to us by the curious and laborious investigations of Anton Dohrn and other naturalists. The young barnacle is a beautiful swimming creature with the traits of its long descent written plainly all over it. The adult barnacle, as it adheres to ship-bottoms and logs of floating wood, is a long-stalked, ungainly animal, provided with a sucker to fasten itself, a mouth, a stomach, intestines, and a bunch of tentacles sticking out of its shell, forever employed kicking its food into its mouth. The contrast between the baby barnacle, highly organised and active, with the adult, a fixed, simple, senseless glutton, does not make evolution quite admirable. But the sea-squirt is an instance of still greater degradation. The 'tadpole' of the sea-squirt has an eye, the adult has lost it. The 'tadpole' has a brain, the adult is all but brainless. Its notochord or primitive backbone has by evolution got squandered away. The agile youth loses agility and becomes little better than a leathery sack with a hole in it to receive victuals. The same sad lesson is read to us by the mites, the degenerate offspring of spider ancestors, the most degenerate of them all being the curious thread-like fellow whose dainty abode is the skin of the human face, and whose eight spider legs are merely present as eight stumps pushed far forward near the head.

Nor when we leave off the domain of natural history and betake ourselves to the history of our own species, can we be assured that our gains are all safely insured to us. Throned races have toppled from their high position. Galton, in his interesting book *Hereditary Genius*, has called our attention to the fact of a small portion of ancient Greece, with a scanty population producing, in the age of Pericles and a few years afterwards, a greater number of men of the highest order of intellect than ever has appeared since in the same population and time in the whole historical period. Who that has ever been to many of the world-famous cities of the Eastern hemisphere but must have had grave doubts of the progress of the species. Could the ancient Incas of Peru arise again and see their poor, wasted, thinly-peopled country, their theme would be retrogression rather than progress. In a striking passage in the work already cited, Galton endeavours to account for the present degradation of Spain by showing that bigotry and intolerance had burned or banished a large percentage of the most intellectual, thrifty, and honest of its inhabitants, and made bachelor priests of many of the same class who remained and conformed, leaving only a considerable mixture of the tyrannical, greedy, short-sighted, and superstitious to continue the race. Considerations such as these are enough to show that we lose our jewels on the way, that there is a dark side to the doctrine of evolution, that, if it be a trustworthy hypothesis, it is one which requires us to join trembling with our mirth, and that it does not lend itself so easily to rosy dreams of the millennium as some of its sanguine preachers might suppose.

SONNETS ON NATURAL SELECTION

I.—WHY ARE FLOWERS AND FRUIT BEAUTIFUL?

At gayest hour of willow, heath, and rose,
  As lover to beloved, come the bees
  And sow the golden pollen. Summer leas
That know the painted butterflies, or doze
  While gnats are dancing to the droning flies,
  Fulfil the ball with flowers, whose rainbow dyes
Show insects where the nectar drops to reach;
  So of the pale gold pollen-dust each flower
Is but the pretty tell-tale ; while the peach,
  The purple bloom of grapes, the golden hour
Of full-orbed orange, and the flesh of flame,
That wraps the seeds of rose and row'n the same,
Inform the birds to snatch and bear the fruit,
And sow the wilds with germ of branch and root.

II.—WHY ARE FLOWERS AND FRUIT ODOROUS?

Show me a flower that hath a carrion smell,
  And lo ! 'tis haunted by a carrion fly ;
  Both bee and butterfly will pass it by,
Even should its red lips hold a honey well ;
  For like ourselves are butterfly and bee,
  And surely like the ancient gods are we,
Loving the offering while the perfumed shell
  Swings with the incense. Nay, friend, pluck for me
  A plant that hath no blossom gay nor scent—
  What living thing rejoicing ever went
To fertilise it ? Its spores went alone
With the cold winds—like dull dust were they sown.
What citron, or what apple breathing sweet,
But birds would quarrel the dainty food to eat ?

Glasgow Herald, 19th Oct. 1872.

CHAPTER IV

Miscellaneous Poetry

Two Sides of a Question—Snow—The Skylark—We're a' Mismarrowed Thegither—Sonnets on Evolution and on Antiquities.

Two Sides of a Question

'Honesty's the Best Policy.'

I. FROM DUNCAN'S POINT OF VIEW

Both when you buy and when you sell,
Look to your weights and measures well ;
And when your soul and fingers itch
For pelf, and still you are not rich,
Remember, in the race for gold,
They stumble who rush over-bold.
Keep the plain middle of the way,
And always run with light of day ;
Don't break your word, don't tell a lie,
Don't put dust in your neighbour's eye.
And the reward will come with time,
The money bags will clink like rhyme ;
The knave and cheat will credit lose,
Whom honest you may then abuse,
Standing high on your own good name,
While up and down there runs your fame,
And customers besiege your doors
On foot, on horse, in dozens and scores ;
Small profits then and many sales,
Like favouring winds, will fill your sails ;
Meeting you, men will doff their hats,
And ladies round you purr like cats ;
Your banker in your face will smile,
Your hands get white, released from toil,

And what, although much wordly care
Should make the pate too scant of hair,
Fortune will fit you with a wig;
And—Oh, blessed thought!—supply a gig.

II.—FROM DONALD'S POINT OF VIEW

Speak out like a true honest man,
And use no flattery to your clan;
Tell them, without conceit or fear,
When you see pinchbeck or veneer.
Let the rogue learn he has a smell,
By which, though dark, you know him well:
Snap at the wolf, though hid with wool.
Be ready with your square and rule
To see that word and deed are one,
Expose each biscuit and each bun
That aren't as they advertise;
Or, when you hear the crowd with cries
Salute some idol of the street,
Be dumb, and turn away your feet.
Will that secure for you applause?
Will that buy nuts to fill your jaws?
What kind of policy is that?
'Twill neither bring you ease nor fat,
Guineas nor gigs, but showers of stones,
And you shall ache through all your bones;
Be named a cynic when you hoot,
A stoic when your tongue is mute.
Ne'er mind! though no reward be given,
Though bones should ache, and skin be riven;
Be honest—stars shall brighter roll,
And heaven grow wider in your soul.

Snow

Light as May blossoms, those snowflakes can pile
Great pyramids, grander than those of Nile,
Walls not to be taken, strong ramparts and towers.
With flake upon flake, through the dreary hours
Mighty armies are stopped; those petals small
Stop and defy them like thundering wall.
As mute as stars in the Milky Way,
Dancing in myriads like insects gay,
Speck upon speck clothes the mountain rock,
Till the avalanche falls with a crashing shock;
Small harm to the homestead or grief to the glen,
When it smothers no kine and buries no men.

N

Snow, soft and bright, like a schoolboy's toy,
You are welcomed at first with a strange sense of joy ;
But you scarce fall a day ere you try to creep
Over the mouths of the thin hungry sheep.
As you circle with glee in the wind's embrace,
Like a death-sheet you cover the wanderer's face.
While all manner of beasts are dumb with woe,
Like a highway of glory you choose to glow
Near the face of the sky, on the mountain's crest,
When sunset flames o'er the frosty west.

Dumb snow of the forest, you love to hear
The howl of the wolves, and are glad to be near
The hoot of the owl, when the starving mole
Peeps at the moon from a wormless hole.
Snow of the hamlet, you drift like a guest
To our windows and doors, as for warmth or for rest ;
You muffle, as if for a sick man's ear,
All creaking of wheels, but be off, for we fear
Your caress as that of the venomous snake ;
In your silken folds we may never awake.

Snow of the old man, cold and thin,
Who creeps to the hearth and gropes for his gin ;
Snow of the errand-girl, ragged and mean,
At the points of whose shoes red toes are seen ;
Snow of the soldier, smothering his cries,
And hiding his wounds from the angel's eyes,
May a genial thaw, or a mighty spate,
Sweep you from earth to the ocean's gate.

The Skylark

With speech as varied as its woods and streams,
The peopled garden of our planet teems ;
Each age and nation boasts its native tongue,
Nor Homer would have known what Shakespeare sung.
But thee, O skylark ! great hills, crowned with snow,
May separate from thy kin, or thou mayst know
Only some isle, far exiled o'er the sea,
There still remains the self-same speech to thee ;
Thy birthright is the old immortal song,
The language universal, deep and strong ;
The love-tale which, ere yet the world was old,
Above the shepherd's dawn-kissed lambs was told ;
The love-tale which, now that the world is grey,
Holds Hesperus in trance at close of day.
Thy glorious music courts no earth-born bower ;
Even where the spheres are choral dost thou tower.
One could imagine the stern god of war
Snatching short sleep within his scythe-wheeled car,

Hearing thee, smile in dreams ; or in her skies
Of April morn, Aurora with surprise
Cease to strew roses, listening to thy lay,
And for an instant all her courts grow grey.
Fair is the blue of yonder sea at rest ;
But ah ! beneath its azure sparkling breast
What numerous teeth are whetted ! and what strife !
There the dumb monsters seeking life for life
Utter no songs.   There's blood within the grove,
And shouts of power and terror, not of love.
O'er stagnant pools, zigzag, the dragon-fly
Leaps like the lightning when its prey draws nigh ;
But yet amid the turmoil of the deep
Are milky mothers nursing babes asleep ;
But yet amid the strife that mars the land
Some emerald gem set in the Syrian sand,
Some painted train of bird or jewelled crest
Or rose of glory sparkling in its breast,
Some honest utterings of a dog whose eye
Says, 'Master, 'tis for thee and thine I'd die ; '
All these redeem the promise of our youth—
The fond warm wish that there is joy in Truth.
But proudest gain from hate, and strife, and war
Is the full music of this earth-born star,
No Syren's song, but one that, wreathed with flowers,
Eves might have sung in unlost Eden's bowers,
Caught from the sons of God and morning stars,
Ere slavery wailed, or trumpets stirred to wars.
O love ! you mind that day of sun and rain,
When lark on lark uprose, and with their strain
We heard the quavering lambs and sparkling rills ;
And there, far up amid the smooth green hills—
Our feet on fragrant thyme—a rainbow rose,
And disks grew broader of the wild briar rose ;
And as the unseen choirs with quivering throats,
Flung through the sunny air their liquid notes,
We thought the ancient gods, once deemed divine,
Were raining down from heaven their own sweet wine.

WE'RE A' MISMARROWED THEGITHER.

Tune—'*Wooed and Married and A'.*'

O we're a' mismarrowed thegither,
     O we're a' misfitted and wrang,
Jean Johnstone's taen up wi' anither,
     And cares na a doit for short Tam ;
Short Tammas he's standing dumfoonered,
     Though Nanny keeps becking at him ;
And Rob's like a dog that's been lunnered
     'Cause Nanny's so dry and so mim.

O we're a' mismarrowed thegither,
　　Lang Lizy has married a dwarf,
Jock and Jess are as like ane anither
　　As an auld pin's like a new scarf.
Douce Davie deserves to be paikit,
　　He's spoony on muckle-neeved Meg,
A hizzy licht-headed and glaikit,
　　Wha takes a sly dram frae a keg.

O we're a' misfitted thegither,
　　Big Will's taen the best plan of a';
There's a heap he can say to his mither,
　　A fremit wife would but misca'.
For Bessie—sa braw as she's buskit—
　　Od! she's on wi' creeshy Pate Graham,
Wha looks as he should hae been wispit,
　　Or cleaned wi' a stick and a kame.

O we're a' mismarrowed thegither,
　　Sour plums, she has got a sweet pear,
Rose leaf's got a piece o' ben leather,
　　China cup's got a flat o' earth-ware.
Like a basket o' eels when they're whummled
　　We wriggle and rax for our ain ;
We're sore disappointed and bummled,
　　The richt ane but seldom we gain.

Ill folk how they giggle and hotch, man,
　　The last news is warst news of a',
Lady Ann has eloped wi' her coachman,
　　Wi' a black bristly beard like a craw.
For we're a misfitted thegither,
　　We would need to be paired anew,
And tied, arm to arm, wi' a tether,
　　For fear that we ever should rue.

SONNETS

I.—ON READING DARWIN'S 'SEXUAL SELECTION.'

Why have birds lustrous colours like the dyes
That paint heaven's clouds on summer eve or morn,
Making these glorious ? Birds are never born
In gold and purple. It is Love that cries
For crowns and coronation robes, and sighs
For vests of scarlet, crowns of gold, and trains
Sparkling with stars and eyes.   'Tis Love takes pains
In books illumed to write about her prize,
And tell the world how like a queen she reigns,
And how 'tis by her own selecting power
That beauty blooms most at the bridal hour.
Ah ! light, like life, is dear to human eyes ;
We love the Sun-god and the coat of flame—
Poor birds and insects, ye too love the same !

II.—ON READING WALLACE'S 'MIMICRY.'

Yet life is more than light, and fiercest wars
Teach the gay soldier that his scarlet coat
(His sweetheart's joy) and every glittering mote
Be hid betimes, that he without his stars,
Unseen, may slip from or surprise his foe :
And so hath Nature in her cycles wrought ;
The weaker she-fowl rears the brood, and lo
She flaunteth not with wedding-gown for show,
But dons a sober dress that none may note
She hath a nest—her home.   Sometimes quick fear
Makes the gay lizard like dull stick appear,
To aye-green woods green birds their safety owe.
And, trusting to brave shams, weak insects use
Strange masks, forged like strong insects' shapes and hues.

Sonnets

I.—ON A PALÆOLITHIC FLINT FLAKE

While Earth was young and baking up its clay
To stones for Pharaoh's pyramids, a hand
Grasped this old weapon, which a head had planned,
And a heart thrilled on some forgotten day,
When the great mammoth, or hyena grey,
Or the cave-bear, cowered backwards and was slain
By Thought's first weapons—Man's first mighty gain.
Oh for a cunning glass by which to peep
Backwards to those old days and see them plain !
When gestures, more than words, explained the deep
Longings of wild sad folk, now all asleep,
Whom caves concealed from bitter glacial rain,
And naught was temple save the black pine trees,
And organ lofts were branches in a breeze.

II.—ON A STONE BEAD OF UNKNOWN ANTIQUITY

A drop of tenderness where all was rough
And jagged, like a wild beast's tooth, is here.
Harpoons, lance-heads, flint-knives, we have enough,
But these kept company with blood and fear ;
Whereas, upon the neck of one held dear
This relic may have hung, like the first bud,
Whence bloomed the rose of Art ; like the first mud
Statue, whence rose the marble queen of love—
The crown and flower of ages.   When a tear
Steals down a cold hard face, we like to think
That amid granite rocks and dry-blown sand
A well hath opened with a grassy brink ;
So hope we in an old and cruel land
This bead came from an artist-lover's hand.

CHAPTER V

THE EIGHTH DUKE OF ARGYLL

THE days are gone when soldiers and sailors stood highest in the Pantheon. Leaving Mars and Neptune, the world turns its worshipping eyes to other stars. Horsa the horse, Hengist the stallion, Hildebrand the war-brand, Mathilde the mighty Amazon, Adolf the noble wolf, Arnold the valiant eagle, must relate and combine facts, and invent new applications of laws conducive to well-being, instead of drilling soldiers and dealing blows, if they would maintain the honours of their house. The Duke of Argyll is precisely the reverse of Hercules. Could the mailed barons, his ancestors, after harrying a neighbouring clan, have looked through their visors across their mighty and deep potations to the late President of the British Association for the Advancement of Science, to the late President of the National Bible Society, Lord Rector of Glasgow University, Chancellor of St Andrews, and all that kind of thing, no words would have been strong enough to express their amazement and disgust. They would have tossed the 'Reign of Law' to Bertha

to illuminate in her bower, and among their hawks
and hounds have tried to forget the 'wraith' conjured
up before them. A short, reddish-haired, lithe man,
next door to a teetotaller, and skilled in all manner
of tongue-fence and chopping of logic, Oh how unlike those brawny shoulders and muscular, naked,
hairy legs, which seemed in keeping with the granite
peaks of their fastnesses, and which hurled defiance
to Scottish Kings from the far-off regions of Loch
Awe!

> 'To crack the croun o' Highland loun,
> To harry knowt from Southern lout;'

or later, to lay down one's head on the block for 'Christ
and the Covenant!' These are chances never again to
come the way of the chief of the Campbells. Captain
Sword has resigned to Captain Pen. The world of letters
was startled about a quarter-a-century ago (1842), by the
precocity of the then Marquis of Lorne. *A Letter to the
Peers from a Peer's Son* will be remembered perennially
in the literature of the 'Disruption.' Precocity is always
startling. We love it, and yet we are afraid of it. We
recollect the saying about the gifted, the beloved of
gods and men, dying early. We remember the frost
which spoils the blossoms of spring.

> 'Every month in the year
> Curses a fair Februar.'

An undefined pathos mingled with the admiration elicited
by the production of a lad not yet out of his teens. The
evil prophecies in this case have fallen, and the matured
intellect of the Duke of Argyll has maintained its early
promise. In some of the highest ranges of thought no
nobleman in Scotland is so much an aristocrat, so much
the 'strongest and best,' as he.

The Duke of Argyll and Mr Gladstone have been
compared. Both are what is called liberal in their views,

both are versatile and literary, but to us there is no comparison between the two. Excellent practical commonplaces—tracts that sail in the wind of popular sentiments with a ballast of classical learning—lectures to a class of history on the left, and a very promising class of arithmetic on the right—the knowledge of the masses put into order and uttered with due regard to grammar and proper emphasis, and a saying of what you do say like the singing of the old Presbyterian lady who 'praised the Lord with all her "birr"'—those are ever prominent qualities in Mr Gladstone's books and orations. It is altogether different with the Duke of Argyll. His position with regard to questions of public interest is almost always a central one. He lives in the thoughts and feelings of his opponents as well as of his friends. He never thoroughly closes a subject. Beyond and around all that he has said, he suggests a more wonderful knowledge, which has yet had no prophet to utter it. He seems to understand that much of what is so solid-looking and fixed is but a cloud of slower motion, and that habits and modes of thought are ever at the mercy of new generalisations. He stands in the middle of a wood, and vistas open on every side, tempting you to explore them for some newer secret. Oh, poor Icelander, you are indeed in the Arctic zone. Frost and snow and mud are giants, but are there no other giants? What far volcano is yon sending up the colour of the rose above the snowy limits of the hills? The Frost-King is powerful, but he has not exhausted strength. Yon neighbour of his, so unlike him too, brings up in other modes a message of force from the innermost depths and darkness of the earth.

Gilfillan has well expressed one grand idea in his recent poem. He says in effect, that every thought that strongly moves man's mind, and makes itself a worship in the soul, is a thing beyond the power of death. It may get transmuted,

but it will one day assert its divinity. In a recognition of
this idea, we had better try to understand our fellow-
creature's belief. His belief, if you can really get it, is
the grandest thing about him. There is always truth at
the bottom of that well. The Duke of Argyll must
understand what it is to believe. He finds that faith is
still upon the earth, and so he preaches neither wrath nor
maudlin toleration, but defines a toleration which is at
once generous and also fit for self-defence. No man
knows better than he the courtesies of debate. He is
polite without imitating a flunkey. He is frank without
being surly. He does not incline to stamping and hallooing, as if strong language were better than convincing
language. He has a modest fear of adjectives which
make sentences often too sweet to be wholesome, or too
noisy to be terrific. You never find him peering into the
consciences and brains of his antagonists, discerning dullness and turpitude with owlish glee. I once saw a prize
fight. Brown entered the ring, and after having been
blown with a few rounds of conflict, instead of fighting
steadily, he came out and harangued his friends about
what a weak fellow was Jones, what tricks he resorted to,
violating all the rules—that though he (Brown) was under
in the fall, he ought to have been upper, but that, being
magnanimous, he did not put out half his strength, and
could not think—the lion that he was—to play the part
of tiger. That prize fight often recurs to me when I find
some writers believing in no miracles save the strength of
their own arguments and the wilfulness of their
opponents.

It says much for the improved temper of our public
meetings that a man like the Duke of Argyll can be welcomed there, and listened to with interest and deep respect. We are surely beginning to see that 'error needs
light rather than heat,' and that 'truth is more than

triumph.' This, however, is but occasional as yet, and in
general the mass meetings take very kindly either to
honey-smearing or the showman's pennyworth of thunder;
and our epitaphs are too often written in the spirit of our
advertisements.

The Duke is a geologist, and this is a branch of science
which has a rich reflex development in the minds of those
who pursue it, and who have got considerably beyond the
pride of being merely collectors of fossils.   Think what it
is to handle a trilobite.   Immediately by successive stages
all the green fields and browsing oxen around you pass
away, and your verdurous meadows are the home of
glaciers.   Then the sun of a farther-removed yesterday
rises, and in the glare of intense heat crocodiles from the
Thames bask in the site of Westminster, or dull, warm,
moist ages nourish the plants which are to be stored for
coal.   But the beginning is not near.   Cycles on cycles
have to be swam through, and on the muddy shores of
the Silurian seas you get among the living trilobites,
having seated yourself on the back of a ridge of coral,
with its covering of lichen, waiting patiently till, by a
grain per day, Europe and Asia at a far future date be
formed.   What of our own lives, when the trilobite thus
puts our imaginations out of breath and weary of wing
by the flight to get at it?   Do they not contract to the
thin sharp squeak of a bat, or the quick vivid song of a
swallow?   All things that are known as old become young
before this venerable three-lobed sailor.   Even Alps and
Apennines have rolled themselves together like vapours,
and like vapours have melted away.   And yet in that
distant past there are links connecting it with the present.
In the silent stony trilobite you can see that there once
were eyes—if eyes, therefore, there was light, so that
light, which is dear as life, is the magnificent arch connecting at once the geologist's past with the politician's

present, and the undefined and enormously distant nebulæ with the charms of our own fireside.

Have these conceptions no relation to duty? Verily, we think they have. The unbroken continuity which stretches backwards in time, linking all events, so that the present is born of the past, imposes upon us the awful thought that our good or evil deeds will influence a future of illimitable extent.

I once read of a monkey being shot. In the agonies of death it threw its offspring high up into the dark bosom of an adjoining tree, and so secured life to its posterity in the hour of its dissolution. If there is anything which modern science teaches and Christianity exhorts, it is that we by our example should so live that untold generations may have reason to thank our efforts for their welfare. Woe not only to us, but to the coming ages, should we exhibit more selfish regard for our temporary interests than the brutes we affect to despise.

Ill-expressed as this ethical and poetic side of geology has been by us, still we think we can see traces in the writings of the Duke that science does not detract from wisdom and reverence, but exalts the moral tone of her disciple. It has taught him to treat of the questions of the hour with caution, patience, and hope, qualities which are required if one is to be successful in exhibiting natural laws, which admit of more exact and ready verification than political postulates.

In his lecture on Mahomet, in which the nuggets of thought are very closely packed, Carlyle represents the fervent Arab as trying to solve the Mystery of Existence outside of himself, from the rocks, and plains, and stars. But only 'from his own soul, and what of God's inspiration dwelt there,' could he find an answer to his questions. Tennyson in *In Memoriam* takes up the same strain. 'I found him not in world or sun, or eagle's

wing, or insect's eye,' but in the warm depths of his own
heart. Outside that sacred circle there is a vast immeasurable field of glory and of shadow, on which 'time like
Chronos devours all its children,' whose ceaseless winds
and waves are ever on the side of the ablest navigator,
but whose dreadful and inexorable doings have also sent
'an ancient song steaming up a tale of misery, desola-
tion, and woe,' so that the very words we coin from
planet earth—' worldling,' ' worldliness,' 'the cold world,'
' earthly,' etc., have come to have a bad savour. Matters
don't mend when we get beyond the planet, for though
ten thousand orbs shine on us from afar, they are like the
faces flitting past a stranger in a crowded city. 'Our
soul does not enter into their secret.' They are dumb
as our graves, and raise questions as keen as they are
vain.

> 'The Plough was silent—silent was the glow
> Of the great Dog-star, while Orion stood
> Haughty, and cold, and speechless—the same mood
> Met me in Milky Way and Polar Star—
> One Father's Children, and apart so far !'

The Duke of Argyll is of no such despairing mood.
Certainly he has found in 'eagle's wing' the realised
solution of many exceedingly different and complicated
problems. Notwithstanding, after one has read the very
clever contributions His Grace has made to natural science
and natural theology in his remarkable book, the *Reign of
Law*, the old puzzles somehow recur.

Mind without a brain, invention without necessity
for its mother, genius without gradual growth, and agony
ending in triumph, contrivance, where the very difficulties to be overcome are contrived by oneself, design with
no new thought illumining one's former ignorance,
planning without acquisition of knowledge, without fear
or hope, affections without the ruddy drops which visit

the heart—are as hard to conceive of as laws without a
lawgiver, or order without purpose.

We have had our own misgivings as to whether the
so-called primeval flints were man's work. We have
found it difficult to draw the line of demarcation between
what was natural and what was artificial. Our forefathers would have seen witchcraft in rinderpest. The
Indians thought the Spanish Knights were Centaurs.
The Highlander mistook a watch for an animal, and
thought when it stopped that it had died. We once believed the rings in the grass were made by fairies, and
the dentist and wig-maker deceive us daily. In summer
wax-flowers look like the product of the garden. In
winter, garden flowers, especially exotics, suggest wax
ones; but no such puzzles present themselves with more
familiar objects. We know that a joiner made our chairs,
but not the trees of which they were made; and so we
find that the design argument is of most practical use in
those cases in which we can test its correctness by reading
its history, and verifying the processes by our own or our
neighbour's experience. Without a Bible and a belief,
natural theology does not accomplish much. Leaving this
grand argument, we should like to have looked at the
Nigger Question in the light of His Grace's views *versus*
Sir S. Baker's or Carlyle's. It is one of those many-sided
questions which seems to have particular charms for him;
but space forbids that we should touch on it just now.

When we look at the British aristocracy as pictured by
Thackeray, and then turn to the Duke of Argyll, we acknowledge a rare chieftain—one who stands apart among
the haughtiest featherheads, as George Stephenson did
among the dullest clodpolls. Here is a man to whom
knowledge has more charms than star and garter—one
whose wisdom can inspire us so that we are forgetful of
wine—whose sympathy soothes like an opiate—one who

looks a fact in the face though it should appear like an
Egyptian skull at a banquet.

We shall not soon forget poor Alexander Smith's description of his kind reception at Inveraray Castle, although
he felt ill at ease when he considered the enormous
difference of position. A Duke who could thus interest
himself in a son of toil because he had genuine poetic fire,
and who could dine for fourpence in a Glasgow cooking
depôt, that he might find out for himself how honest
labour fared, makes himself of more consequence to his
fellow-citizens than if his blood were Norman, his hand
small, his heraldic devices without a bar sinister, and
his foxhounds and hunting horses brooking neither
superiors nor equals.

The Reverend George Gilfillan

More than nineteen years ago there was a magazine
published in Edinburgh, in the Liberal interest, at one
shilling monthly, named *Tait's Magazine*.* It was well
edited, and why it has become extinct is as mysterious to
us as why the Saurians have become so. De Quincey,
Theodore Martin, under the sobriquet of *Bon Gaultier*,
and various other clever people, wrote in it, and there
was Sir Thomas Dick Lauder who gossiped nicely about
Scotch streams, being quite an authority in the art of
angling. But to us, in those days, the writer of chief
interest was the one whose name is at the head of this
article. The times were stirring times. Chartism was
in the wind. Large posters, the size of banners, would
suddenly appear at street corners, telling people that
progress could no more be bound than Xerxes could bind
the waves of the Hellespont. Murmurs, both loud and

* *Tait's Edinburgh Magazine*, begun in 1832, ceased to appear
on the death of William Tait, its founder, in 1864.

deep, chiefly fed by low wages, bad trade, stump orators, and cheap publications, were rife among the working-classes. Like 'Jerusalem the golden' bending under the Roman yoke, the British aristocracy, under the tyrannous and strong blast of the agitators, seemed fast approaching its final hour. Nor were there wanting factions, who brought the whole weight of their battering-rams and mining operations against the temple itself. In important sections of the working classes in manufacturing towns, the question was not whether the Free Church or the Established Church was founded on the widest Scriptural basis, but whether Scripture itself had any proper basis at all.

Meantime, to the more intelligent rationalists, the clergy seemed to shirk discussion—to be unequal to the defence, or unwilling to defend. They quarrelled among themselves, as if no enemy were at the gates. They entirely ignored what was dearest to the hearts of sincere dissenters. They were unwilling to compromise matters in the least, and they granted no parley. Now, most moral and intellectual upheavings contain within them some portion of truth. At the bottom of them, blindly and roughly, there struggles some principle which deserves wider recognition, and no ponderous many-leaved volumes on 'plenary inspiration'—no prize Sabbath essays by working men—no legacies spent on popular editions of the 'Evidences'—no whimsical or spasmodical efforts of Ritualism or Revivalism—will continually put out of sight the demand of growing thought to be taken up and discussed. And so at length some Dr Chalmers, or Hugh Miller, or Dean Stanley, or Dr Macleod, risks or gains popularity by new and careful expositions of doctrine falling in with the continual flux of outward conditions, increased knowledge, and new social arrangements. Looking back upon that time—its arguments, its struggles, its orthodoxy,

and its heterodoxy—we seem to perceive in it the dawning of a wider recognition of the principles of toleration
in matters of opinion, and a more pious spirit towards
much that environs mortals here now in this present
century. Not in Palestine alone, and in far past ages,
had miracles been wrought; but the Great Miracle-
worker, who never slumbers, was every morning clothing
the world in beauty, and every night was hanging
wonders in the sky. Neither was any planet, dawning
out of the depths of space, more worthy in a certain
sense of reverence than the young boy or young maiden
on whose cheek the first blushes of 'divine shame' made
themselves known. Now, we have to thank the Rev.
George Gilfillan, that while too many of his brethren
were walking in narrow enough ways, he recognised that
there was nothing common or unclean, and that the
world had still a grand catholic interest to its inhabitants.
At the period we allude to, he was almost the only
literary clergyman in Scotland—at all events the only one
whose words were winged and permeated through the
masses. Indeed, when we consider what that means—
that literature is an element without which civilisation
would be at a stand-still, and that the song-maker is in
some respects the law-maker; when we consider in this
country the influence of the Press, and that, as Disraeli
wisely remarked at the late Edinburgh banquet (1867),
the newspapers and periodicals are an important factor
in national education; then, to say this much of Gilfillan,
is to say a great deal. Not to recognise that Burns and
Byron, Wordsworth and Shelley, had written books of
deep and original thought, of burning eloquence or
tenderest pathos—albeit, it could not be said positively
whether they were Calvinists, or Unitarians, or Pan-
theists—was a serious thing for a young man whose mind
was opening to the beauties of these writers, especially

when the blindness was on the part of those who had
been traditionally represented as the bearers of light and
knowledge.

Fearlessly did Gilfillan open the dreaded books—
impartially, justly, sympathetically did he very often
comment upon them, and when he was done with his remarks you felt relieved. It was as if the fire, which the
child or the savage dreads, had become in his hands the
talisman to open up new sources of comfort and enjoyment. You might doubt whether Wordsworth was
sound, but you did not need to become tainted with his
unsoundness, while his wit and wisdom was a new
treasure to your mind. Shelley blasphemed terribly, but
then, when Gilfillan explained that the poet was, as
it were, an angel inflicted with lunacy, you chanted the
angelic strains, and allowed the madness to ebb away forgotten. There was a fine fluency in Gilfillan's *Gallery
of Literary Portraits,* combined with great plainness.
His instinct first for picking out the finest utterances of
any writer he was criticising, and then for putting these
utterances in the best light, was surprising. Two most
useful things he kept doing almost for a while alone as a
Scotch pastor; he came with religious reverence to the
store-houses of poets and essayists, and wove around us
their aspirations after a better and holier life, and he came
with a poetical and loving eye to his Bible, and showed
that wonderful as it was, considered as a book upon which
to found dogma, it was equally admirable and interesting
as a picture of what had really passed in men's hearts, and
in the world which was their home. Certainly Gilfillan
was in advance of his age. He opened his chapel to
Emerson shortly after Emerson had found that the Chan-
ning Unitarianism of America and himself could not go
on together in harmony, and he was the first Scotch
clergyman who saw clearly the greatness of Carlyle.

O

Quoting from memory, we yet remember well how he described the former as 'one of a race of Titans running
over the mountains of the west on the errands of genius
and of love,' and we have an unmistakable impression
of the high value he set upon Carlyle when the latter was
merely considered whimsical by *Punch*, and sneered at
by all respectable people.   Emerson was then very far
from being the subject of an article in a *Quarterly Review*,
and Carlyle's Edinburgh apotheosis was a thing the most
sanguine dared not to have dreamed of.

It must exist, we suppose, as one of the annoyances of
being famous, that you become the target for all manner
of letters — boring you incessantly, and making the
postman's bag as intolerable in your eyes as that other
bag, accompanied by the pipe, held beneath the arm-pit
of a Highlander, especially if, beside the dreadful reality
called music, you have been cowed, when a sulky child, by
threats of being sewed into the aforesaid wind instrument.
We recollect that our boyhood began to revolve at such
a rate round the Gilfillan luminary that we too must take
advantage of Rowland Hill's discovery, and invest a
penny in giving G. G. the benefit of our lucubrations.
One thing in our favour was that we were desperately
sincere, although, we don't deny, some vanity at the
likelihood of a forthcoming answer mingled its dross
with the genuine metal.   We shall never forget the
kindness, and patience, and good-humour of Gilfillan
in his replies of those dates, written in letters that have
long since become brown.   The worst thing that happens
to the successful humble party in these circumstances
is, that he is apt to gain a little too much intellectual
pride, and look at himself as being from the shoulders
upwards higher than a good many of his acquaintances.
A few hard blasts, or some unexpected lull, are sure
to happen; and if the wind is not taken out of your

sails, you at least learn to bear your honours more meekly.

That sea-simile puts us in mind of a very grand one which Gilfillan used long ago in *Hogg's Magazine*, in which he compared Burns, in his worst and latter days, to a noble ship deserted, stowed with powder and a fusee left burning, so that it was dangerous to go near it. The paragraph was written in the most kindly and generous manner, as of one mourning that the poet's sun should go down in sorrow and shame before noonday; but there is bigotry in Scotland about Burns as well as about Calvin. A most amiable friend of our own, who has since gone to his account, Macdonald, author of *Rambles Round Glasgow*, etc., was bitten, and a kind of Burns' fever ensued. The argument was conducted unfortunately with some temper on both sides across the pages of a Glasgow newspaper; and we were only sorry to see two such men, really admirers of our national poet, getting in arms at all upon the subject. Macdonald's reading was the narrower, and his zeal burned the fiercer of the two. For a sympathetic sketch of Macdonald—a really remarkable son of toil—we refer the reader to Alexander Smith's *Summer in Skye*.

Very many years had passed since our correspondence with Gilfillan, when at last we had an opportunity of seeing him in the flesh in a U. P. Church in Nithsdale, delivering a lecture on Norway. He was stouter and ruddier than we had anticipated, but his fingers showed that they used the pen and not the plough. The matter of his lecture was very good; but his manner, especially the tone of the voice, was not precisely so natural as we expected. Of course, the poetical and pictorial elements were strong in the discourse, and a farmer objected to it because it was not so practical as it might have been, and did not inform us about the agriculture of the country,

nor the way in which the lecturer had spent his Norwegian Sundays.   We do not intend in this short
sketch to begin criticisms of Gilfillan's numerous books.
Some of them we have not read, nor otherwise do we
consider ourselves equal to the critic's task.   We believe,
however, that the leading literary journal, the *Athenæum*,
has been as unfair towards him in reviewing his last poem
of *Night*, as it was to Alex. Smith's *Life Drama*.   *Night*
is not free from faults, but it contains many noble
thoughts well expressed, as may be remembered even
from the short extracts given in the *Athenæum*.   This
journal had not a single word of encouragement, and
this, of course, suggests strange thoughts.   Is it necessary for the ill-natured and envious readers that an un-
usually bitter article must occasionally appear as pepper to
the dish?   It looks as if that were needed, that wrath and
sourness must have their turn ; and the solemn sneer and
ponderous satire may thus serve to balance the whole and
keep away the monotony of less emotional writing long
drawn out.   How do they get at the book which is
doomed to such a tremendous underrating?   Is it by con-
sulting the doctrine of chances?   Three years ago they
attacked Strauss in a style perfectly outrageous ; we mean
by that, inconsistent with the use and wont of the journal,
for they pursued that wounded deer through several successive numbers, and having unrobed him of every wrappage
of truth and learning, left the great German ready for
the doctors and Samaritans.

Gilfillan's recent work * on obscure but worthy
ministers gives a most interesting sketch of his poor but
industrious father.   Whoever reads it will thrill with the
thought that—

> ' The rank is but the guinea stamp,
> The man's the gowd for a' that.'

* *Remoter Stars in the Church Sky*, 1867.

The Reverend Norman Macleod

Dr Macleod's Church of the Barony occupies a site in the midst of the stranded wrecks of 'Old Glasgow.' Near it are the Cathedral, the Molendienar Burn, the Drygate, the 'Bell o' the Brae,' where Wallace had a skirmish with the English, the College, the Rottenrow, and other places known to history and biography. It is a mean, square, capacious, and dirty building, and is utterly contemptible in presence of its grand old companion the Cathedral. The last relics of two and one-storied thatched houses, with outside stairs jutting into the streets, and modern improvements tacked on to them which were never stipulated for by their original architects, render the locality sombre and odd even under the brightest summer sun. Yet, when Dr Macleod preaches in this church on Sundays, fashionable people may be seen waiting long after service has commenced, until the beadle has found holes and corners in the pews and passages into which he may cram them; and not fashionable people alone, but those whose face and hands speak of hewing wood and drawing water. It is strange by what mysterious instinct the insect, like an able botanist, avoids all plants and flowers but those which minister to it a suitable nutrition. Something like this instinct is the feeling or mental process by which churches are filled and schools are crammed. When logic and every process of training and trial has fitted out your preachers or schoolmasters, there remains the problem of how the aforesaid will fit themselves to their work after all. We recollect our first impressions of Dr Macleod. It was on a high fast-day, ordained to be held by the nation on account of the Crimean War. With a company composed chiefly of hard toiled artizans, we walked eight miles to the

Barony to hear him of whom Fame had already spoken.
We were not disappointed. There entered into the pulpit
no chance sapling—sown by the fountain, of slender
make, and suggestive of evanescence—but a man like
Roderick Vich Alpine's own pine tree—a round, brawny
Highlander, with a tone of voice perfectly natural—no
nasal humming, no falsetto (by indulging in which
Emerson says clergymen bring on bronchitis)—but a voice
that ebbed and flowed like the wind through woods, or
the waves against an iron-bound shore. He read a
chapter in Isaiah—something about the Assyrian, his
pride, his pomp, his boasting, and his inglorious over-
throw. There was a challenge to the Emperor Nicholas
in every verse he read, and a consciousness of strength as
well. As he proceeded to preach you began to think that
it was well that the Celtic race musters so numerously in
our army, and holds such high rank in our councils of war.
The preacher became the general of a division, and
transformed his audience for the nonce into soldiers, and
through the charging cheer you heard the pibroch, and
got glimpses of Highland bonnets. And then there was
a pause. Like every careful general, and almost every
successful general, he thought about his men. The dying
and the dead, the wounded and those flushed with victory,
their sorrows and their joys, their rations, and medicines,
and housing—all must be attended to, aye, even up to
those thoughts (for soldiers have them too) which take
hold of eternity and of the throne of God. This discourse
was a good sample of the preacher and his manner. Dr
Macleod preaches no abstractions. He does not come
down from the manse neatly dressed in broadcloth without, and neatly lined with Calvin's postulates and dogmas
within. Inside the broadcloth there beats a human heart.
When he looks on the passage which pictures wretchedness, he does so with eyes that have gazed on the steam

of sewers dripping from the black ceiling of the poor
man's dwelling. When he talks of Trades Unions, he
does not see in them a threat that the employer must
have by-and-by fewer courses to his dinner, and therefore
get sulky ; but he recognises in them the outcome, in mad
shape or sane, of a real agony. He knows that amelioration is the aspiration and the destiny of humanity, and he
has seen the hells of sweating tailors, and the ill-ventilated,
badly-lighted, ill-heated apartments in which Gradgrind
keeps his apprentices with a view to grind gold out of
them, whatever else may be ground out. Selfish, cruel,
greedy, he knows workmen too often to be—lazy also at
times—but of these dazzling qualities unfortunately they
have no monopoly. Employers have them too, and these
qualities in employers are no less odious, because they
know better how to veil them. And thus this man, knowing and feeling deeply both sides of a question, steps in as
reconciler, as a servant of man and his Maker ; he
preaches from the life, he recognises in man his brother's
keeper, and that what is my interest in the long run will
also be yours.

Emerson says that of the bad preacher it may be
predicated that he never enters into autobiography. You
are not fit to discover while he preaches that ever he
lived on this earth at all. We think at rare times we
have met with this bad preacher, we cannot tell where,
but certainly it was in the days of clocks and watches,
either when larks and gowans were inviting us out of
church, or beautiful flakes of snow kept us gazing at the
window. If we looked attentively at him at all, it was
like the little boy, to see when he would turn the last leaf.
We knew that the Red Sea and certain towns in Palestine
existed, and were known to him as the moon to astronomers,
or as the various species of willows to German botanists.
Certain names, too, he knew or read as one reads them on

tombstones, but no indication in all his sermon told you
whether ever he had courted, married, wept, laughed,
eaten, drunk, slept, had dreams, had seen flowers or
trees, or read newspapers, or mingled in the busy bee-
hives of men, or been abroad in the solitudes of Nature.
Of the world into which he had been born we had no indication any more than of Saturn and its rings.   Far
otherwise was it with Dr Macleod.   When he discoursed
of Job, he had seen Job—many a poor, patient, sensitive,
proud heart of either sex overtaken by poverty and sickness and despair.   He had been in the lonely room with
the undertaker, he had stood when the doctor felt the
pulse, or when the tardy messenger announced that the
doctor could not come,

> 'Where helpless anguish turns to mourn,
> And lonely want returns to die.'

And you believed him all the more, because he had sat at
great men's tables, groaning with the choicest morsels of
creation, and laughed with all the exuberance of joy; for
that was human too.

One who is sincere in his pleasures and amusements,
gives a guarantee of his sincerity in the presence of
distress and woe.   Dr Macleod's moral and physical nature
suggests balance, and a fine harmonious composition of
forces.   A physically feeble man is tyrannised over by his
intellect or his emotions.   He falls into a fine train of
thought or feeling, but it runs off with him.   He cannot
recover poise.   Like a light bark with crowded sail, the
wind carries him away.   He gets strained or leaky, and
takes a long time before he can recover his usefulness;
or he becomes the victim of a fixed idea.   And so while
he is making an extremely fine and clever lad of his son,
he is spoiling his daughter; while he is busy with Revival
meetings, he is neglecting the ragged school; while he is
preaching teetotalism, he is forgetting sobriety of speech.

No preacher knows better than Dr Macleod when to get done with a sentiment, an idea, or a train of thought. The impulsive nature of the Celt is in him, but it is checked by culture, common sense, and healthy blood. He came down upon the Sabbath question as his ancestors swept down upon a Lowland strath, hot and hungry, and for a moment carrying all before him. The impetuosity and formidable nature of the charge lay in the sincerity of his convictions and in their strength. His utterance was illogical and tautological, but always frank and clear. In pure intellectual wrestling, in reasoning from a vast store of acquired facts lying orderly in a ready memory, he was no match for many of his opponents; but he had more than intellect, more than history, he had his own experience and convictions to stand on, and his words came warm from his heart, and not from the books of a logic-chopper. The healthy elastic nature of him soon threw off all the wounds inflicted on his retreat. But these very qualities, the source of his popularity and his usefulness, forbid us to look upon him as a great man, as a beacon for the future. To be such requires a towering intellect or a lordly will, whereas the very uniformity of his nature, the fact of it being

'totus teres et rotundus'

militates against far-living influence. He is rather a pioneer clearing the forests, than a lawgiver consolidating states. He is neither scientific, theological, nor literary, in the strict and special meaning of these words. He is a preacher of the highest qualities—may his race multiply and grow. His work—hard practical work—on social questions, deserves every praise; but as a writer, men ten times less useful in their day will live ten times longer than he; and yet, through his service, what a boon has he conferred on the humble in bringing home monthly to their hearths *Good Words* from some of the wisest and best of their living brethren.

SONNETS ON SAGES

I.—PERICLES

The stars of heaven look glorious in the night,
Wonders of space—but in the night of time
What star shines like the sage's brow sublime?
Few orbs so bright as Pericles. The sight
Of Athens glorious, active, great, and free,
Sailing down time, as down an unknown sea,
And this brave pilot at the helm—whose voice
And eye bring triumph—gives me stern delight.
Men are not in his hands like gamblers' dice;
He knows the subtle laws that govern mind,
And battling for the greatness of his kind,
In few short years weaves Greece a statelier crown
Of living lustre and of far renown
Than ages wove for Persian slaves so blind.

II.—MARCUS AURELIUS ANTONINUS

Firm, tender, just—sad in his very smile,
Tears in his wrath—a godlike noble king:
Let us join hands with Marcus who did bring
For crown, a soul of truth, hating all guile,
Vain shows, luxurious living, every wile
Lying in ambush for a monarch's feet
To trip him. Sun, and rain, and snow, and sleet
Saw thee, poor king, on that wild horse of thine,
The Roman people—an uneasy seat;
For the rough barb—ill-trained, though strong and fleet,
Kicked, plunged, and bit thee. But an aim divine
Upheld thee, stronger than applause or wine;
'Life is full short—work well while it is light;
No riot! Harvest must be home ere night.'

III.—PLATO

We cannot climb the heights which thou hast scaled,
We cannot see the stars which thou hast seen,
We cannot dive for pearls where thou hast been,
Deep in the sea of knowledge. Unbewailed
Shall be our lot, however, for we've sailed
Some humble, pretty voyages with thee—
Heard thy sweet talk like murmur of the bee

Half-buried among roses—that pure Greek,
Than which, 'tis said, the gods no better speak—
Grateful that standing reverent at thy knee,
Our weak good wishes were by thee made strong.
'Death rather than dishonour' didst thou teach;
'Ruin is better far than doing wrong'—
These were the fruits which thy kind hand did reach.

IV.—DANTE

Poet of duty. Sternest views of life
Were thine; and in thy deep sincerest soul
Thou seem'st thy every idle word to roll
Tormenting thee, like many-bladed knife.
Thine eye saw in the green the ripened tree,
And in the seed the harvest which would be
Sad harvest for the sinner. Thou didst toll
The knell of retribution in thy song;
And down in deeper circles far along,
Just as its deeds were blacker, didst thou sweep
The affrighted spirit. Yet thy hopes were strong.
The adoration of an angel's face,
When Christ-ward thy triumphant pæans leap,
We in thy marble countenance may trace.

V.—JENNER, THE DISCOVERER OF VACCINATION

Old faces, ugly, scarred like sin itself—
These sat before our grandsire's cheerless hearth—
Young faces too all pitted, and a dearth
Spread o'er the land, for as by hand of elf,
Strong men had been laid low in the cold earth,
And there were few to cut the grain, for, lo !
Small-pox had been at work—that deadliest foe—
Far worse than modern armies. Jenner came ;
And as when woods and prairies are on flame
Men burn a circle round them, and the glow
Of lesser fires endure, and waste their corn
To save their lives and hold great fires at bay,
So Jenner taught us our great foe to scorn,
With his own weapons beating him away.

VI.—NEWTON

Through unknown time the firmament of stars,
Dumb as our graves, like them too raised anew
Questions as keen as vain, till the great Few
Banding their strength wrung answers, 'Brother Mars !'
Earth cried at last—'Venus my sister too !'
But joy was yet unfilled, when in the pause,
Rose from the silent halls of human thought,
Mild, pious, wise, an earnest king who brought,

Learning for robes and throne, and by his laws
Were bound together in one mighty whole
Comets and constellations—these shine bright
Undimmed though old, and if a grander sight
Be ours, 'tis this that these far orbs enrol
In deep fixed splendour that majestic soul.

VII.—GEORGE STEPHENSON, THE INVENTOR OF THE LOCOMOTIVE

The sore-worked boy, earning a plack per day,
Hoeing his turnips—how he fought and grew
Great in life's battle, till the favoured few,
Bent down before him when his head was grey—
There is a subject worth a poet's lay !
Yea, and there bursts to him a kind of hymn
From every railway carriage on its way,
Sounding o'er viaducts—through tunnels dim.
Space, that keeps earth still ignorant of the stars,
And nation shut from nation, man from man—
Dull vacant space—was by his subtle plan
Conquered in part ; torn were its iron bars.
Far wider rooms did he to dear friends give,
In which to meet, to part, to talk, to live.

VIII.—THOMAS CARLYLE

O how I mourn, when he who tells the tale
Of duty is himself a graceless scamp,
Firing men's souls, and yet his own soul damp !
O how I stronger grow—feel young and hale,
And seem like Hercules in coat of mail—
When he who makes my inmost heart abhor
Shams and veneering, is himself no show !
But a right noble worker with the sore
Sweat of his brain undried—his heart a-glow :
Whose life is like the book o'er which he broods ;
Who, slaying dragons for his weaker kin,
Holds no foul orgie his own house within.
Sincere old man, with wild or tender moods,
Thy music leads to dawn through deepest woods.

IX.—JAMES WATT, INVENTOR OF THE STEAM-ENGINE

Horses, the pride of kings in ancient days,
Neighing in working harness, strong and fleet,
Made human labour light through cold and heat :
But now we've got the steam-horse, which might craze
Those who first looked on its gigantic powers,
And saw it work unwearied through long hours—
Even that great engine, with its strength and speed,
Needing no whip, and uttering no complaint ;

Like Pallas from the brow of Jove, this steed
Came forth from Watt's own soul, whose force was spent
Reading for us hard riddles—his the pain,
Which also had reward ; for as he grew
In knowledge, he grew wiser—ours the gain,
Getting such boundless help our tasks to do.

X.—ZOROASTER, THE PERSIAN SEER

Another Moses—in times dark and old,
Among the herdsmen of the East, who bent
Before rude idols in a skin-roofed tent,
Or those whose Providence was Luck—he told
The open secret of a God who rolled
His thunders, or His living lightning sent ;
But also sent the murmur of the rills—
Filled night with stars, and His vicegerent sun
Ordered to clothe with light the ancient hills,
O sun ! thou symbol of the changeless one,*
Stronger than death, or hell, or all our ills,
Even as our God is stronger, who fulfils
His righteous edicts as the ages roll ;
For He is Nature's living central soul.

SONNET ON IRONGRAY PARISH

My ' Bishop's Forest ' has a secret glen,
    Far up the hill where glens are seldom seen,
    And in a sword-swept land this glen was screen
To anxious pilgrims ; there as in a pen
    Christ's sheep assembled and partook the feast
Which he ordained—the sacred bread and wine—
    Sitting on the Communion stones ; while east,
And south, and west, the sentries watched for sign
Of the wolves' coming—whose teeth once had met
    On six stray lambs beside the church's wall,
And whose lank jaws were with their warm blood wet.
    Shed not these memories sadness over all
My streams, and moors, and woods, not vanished yet ?
    Am I not mansion with a haunted hall ?

* *Vide* the *Zend-Avesta*, which is the Bible of the Zoroastrians.

CHAPTER VI

Astronomy

The Terrible Stars—With the Stars—The Use of the Moon—
Motion a Finite Phenomenon—Astronomy and Religion—The
Infinite Divisibility of Time — Sonnets on Utter Solitude,
Winter, and June.

The Terrible Stars

As man began to look with greater interest on the stars,
his reverence and delight passed into adoration. He
kissed his hand towards them, and connected them
closely with his divinities. Thousands of years passed
over him, and still those bright and countless orbs were
credited with occult influence. According to the al-
chemists, while the sun governed the heart and the
moon the brain, life itself was an emanation from the
stars. Byron belauds them as the poetry of heaven,
beautiful, mysterious, alluring, so that Fortune, Fame,
Power, Life, have been named Stars. All who gaze upon
them, he finely says, wish for wings to fly towards them
and mingle with their endless day. In *Faust* they rise
every night in beauty and in love. In Shakespeare those
holy vessels of bright gold, each in its place, utter angels'
songs. If the stars, says Emerson, had appeared only
once in a thousand years, what a tradition of their glory
would have been handed down to us! Robert Chambers,
in his collection of popular rhymes, has preserved to us

four melodious, metaphorical lines, chanted by the
children of Scotland to a star :

> ' I had a little sister, they called her Peep-Peep,
> She waded the waters deep, deep, deep,
> She climbed up the mountains so high, high, high,
> And, poor little thing, she had just one eye ! '

Into the midst of these dreams science steps with im-
perturbable foot. She lifts away the veil of enchantment.
She substitutes mechanical and chemical theories in place
of visions. Yet the melting of the visions disconcerts us.
When in 1891 Dr Huggins discoursed at Cardiff before
the British Association, one could have wept if tears had
availed aught. ' Happy are they,' said the learned
President, ' who are still in the east of life's meridian line.'
He did not mean they were happy because of their
ignorance, but because, having a longer probable future,
they would have larger opportunities of learning. No
doubt knowledge is gain. Still it is pleasant, with the
American poet, to recur to our own little age of faith,
when we were easily pleased and never asked why a rose
was so beautiful, thinking only that the self-same Power
made the flowers of earth and of heaven, and placed us
among them that our eyes might be delighted.

Perhaps the first revulsion of feeling in studying the
new astronomy, armed with its telescope, spectroscope,
camera, and spider-web lines, is produced by the tidings
of the exceeding swiftness of the ' fixed stars.' They
seem all to be in a hurry and a heat. Neither do they
run together, but like scared wild-fowl are found rushing
in every direction, so that were it not for the immensity
of the arena, the billions of miles of separation, they
might be the victims of most serious collisions. Carlyle
wonders what Bootes thinks of it as he hunts across the
zenith with his leash of sidereal fire. Now there is a
great red star in Bootes, of physical constitution some-

thing like our own sun—Arcturus, to wit, mentioned in a sublime verse in the book of Job—which, if half be true that Greenwich astronomers are telling us about it, could rush from London to York in a second, and cross the earth's orbit, enormous as that is, in a handful of short winter days. Now this same star has another alarming characteristic, and in a much lesser degree this characteristic belongs to many remote bright stars, namely, enormous bulk. Conceive a heavenly body with a diameter, to put it mildly, equal to the distance of Venus from the sun, although those who argue for a longer diameter to it are perhaps more correct. Think if it rushing even with half the calculated speed, so large, so swift, through the most thickly star-strewn portion of the Milky Way, and there is no saying what dreadful black holes, what ' coal sacks,' as some portions barren of stars have already been named, would be produced in that radiant arch. The Ettrick Shepherd thought of a comet sweeping aside the twinkling orbs of night as if they had been foambells in a tranquil sea. But the tremendous attractive power of a sun manifoldly larger and heavier than our own could not fail to make itself felt, even through countless millions of miles, to the smaller orbs of that part of the galaxy.

That is an uncomfortable feeling which the attempt to realise the enormous light and heat of each individual star produces. Indeed, their whole stellar surfaces seem to consist of whirlpools and hurricanes of flame and molten matter. Hurricanes that move not like our laggard typhoons at eighty miles an hour, but at ten times, or it may be a hundred times greater speed. In those blinding, dazzling tempests, there is no rest, no hiding-place for the lowliest forms of life. Not for one moment can we concede enjoyment to any created thing in those awful abysses. Neither in the sun, nor in his brother spheres

can we expect either the germs or spores of anything
organic. The music of the spheres is an ancient thought,
a grand idea. Shakespeare, as we saw, repeated it, and
Goethe introduces it into his grandest drama. But
suppose our guardian angel could convey us to the proper
distance from any star, so that the vibrations of its
hydrogen, or more composite atmosphere could be conveyed to our ears, how those ears would be astonished to
listen to explosions and chemical and mechanical combina-
tions on such a scale and with such velocities! Thunder
appalling as the crack of doom, noises such as no artillery
on earth could render, from diapason to treble, would rend
the skies in which we were placed. We have only
analogy to guide us, but taking what happens in our
chemical laboratories as guide, and assuming Jules Verne
could take care of us and place us at a suitable distance
away from harm, is it not possible that from Vega, in
Lyra, from the Pole Star, from the splendid jewels which
compose Orion and the Pleiades, or sparkle every night
for us in the constellation of the Plough, our sense
of smell would be able to distinguish one luminary from
another, just as fertilising insects discriminate garden
flowers by their odour?

Another uneasy feeling we can scarcely escape, while
gazing at the stars is this, that we surmise they are all on
the road to death. First, we have nebulæ, some of
wondrous forms, spiral and other. Then there be infant
stars, so we are told, bluish-white and little condensed;
besides these, there are young stars, white and resplendent;
adult stars, large, dense and red; aged stars, dull and
murky. Perhaps, going forward another step, and
guided by planetary analogies, we have huge dark masses
shrunk and cold. Yet, sooner or later, so says the great
doctrine of the conservation and dissipation of energy, all
the suns we see, even as they have waxed through ages

P

and æons, so through ages and æons shall they wane.
They are fires kindled we know not how, we know not
when, we know not why. We can only guess. But like
any fire that ever was kindled, they will all go out. No
discovery has yet been made to prove that our sun can
for ever give out energy while it receives none, or at least,
far less than it parts with. If one doubts that a star
should ever so wane, we have only to look at the moon, or
at our own earth. The very shape of earth and moon
suggests they were once more plastic and had greater
heat. But a tithe of the earth's original heat remains
underneath its crust.

Meantime, let us be thankful for these billions of miles
separating us from those terrible millions of stars, just
as we are thankful for an atmosphere whose friction
reduces to fine ashes almost all the numberless meteors
for ever bombarding us, and which would otherwise work
us woe. It has been calculated, that although moving
towards us at sidereal speed, or it may be our sun and
system moving towards it, or both motions bringing us
nearer, that it would take a century ere a star, rushing
towards us, would appear one-fortieth brighter. The
spectrum and camera have assured us of the existence of
stars which we may call invisible, since no telescope has
ever been able to make them out. Some of these are
binaries, such as the two great bodies each much larger than
our sun, revolving round each other with enormous speed,
and at a comparatively short distance from one another,
the first indications of whose existence were lately supplied to us by a lady studying stellar photography at
an American Observatory. These compose Beta Aurigæ.
Another binary star, longer known, is Algol in Perseus.
The speed of its members has been calculated from micro-
metrical measurements of the displacements of the
spectrum lines caused by the approach or retrocession of

either star in our line of sight. These twin stars revolving round each other, and having together a bulk nearly equal to that of the sun, are approaching quickly, if we measure by terrestrial standards, but so slowly if we measure by sidereal, owing to the vast abyss that separates us, that not for a million of years need earthly inhabitants entertain any fears of serious results. It is thus that extreme distance saves us from supreme inconvenience. [December 1891.]

WITH THE STARS

The terrible hurricane of the 14th October 1881 which wrought such devastation to the Eyemouth fishermen, and whose havoc was felt so widely throughout western Europe, was followed on the 15th by a day of unclouded serenity. The air, thoroughly washed with the rain of the preceding day, was so perfectly transparent that walking or riding westward in front of the declining sun was irksome to the eyes.

The sun set and there was a moonless night. No evening for weeks before had been so favourable for star-gazing, and there have been few since. Not a cloud disturbed the translucent atmosphere. It was a gala night with every constellation, and astronomers tell us there are not more than thirty or forty such celestial fêtes in a whole year. Not only the stars of greater magnitudes were present, but lesser lights on rare occasions visible to the unassisted eye. How they crowded, and swarmed, and twinkled! Shy stars, that in their far abodes distrust the gaze of curious seekers; pale streaks of light, that refuse to be luminous under the thinnest veil, sparkled sharp and keen, as if they had silently glided millions and millions of miles nearer to the front. The

constellation of Ursa Major, or the Plough, showed not
only its seven great diamonds, but there was the little
gem that shines near the middle star of the seven, called
by the Arabs the 'tester,' as requiring good eyesight to
detect it.

Early in the evening, in the West, Bootes was gliding
towards the horizon warily holding in his hounds with his
leash of sidereal fire. Modest Mirac shone upon his tunic.
Great Arcturus glittered near his knee. But as the hours
advanced and I began to clamber up a steep bridle-path
that led across the hills and ascended to one of the water-
sheds of the Southern Grampians, the Milky Way, that
paradise of flowers overhead, stretching from east to west,
like a triumphal arch, showed its every star, like petals
unfolded by genial wind and sun. How grand it looked,
reminding one of a glorious river parting into two streams
at the point where Arided in Cygnus shone like a beacon-
fire piled on a rock, overlooking the foaming waves ;
while closer the one, and further apart the other, from the
outer bank of either divided stream, Altair and sapphire-
tinted Vega flashed out their watchfires of the night. High
in the heavens, south of the Milky Way, pranced the Poets'
Pegasus enriched by stars with Arabic names. Drawing a
line through two of the bright stars of the four forming
the Square of Pegasus, and prolonging the line scaling the
eastern walls, behold Aldebaran ! No wonder we did not
know them at the first blush. These are stars of the first
magnitude in Orion. Orion is a haughty constellation,
and brooks not to show his face in the heavens when a
summer sun reduces his hunting-ground to a mere crumb
of night. Why should one get up from bed, dress, see
that his club and other hunting gear are in order, to chase a
troop that disperses and vanishes as soon as it is herded
together ? To-night he will not yet display himself
wholly ; but mid-winter will have all his retinue ; as well

as Sirius, the first-born of stars, roaming for hours at a
stretch from the gates of the east to the happy hunting-
grounds of the west.

Near me was a lonely loch or mountain tarn. It had
been scooped out by a glacier and was still dammed back by
an old moraine. It contained a little boat with oars, used
for angling or for pleasure. I loosed the rude cable that
held it, half-beached, and pushed it into the loch. I
pulled on to the deep part protected from the wind by
the frightful warlocks' crag. Then I sat still until the
ripples of my oar had died away. The glory of the
celestial was one; the glory of the terrestrial was another. Half the heavens hung below me, half the
heavens sparkled above my head. Occasionally a meteor
passed leaving a train of light. How I wished for wings,
swift as sunbeams, to carry me through the lighted streets
of that great mysterious city! Questions like a child's
arose. What sort of world will ours be, when Vega is the
Polar Star, some 12,000 years after this? Has any one
ever calculated how many hundred degrees below zero
must be the cold of the interstellar spaces? Have these
mighty suns got planets, and those planets moons; and
do lovers walk in their moonlight, and warriors fight in
their day? Do these suns waste their light, and heat,
and energy, as our sun seems in great part to do, striking
on a lonely planet here and there, to comfort and to
nourish; and transmitting the vast overplus to insatiable,
cold, hungry, vacant, ungrateful space?

To all such questions they are dumb. We cannot hear
the crackling of their flames. Articulate message they
have none; or else our ears are gross and hear no better
than the fisherman's, whom yesterday's cyclone put under
the waves.

I left the lonely loch, where I seemed to be at the
centre of immensity, and was glad to reach the vale

where the owls hooted, where the voices of woods and
waters rose and fell, where firelight made ruddy the
window curtains, where honest collies barked, and where
children were saying short prayers in bed before composing themselves to sleep.

THE USE OF THE MOON

The planet Earth is a demure old cat. Like most
young creatures she was more frisky and agile in her
tender years. Some millions of millenniums ago she kept
whisking round on her axis as if to overtake herself.
Instead of taking twenty-four hours to make up a day
and a night, she took little more than three. No wonder
she got humped up at the equator and flattened at the
poles. As Humboldt long ago remarked, the shape of
the earth betrays one of the earliest chapters in her
history. Her diameter at that time was much larger,
and she behaved like a viscous fluid. She had hardly
lost all her original luminosity. Her diurnal speed was
so great that large masses like foam flew away from her,
rushing through her steamy atmosphere and above it, in
the same direction as herself. These moonlets were of
different sizes, but the same law which gives us round
tears, and round spheres, tended to make them spherical.
Armed with gravitation, in the process of the ages, the
bigger spheres began to pick up the smaller, until mother
earth, instead of being surrounded with a ring such as we
see round the planet Saturn, became surrounded with
moons like Jupiter. Enormous tides were formed, both in
herself and satellites, due to mutual attractions. These
and other causes widened the orbits of the satellites, and
in their viscous fluid state they and their parent earth
still shone with auroral splendour. But the inequality of

the moonlets was their ruin as a system. The larger claimed the smaller, until at last all the mass of matter, lost to the earth by its headlong diurnal rotation, was reduced to one single lump, 'the orbed maiden, with white fire laden, which mortals call the moon.' But while the moon, now far removed from the earth, still retained her fluid, or semi-fluid, state, the enormous tides formed on her by the attraction of the much greater primary, began like a tight belt to restrain the axial motion of the secondary planet. Slower and more slowly the moon began to turn on its axis, until the last stage was reached, when it made one rotation on its axis in the same time that it made one revolution round its primary, and one-half of its surface was for ever hid to natural or telescopic eyes, so far at least as man is concerned.

Changes succeeded each other in the moon as they succeeded each other in the earth, but everything went on more rapidly in the smaller planet. It cooled much quicker than the earth, just as a pistol bullet red-hot cools quicker than a red-hot ball, in volume fifty times bigger. Dry land, condensation and evaporation forming seas, rain, and rivers, mighty volcanoes upraising mountains, wide chinks out of which oozed liquid lava, during its shrinkage and consolidation, made the moon look like a habitable globe for bacilli, for algæ, for mosses, for low forms of animal life, long before mother earth became ready for the display of such phenomena. Whether there was ever enough of time vouchsafed to allow the moon to have a thick series of sedimentary strata, or whether old age, creeping upon her all too soon, arrested development of flora and fauna at a very humble stage, can only be guessed. Old age, however, has crept upon her. Her volcanoes are extinct. Her atmosphere cannot be distinguished. No signs of vitality, change, polar snow, or summer verdure, ocean waves or leaping cascades, can be at all discerned on her surface. In the long night of fourteen days to which every month she is subjected, an intensity of cold would prevail, sufficient of itself to kill all vegetable or animal life as such are known to us.

To me the moon is an awful and terrible sight. It is like a white corpse hung up in the firmament. Use it has none beyond ' ruling the night,' and that only as a half-timer and in certain conditions of our atmosphere, and giving us a source of energy not much utilised in the tides. In short, she is a gay deceiver. Which of us has not penned a youthful sonnet to her praise ? ' Fair Dian's crest hangs in the azure air an island of the blest.' Does she? No; she is 'joyless in her voiceless woe.' If we stood in her and cried, no sound could be heard. If we breathed, the odour would not approach. Sad it is. We have only one little sister, the child of our mother, and her gambols are all over. She has become wrinkled and old, while the mother is still in the heyday of her splendour.

But the message that comes from her is a heavy one. It says to the living earth,—' As I am now, so will you in the future become. You are already getting cold at the extremities—the hand of death is there. Nothing lives at the poles. Colder you yet shall become. Ingenious man may get over the loss of coal and bore for heat to generate steam deep down nearer the centre of the earth. But though he clothe himself with electricity as a garment, what shall it avail when the cold which can now freeze brandy triumphs over every imaginable source of earthly heat ? Don't fear the universal conflagration. It is the universal refrigeration that is slowly but surely approaching, with ebbings now, and flowings then, of which you ought to be afraid.' I notice that in his *Evolution and Ethics* our philo- sophic Professor Huxley does not overlook some of these possible cosmic processes.   He points out that the 'survival of the fittest,' although a happy phrase, may also mislead. 'Fittest' is a connotation of 'best'; and about 'best' there hangs a moral flavour.   In cosmic nature, however, what is fittest depends upon the conditions.   Long since, I ventured to point out that if our hemisphere were to cool again, the survival of the fittest might bring about, in the vegetable kingdom, a population of more and more stunted and humbler and humbler organisms, until the fittest that survived might be nothing but lichens, diatoms, and such microscopic organisms, as those which give red snow its colour.—[The alga, *Protococcus nivalis.*]

The message of the moon is therefore a melancholy one, and the 'use' of the moon as compared to earth and sun not a particularly grand one.   If any student would like relief from the dark side of Evolution, there are tremulous rays of hope to be found in Herbert Spencer's *First Principles*, section 182, p. 529.   [December 1894.]

MOTION A FINITE PHENOMENON

In the systems of Nature of the atheistic philosophers of France at the end of last century matter and motion were assumed to be indissoluble and eternal.   This mode of regarding the universe is paraphrased by Pope, from Bolingbroke : 'See through the air, the ocean, and the earth, all matter quick and bursting into birth.'   Young, the poet, assumes a necessary connection between the two, for he asks, 'Has matter more than motion, has it thought, judgment, and genius ?'   In the latest *Primer of Evolution* we are informed that the universe consists of matter and motion.   We can conceive of matter without motion, but motion without matter is unconceivable.

The modern doctrine of the dissipation of energy allows us to consider the matter from a new standpoint.

Taking this doctrine as already proved, and looking not only at the earth but at the solar system and the starry heavens, we are confronted with the fact of matter being busily engaged everywhere in getting quit of motion, and tending towards absolute rest. Taking our own satellite to begin with, it is curious to note that in order to describe it we had best employ terms which are the negation of motion. There it shines with its burnt-out volcanoes, with its dried-up oceans, without leaping streams or roaring winds. No springs, summers, nor autumns succeed each other on its surface. True there is some change in its condition, namely, a monthly change of temperature at its surface, the difference of its exposure to the beams of the sun for fourteen days, and again, its deprivation of them for the like period of time.

Compared to the earth, however, it is motionless, dead, and cold. But what the moon is now the earth shall yet become. Once the earth shone as a star. Now it is only a solar mirror. Its fires are concealed at lower depths, and the flames that crest its active volcanoes are the only torches it can uphold. Already death is beginning at its extremities, and the waves of its Polar oceans are becoming fixed and gelid under the influence of ice that refuses to melt.

Supposing, as is likely, that stars arise from the condensation of nebulæ, whether nebulæ be clouds of meteors or burning gas, or both, and supposing further that many stellar bodies are of different ages, then there are certain physical conditions which they are likely to pass through. For a long period they become brighter and hotter, but by the doctrine of dissipation of energy the doom of absolute darkness, coldness, and silence is written over the faces of the stars. It is somewhat the same with human life itself. We have the noise and restlessness of childhood, the strength and fleetness of the adult, the senility and slow-

ness of old age. Red, dim, and discrowned are already
Aldebaran and others of its brethren, and we have reason
to believe that numerous dark suns, their fires all burned
out, are groping their way through the depths of space.

This tendency of matter to get quit of motion is shown
in the limitation of the rotational motion of the moon,
so that it now presents only one side to the earth, and
astronomers are divided as to the fate of the rotational
motion it is presumed the planet Venus once had,
some thinking that, from retardation caused by tidal
friction, Venus now presents only one face towards the
sun.

The nebular theory of Laplace, which asserts that
planets have been formed from suns in concentric circles,
has long been favourably received. Professor See, however, has questioned its application to many sidereal
systems. Nebulæ, he says, appear to part asunder in
masses at the weakest point, whence result binary and
ternary suns revolving around each other in elliptical
orbits, each member of the group vastly nearer its fellow
than our sun to the nearest fixed star; so near, in short,
as to revolve more like the inferior planets round our
sun. Revolving around each other in highly elliptical
orbits with physical conditions analogous to those which
obtain in our sun, they form immense tides on each
other's gaseous or liquid surfaces. This again, as we have
seen, by friction is destructive of rotational motion.

The doctrine of dissipation of energy has been the
greatest stumbling-block hitherto presented to the
evolutionary biologist. Lord Kelvin is loth to allow
more than about 20,000,000 of years as the period during
which the sun can have been shedding his life-giving
rays. Most evolutionists ask for a far greater period for
the slow and gradual advance from the lowliest organisms
to those highest in the scale. One professor asks for

100,000,000 years, others for four times that period.   The
late Dr Croll in his *Stellar Evolution* tried to reconcile the
conflicting claims by supposing the sun to have been
formed by the collision of two solid bodies moving at
enormous velocities.   By the conversion of the proper
motion of such bodies into the molecular motions of light
and heat, his calculations assured us of a sun that would
shine for a much longer period than the calculations of
physicists.   Even were such a hypothesis true, every
reader must see that it is obtained by an enormous loss of
proper motion, and that what these supposed dark solid
bodies did once they could not do again.

In the presence of these great mysteries we are ready
to bow our heads in reverence.   Some cause, beyond and
above Nature, is required to set the immense machine
a-going.   We are led to imagine that what seems destined
to have an end must also have had a beginning, and
that motion is a finite phenomenon.   If we had other
senses, and that is not inconceivable—witness the sense of
electricity developed in some animals which man has not—
we might be better prepared to apprehend the necessity
of postulating an intelligent cause of motion.   After all,
the true miracle in the midst of Nature is intelligence and
life.   Compared to the brain of the lowest savage the
mighty sun itself looks mean.   How great are prudence,
audacity, curiosity, love of relations, mechanical inventions,
compared to cosmic hurricanes.   The savage knows the
sun warms and lights him, but the sun knows neither.
The poet sings :

> 'Once slept the world an egg of stone,
> And pulse, and sound, and light was none ;
> And God said 'Throb' and there was motion.'

We would rather believe with the poet than doubt with
the astronomer. [November 1895.]

Astronomy and Religion

It has often been triumphantly asked, What is our earth but an insignificant satellite of a sun, which again is only one, and not by any means the largest, of millions of other suns? Would the Creator have sent His Son into the world, when the world we inhabit is a mere speck in infinity? Dr Chalmers sought to meet this difficulty by referring to the parable of the Shepherd leaving the ninety-nine sheep to seek that which had gone astray, as if the single world which had revolted against the Creator were of more importance than all that had remained faithful.

Another method of meeting the difficulty is one suggested by astronomy itself. As far as the modern astronomy can carry us, we have no proof, no likelihood, of any other globe being inhabited by rational' beings except our own earth. The inferior planets circle too near the heat and light of the great central luminary, and are so light and gaseous that no astronomer has ventured to hint they are the abodes of life. The most of the superior planets, on the other hand, are so remote from the sun, share his heat and light to so small a degree, that we cannot conceive of their being inhabited. True, of late, certain guesses have been ventured upon concerning Mars. But the discoveries upon the surface of that planet point more clearly to sterility than to luxuriance. At the snowy poles of our own earth death reigns supreme, and the clearest fact revealed about Mars is that he has polar caps. Change only manifests itself in a limited area of his surface. One of the clearest-eyed investigators of the planet has lately told us that the part corresponding to our torrid and temperate zones is very much a waterless desert. The two giant superior

planets are so fluid and so hot, that neither vegetation
nor life are likely to find harbour on their surface. But
the body external to the earth, of which we have the
fullest information, is the moon. It appears without
water and without atmosphere. It rotates once in
twenty-eight days, consequently every portion of its
surface must be exposed for fourteen days to the sun's
heat and alternately deprived for fourteen days of the
same, so the tremendous difference of temperature at
any given point in its surface, between its long night and
its long day, would kill all life such as we can realize.
Add to all this difficulties connected with the attractions
of the planetary masses to objects on their surface, and it
would appear, no beings such as enliven the streets of our
cities could exist. On the smaller planets people would
require to be very much heavier and very much larger;
on the large planets their muscularity would need to
be enormous to overcome the mighty power of gravitation.

Another consideration which ought to weigh with us
before allowing ourselves to be overpowered with a sense
of our own insignificance is this, that astronomers are
losing faith in the nebular hypothesis of Laplace. It is
seen that this theory, however it may suit our own
planetary bodies, does not apply to other stellar systems.
By far the greater number of stellar systems, it has been
remarked by Professor See, appear to be composed of
only two stars—two vast suns; but a few systems are
made up of three and even of four such bodies, all in
fluid heat, all having fiery hurricanes troubling their
surfaces, all creating in each other enormous tides, shaking
them to the very centre, as they revolve around each
other. 'Viewed as a stellar system,' he continues, 'our
own system is quite unique, and its development has
apparently been radically different from that prevailing

among the double stars, which would seem to be the normal form of celestial evolution.'

Ranyard and, in his later articles, Norman Lockyer, depart considerably in their views from the beautifully spun theories of Laplace, and even go so far as to distrust them, in their application to our solar system.

Now if it can be shown that our solar system, both in its constitution and its history, is perfectly unique in the celestial worlds, there is, to say the least, a probability that life, and above all, rational life, is a phenomenon of rarity so extreme and so rare, that it does not appear, *prima facie*, a thing improbable that God should send His Son to earth to die that man might live.

Modern astronomy has told us much of the heavenly bodies, but it has made them terrible to our imaginations. Not in all the suns that brighten the Milky Way, not in all the constellations that bespangle the sky, is a single island, continent, forest, valley, or mountain on which we could suppose a mammal to graze, a squirrel to swing, a ploughman to turn the soil, or an eagle to soar. Neither amœba nor bacillus could exist for a moment in those fearful fires, in those resounding seas of death.

THE INFINITE DIVISIBILITY OF TIME

The infinite divisibility of matter, although difficult to realise in thought, is a doctrine which holds the field owing to the still greater difficulties attending the alternative hypothesis that matter consists of ultimate parts. 'For each of such ultimate parts, did they exist, must have an under and an upper surface, a right and a left side, like any other fragment. Now it is impossible to imagine its sides so near that no plane of section can be conceived between them, and however great may be the assumed force of cohesion it is impossible to shut out the idea of a greater force overcoming it.'

But the same line of argument, favourable to the supposition of the infinite divisibility of matter, may help to bring home to us the concept of the infinite divisibility of time. In our familiar divisions of time we begin with seconds and end with centuries. The idea of a shorter fragment of time than a second is rarely entertained. Napoleon, who knew the value of time, remarked that it was the quarters-of-hours that won battles. The value of minutes has been often recognised, and any person watching a railway clerk handing out tickets and change, during the last few minutes available, must have been struck with how much could be done in those short portions of time.

At the appointed hour the train starts, and by-and-by is carrying passengers at the rate of sixty miles an hour. In a second you are carried twenty-nine yards. In one-twenty-ninth of a second you pass over one yard. Now one yard is quite an appreciable distance, but one-twenty-ninth of a second is a period which cannot be appreciated.

Yet it is when we come to planetary and stellar motions that the notion of the infinite divisibility of time dawns upon us in a new light. It would seem that no portion of time, however microscopic, is unavailable. Nature can perform prodigies, not certainly in less than no time, but in portions of it so minute as to be altogether inconceivable.

The earth revolves on her axis in twenty-four hours. At the equator her circumference is 25,000 miles. Hence, in this part of the earth a person is being carried eastward at the rate of 509 yards per second. That is, he is moving over a yard, whose length is conceivable, in the period of 1-509th part of a second, of which we can have no notion at all.

But more: the orbital motion of the earth around the sun causes the former to perform a revolution of nearly 600,000,000 miles in a year, or somewhat less than 70,000 miles an hour, which is more than 1000 miles a minute. Here, then, our second carries us the long distance of about nineteen miles. The mighty ball thus flies about a mile in the nineteenth part of a second.

Still higher values seem to be set on the meanest fractions of time when we make stellar motions the subject of inquiry. Our poor moments and minutest fragments of moments appear to be exalted to a new importance when we are told that the first magnitude star Arcturus, in this same nineteenth part of a second, can clear six miles of distance—in short, is flying through space at such a rate that, if the earth sped at the same rate around the sun, we would have half-a-dozen Christmases in one year!

But the marvellous velocity of light, or rather the incredible swiftness with which the waves or undulations of the luminiferous ether succeed each other as antecedent and consequent, impresses us most vividly of all with the feasibility of the notion of the infinite divisibility of time. Light travels at the rate of rather less than 200,000 miles a second.

Suppose we could clap to our sides wings of such a quality that they could carry us through the air at the rate of 12,000 miles an hour. If now we left London at noon, we could be in New Zealand at one o'clock. This we would esteem a miracle indeed. Suppose we quicken our pace, and instead of, at the end of one hour, being conveyed to the Antipodes, the same time served to carry us to the moon, 240,000 miles distant, how would a fairy mounted on a sunbeam laugh at our leisurely way of

Q

taking it! Why, this fairy, in the same hour's time could take and bring back fourteen hundred consecutive messages between England and Diana's orb. Suppose the moon were a torch, kindled instantaneously to lunar or solar brightness, in little more than one tick of our clock or one beat of our heart the light and heat there originated would be striking with its millions of waves upon our eyes.

Think well of the value of time, when, in the two-hundred-thousandth part of a second, billions of red, blue, and yellow undulations (occupying, the red, 33,000 waves, the blue or violet about 60,000 waves in the length of an inch), can be hurled one mile from a luminous centre like our own sun, or any of the visible stars. We may laugh at the idea of such a fraction of time, but we dare not laugh at the work done in it. Life though prolonged to the normal term seems too short for man. Yet before we can live a second we must have lived through the immeasurably shorter period mentioned above. Those who treat time as an enemy, those afflicted with *ennui*, may well be amazed at the activity of Nature.

As man through the process of the ages acquires wisdom and knowledge, his own activity is quickening and approximating more to the planetary and stellar motions. In war, in means of communicating news, in transport from place to place, in agriculture and in architecture, the pace is swifter now than in the days of yore. The aim of civilisation seems to be to get through the greatest quantity of work in the smallest quantity of time. It may be even that we are hurrying on too quickly, losing sight of the old saw, that there is luck in leisure. It is to be hoped that, while our brains work harder and our fingers are busy for longer stretches at once than those of savages, they are also working to better purpose. A modern novelist * lately introduced us to a figment of his

* Rider Haggard in *She*.

own creation—a coquettish lady three thousand years
old, whose light feet pacing up and down the granite steps
of her subterranean palace stairs, had at last rendered
those hard steps concave; so that changes can succeed
each other at any imagined rate of slowness as well as of
quickness. The speed of light, no less than the extraordinary slowness of the wearing down to ocean's floor of
the all but everlasting hills, brings before us the marvellous conception of an element, a condition, an attribute,
or an entity, which both in its narrowness and its breadth
proclaims itself infinite. Divide time as we like, we cannot reach a part of a second so short that something may
not be done. On the other hand, its expansion is so
elastic, that we cannot contemplate changes so gradual,
but that there is enough duration, enough of ages and
æons, for those changes to be stupendous.—*Good Words,*
1895.

Deep Solitude

'O tribes and nations in the same bright sky!'
The Earth said to the stars—Why has it come
That we for countless ages have been dumb?
No signs have passed between us—we shall die
With our great load of secrets. Not a sigh,
Nor smile, nor throb of joy, nor pang of woe,
No thermal burnings, and no glacial snow
Have changed me, but to Heaven there was a cry
From Earth, yet back to Earth came no reply;
The Plough was silent—silent was the glow
Of the great Dog-star, while Orion stood
Sparkling, but fixed and speechless—the same mood
Met me in Milky Way and Polar Star:
One Father's children, and apart so far!

The Solitude Breaks

Thus with my child the Moon and parent old,
The Sun, cycle on cycle, did we live,
For the mute myriads would not take nor give.
Heat, light, the tidal wave that round me rolled
Came from these two. Far from me—haughty, cold—
The rest were ever. Through great gulfs of space

We three kept close together.　By degrees,
Conning intent, like one on bended knees,
The brightest wanderer in the mazy race,
Slowly I saw it in my sister's face
Lit by our Sun—I cried, like a crazed boy,
'Venus!'　She whispered, 'Jupiter and Mars
And jewelled Saturn are not with the stars
But brothers—thine and mine.'　I ached with joy.

WINTER

Thou dark-robed man with solemn pace,
And mantle muffled round thy face,
Like the dim vision seen by Saul,
Upraised by spells from death's dark hall :
Thou sad, small man—face thin and old,
Teeth set, and nose pinched blue with cold :
Dark man, with old, snow-bearded face,
Who lov'st on plague-struck leaves to pace.
Ne'er mind !　Thy coat, so long and black,
And fitting round thee all so slack,
Has glorious spangles, and its stars
Are like a conqueror's fresh from wars,
Who wove it in time's awful loom
With woof of glory, warp of gloom !
Jove's planet glitters in thy breast,
The morning star adorns thy crest,
The waxing or the waning moon
Clings to thy turban late and soon ;
Orion's belt is thine—thy thigh
His jewelled sword hangs brightly by ;
The Pleiades seven, the gipsy's star,
Shine as thy shoulder-knots afar ;
And the great Dog-star, bright, unknown,
Blazes beside thee like a throne !
Take heart ! thy coat, so long and black,
Sore-worn, and fitting round thee slack,
Is broidered by the Northern lights,
Those silver arrows shot by sprites—
Is powdered by the Milky Way,
With awful pearls unknown to-day,
Which well make up for all the hues
Proud Summer, bridegroom like, may use.
Proud Summer, with his roses sheen
And dress of scarlet, blue, and green,
Floods us with such a sea of light
We miss the faint far isles of night,
And thoughtless dance, while he with lute
Beguiles us, or assists to fruit.

But, like a shade from spirit land,
Dim Winter beckons with his hand—
He beckons, all things darker grow,
Save white-churned waves and wreathing snow;
We pause, a chill creeps through our veins,
We dare not thank him for his pains,
We fear to follow, and we creep
To candle-light, to cards, to sleep.
Yet, when we follow him, how deep
The secret he has got to keep!
How wonderful, how passing grand!
For peering through his storms there stand
The eternal cities of the sky,
With stars for street-lamps hung on high—
No angel yet can sum their worth,
Though angels sang when they had birth.

Chambers's Journal.

JUNE

Come with bridal wreaths and song,
　Come with perfume and with tune,
Come with sunny days and long!
　Welcome, lovely June!

Who names thee names the queen of heaven
　June with eyes and wings of light,
Whose glittering arrow-beams have driven
　The pale stars out of sight.

Diana's moon seems thin and weak,
　Thy twilight makes her pale and worn;
As silent as a ghost, and meek,
　She flies thine early morn.

Three hours of twilight pass, and hark!
　The blackbird from the coppice sings,
And near Aurora's car the lark
　Spreads out his quivering wings.

And soon long shadows of the trees,
　And light upon the eastern hills,
And cattle lowing at their ease,
　And trouts a-leaping in the rills;

And odours from the flower-paved wood,
　And from the trees no longer dumb,
Foretell another day as good
　As any day that yet has come.

CHAPTER VII

BIOLOGY

Laughter—Dandies, Animal and Human—Right-handedness—
Left-handed Folk—Are Wild Animals Happy?—The Prairie
Dog—Sonnets on Animals—The Aviflora of Upper Nithsdale
—Bird-nesting—School Children Among the Hills—Glimpses
of Bird Life—The Pleasures of Field Botany—A Strange
Vegetable Parasite.

LAUGHTER

THE gulf separating man from the inferior animals is
pretty well marked in the matter of laughter. Not the
ghost of a titter can be extracted from any of the other
members of the animal creation, whereas all of us, and
our ancestors before us, have had our gusts of merriment
culminating in 'laughter holding both its sides.' Moreover, it is to be hoped that our diaphragms once set
a-going will in the future continue to respond to the jests
of humorists and comedians. Any excess of pleasant
feeling in a healthy child is readily relieved by laughter,
just as irritation is relieved by crying, and strange to say
in both cases there is often the accompaniment of tears.
Quick and violent motions, such as leaping, clapping of
hands, laughter or crying, express the inward joy of all
races, binding us together in one common brotherhood.
As an explosion of emotion our cachinnations have a far
wider range than our kisses. Dick Steele was mistaken
when he said of these, ' Nature was their author and they

began with the first courtship.' We have the authority of travellers and naturalists that these pleasant osculations are unknown to Fuegian lips. New Zealanders, Papuans, Tahitians, Australians, and Esquimaux, up to the latest notices of them, are also ignorant of the honeyed bliss; although, to be sure, many of these unfortunate races indulge in less satisfactory substitutes, such as rubbing noses, patting arms and stomach, blowing lustily on each other's faces, or clawing countenances with each other's hands.

Doubtless some nations are more saturnine, others more jovial. The Jews did not appear to throw themselves much in the way of jests, but to have been an 'as-sure-as-death' sort of people; so much so that Carlyle, who liked their earnestness, finds fault with their want of humour, which he avers contrasts unfavourably with the 'inextinguishable laughter' of the Homeric heroes. The historian Mommsen, on the other hand, notes the droll humour and love of practical jests displayed by the Celts subjugated by Cæsar. They were passionately fond of oratory, and one of their rules was to the effect that should any one interrupt a person speaking in public, a very visible hole should be cut, as a measure of police, in the coat of the disturber of the peace. In the far-off old unhappy times when Hesiod wrote, there seemed to be nothing laughable—man was born to labour and sorrow. In the *Iliad* life appears full of war, its causes and its consequences, but in the *Odyssey* the grey world becomes gay, and amusing situations abound. Old Herodotus must many a time have laughed in his sleeve at those Egyptian priests with their prolix serious stories, their mummified animal deities, and their endless statues and paintings without the variety of a single caricature. What a relief to the old Greek must have been the diverting story of clever rascality, the *Treasury of Rhamp-*

sinitus, a tale worthy of the *Arabian Nights*, but the solemn seers who told him no doubt were only winking like owls. It needs all the comedies of Aristophanes to put us into good humour after having digested the three awful Greek tragedians. The two first, Eschylus and Sophocles, are a little heavy, but no less divine. They affect our risible nerves as remotely as do Victor Hugo, Herbert Spencer, or Algernon Swinburne. Boccaccio is needed to qualify the awful Dante. Shakespeare could season himself. The sublime, pathetic, and ridiculous are 'warp and weft' in his dramas as in human life itself. The flippancy and grossness of the poets of the Restoration are a sad contrast to Milton. The moods of individuals seem only thrown upon larger canvas with the life of nations, which also oscillates 'from grave to gay, from lively to severe.'

What may be the age of a small specimen of humanity when its happiness clucks audibly in our ears is perhaps not yet definitely made out. During the first moons of its existence it is such a sleepy, pulpy, hungry little cherub that not much of its history is available. The beautiful Persian stanzas which inform us that we came into the world weeping, and hope that we shall leave it smiling, do not convey an accurate picture, since it has been observed that tears never trickle down the cheeks of childhood until three or four lunations have passed over them. With boys laughter is rather the outward manifestation of good health and enjoyment of life, than the result of abstract mental cognitions. The mental moods, of which laughter is the expression, are difficult to analyse. Hobbes hit upon one of them when he averred that laughter betokened a sudden exultation, arising from a sudden conception of some eminency in ourselves, compared with the inferiority of others, or our own former inferiority. The unexpected mental image or event which brings down the proud a peg, or allows freedom from the restraints imposed upon us by the austere, is sure of a hilarious welcome, provided the degradation be not too severe, otherwise our feelings of compassion are awakened. Don Quixote and Pickwick were each of grave and decorous habits; so, when they trip on their staid and solemn march, we giggle more readily than at a merry Andrew's fall. When Pickwick shows less technical skill than a schoolboy at his first slide on the ice, we seem to grow greater as the wise man grows less. The vicar running after his hat in a breeze is amusing in proportion as he is stern and pompous. The man trotting to catch a train is ludicrous in accordance with his dress and social position. But degradation of dignity, to yield pleasure, must be within limits. Many incidents are on the borderland between the grand and the ridiculous. From the one to the other is but a step.

Lord Byron declares that if he laughed at any mortal thing 'twas that he might not weep; and in the course of his long narrative, the historian Gibbon once or twice pauses, not knowing whether he should laugh or weep over illusions which once roused a world to arms.

From of old the Muse of Comedy has had her preferences for which she is careless to give reasons. Why, while so many of our features should be flattered by the poets, our indispensable noses and thumbs should be held in ridicule, is not easy to make out. George Eliot pokes fun at Bob Jakin's thumb, and Carlyle has made merry with Queen Elizabeth's nose, when her tire-woman rouged it along with her cheeks, after she had given over looking at her wrinkles in any mirror. Shakespeare, who sings of eyes like the break of day, 'lights that do mislead the morn,' is no flatterer of noses, but notes when they are 'red and raw,' or otherwise out of sorts. As with features, so with professions. The Scotch, who boast

of their schoolmasters making them what they are, are
never done jesting at them as 'dominies,' and one of
those unfortunates, Dominie Sampson, brings down the
gallery in Scott's *Guy Mannering*; while another has been
rendered immortally ludicrous on the canvas of Wilkie.
In England, tailors could hardly gain the franchise even
with one man one vote. With the heavenly bodies
themselves, folklore picks out the moon for a farce,
but the stars and sun are never spoken of with levity
—no comical cow ever daring to leap over them. The
horse is poetical and sublime, but the ass is as a chimney-
sweeper or street scavenger. A sirloin of beef is noble,
but a potato, mean, wrinkled and ragged.

Fossilised laughter is not always cheerful; yet extremely comical faces, and more especially marks, still
reward the explorers of classical realms, either in bronze
or bas-relief, often, like a ray of light, brightening up
the sombre halls and quiet galleries of our museums.
The words 'ludicrous,' 'comedy,' and 'mimicry,' are from
classic sources. 'Fun' is not the least welcome of Irish
imports, nor is 'merry' a Teutonic word, but comes to us
from the Gaelic. Buffoons, strange to say, were frequently
employed at funerals of the great, at which they danced
grotesque dances, their heads decorated with the fool's
cap, as witness the figure on a sepulchral lamp from a
tomb in the Villa Corsini.

DANDIES—ANIMAL AND HUMAN

The love of ornament is no merely æsthetic faculty,
confined to artists and amateurs in civilised society. As we
descend in the scale and obtain glimpses of man in poor,
ignorant, rustic communities, or in the savage state, we
find him passionately fond of his simple melodies, dances,
and strongly pronounced pigments. In this respect the

simple peasant, or the still simpler savage, is like the child, showing fondness for toys, beads, and everything that glitters brilliantly. A pregnant passage, bearing on this subject, is to be found in *Sartor Resartus.* The miserable condition of the naked savages, our ancestors, is graphically depicted by Carlyle. They are represented as having no covering save their fleece of shaggy hair, and possessing implements of the rudest type. 'Nevertheless,' says the writer, 'the pains of hunger and revenge once satisfied, man's next care was not comfort but decoration. Warmth he found in the toils of the chase, or amid dried leaves, in his hollow tree, in his bark shed, or natural grotto ; but for decoration he must have clothes. Nay, among wild people we find tattooing and painting prior to clothes. The first spiritual (ethical) want of a barbarous man is decoration, as indeed we still see among barbarous classes in civilised societies.'

Recent observations have very much added to the force of the above remarks. The men who etched the extinct mammoth on its own tusk, or sculptured the reindeer on its own horn, or in the caves of the Pyrennees drew outlines of their own shaggy selves on the teeth of the cave-bear, are among the earliest of whom we have traces. The ornaments which have been found in American mounds consist of gorgets, bracelets, necklaces, pendants, plates of mica, shells and beads. A good account of these mounds and of savage ornaments generally will be found in Lubbock's works. The number of beads in the mounds is astonishing, and various materials, shell, bone, teeth, have been employed in their construction. In the mounds of Ohio are smoking pipes, highly ornamented. Several of them have been found with spirited representations of the manatee, a sea-mammal, not now found nearer than a thousand miles southward. These ornaments have been found in situations indicating their great antiquity.

In the New Stone Period and in the Bronze Period decoration advanced apace. Modern savages, and the lower classes in civilised societies, put a high value on ornament. A child's lozenge, and a child's wooden horse, are nothing if not painted. Tattooing is one of the most universal and venerable of all fine arts. No barbarous nation can do well without it, and it is in vogue with sailors both in France and England. The New Caledonians are fond of dress, which, in the case of the man, is purely decorative. A dandy wears a bright red flower stuck behind his ear, as did the dandies of Queen Elizabeth's time, but then he wears scarcely anything else. The skirts of the women are scanty, but there is plenty of tattooing. Westward of the River Mackenzie the natives have a peculiar cheek-stud. It consists of a stone ornament inserted in holes made in the cheeks. The Dyaks, on the other hand, affect teeth studs. They pierce their front teeth, driving into each hole a round brass-headed pin which glitters like gold every time they grin or raise the upper lip. Sometimes in tattooing the women are the artists, their tools being a branch of thorn and a small mallet. The Fijian modes of dressing the hair are most painstaking and elaborate, and give their heads an appearance not unlike the odd arrangement and development of hair on *Semnopithecus rubicundus* and *S. comatus*, and of the monkeys of the species *Cebus* and *Ateles*. The precious metals and stones owe no small part of their attraction to the fact that they glitter. In Peru, when discovered by the Spaniards, gold was employed not as a coin but as an ornament. Recruiting sergeants know how much easier it is to induce enlistment when the uniform is showy, rather than dull grey. Printing-masters in Glasgow and Manchester know how to get up patterns, whether they be dresses, handkerchiefs, shirts, or turbans, for the foreign market, or mufflers and handkerchiefs for

Wales, Ireland, or the lower classes of the large towns.
These patterns are showy almost in inverse proportion to
the culture of the classes for which they are intended.

Popular ballads represent the dandy soldier, with his
captivating plumes and tinsel ; and popular songs never
forget the rosy cheeks, the ruby lips, the teeth of pearl,
the diamond eyes, the golden or raven locks of those whose
praises they celebrate.

In that neglected class of mankind, denominated ' half-
witted,' who, like the lower animals, are more guided by
their instincts and impulses than by reason, we frequently
find the strong taste or passion for what is odd and gaudy.
Let the reader compare the descriptions of dress of
Madge Wildfire and of Barnaby Rudge, by Scott and
Dickens, or remember the flower-crowned Ophelia of
Shakespeare. Dickens' description of Barnaby Rudge
looks not unlike the description of some broken-down
Indian chief—' His dress was green, clumsily trimmed
here and there with gaudy lace. A pair of tawdry ruffles
dangled at his wrist, while his throat was nearly bare.
He had ornamented his hat with a cluster of peacock's
feathers. Girt to his side was the steel hilt of an old
sword without blade or scabbard ; and some parti-coloured
ends of ribbons and poor glass toys completed the orna-
mental portion of his attire.' It will be recollected of
Shakespeare's crazed Lear :

> ' Alack ! 'tis he ; why, he was met even now
> As mad as the vexed sea ; singing aloud ;
> Crowned with rank fumiter and furrow weeds,
> With harlocks, hemlocks, nettles, cuckoo-flowers.'

In these cases in which man reverts animalwards, he
reminds us of the savages' delight in colours and in painting their skin black, white, red, yellow; or of cutting,
as the inhabitants of Tanna do, pictures of plants, flowers,
and stars upon their chest and arms. The great men of

Guinea have their skin cut into imitation of flowers; and in the Deccan, the women, notwithstanding the great pain of the operation, cook their foreheads, arms, and breasts, into elevated scars painted in colours to resemble flowers. Nose, ears, fingers, wrists, ankles, legs, and body are alike honoured by the savage dandy, and his materials are as varied as the contents of a magpie's museum.   Teeth of quadrupeds, bones of fish or fowl, shells, glass, ivory, leather, seeds of plants, or bits of wood or bark, are all forced into service, or thankfully received.   Plumes of gay feathers, wing-cases of beetles, glowworms and fire-flies mingling with their hair, enhance the beauty of braves and their fair ones for the revels of the season.   Even in Europe amongst the hills and valleys of Germany, Spain, Switzerland, and Italy, many costumes approach the savage ideal.   In the Black Forest the marriage head-dress of a St George maiden sparkles with gaudy glass beads; there are hats resembling the headgear of Welsh women, and hats studded with bright-coloured balls of worsted.   Nothing can be gayer than the dresses of the 'bandilleros,' and others composing the procession at the Madrid bull-fights on Sundays.   Savages take great pains to decorate their destructive weapons and other imple-ments, and semi-civilised nations make beautiful toys, as the Burmese, whose puppets for their puppet-shows are elegantly carved.   The darts or 'bandilleras' used at the Spanish bull-fights are as highly ornamented as many a jockey's whip or shepherd's crook among ourselves.

It is strange that in order to obtain any direct evidence of other beings than man having a taste for ornament, we must pass over the order *Mammalia* in favour of that of *Aves*.   The bower birds of Australia are the most re-markable for their appreciation of the beautiful, so much so that the account of their bowers when first related was received with distrust.   There are several species, each exhibiting peculiar habits and characteristic architecture. The bowers are quite distinct from their nests, and are built, as assembly halls, wholly for the purpose of courting. Here they race about, performing strange antics—for dandies, whether they be human or animal, are all fond of dancing. But the most extraordinary thing is their taste for decorating these bowers with prettily striated shells, parroquet feathers, bones, leaves, beads, or any gay glittering objects. They will at times pick up a gay feather, or large leaf, set all their feathers erect, run round the bower, opening first one wing and then another, uttering a low whistling note. The great bower bird is described as amusing itself flying backwards and forwards, and taking a shell alternately from each side. In some of the larger bowers, which had evidently been resorted to for years, Gould says that he has seen nearly a bushel of bones, shells, and small pebbles. The building and decorating of these bowers must have cost much trouble, and are certainly wonderful specimens of bird-architecture.

The hammerkop of South Africa has been described by Layard. It is exceedingly active about dusk, and is a strange uncanny kind of bird. These birds collect curiosities and arrange them about their nests. Bits of brass, buttons of bone, bits of crockery, and bleached bones are gathered to their brooding-places. If a resident had lost his knife or tinder-box on the farm, or within some miles of the place, he made a point of examining the brooding-places or nests of the hammerkop, and frequently with success. At times, when two or three are feeding at the same pool, they will execute a singular dance, skipping round one another, opening or closing their wings, and performing strange antics. Evidently they belong to the dandy family, and have much in common with bower-birds.

Gould informs us how certain humming-birds adorn their nests on the outside with the utmost taste; how they instinctively fasten thereupon beautiful pieces of flat lichen, the larger pieces in the middle; while, now and then, they intertwine a pretty feather, the stem being so placed that the feather stands out beyond the surface.

While reading such accounts as these by credible narrators, one cannot forget the little rag and broken-crockery houses, ornamented with coloured fruit, shells, and pebbles, which children in rural districts improvise at their leisure.

But the passion for odd and glittering articles is not confined to birds belonging to foreign climes. The magpies' museums have already been alluded to.

Light has a fascination for some birds, similar to the cry of their mates; and so, by small revolving mirrors, larks are caught in the rural districts of France. Well authenticated anecdotes of exhibitions of pugnacity or courtesy in the presence of mirrors, or even of well-executed pictures of themselves, have been adduced. To keep a looking-glass in a dovecot is sure to attract pigeons; and these are more at home with a beautiful white-painted cot than with a dingy one. Peacocks display themselves all the more readily in presence of glass doors and windows that reflect their image; and one has been caught admiring himself reflected in a smooth granite tombstone. So vain are these birds that any pair of eyes coming into the court, let them be a dog's, is enough to produce a display, and we have caught one strutting before a half-dozing cat. Pet canaries and larks have displayed aristocratic tastes, and shown more attention, by antics and songs, to well-dressed than to dull and dirtily-clad individuals. In the Ionian Islands, as Darwin mentions, the ruff, even while the sportsman is firing at it, cannot withstand the seduction of a bright-coloured handkerchief dropped on

the ground, but will dart down to it at the risk of its life.
It is a long road that divides ants from birds, both in
organisation and habits, yet, strange to say, with these
comparatively diminutive, but highly-gifted insects, there
is recorded an instance of a feeling for beauty, for in
Idaho, the mounds of the red or agricultural ant are made
of gravel, and are usually about two to three feet in
diameter at the base, and one foot high. 'Frequently,'
says an observer, 'they are ornamented with bits of
crockery, beads, or pins, as opportunity may offer.'

It is singular that animal and human dandies display
their charms most eagerly and to greatest advantage at
the period of courting. We need not dilate on the
splendour of the male birds at the breeding season; how,
like savage braves, they are ornamented around the head,
and painted on the cheek, neck, and eyes. And as no
wedding in the country is complete without music and
dancing; so our late great naturalist [Darwin] has been
at pains to collect a volume of facts, bearing upon the
vocal and instrumental music of animals, their wedding
dresses, courting dances, and eagerness to display their
charms. It is also a curious coincidence, that, like our
own crowns and coronation robes, ear-jewels, breast-knots,
and shoulder-knots, the brilliance which attracts in the
feathered creation is not hidden away on the underpart of
wings which are never raised, but is either exposed to view,
or, if it is normally concealed, there are muscles which,
at the suitable hour, expand tail coverts, or erect shining
crests. One bird, the 'Caracara,' has the power of
changing the colour of the bare face, at will, from purple
to yellow, and from yellow to red. It is not in the
plenitude of summer and autumn, when woods are in all
their foliage, so as to conceal, and when the means of
subsistence is at hand, but in the hungry season of spring
and early summer, when fruit and insects are scarcely to

R

be had, that the bird dandies of the extra-tropical zone trip
upon the scene, like conspicuous marks for their enemies
to strike at. The long feathers of some of them are often
cumbersome for fight or flight; and the vocal and instrumental music which gladdens fields and groves, uttered
by throat or wings, betrays the haunts of others. There
is some slight analogy between savages and animals even
here, for the braves or males are, as a rule, more
elaborately tattooed than the females, and there are those,
as among the Esquimaux, who appropriate the lion's share
of the ornaments to themselves and let the squaws go
plain.

Everybody knows that Darwin contended that these
ornaments were useful to their animal possessors. But
being acquired and maintained at such cost and risk
to the possessor, they were, he argued, of utility to
him as a sexual attraction, just as some naturalists
maintain the gift of song is of use in securing
mates. Deny this, he says, and it seems as if all the
assiduous display of the males before the females is
unaccountable. Few naturalists have dared to follow our
gifted countryman into this new field. The consideration
of the whole subject is beset with difficulties. Many
problems in connection with the colour of animals seem to
yield to the doctrines of protective resemblance and
protective mimicry. Again, gaudy colours, in insects and
in their caterpillars, among which last it is impossible to
conceive of sexual selection playing a part while the
animals are still a-sexual, have been explained as giving
warning of how nasty to taste, or fatal to touch, the
animal is. Nevertheless, especially with birds, there may
be a residuum of truth in the sexual selection theory.

The eloquent descriptions of the grand displays made
by the peacocks and birds of paradise in their native
woods on a shining morning to their mates, the waltzing

of the cock of the rock, *Rupicola crocea*, the famous partridge-dances, described by North American hunters, the 'baby' or love-dances and love-song of the black-cocks would, under Darwin's theory, have, at least, more meaning. Indeed, it is impossible to read that naturalist's description of the different ways in which the golden pheasant and polyplectron display their charms, as compared with the peacock, and yet in the very difference of manner exhibiting to their gratified females in the best possible fashion their peculiar adornments, without being strongly impressed with his arguments in favour of his contention.

In the spring, our poet-laureate informs us, a brighter iris glows upon the dove, and in the spring youth goes a-wooing. Dr Kulischer has collected more fully than had before been done, evidence of primitive courting dances among our early ancestors in the seasons of spring and autumn, the one being the season of returning warmth, the other of returning plenty. These dances becoming more decorous with advancing culture, exist now sporadically as curious relics. The Ascension Day Festival in Gotha is still marked by the dance under the linden tree, symbolising the union of the peasant couple. Girls and boys in Old England were wont to dance round the midsummer bonfire, and it was considered lucky to wear new clothes on Easter and on Whitsunday.

Lastly, in order to knit closer the analogy between our human and animal dandies, we will call in the evidence of the physiologist. The physiologist has a story to tell about eyes, which bears pretty closely on this question. The yellow spot, which is the most favourable portion of the eye for the perception of colour, is the spot in which we find cones very closely packed, and very long. 'A little beyond the macula or yellow spot, the rods, or elements which give us the sensation of light, irrespective of colour, make their appearance, and soon gain in numbers until they exceed the cones in the proportion of three to one. As the cones become fewer and shorter the colour sense gets poorer; until at the region where we are totally blind, we find that the cones have altogether lost their outer limbs and are otherwise degenerated.' Alfred Russell Wallace, in reviewing Grant Allen's book on *The Colour Sense,* admits that there is good reason for believing the sense of colour in birds is more acute than in man. Among mammals the yellow spot exists in man and monkeys only. Your average monkey has not the cut of a dandy, nevertheless many of them in captivity have been amused with glittering objects and appeared vain of gaudy apparel; while, in a state of Nature, some of them have on their naked skin bright blue and scarlet patches, which in fine weather they are anxious to display. Their curious Fijian-looking head-dresses we have already alluded to. In birds the cones of the retina, or colour organs, are three times as numerous as the rods, while in mammals they are less numerous. Nocturnal birds have few cones—which is just what we would expect—while nocturnal mammals have none.

Whatever may be the meaning of gay colours with animals, we know that Nature is thrifty rather than prodigal. It is only lately that the use of the colour of flowers has been scientifically demonstrated. The colour of fruit is partly explicable and partly awaits explanation. The colours of animals have not yet been so satisfactorily explained as the colour of fruit. Most animals are lighter coloured beneath, and darker coloured on the back and sides, and it has been suggested that white, being a bad conductor of heat, suits better in cold latitudes and seasons those animals that have the habit of lying down on the cold snow or frozen earth, either for sleep or rest. It has been asked, why, if sexual selection

be a *vera causa* of gay colours, are not birds of prey the
most radiant, seeing that these warriors could sport
brilliant hues with less likelihood of being marked out by
them and attacked by enemies. It has been answered,
that as among our police, we have detectives in plain
clothes, so sober colours may be an advantage for
taking prey by surprise. Not only slow-moving, defence-
less caterpillars are green like the leaves among which
they feed, but the tyrant spiders are sometimes green;
so that protective resemblance protects alike the tyrant
and the feeble.

In populous countries large game, bright-coloured
birds, and showy flowers on the wayside have a tendency
to disappear; and one regrets to think of the future, in
which fertile New Guinea will be an Australian Colony,*
and all its birds of paradise will be extirpated. On the
other hand we have, within historical time, at least
one instance of a new domesticated animal, and that
the ostrich, whose beautiful plumes bid fair to insure
the continuance of the species. It is scarcely possible,
from geological evidence, to make out whether beauty
got gradually built up since the first introduction
of mammals and birds. Hues are evanescent. By a
wonderful chance we know that the Siberian elephant
was red. Prof. Duncan has called attention to the large
fossil representative of the armadillo, whose gigantic tail
was of great beauty; but which, like the patches of colour
on the bodies of some of our monkeys, could not possibly
be admired by the eyes of the animal owning it. He concludes that the male glyptodons displayed themselves
after the manner of monkeys and crested birds, to be
admired by other eyes than their own. The great law of
the association of ideas whereby frugivorous and nectar-
seeking birds might be expected to admire in their mates

* The first part of this prophecy is not now likely to be realised.

the colours associated with their repasts has not yet been sufficiently discussed. But to understand a bird's acquired taste in this respect, we would require to know more of its history and the habits of its ancestors. In New Zealand, within the last half-century, a frugivorous parrot, *Nestor notabilis*, has become a carnivorous pest, preying on the sheep of the colonists. The law of the association of ideas would in this case, without the previous history of the bird being known, be inapplicable. Many of the difficulties presented to a student of Nature in the appearance of the external world still await solution at the hands of the observer and the patient experimenter. A new generation will discourse more learnedly on 'Dandies —Animal and Human.'

RIGHT-HANDEDNESS

Although at first sight, the four-handed mammals might appear to have a superior organisation to man, yet, because locomotion and prehension have both to be accomplished by the limbs of the former, whereas in man there is a division of labour with his limbs, the upper pair being almost entirely prehensile, the result is that man's two hands are worth more than the ape's four. In extreme youth there is little appreciable difference between the functions of the hands and feet, which alike shove and twist awkwardly in the nurse's arms. At a later period both hands and feet assist in locomotion. Nor is it until a child has acquired the power of language that the difference between the right hand and the left becomes discernible. This difference does not quite come of itself, like the difference of voice, or like the beard announcing puberty, but it is guided into distinctness by precept and example. Around the youthful pupil stand parents, nurse, and preceptor, all anxious that he should leave off the use of the 'wrong hand,' either in labour, or as a matter of courtesy. So persistent

and universal is this education that some authorities have
deemed the difference between right and left hand wholly
an affair of fashion ; and that if both hands were educated
alike it would be a great gain, since in case of any
casualty depriving a man of the use of the highly-
favoured limb, the tedious operation of educating the
left hand to do the right hand's work would be avoided.

Nevertheless, if right-handedness be a fashion, it is all
but universal, and the most ancient fashion we know of.
The history of writing, the evidence of language, and the
drawings and tools, not only of Egyptians, Assyrians,
Greeks, and Romans, but of races the memory of whose
existence had passed away ere the earliest extant
records had been penned, and whose rude tools, and
weapons, and artistic representations have been disinterred from caves, kitchen-middens, and crannogs, give
us early evidence of right-handedness. These drawings represent faces in profile, looking towards the
left, just as a street Arab, unless he be left-handed,
chalks them on any unoccupied surface. Such is a
sketch of the mammoth, on a piece of ivory, found in the
rock-shelter at La Madeleine, in the Dordogne. So, also,
'is the reindeer etched with great spirit and skill on bones
procured from a cave near Bruniquel. Another drawing—
in which an eel, two horses' heads, and what Dr E. B.
Tylor has pronounced as possibly the earliest known portrait
of man, are depicted—represents the implement held in the
right hand. Sir Daniel Wilson has given three engravings
of bronze sickles from the Lake of Brienne, all constructed
for right-handed men of the Bronze Period. One such
handle, found in 1872, was the first example of a complete
hafted instrument ; and, as Wilson remarks, it is carefully
fashioned, so as to adapt it to the grasp of a very small
hand, and as incapable of use by a left-handed shearer as
a mower's scythe.—*The Right Hand and Left-handedness.*

In drawing or copying a print, especially if the ornament be of a small and repeating character, we begin at the top of our sheet or tablet on the left-hand side. The reason for so doing is that our hand may not rub upon what is already finished but not quite dry. This reason seems to have determined the method of writing, which is from left to right. Nevertheless, the most ancient Egyptian writing is like that of a left-handed race, and proceeded from right to left. The figures of men and animals in their hieroglyphics do not shed light on the problem of which was the favourite hand ; but their ancient drawings and sculptures are evidence of right-hand superiority. The universality of the preference given to the right hand is as striking as its antiquity. It was wont to be believed that kissing was a sign of affection known all the world over ; but our anthropologists have rudely dissipated this pleasant dream, by showing that there are races so benighted as never to have heard of it. Not so with right-handedness. The Esquimaux, American Indians, Maoris, Negroes, and natives of the Oceanic Isles place the sword, staff, or whip in the right hand ; the shield or reins in the left. The arrow is guided to its mark, the assegai thrown at the enemy, the boomerang aimed at the bird, by the same hand, as a rule, in whatever regions these missiles are employed.

All languages lift up their testimony in favour of the antiquity and universality of right hand preference. Our words 'sinister' and 'dexterous' are from the Latin for left and right, and our Anglo-Saxon word 'left,' expresses, according to Trench, the little-used hand, being left out of work so frequently compared to its neighbour. *Gauche*, the French word for 'left,' is, says Brachet, 'literally the weak hand which has not the qualities of strength, agility, address, compared to the other. Strange as this may seem,' he continues, 'it is confirmed by the existence of analogous metaphors in other languages. Thus in Italian the left hand is *stanca*, the fatigued; or *manca*, the defective. Modern Provençal calls it *man seneco*, the decrepit hand.' The exceptions to the honour given to the right hand are few, and some of them such as seem to strengthen the rule. Lucky omens were seen to the right of the Roman armies; but, inasmuch as these omens would be considered unlucky from the barbarian's point of view, there might grow up a prejudice against right hand initiative among the latter. In the Hallowe'en superstitions of the Scottish peasantry, luck was secured by dipping the left arm or looking over the left shoulder. With the Chinese the place of honour is towards the left.

As man rises from a state of barbarism to that of civilisation, the education of the right hand becomes more urgent. A hunter of wild beasts, or a cattle-drover losing a right arm, would not sustain so serious a misfortune as if the same loss occurred to an engraver or clerk in modern times. We can easily imagine that the transfer of a spear or stick to the other hand would be less irksome than the many trials to write well with the left. As men began to unite in bodies, requiring simultaneous combined movements, the pre-historic drill-sergeants would not be slow to discover the advantage of troops covering the heart with the shield by the hand that lay nearest it, and having the sword hand free throughout the whole line, ready for offence. As tools became more numerous, varied, and complex, it would be a matter of importance to make them to suit one hand rather than the other, and so now we find that a left-handed man is handicapped, since many of our most useful tools, etc., the screw, the gimlet, scissors, carpenter's benches, printcutters' gauges, and even that latest novelty, the 'moustache cup,' are all made for a world of right-handed men. This tendency to specialisation may be seen in clothes, the buttons being placed on one side, the loopholes on another. In the struggle for supremacy, left-handed persons are, amongst us, like foreigners speaking no other language but their own, and from their want of fitness are apt to fall behind. The duty of giving preference to the right hand seems more imperiously enjoined in families whose education and social position are most advanced, and it has been remarked that the number of ambidexter or left-handed individuals is proportionally larger as we descend the scale, being greatest in such localities as the Fiji Islands and places remote from civilisation.

Is all such anxiety to educate the right hand exclusively not somewhat misdirected? Would it not be an advantage to have each hand equally deft? There appears to be no inherent deficiency in the left hand of the violinist, or of the charioteer, for the hand that regulates the delicate chords of the violin or the reins of the spirited steed takes upon itself more responsibility than the one which guides the bow or the whip. Eminent painters, surgeons, musicians, athletes, have been enumerated who were either left-handed or ambidexter. Why should not hands be trained like eyes, giving a free field and no favour to either? Then should the king meet with accident, there would be a prince equally accomplished to take his place. Perhaps it is too late to expect for this question the answer which one, prepossessed in favour of an ambidextrous education, would desire. The antiquity and universality of the preference are enough to cause suspicion that it has now got into the blood, and is not likely to be easily eradicated.

Various theories have been set forward to account for this peculiarity of the sons of Adam. Aristotle seems to have been the first to display philosophical curiosity on the subject. He tells us that there is a right and a left in animals, which different sides must be determined, not by position, but by function. He goes on, in his own way, to give a reason for right hand predominance, and why it is that burdens should be carried on the left shoulder. In a memoir, published by Professor Buchanan of Glasgow, the preference of the right hand, as well as the equally old and prevalent custom, attested by the most ancient monuments, of carrying burdens on the left shoulder, was alleged to be due to the want of symmetry in the human body. The centre of gravity, it was argued, was not in the medial line, but inclined towards the right, the right lung being larger than the left; and the liver, the heaviest of the internal organs, occupying a place towards the right. Owing to this cause a mechanical reason was given for the right arm acting with greater power; while it was argued that in carrying a burden on the left shoulder, the porter stooped forward towards the right, thus bringing the weight to be upheld more directly above the stronger right limb. The weakest part of the argument was that which required transposition of the viscera to account for left-handedness.

Transposition of the viscera is extremely rare, but left-handedness is a phenomenon with which everybody is acquainted; it is accompanied by the same larger size in the left limbs that exists normally in the right, and can be shown to run in families. Indeed, in at least one case of transposition of the viscera the subject was right-handed. Anatomists, who have made additional observations, confirm Dr Buchanan's remarks on the relatively greater weight of the right side in adults, and consequently of the position of the centre of gravity being towards that side, although pointing out that in children and quadrupeds the body is more symmetrical.

Another theory is founded on the fact of the brain being composed of two hemispheres, which work the muscles crosswise, so that disease or weakness of a hemisphere affects the whole opposite side of the body. Gratiolet had observed that the right side was worked with more nervous energy, since, even at an early date, the anterior and middle lobes of the brain in the left side were more largely developed; and the late M. Paul Broca records that in forty brains which he had examined, he found the left frontal lobe heavier than the right. Further independent observations are needed to confirm the theory of right-handedness depending on the greater energy supplied to the right side by the larger left hemisphere.

Nature, when there is a purpose to serve, is nowise loth to depart from symmetrical form. This may be observed in our Crustaceans, especially the hermit crab of our coasts, which has one set of limbs, notably those in front, which protrude from the shell longer than the set on the other side. The tusks of the narwhal are very unequally developed. In serpents the lung most developed is the right. In birds the aborted ovary and oviduct are the right. The sole's eyes are twisted to the right, the turbot's to the left. Parrots perch, for most part, on the right leg. Training induces preference, as in the case of the dog which 'gives paw' with the limb so trained, and the horse which leads with the right foot in a canter. The African elephant uses one of its tusks more frequently than the other for digging roots, etc. This tusk, from being often broken, is called the 'servant' by the ivory traders, and is of less value. It is most frequently the right. In the two eyes of many persons the focus is different, the right eye being the one generally, it is thought, with stronger vision. The curious circumstance of travellers, bewildered on a prairie, or amid mists, and striking their own footmarks after completing a circle, has been referred to the agility and strength of the right limb unconsciously pulling on slightly in advance.

But this belongs to the pleasant guesses that attend every theory not sufficiently submitted to the ordeal of experiment, and need not be too seriously considered in the question under discussion.—*Science for All.*

LEFT-HANDED FOLK

Why anybody should be left-handed is one of those matters in which the question is easier put than answered. The reason why we are right-handed has been met by statements and theories more or less plausible. In the first place, it has been shown that the human body is not symmetrical. It has also been pointed out that the left hemisphere of the brain is larger and better supplied with blood-vessels than the right, and that it is the left hemisphere of the brain which, working crosswise, controls the muscles of the right arm and hand. Then there is the sword-and-shield theory. True, against these is the wet-nurse theory, which supposes left-handedness to be favoured in youth by the fact of the infant being carried most frequently on the left arm, thus giving more scope to the early use of the child's left hand. Fashion, however, is always alert, and to this imperial mistress even our limbs must submit. Fashion incessantly demands that the right hand should have the preference. So that, with all these weighty reasons why we should be right-handed, it is marvellous why left-handed people should be found at all. Yet such are by no means uncommon. The teacher of an elementary school who watched the proportion for many years, gave it as his experience, that, in the rural district in which his school was situated, more than five per cent. of the children were left-handed. In these cases the tendency could be shown to be hereditary; and the left hand, even to the size of the thumb nails, showed itself larger than the

right.   It was painful to see the attempts made by the
left-handed pupils to write and cipher normally ; and,
after the right hand had been forced into service, the
result was a compromise, the writer generally developing
a handwriting inclined neither to right nor left.   In the
making of figures, both the 3 and the 6 were for a time
reversed, and 8 in some cases formed by drawing the
straight line down and curving the other from below.

Here are some additional illustrations of how incon-
venient a world this is for the left-handed. Purchase a
scarf, and the left-handed owner finds the slit, through
which the part requires to be pushed to catch the pin, on
the wrong side for him.   Let him sit down to dinner, and
the waiter brings the dishes, from which he selects a part,
to the wrong shoulder.   Let him attempt to mow, and he
fain would reverse the shape of the scythe.   Let him
learn drill or dancing, or endeavour to work in harmonious
combination, and his awkwardness is for ever brought
home to him.

It would appear that as life becomes more and more
complex, we are becoming more and more specialised, and
the difference between our limbs is encouraged, rather
than hindered, by every pair of scissors turned off at
Sheffield, by every screw made at Birmingham, and by
every slap administered to the young offending fingers
that would dare to shake hands incorrectly.

It is curious to notice the vagaries of humanity in cases
where no hard and fast line has been already drawn.
Although most right-handed persons put on their coats
left arm first, a considerable percentage thrust in the
right first.   Soldiers fire from the right shoulder, but
sportsmen are found who prefer the left.*   In working

---

* This is, in some cases at least, when men, of whom I have
personally known a number, are unable to close the left eye and
keep the right open.

with the spade, a proportion of right-handed men grasp the spade with the left, and push with left foot and right hand; though, when using an axe, the same individuals would grasp farthest down with the right. The Persians mount their horses from the right or 'off' side, which is the different side from that mounted by Europeans.

The buttons on coats, etc., are placed on the right side, and the shed of the hair in boys to the left, evidently to suit manipulation by the right hand. The great philosopher Newton records that at first he confined his astronomical observations to his right eye, but afterwards he managed to train his left. But there are persons who could not do this owing to the unequal strength of their eyes. At Kunyenyé, in Africa, Cameron relates being introduced to the heir-presumptive to the throne, the nails of whose left hand had been allowed to grow to an enormous length as a sign of high rank, proving that he was never required to perform manual labour, and also providing him with the means of tearing the meat which formed his usual diet.

The falcon in Europe is carried on the left wrist, but in Asia on the right. As we have seen, the Latin races hold omens to be favourable when towards the right; but the Teutonic races, including our own, when towards the left. The Saxon races, as masters of the sea and pioneers in the laying of railways, have imposed their own rules of the left side on the French and other Latin races, who, however, still in driving and riding keep to the rule of the road derived from their progenitors.* The hands of

---

* The almost forgotten rhyme, by the great-grandfather (Reid) of the present writer, states the rule for meeting from the British point of view :

> 'The rule of the road is as plain as my hand,
>   To explain it I need not be long.
> If you keep to the left you are sure to be right,
>   If you keep to the right you are wrong.'

The reverse is the custom among Anglo-Saxons in America.

clocks and watches travel from east to west like the sun,
or as we draw a spiral from the interior outwards; and we
hand around our playing-cards and our hospitable bottle
after the same fashion, which like fashion we adhere to in
turning a horse, so that the violation of it, or the turning
'widdershins'—that is, against the sun—is considered unlucky.   It is a curious circumstance how few people ever
clasp hands otherwise than having the right thumb outwards, or coil thread save one way.

With regard to 'symmetricality,' Nature, when she has
a purpose to serve, is nowise loth to depart from it.
Indeed, there is hardly a symmetrical human face to be
found.   The right eye and ear are generally placed
higher, and the left leg is frequently the longer.   Aristotle declares that motion begins from the right.
'Wherefore the burden should rest on the part moved,
and not on the part moving, otherwise motion is more
difficult.'   He also looks on the spiral curves of shells
as suggesting a right-handed designer.   Another ancient
philosopher assures us that our dreams are least egotis-
tical and selfish when we are sleeping on our right side.

Curiosity was naturally highly strung when discoveries
were made of exceedingly ancient engravings and sculptures, fashioned by cave-men at an era further removed
from the earliest Egyptian records than ours is from those.
We have the authority of Sir Daniel Wilson, that the
earliest records of the human race show a preference for
the right hand, although not so completely as that shown
in modern times.   In the scarcely so remote Bronze Age,
the preference still holds good.   One has only to look
over Egyptian, Etruscan, Assyrian, Greek, or Roman
pictures, engravings, or sculptures, to see that man was
right-handed as he is now, and that he carried his burdens
then, as now, mainly on the left shoulder, while his dress
and decoration followed in the same lines as the soldier still

wears his sword, or the shepherd his plaid. At the same
time shoes made especially for each foot, and gloves de-
signed for each hand, have more of a modern aspect.
The sandals of ancient times are extremely alike. Among
the humble classes in Scotland, sixty years ago, shoes for
young people not made for right and left were preferred.

It is pleasant to be able to record that, notwithstanding
the sinister ridicule of ancient and modern language and
literature, and the antagonist pen and ink demonstrations
of doctors, there are, and have been, many eminent left-
handed individuals, both professional and gymnastic. A
list of these has been preserved to us through the labours
of Sir Daniel Wilson, and of Charles Reade, the novelist.—
Chambers's Journal, 21st January 1893.

ARE WILD ANIMALS HAPPY?

I read with interest the communication of your correspondent 'Ornis.' Kingsley's *Chirm of Birds* and Jules
Michelet's book on *The Bird* I look upon as poems not
to be too strictly criticised—splendid exaggerations, which
have, however, the good effect of enlisting our sympathies
in favour of animals, and making us kinder and more
considerate towards them. It being more than twenty
years since I read Kingsley in *Fraser*, I aimed more at
giving the spirit than the words of the essay, and now
when I think of it, it must have been the wood-lark, and
not the willow-wren, that sung so sadly in the prose poet's
ears. I, never having heard the wood-lark, and not being
acquainted sufficiently with the song of the willow-wren,
must refrain from expressing an opinion, although I
sympathise with Shelley in the *Skylark*:

> 'Teach me half the gladness
>   That thy brain must know,
> Such harmonious madness,' etc.

It is strange to me if something somewhat akin to ecstasy
be not in the breast of the little speck singing to Aurora,

S

or bidding melodious farewell to the evening star. 'Ornis'
separates humanity too deeply from the brute creation.*
The old theological idea, that man's suffering was due
to sin, never answered the far wider question—'Why
has the whole creation groaned and travailed together
in pain until now?' That sublime picture which Milton's
angel shows Adam of the lazar-houses and pests which
should cling to humanity by reason of the fall has diverted
attention from the living and fossil teeth, stings, poison-
bladders, claws, etc., which proclaim that suffering is
restricted to no species, no locality, and no time. It remained for a later science to show that 'fleas had little
fleas upon their backs to bite them, and little fleas had
lesser fleas, and so *ad infinitum.*' Young, of the Paisley
Museum, showed me lately some horrible little parasites
taken from the brains and tender parts of animals widely
separated in the scale. As for emotion, I have had a
welcome from my dog after a month's absence such as I
never had from a human being.† Has 'Ornis' never
heard of dogs dying on their master's grave? I could
tell him an anecdote of a canary dying because left alone
in the house and fed only occasionally by a stranger.
It was young enough and healthy enough, but company
seemed to be the life of it, at least it did not 'live by
bread alone.' As George J. Romanes says, 'The pining
of the "love bird" for its absent mate, and the keen
distress of a hen on losing her chickens, furnish abundant
evidence of vivid feelings. Even the stupid-looking
ostrich has heart enough to die for love, as was the case

---

* Service, as 'Ornis,' denied in the brute the human passion of love.
† The little, black, curly-tailed mongrel here referred to, was
near the end of its days left alone with a solitary housekeeper.
After restlessly pining for days for its absent master, it fell into a
state of patient and profound melancholy, from which it did not
recover even after his return, and seemed to take no further interest
in what were its earlier pleasures.

with a male in the Jardin des Plantes in Paris, who,
having lost his wife, pined rapidly away.' Indeed, the
whole discussion of the affection and sympathy of birds
in this author's *Animal Intelligence (International Scientific
Series)* will repay perusal. 'Ornis' might also read the
account of the Anthropoid apes in captivity by Hartmann,
in the same series. The account of Mafuca is extremely
interesting, and her death pathetic. 'Just before her
death from consumption, she put her arms around her
keeper's neck when he came to visit her, looked at him
placidly, kissed him three times, stretched out her hand
to him, and died.' I must be brief. Timidity is an
almost habitual state of wild animals, and timidity often
becomes terror, which is wretchedness. Wild animals
have no immunity from disease, lingering or galloping.
Witness Joseph Thomson's buffaloes in Africa. Witness
the seashore which I had to avoid, owing to the stench
of dead fishes cast on it in West Kilbride. My dog's
welcome of me was 'ecstasy'—at least the word fits
better than 'madness.' Of course, the higher the
organisation the wider the extremes of feelings :

> 'Chords which vibrate sweetest pleasure,
>   Thrill to deepest notes of woe.'

The beetle does not feel a giant's pangs, but with the
higher animals the brain and nervous system is marvellously like our own.—*Dumfries Courier and Herald.*

THE PRAIRIE DOG* AS A PET

About five years ago a couple of prairie dogs were
brought over to our rural parish in the south of Scotland
from Coleman County, on the basin of the River Colorado,
Western Texas. The surface of the prairie-lands in that
quarter, which is now being occupied extensively by sheep,

---

* The prairie dog is a ground squirrel (rodent) allied to the
European marmot, and gets its name from its sharp, barking cries.

is either nearly level or slightly undulating. In an extensive district, Santa Anna, the highest eminence only reaches two or three hundred feet in height. The region is fairly open country, here and there a short scrub. It is a flowery land in spring, after which the grass grows high ; and if drought set in, there is danger of its taking fire. The climate is so warm and salubrious that for a great part of the year the shepherds can sleep out of doors with impunity. In this region the prairie dog is very numerous, and it is little liked, for the holes it burrows often trip up the horseman at night. It is frequently to be seen sitting upright near its burrow, barking in its own way at the stranger. Then it bolts, tail quivering, headlong into its hole, turns itself, and peeps out as the wayfarer approaches, thus giving animation to an otherwise lonely region.

Our two prairie dogs were brought over to this country in boxes, and were far from being in good condition when delivered from the irksomeness of confinement. The house * into which they were received as lodgers is a humble dwelling of two small apartments, close to the church and churchyard, and occupies the middle of a small row or hamlet. Their appearance was a subject of great curiosity, being somewhat like that of a squirrel, and somewhat like that of a water-rat. They were not so large as a common rabbit; were pretty broad for their length, had short forelegs, small tails, no external ear, long claws, and soft, short hair, which was of a dull red colour, changing to grey. They were very playful with each other, and made excursions to the churchyard, the grass of which they seemed to enjoy, plucking it up with their forepaws, and then sitting eating with the greatest

* The house of William Brown, postman and elder, Tynron—one of the cottages to the left in Plate III, representing Tynronkirk and village.

avidity the least coloured portion of stem nearest the root. At the end of a year the older of the two died. He was supposed to be two months old when first caught. Our remarks now mainly concern the younger and stronger one, Yap, which is still alive and lively, being now at least six years old. [He died very soon after.]

The great trouble with them was to keep them from gnawing the mats, rugs, bed-hangings, and furniture of the kitchen in which they were located. For this purpose they required to be locked up at night. A strong box was procured, provided with a lid that could be closed down. A partition was made in the middle of the box with a hole in it, so as to give each an apartment. One side of the box was made of strong wire; and the wood of the other sides and of the lid was lined with perforated zinc. A motley quantity of rags was procured, and they were allowed to make their own beds. It was observed that the stronger of the two mainly occupied himself in arranging the patches within the box, while the other carried them from the floor. An empty tea-chest containing some newspapers was also placed at their service through the day. This was set in the dark under the bed. To this day, Yap objects to newspapers, which he turns out, much preferring the woollen rags. A singular fact in regard to the arrangement of the particoloured patches may be noted. In arranging them, the brighter colours are always turned to the surface, and the red rags are more exposed to view than those of other colours. It takes Yap a long time to make up his bed; but he does it neatly, keeping a hole in the middle, into which he plunges and covers himself well up. When tired, he goes to bed in the tea-chest for an hour or so throughout the day, but likes to get into his strong box near the fire at evening. If the lid be closed, he becomes restless, scrapes at it, stands on his hindlegs, and plucks at the clothes of his friends. His time to go to bed, even when the days are long, is very nearly about the time of Texan sunset, seven or eight o'clock.

Although West Texas is a sheep-country, the shepherds employ no dogs; they trust to stone and sling. When a sheep inclines to bolt from the main flock, they dexterously throw a stone right before, which causes the runaway to go back into the herd. The slinging is accompanied by shouting, and by-and-by the sheep understand the shout without the stone. This may account for the fact that Yap has never shown much timidity towards dogs. The dogs, on the other hand, generally bridle up, however loud and swift their assault, whenever they come near him, as if they noticed something uncanny. In Texas there are a few wolves, now getting very wary, and several rapacious birds, having far less fear of man than those in this country. Perhaps that is the reason why Yap is much more terrified at a rook than a dog, and runs quickly into the house if one or more alight in the tree opposite and begin to caw.

With regard to sounds, Yap is capricious, and can never endure that of a barrow passing, although no notice is taken of that of the church bell. His food is strictly vegetable and his diet light. Dry oatmeal, a bit of oatmeal cake, and oats, are his favourite food. He likes milk, but can never be induced to take porridge. He does not object to fruit, and is particularly fond of almonds. The average temperature of this country being so much lower than that of Texas causes him to be extremely anxious to creep near the kitchen fire, where he sits close to the cat, which he fondles, bestowing on her many gentle strokes with his little paws. When out of doors, he is particularly fond of the company of the little bantam hen. Of the two persons with whom he resides he prefers the mistress to her husband. Nevertheless, at night, the mistress having left for some time, he sat close to the feet of his male friend, and did not wish to go to bed until the master retired to his, as late as eleven o'clock; and, strange to say, when, after a few days' absence, the mistress arrived, it took her some time to regain his affections.

Although his ancestors never were domesticated, he seemed capable of a certain amount of training. One strange peculiarity of both dogs was that they lacked the sense of vertical distance. When they got on a table, chair, or window-sill, they stepped from them and fell as if unaware, hurting the face and nose. When they attempted to leap from two chairs a bit apart, they would also miscalculate, and fall between them. They soon got over this, and correctly judged the horizontal distance; but it was a long time before Yap could do the same from a height. Now, however, experience has taught him this also, and he can leap from box to chair, from chair to bed, and *vice versâ*, with the utmost precision. Perhaps the nearly level nature of their original habitat may have something to do with this blunt sense of vertical distance.

Yap has intelligence enough to notice any strange piece of furniture or utensil brought into the apartment, never being satisfied until he has smelled and examined it. Once when a new rug was put down before the fireplace to grace the ministerial annual visit, he sat down on it with great enjoyment. And when the old faded rug was again laid, resentment was shown, and he began to gnaw and tear it. The indomitable habit of gnawing stands in the way of any of his kind being made a household pet. Even the perforated zinc of his strong box gave way before his incisors, and he succeeded in making a hole through the lid. Here, also, he has learned by experience; and if caught in the act of gnawing any household article, instantly stops, lest a hard word or a cuff should be administered.

He expresses his affection mainly by pressing gently with his teeth the hand of one he loves. If a stranger lay hand on him firmly, he shows no resentment; but should he touch him in a timid, hesitating way, he is apt to give him a pinch. Yap, after his companion's death, grew much more timid about going out of doors, and never afterwards ventured as far as the churchyard in which the two used to play together.

During the last nine months Yap has fallen off considerably. He now weighs two pounds, is nine-and-a-half inches in girth, and from the snout to the tip of the tail fifteen inches long. Within the last three months he has developed a taste for meat, which he begs for, holding up his forepaws, and prefers cooked to raw. In this summer weather he gratifies his instinct, filling up holes with earth, and beating it in with his head as, in the wild state, his kind seal up rattlesnakes should they enter their funnel-like burrows.—*Chambers's Journal*, 25th July 1891.

SONNETS ON ANIMALS

I.—THE ASS

Thou art as old's the Nile—crimson and gold
Thy trappings were when kings thy back bestrode.
The self-sufficient prophet on thee rode;
Oracular wast thou,—he blind and bold,
When thy reproof like thunder through him rolled.
Pleased with a thistle and a bed of moss,
Humble and patient thou dost bear thy cross;
And yet the Saviour was himself thy load!
Sometimes a little stiff, yet come and thrash,
O ghost of Sancho! them that smash at thee.
When whisky makes him utter curses rash,
Why does my enemy cry 'ass' at me?
Wild beasts might shame us, soberer if not gladder;
Monkeys, the more like men they grow, turn sadder.*

* *Vide* Humboldt's Travels.

II.—THE MOLE

Come out from thy curved tunnels damp and dark,
Black sightless miner. Dost thou feed on roots?
' Neither on these nor any corn or fruits.
I feed, O man ! on grubs and insects—hark !
I'm a good drainer, therefore do not bark,
And set your traps for me—a ploughman, too,
I turn your soil up to the rain and dew.
And though not bound to do whate'er you suits,
I, with my front teeth, sometimes kill your mice.
You sleep—we do your work—I and the owl.
Flesh is my cry—I am not over nice,
But greedy as the very wolves that howl.
Those who kill friends with spades and traps may find
This query puzzling—who is the most blind?'

III.—THE HORSE

The noblest poem of the noblest book
Gets more inspired when thou becom'st its theme ;
In oldest Vedic hymns, too, men did deem
Thee nearest to a god.   Greek sculptors took
Thee for a model with thy peerless look.
Courage ! though lost—that chariot of the sun,
Cities still rush to see the Derby run.
Thou pull'st the sober plough in rustic nook.
With thee we break the bloody bristling square,
Thou, with thy rider, art a centaur named,
When savage eyes do first upon you stare,
Hengist and Horsa, by our histories famed,
Clothed themselves with thy names, and knew thy force :
And England once was offered for a horse.

IV.—THE HOG

Through the great virgin forests crashed thy sire,
With tusks that ripp'd the hunter on his horse,
When kings and nobles matched its furious force.
The boar's head ! how our fancy gets on fire
Picturing the iron knights of fierce desire—
Ladies and lords with foaming tankards deep,
All circling round thee in the feudal keep.
Poor hog ! what vision dost thou now inspire?
Too oft, I fear, in greedy owner's sty
Thy ears droop down—thy instincts fall away.
Eat, eat, no doubt, is thy continual cry ;
Cramming's thy training—cramming night and day.
Outraging Nature with our prize-pig scholars,
She sends a worm betimes to gnaw our dollars.*

* *Trichina spiralis*, for instance.

V.—THE SHEEP

The skin-clad pre-historic herd in May,
Watching his lambs, was armed against the dread
Hyena, eagle, wolf. Judah, we've read,
Shore sheep three thousand years ago. To-day
Both cook and weaver make our ewes their prey ;
But chiefly for the first now reared and fed,
The 'lilting at their milking' all has fled.
We call them stupid—no—in their own way
They worship heroes, and so in the East
A well-trained leader is the shepherd's prize.
There, in one noble parable at least,
Nathan embalmed one for our mental eyes.
The golden age—that loveliest dream of sleep—
Had all its breezy uplands 'dorned with sheep.

VI.—THE LARK

Those breezy uplands of the age of gold,
Flaked thick with lambs, were musical with thee.
To-day was dull and rainy—through the tree
The wind moaned harshly—evening came and rolled
The clouds away, and then a rainbow told
The lark to sing—he rose, and from afar,
We heard him singing, till the evening star
Shone on Night's forehead. The sky was a sea
Of glory, which that little quivering speck
Seemed praising. Would his sober listening mate
Not think him music-mad and much too late?
This songster, whirling up to heaven erect,
Is served in pies to suit the Frenchman's taste,
Whose crops, for that, the swarming insects waste.

VII.—THE NIGHTINGALE

We know his song only from poets' books
Suggesting it, as high bright peaks may tell
Of unrisen Sol, or as the murmuring shell
Hums like the sea. He sings, they say, in nooks
Darkling in happy England, while the brooks
Mirror the moon, and many a honeyed smell
Invites the moth to search the glowworm's dell.
Plumage rich brown—less than a thrush he looks,
Yet love and music make his soul their throne.
Cage him before he courts ; if not, he cries
For ever for his mate, and pines and dies,
So much our fancy's held him for her own,
It almost fears us to seek out the real,
Lest it should lack aught of the high ideal.

VIII.—THE HOUSE-FLY

If being too familiar breedeth scorn,
Then scorn we thee, for on our very nose
Thou seekest nectar. Should we pare our toes,
Doze in our chair, drink tea at even or morn,
Then must thou know about it ; and if borne
On the steam-horse to cities, still thou'rt there,
In black battalions, tasting all that's rare,
Thou and thy large blue friend who blows a horn ;
Despising gravitation's far-felt laws,
Thou walk'st upon our ceilings and our walls,
With compound eyes—with lancets in thy jaws—
With glistening wings—in spite of all our saws
To catch or poison—till some dexterous spider
Leaps on thy back, and death becomes thy rider.

IX.—FOSSILS

Geology has caused the dead to rise,
Its shells and bones and teeth reveal the past
Crushing us with a thought of time so vast,
So silent, so unknown, that our surprise
And awe are speechless ; and our inward eyes,
Gazing like eagles o'er the boundless deep,
Worn with the vision, make us sigh for sleep,—
Dizzy upon a peak whence we behold
Great Alps and Apennines like vapours form,
Like vapours go,—and all things known as old
Grow young compared to cycles that have rolled
Since, following host on host through calm and storm—
Molluscs, fish, reptiles, birds, and mammals strange—
Across a world unseen by man did range.

X.—THE TRILOBITE

A small stone mummy—strange symmetric thing.
When did it live ? Conceive in space afar
A point that's so remote from every star
Studding our skies, that through a finger ring
Those shrunk-faint hosts are seen ; go further—bring
The nebulous streak of worlds to look so small,
That like a needle's edge it seemeth all !
'Tis so with time—it hath a stretch so long,
Our lives contract even to a swallow's song
Or bat's quick shriek ; we are as clouds or flowers,
Measured by the enormous chain of years
Fled since this three-lobed sailor first appears
In dull Silurian seas, whose treeless tracts
Of barren isles shot up their lifeless backs.

XI.—SEA LIFE

Tremendous ocean, like a cradled child,
Dozes betimes—the type of happy rest.
Short space beneath that azure sparkling breast
Millions of teeth are whetted, and the wild
Sharks and sword-fish are gliding—for the mild
Liquid expanse holds creatures strong and fleet,
Fleeing the eater, while they rush to eat :
Thus, without pause, the spoiler is despoiled,
The render rent—if not—how could the sea
Contain the shoals—the myriads—that would be ?
Around this battlefield the strong birds sweep,
And it becomes a field of woe or glee
By turns to man who reaps it—yet the deep
Holds milky mothers watching babes asleep !

XII.—THE SONG OF BIRDS

That endless reign of hunger and affright,
Within the sea, admits no time for song ;
Though dolphins play, and to the waves belong
Beings whose wondrous hues of flame and light
May fill their savage mates with fierce delight.
But on the land alone, in sky or tree
Are poured those careless notes of love and glee,
Soothing our toils at morning, eve, or night.
It marks a little truce with death and fate,—
Greed, hunger, terror, rage, and cunning, lie
In caves forgot ; angels are in the sky,
Nymphs in the groves, and open is heaven's gate
When the poor peasant's child comes out to play,
Lured by the song of birds in merry May.

XIII.—THE ELEPHANT

Lord of the earth, ere man the earth did own,
Social, slow-breeding, wary, wise, and grave,
Thy palaces were jungle, wood and cave.
The flint-folks came, and then thou lost thy throne.
A magic circle with those wondrous tools
They drew—the quadrupeds shrunk back in dread,
Nor could thy supple trunk and wise old head
Longer preserve thee king of plants and pools,
And slowly man grew master—brute grew slave.
Battles and coronations thy small eyes
Have seen, and Eastern splendours set and rise.
Not bred with care—wild-born—there lies thy doom :
When a new Polar star winks in our skies
The ivory-seekers will but search thy tomb.*

* Vega in Lyra will be the pole-star in 12,000 years, and long before that, at the present rate of diminution, the elephant will be extinct.

XIV.—THE DOG

Why had the Jew, with those deep earnest eyes,
No kindly word for thee? Why through the East,
In Turkey, or in haughty Spain, dost feast
On garbage, houseless and unowned? The skies,
Which the Red Indian gives thee for a prize,
Repaying thus thy services with share
Of his immortal glorious hunting there,
I own I think of with much less surprise,
Knowing how much thy master's care is thine.
The large brained spaniel, sledge-dog from the snows,
Warm-hearted greyhound, dog with blind man's line ;
Wise watch and shepherd dog—we've seen all those ;
And, since each man still for the best dog tries,
Who knows how far your wondrous powers may rise? *

XV.—ATTRACTIVE COLOURS

Colours that match the rainbow, or the dyes
Which paint heaven's gates at summer eve or morn,
These make you glorious. Yet you are not born
In gold and purple. Is it Love that cries
For crowns and coronation robes, and sighs
For vests of amber, scarfs of pearls, and trains
Spangled with stars and eyes? Doth Love take pains
In books illumed to write about her prize,
And tell the world how like a queen she reigns,
And how 'tis by her own selecting power
That beauty blooms most at the bridal hour?
If light, like life, be dear to human eyes—
Pleased with the day-god, or the coat of flame—
May the poor glowworm not enjoy the same?

XVI.—PROTECTIVE COLOURS

Yet life is more than light, and bloodiest wars
Teach the gay soldier that his scarlet coat
(His sweetheart's joy) and every glittering mote
Be hid, that green or grey, without his stars,
Unseen, he may elude or fight his foe.
And so hath Nature in her cycles wrought.
The weaker female rears the brood, and lo !
She is less gaudy ; or her plumes become
Like heath, or fern, or bark, where she sits dumb
On her warm eggs unmoved. Sometimes quick fear
Makes the gay lizard like dull stick appear ;
To greenest woods green birds their safety owe ;
Sparrows are like the dust—weak insects use
Strange masques, forged, like strong insects' shapes and
    hues.

Vide Darwin's *Origin of Species.*

XVII.—THE OX

I see thee, ere the pyramids, in time,
First plougher of our fields for golden grain ;
First bearer of our burdens o'er the plain :
Or lo ?—what crowds ! wreathed—led to death sublime,
With blood thou washest out our spots of crime.
Thy horn is symbol of all strength—thy fame
Has reached the stars*—coin first received thy name.†
Egypt bowed down—for thou, its god, did'st rule !
Then came thine iron age—butchers for priests.
Roast beef and dairies fattening dear John Bull,
And Britain's empire propped by ox-flesh feasts.‡
Daisies themselves denied to stall-fed beasts !
On 'model farms' not by your breath or lowing,
But by your price your master's breast is glowing.

XVIII.—THE WREN

The Negro holds his fetish stone divine ;
A schoolboy's fetish thou—he says with glee,
At God's right hand there is a place for thee,
My little wren, out hopping there to dine
On beech tree table—flies thy cakes and wine.
'Tis sunshine, and a string of wood-notes wild
Flits blithely through green leaves, where none can see
Cock-tailed papa the piper—though our child
Has got a heart half dancing to its notes :
Then all grows silent, save fifteen small specks,
Whose yellow tongues yelp in their open throats,
Waiting mamma's supplies with outstretched necks.
Hard work for Jenny in this world of beauty ;
But love makes silken all the cords of duty.

XIX.—THE WOLF

No bloody finger, writing on the sky
Threatenings of Egypt's plagues, could move men more
Than when the traveller hears the sullen roar
Of wolves in packs—fierce famine in each eye,
Or lists their measured tread ; he heaves a sigh,
And stands a moment, like a man near shore,
Who feels his ship is drifting on a coast

* The constellation Taurus, the Bull.
† A bit of hide, stamped with the image of his *pecus* or ox was
the first bank-note, saving its owner from taking the original to
market for exchange ; hence *pecunia*, money.
‡ Carlyle gives *hunger* as the efficient cause of the French
Revolution.

Black-speckled with the points of iron rocks ;
And whether he should quickly load his gun,
And, wheeling round, should face their utmost shocks ;
Or whether he should leave his horse and run
To yon high tree, white with the moon and frost ;
Or whether, putting spurs in, he should flee
Across that boiling river—knows not he.

XX.—THE APE

Poor friend of ours—made by the self-same Hand,
How often have we wished that unseen coat
Our nursery giant-killer wore, to note
Thee in thy native woods—to take our stand
In the green arch-ways of thy tropic land,
Where heat and moisture make thy thick rank bowers
Gorgeous with reptiles, insects, birds, and flowers,
Or fierce strong light smites yellow on the grand
Old columns of thy palaces, to see
How thou dost with thy family agree,
How build'st thy shed—how fight'st for precious life,
With twenty fingers—nuts and sticks—and wife.
Much better way, if thus we could, to see him,
Than caged and sick—or stuffed in a museum.

XXI.—FINIS

Our little Noah's ark is emptied quite ;
We've pulled the puppet-strings and talked awhile
Of some mysterious creatures—of their guile,
Their beauty, and their strength—for from the mite
Up to the mammoth, from the beasts of night
On to the pets that bask in ladies' eyes,
Each is a temple of that holy light
Called Life—than which the glory of the skies
Strikes less with love, with awe, with great surprise,
Portraits of beasts were drawn by early man :
He scratched them—the poor symbols of his thought,
With flint on flakes of bone, and so began
His jewelled crown of letters—has it taught
The lord of brutes to treat them as he ought ?

THE AVIFAUNA OF UPPER NITHSDALE

After a long residence in one of the beautiful glens which
converge at Thornhill on the Nith, Dumfriesshire, I have
taken the following notes of the birds of the district.

During the last thirty years there has been a serious
diminution of the birds of prey. The peregrine falcon

and merlin are rare, the kite is extinct, while the
sparrow-hawk and buzzard are becoming very scarce.
The kestrel, however, is common, and may frequently be
observed gliding over the cliffs near the sources of our
upland streams, or pouncing on barn-door sparrows.
Owls are very plentiful. The woods around the ducal
residence of Drumlanrig, and the large quantity of natural
wood which adorns the hillsides along the banks of the
tributary streams, afford them protection. The tawny owl
is the most common. It delights to utter its screech
perched on a coniferous tree, and it is the boldest of its
kind. The barn-owl is common. The long-eared owl is
both rarer and shyer. On one occasion the nest of a
barn-owl was found in a rabbit-burrow.

The missel-thrush and blackbird are very common,
although, one summer about nine years ago, we missed
their delightful songs entirely. They seemed to have
succumbed to the previous severe winter. The song-
thrush is rare. The fieldfare comes to us in immense
flocks in October, and in a few days strips every mountain-
ash of the glittering red berries which make these trees
so conspicuous after their leaves are shed. The dipper is
found in all our streams. The ring-ousel is not uncommon.
Everywhere in early spring the simple song of the hedge-
sparrow greets us. The redbreasts and chaffinch are
plentiful. The redstart and night-jar are rare. The
whin-chat is heard as it hops along our fences built of
uncemented whin-stones. The grasshopper-warbler and
the sedge-warbler are rarely heard, but the wheatear is
common. Its nest is far from being easy to find, on
account of these same stone-dykes.

The wood-warbler and the willow-warbler have increased of late years. The golden-crested wren is
plentiful in our fir-woods. Its nest, lined with feathers,
is sometimes blown down from the pendent bough. The

wren and the willow-wren are common. ¶The lesser
white-throat and chiff-chaff are rare. The tree-creeper
is more common than appears, for its nest is most difficult
to find.

The great-tit is rare, the blue-tit and the cole-tit
common. The long-tailed tit—to which Dr Bowdler
Sharpe has given a new significance by pointing
out that we have a form specialised in the British
Isles — is rather scarce. It makes its wonderfully
artistic nest in almost inaccessible black-thorn scrub.
The pied wagtail is much more common than the
grey wagtail. The golden plover and spotted fly-
catcher are rare, but the nest of the former is difficult
to find. The garden-warbler is very uncommon. The
tree- and meadow-pipit are abundant, so are the skylark
and yellow-hammer. We are far from being rich in
finches, putting aside the chaffinch. The common linnet
is seldom seen except in flocks in winter. The same
may be remarked of the lesser redpoll.

The house-sparrow, rook, and starling are ubiquitous.
The cuckoo is plentiful and arrives about the last days of
April. Although it delights to lay in a smaller bird's
nest, such as the meadow-pipit, I have got its egg in the
nest of a kestrel. The carrion crow and jackdaw are
not uncommon. The king-fisher is exceedingly rare. As
it commands a price, it was entirely exterminated by a
band of bird-catchers, more than a dozen years ago,
all along that finest tributary of the Upper Nith, the
romantic and wood-fringed Skarr.

The swallow, house-martin and sand-martin, are common
—but the swift does not come. The ring-dove is abundant, but I have never observed the reed-bunting.

The following birds are very common : pheasant, which
has a stupid fashion of nesting on the roadsides, exposed
to school-children ; black-grouse, partridge, lapwing, and

T

curlew, which latter arrive in March; land-rail, which
come in the first days of May; and moor-hen. The
following are not uncommon—red grouse, heron, wood-
cock, and wild duck. The black-headed gull is very
plentiful, but the common gull less so. The teal and the
little grebe or dabchick I have not observed.

On the upper courses of our mountain streams the
sandpiper may be seen wading. Snow-buntings are
among our winter visitors. About farmyards an occasional pair of bramblings may be noticed. In fields
where *Prunella vulgaris* grows, flocks of twites may be
seen in certain seasons. Our famous naturalist, Dr
Grierson (see Chapter VIII), put into his museum, about
twenty years ago, a golden oriole shot near Kirkconnel.

Enough has been written to show, that although
Thornhill and the three adjacent glens which converge
near it are about twenty miles inland, there is an interesting and well-stocked ornithological district to deal
with—the chief paucity being in the numbers of wading
and swimming birds, and in those birds which are
numerous where cereals are abundant.— *Hardwicke's
Science Gossip.* [About 1893.]

BIRD-NESTING

How pleasant to be born and brought up in the country,
far away from smoke and din, where only on rare, still
nights the boom of the railway train or the shrill whistle
of its engine ever reaches the ear, where gamekeepers are
few and far between, and no threatening notices confine
you for ever to the beaten tracks! Do not think that we
are lonely because we reside in shepherd's cots, remote
from each other. In moonless nights we can steer our
way across the hills by the stars. In summer, although
we do not linger to count the rarities in shop-windows,

we gather chaplets of flowers, and know most of them by their names.

The whisper ran from mouth to ear, making our rosy faces dimple and our blue eyes grow rounder. It is not that the first flower of the *Tussilago* or the little celandine has been plucked, or that the bees are droning like an organ among the catkins of the willows. It is not that the hardiest member of the family shall be allowed to have his feet bare next week, or that the minister is coming to-morrow to baptize a child in far-away Glenwhargen or Stroquhan. The whisper referred to sheds no light on the number invited to a forthcoming wedding, nor informs us of the colour of any summer dress trysted by the prettiest girl. It treats of a matter transcending any of these. It informs us that a ragged loon has discovered a mavis or song-thrush in the very act of building its nest. In the midst of a wood of oak, coppice, and hazel with catkins still unshed we saw it, though some had to pay a marble for the sight, in the midst of a thick hollybush. The peeping during incubation was so strictly select that, in due course, four or five young birds began to gape. The top fledgeling was secured by the joiner's son, whose father made a large cage for it, painted green; and, as he grudged laying out money on wire, he made the side of the cage next to the wall entirely of wood. The nest in which he was born is still in a local museum. It is an honest piece of work, capable of holding water, built with a compost of clay and cow-dung, and constructed externally of moss and small bits of wood.

Who can picture our excitement on that proud day, when one of our number had discovered an owl's nest? It was arranged that the more daring spirits should make a pilgrimage to it first Saturday. We passed over holms where old men were scattering manure. We ascended beautifully rounded hills all aflame, for it was at that

period of spring when the dry withered grass of the
preceding year is burned, filling the long glens with
smoke, and 'cankering,' as the shepherds say, that is,
irritating, the air and causing rain. Other fields had a
blackened appearance, the charred grass smelling heavily.
Curlews and lapwings ran us away from their nests, or
nearly hit our bonnets hovering so close around us. At
last, in a boggy place, we came to a blasted alder growing
near to one of the long uncemented or dry whinstone
dykes that divided two farms. In a hollow of this tree,
made soft at the bottom with bits of wood scraped off the
trunk, three eggs were laid, white and round. Many a
time had we been startled by the owl's screech at dusk.
They were the bogies of the nursery, weird, uncanny
creatures with noiseless wings, the only relation of a
tangible kind that we had with them being that some of
us could so imitate their cry as to get back hoot for hoot.
I confess that when I first peered into the nest, I being
edged upon another boy's shoulder, with the wind moan-
ing through the dark firs of a neighbouring knoll, I
would not have been surprised had the small round
bombs of eggs burst up in my face with a 'too-
whit' and a blue flame. Long after, we tried to
bring up an owl as a pet, but it was too ready with
its talons, and so was let off into liberty and twilight. We were more successful with a kestrel with
clipped wings which was presented to the master. We
easily kept its larder full with mice and voles, which we
brought out of our traps at home, and it was so odd to see
it sitting on the cross-spars of the master's three-legged
stool disgorging the pellets which consisted of the tough
indigestible portions of its prey. Poor kestrel! its
clipped wings were fatal to it, for it was one day found
with its head knawed off, probably by a weasel that had
been seen lurking about the school-house.

Another bit of sensation was the discovery of a squirrel's nest. For years no squirrel had been seen in the parish, and this new vagrant cunningly made its nest in a hawthorn tree, surrounded by hazels, so that while it could easily escape when alarmed, it was difficult to get at. When squirrels became more plentiful they were wont to place their nests on outlying boughs of larches, too high to be reached by a stick, too slender to be got at by climbing. It was not easy to exhibit a 'puppy' squirrel, for blood was sometimes demanded from the intruding hand. When hard chased I have seen them in their nervousness lose footing and fall to the ground, a distance of more than thirty feet, and yet get up and run. It is curious to note how slyly the squirrel interposes the bole of the tree between itself and the human eyes watching it, and how craftily it peeps round the corner. In winter it 'rains' down the outer scales of the cones of the larch and appropriates the tenderer matter within.

We had an accident plundering a wood-pigeon's nest high up in a larch tree, one of a plantation many of which reach ninety feet in height. I think I see these grand trees, newly getting green, the little dark cones of the preceding year mixed with the rosy tufts of the present. The uppermost boy was descending with the pair of eggs in his clouted cap, which he held in his teeth, when his footing gave way, and the result was a fall, with a broken arm, set, however, very shortly after by the schoolmaster, who had once meant to be a doctor, and whose skill in medicine and surgery was frequently useful in a remote locality.

In the ivy which masked an old decaying house for holding tools, close to the manse garden, the blackbirds built regularly. During the sunny showers we used to huddle together in a corner beneath the thick bushes, while the orange-billed rogue, not suspecting we were there, piped his daintiest ditty on a spray above our heads.

One youth from such a nest got into a family that taught him to whistle about the half of a Scotch air. He had more general intelligence than the thrush, but was awfully fluttered on one occasion that a favourite of his approached the cage with an unusual head-dress.

The redbreast, on the whole, gave us most amusement in nest-making, from its habit of building, sometimes inside byres, so that girls could pick up matter for an essay on its habits while milking their cows. Titmice had also comical places for nests. Sometimes in holes in trees, low down and very narrow, so that the collie whelps would endeavour vainly to harry them. Without, the nest of the titmouse is adorned with lichens, tastefully arranged. Within, it is as comfortable as fine wool and feathers from a mother's breast can make it. I need not tell you more about it, for it is an ornament popular at potteries, and often appears on jugs and bowls.

Rooks and chaffinches are our most common birds. Rooks are so much alike, we often wondered how they knew their mates. They begin to build and to steal building-materials from each other on the first Sunday of March, thus breaking one-fifth of the moral law at once. Chaffinches understand the principle of protective resemblance when nest-building, choosing materials of the same pattern as the lichened or mossy tree, in whose fork they build. The females of our game birds trust so far to their tints being similar to the heath among which they brood, that I have seen us betting whether we could touch them sitting.

School Children among the Hills

The school which I attended was in a remote district in the south of Scotland. The number of the scholars was few and their habitations far between. Indeed, we resided at such distances from one another, that assembling at school was enjoyed as almost the sole opportunity of obtaining news and indulging our social instincts. It was curious to see us mustering on a summer morning from various nooks, ravines, glens and sheilings, every little brook or boulder that we passed having its name. From one cot a solitary urchin would set forth, and from another as many as four or five. A bit of old stocking, or the corner of a letter in a hollow underneath a rock, let us know whether we were behind or in advance of a similar group, and moreover, we had all learned to whistle lustily on our fingers. Each scholar was furnished with a strong leathern bag, carried like a knapsack, for holding his books, and in which was also a parcel of soda scone and cheese and a flask of milk. Add to this, in winter, a 'peat' under our arm, which was our daily contribution to the school fire, and only ceased to be carried as railway stations drew nearer us, supplying coals at a cheaper rate. Both boys and girls were provided in the colder months with stout boots or 'clogs' (wooden soled shoes), while in snowy weather the legs of old stockings were drawn across the boys' trousers and the upper part of the clogs, and tied underneath the soles like sandals. The girls wore long pinafores and white hoods, and were tied up in plaids and mufflers. The rose of health glowed on almost every cheek, and the greater proportion were long-limbed, blue-eyed, fair-haired Saxons, although issuing from homes that had Celtic names. It was often in the bargain that the older boys should carry the younger a part of the road, for in some cases the distance

was reckoned by three or four miles, and there was a
good deal of jumping over drains and tiny streams on the
way. In summer our pilgrimages were all performed
with bare feet, and although we walked at first like the
saint with hard peas in his shoes, in a short time our naked
soles became as thick and tough as the hide of a pachy-
derm, and we greatly preferred the free use of our toes
for climbing trees. With bare limbs we built fancy
houses in the channels of the mountain streams, or wading
warily, pulled out betimes a dainty trout from beneath the
flat stone or boulder which concealed it—an operation as
hateful to the angler as delightful to the urchin, and
which was designated by the local name of 'guddling'
(tickling).

Our teacher's temper was uncertain. He had a cheery
face, a red nose, a capital fiddle, which did duty at many
a country wedding, a head in which slept Latin quotations
and Scotch proverbs, and a hand that did a great deal of
the clerking required in the parish. We welcomed
always any of those weeks when he was invited to a
wedding, he was so much less morose and sometimes
positively jocular. He encouraged us to love animals,
and at odd times a pet lamb or superannuated collie
would be in waiting at the school door, the latter often
barking lustily when the parting hymn announced dis-
missal. Spring and autumn were jolly times for us, for
in the former we found out nests, and in the latter season
we rejoiced in wild fruit. The curlews came back to the
hills towards the end of February, and from that time
onwards the incidents of bird life became interesting.

Great promotion awaited us when our years were
sufficiently advanced to allow us to assist in the lambing
season. April caught us at work, and we went on until
May. The rising sun saw our long shadow on the hills,
and the setting orb bade us farewell and allowed the

moon to take us home. But we were not always listening
to the songs of larks. Sometimes we had to scrape the
dead lambs from under the snow, and assist the mothers
with our milk flasks and all our medicines.

Another occasion of promotion took place at the time
of sheep-shearing. Thrice happy he who was promoted
to open and close a gate, stir the pot of tar, stamp the
initials of the owner's name on the sheep, or make himself
generally useful on those auspicious days. These, and
the days when on the moor collecting peats, or assisting
in gathering the sheep towards lowland pastures, when
the snow of winter had lain too long, or in helping to
wean the lambs when all the glens were resonant with the
bleatings of the bereaved, were days in which we were
ascending the steps of the social ladder with rapid strides,
and casting to the winds the fear of failure in our lessons.
How many at this day in crowded warehouse or in narrow
lane, or it may be in the wider areas of our colonies,
think with a happy smile of the days when they were
hardy school children among the hills?

GLIMPSES OF BIRD LIFE

We are pretty much in the dark as to the average age
attained by the members of the feathered tribes. On one
occasion I harried the nest of a mavis or song-thrush, and
kept a male bird in confinement for twelve years. At
first he was ravenously fond of worms and slugs, and
when he saw me pass the window, fluttered joyfully in
anticipation. But a winter of unusual severity having set
in, he subsisted for the most part on pease-meal slaked with
water—'drummock,' we named it; so that when spring
again came round, he had forgotten the slugs and turned
his head saucily at them. We introduced a stout wooden

bowl into his commodious cage, and in this he took his
morning bath. His loud clear song was rather piercing
for indoors, and was never louder than when we were
gathered around the table. He allowed himself to be
caught without much fluttering, and held in the hand
while his cage was being cleaned. About the time he
was approaching his twelfth year, second childhood
overtook him. He became blind and lost his gift of song,
while he would cry for his food like a nestling. Feeding
himself slovenly, parasites began to infest him. In mercy
we put him in a paper bag and finished his days by
drowning. Like the lark, the song-thrush can sing for
a long period without pause. Two years ago, while working in my garden at the beginning of May, I timed one
singing in an ash tree. It sang for forty minutes without
cessation, although it changed the branch while singing
more than once.

Last year, at the pairing season, I was surprised at seeing a pair of partridges frequently feeding together on
the highway which went past my garden. A plat of the
garden farthest removed from the house was in grass
which was cut in June, when to our astonishment there
was found a nest of partridges with eighteen eggs. The
parents continued to brood on them, and one day, June
23rd, allowed me to come so near that I observed both male
and female sitting on the nest, their heads in opposite
directions. Next day the nest contained fourteen living
birds. On the 25th, a great commotion made me rush to
the spot. Our cat had attempted to kill the brood now
out of the nest, and the female partridge, throwing herself between the enemy and its prey, was so severely injured that she died shortly after. The cat was got quit
of, and the male bird took the entire charge of the brood,
covering them with his wings. On the 29th, while I was
from home, the male parent was intimidated by a dog,

and, the shades of evening falling, a well-intentioned
individual secured four of the little nestlings, but notwithstanding every care taken of them, they died next morning. At the lowest part of our garden wall, I got another
dead on the highway, but have reason to believe the remaining nine under their parent's management had
escaped as night advanced. During the period the male
took charge of his offspring in the garden, he seemed to
know the person who paid daily visits for vegetables,
but if any visitor came rather near, he endeavoured to
distract attention from the brood by feigning flight in a
different direction, which he always did by running in
rather a zig-zag manner.

Several years ago, as the days were becoming short,
a redbreast began to enter the kitchen of a farmhouse
adjoining us. It entered early in the morning and
remained in the kitchen until quite dusk, spending the
whole day indoors. It paid frequent visits to the dairy,
and was exceedingly fond of the curd from which cheese
is made. The washing day, when there was much commotion, appeared to be most grateful to it, or when the
floor was being scrubbed. Its liveliness then was remarkable. Its favourite perch was a pan which hung
from the ceiling, where for hours daily it would sit and
sing, frequently in a low strain scarcely audible, but when
the 'hubbub' referred to began, it sung loud and clear.
It sometimes descended to pick crumbs from the floor,
but was much more timid at the approach of a male than
a female. As it disappeared suddenly, after being for a
few weeks a general favourite, it was supposed that it had
fallen a victim to a cat.

In another house near us, for two successive years, a
robin spent part of its time as a visitant. It was known
to be the same bird, by its single foot, the other being
a stump. It sometimes remained all night, perching in a

cellar to which it had access from the lobby of the
dwelling.

To keep watch on a rookery at the next building
season would be interesting. I never observed rooks, in
building, lift a stick from the ground. They prefer to
break them from trees, especially from the larch, nor do
they condescend to pick up the pieces which fall accidentally. They prefer the dead branches as much easier
to snap. It sometimes takes a good deal of manœuvring
to get away from the tree with the stick if it happen to
be broken about the middle of the branches. When they
ascend to their nest their flight is generally a spiral one.
The laying of the foundation of the nest taxes them pretty
heavily. They try to balance the first two or three sticks
very carefully in the fork of the tree they have chosen,
and are repeatedly disappointed as they fall. After the
first few sticks lie securely the rest of the building is
easily accomplished. They do not complete the outside
of their nests until they have first put in the interior
lining, which is of grass or hay. During the whole nest-
building process there is much wrangling, stealing, and
fighting. Bravery seems almost essential to success. The
female, while incubating, depends upon the male to carry
her food, and the sitting bird will recognise her partner
coming at a distance of nearly a hundred yards. Rooks
have fairly good memories. This may be put to the test
by scaring them away for a while from a piece of bread,
or a dead grub they may have dropped, and then keeping
out of sight, when frequently they will return for the
very piece they let fall.

Starlings have grown more plentiful in the south of
Scotland. I can remember when one could scarcely be
had for money, and I would have gone a long way to see
a starling's nest. Now they breed in my pigeon cote,
returning to it annually about the first fine days in

February. Their perseverance is wonderful, for the pigeons at first keenly resent the intrusion. Although I put up a separate box for the starlings, they prefer to incubate in the pigeon holes first chosen. The young are exceedingly voracious. Both parents feed them, and it is surprising to observe what flies, butterflies, moths, and other vermin are brought home to the young, and that even in a period of drought. I have often seen three starlings at the pigeon holes about the breeding time, but in a short while the whole activity was confined to a pair. Their whistle is so human-like that at first I was frequently deceived. While feeding their young, their patience was sorely tried by a pugnacious pigeon filling up the entrance to the nest, and it was amusing to watch them dodging, suddenly slipping in under the very body of the enemy.

The cuckoo is common with us, and arrives, as a rule, on some day or rather night in the last week of April. A shepherd in a pastoral parish near the one in which I reside, while overlooking his hill, descried one morning a young bird lying on the ground. Lifting it and peering around him he discovered a nest, and placed the 'gorling' inside it. Next morning he found the bird lying on the self-same spot. Replacing it again, he arrived a third time near the same-locality and found the poor bird lying dead. He then discovered that both the dead bird and the living bird in the nest were young cuckoos, and that the stronger had ejected its fellow-occupant from the nest. The cuckoo utters its well-known note both flying and sitting. It is a curious sight to observe it sitting and singing. Its whole body heaves like a little boat breasting the billows.

The ring ousel is a very common bird in our pastoral locality. He has a pert chatter which enlivens our rocky glens and grassy hills. He plants his nest on the edge of a steep rock, or conceals it in a bunch of heather. He adapts himself to circumstances, and where the environment is less inviting, conceals his breeding place at the edge of a sheep drain or sloping knoll. His perseverance when his nest is robbed is pathetic. He soon begins to rebuild. On one occasion not until three nests and thirteen eggs were destroyed by mischievous boys did he leave off building in the spot of his choice.

The dipper seems to be losing his fine architectural tastes. When I was young his nests were nearly the size of a small beehive, and entailed a vast amount of labour. Here I have one in my collection, built behind a waterfall, yet lined outside with a covering of moss, making the nest impervious to water. The entrance to it is from below, and the mossy covering shows protective resemblance, harmonising closely with its surroundings. Now he is acquiring the habit of choosing crevices and holes in bridges in which the female drops her eggs. Few birds are so regular in their habits of incubation as these, there being four or five eggs always in their nests by about the middle of April.

The greater and blue tits are shy birds. They have the oddest possible breeding places. A pair of them brought out their family in a piece of tubing resting against my garden wall. I had been in the way of hanging out a piece of fat or even of a tallow candle, of which they are very fond, and this had the effect of allowing me to notice more of their habits. The long-tailed tit is the finest architect in these isles. It is a denizen of the woods, in which it may be seen in family parties. It generally builds its beautiful nest in the heart of a blackthorn tree where it is almost inaccessible.

When the fieldfares arrive in our glens in flocks during the month of October, it is a striking sight to observe how they alight, like locusts, on our rowan trees, and

strip them of their scarlet berries.   One day I reckoned
that nearly two hundred of these birds, with a few blackbirds intermixed, were poised in the mountain-ash which
grows in my garden, and in less than two hours not a
berry was left on the tree.

In the spring of 1886, after the swallows had arrived, a
spell of exceedingly cold weather occurred which destroyed the insects on which they fed, and the poor birds
were picked up dead in great numbers across the
country.   Sometimes they could be observed skimming
close to horses and cattle for the sake of picking up the
slightest morsel of life.   [27th March 1896.]

THE PLEASURES OF FIELD BOTANY

Now is the time to have excursions along the highways
and byways, among the fields and woods, or over the
mountains and lakes in search of wild flowers.   A good
text-book bound up with leathern covers, a vasculum, a
spud, a pocket lens and a bicycle, with health and suitable weather, and any boy at this season of the year may
make the state and happiness of emperors ridiculous, by
simply attending to the gems and gold and lace which
Nature is scattering so widely and profusely.   A few of
our early favourites are already gone, but wonderful
wealth of blossom attests that midsummer has arrived.
From winter to summer, as has been said, there has been
a leap without a spring this season, and so quickly have
the geraniums and veronica bloomed that they can now
be seen with petals expanded beside primroses and
celandines.   Last year there was very little blossom on
our flowering trees, but this year, as if refreshed by their
long rest, first the willows, the males with their golden
catkins, and the females with their grey, invited the

earliest bees to feast among their sweets. Untimely frost
and snow nipped the promise of the hazel and the alder
but the catkins of the fairy birch, the green blossoms of
the massive planes, the dull stamens of the ash, and the
beautiful and numerous seed-leaves of the elm have all
been born into genial times. So rapidly did the blossoms
of the wild cherry trees expand that one almost looked out
of a morning to see them transformed into white ladies, or
not trees, but the ghosts of trees. The bird-cherry's
racemes, of purest white, lay like masses of snow among
the leaves. In gardens the singing birds, the chaffinch,
blackbird, wren, hedge-sparrow, and redbreast conducted
their orchestra among the fruit trees pranked round with
curtains of red and white dipped in the 'delicatest odours.'
Among the verdant hills where the curlew screams and
the lark utters her dulcet notes, beautiful patches of the
cat's-ears or mountain everlasting, the low downy-looking
blossoms tipped with white, were unfolding themselves
beside their nests, while in the thin woods into which the
pheasant loves to cower, the wood-sorrel, with its light
green leaves, and the blue-bell squills or wild-hyacinths
with their purplish bells were filling the air, especially at
evening, with sweetest odour. In those same shady
places masses of the field allium or wild garlic with lily-
like leaves and fringed petals grow, the only serious
objection to it being that it exhales an unpleasant
smell. Now in marshy places look for the marsh trefoil
or bog-bean. Its buds are tipped with dark red, and
when it expands its petals look like lace. Numerous
carices grow in both the marshy lowlands and on the dry
hillsides. The carices and rushes are pretty in their
own way, although more like grass in their appearance
and fruition. Some of them, as the flea carex, are funny
in their appearance, the latter being not unlike the animal
after which it is named. Others, like the 'remote' carex or

the bottle carex, are graceful or pendulous. Grasses are
fast rushing into flower. Already the sweet-scented vernal
grass, the meadow foxtail, the marsh foxtail, and the
early aira can be enumerated, and the flower-heads of the
Poa tribe are nearly ready to burst forth.

Lately we had grand masses of the wood anemone
whitening the fields and woods. To-day the marsh
marigold and the globe flower are flushing our meadows
with orange and yellow. School children among the
hills like to place the globe flower in their hair, helping
with their fingers to unfold its yellow petals. On all our
waysides the pale purple or white of the ladies' smock or
rather Our Lady's smock is glowing beneath the white or
coloured wings of butterflies. That slender and most
fairy-looking of all the Ranunculus tribe, and next to the
celandine the earliest, is thrown about in delightful
patches. Many of our common flowers were named by
our Catholic forefathers in honour of the Virgin Mother.
Witness Our Lady's mantle. The hawthorn in May is late
this season, but soon it will overpower all other perfume by
reason of its own luxuriant odour. Last year scarcely a
blossom or berry was to be had, this year the promise of
both is great. Along the lanes in which it grows masses
of the greater stitchwort are now in bloom, where earlier
ground-ivy was expanding its less ostentatious blossoms.
Robin-run-i'-the-hedge, or goose-grass, dwale, honey-
suckle, and the viburnums are still waiting, but will have
their innings by-and-by. The whitlow grass and dandelion are getting into seed, but early vetches and violets
are filling their empty chairs. The latter half of May and
early June constitute perhaps the most enjoyable season
of the year. Neither the heat of the sun's rays nor the
flies are then so troublesome, while every tree and bush
has on its most exquisite shade of green. The tints may
not be so marked as they are in autumn, but they range

U

through all the shades of yellow, brown, and green ; earl
poplars, oaks and plane-trees, appearing at first witl
leaves almost yellow ; while the grey ash, being in flowe
before the leaves come, is a fine contrast to woods tha
clothe a hillside or are viewed from above. If we wait til
past midsummer we lose the beauty of trees in blossor
and exhaling fragrance, and we lose the charm of th
song of birds and the brightness of their bridal plumage.

The estivation or unfolding of buds is a study tha
is its own reward, from the manner in which the lady'
mantle expands like a fan to the habit of the ferns un
winding themselves as if from a spindle. The oak-fer
and beech-fern have never a more delicate green than jus
now, immediately after unfolding themselves. In a woo
near the writer's house there is a kind of natural rocker
consisting of small and great stones strewed about, the load
perhaps, of some prehistoric glacier, for scratched an
polished rocks all around prove the presence of glaciers a
some remote period. This rockery is at present a fer
garden, the oak-fern, the beech-fern, and the broad prickl
shield-fern being mingled in profusion, while in the masse
of loose stones weathered from the cliffs above, but withou
the shade of the wood, the parsley-fern or rock-brake i
just now, with its curly fronds creeping out of its crevice
The wood-pigeon is cooing in the high larch trees above
and the cuckoo, sometimes on the wing, sometimes seated
but always in motion, swaying its body, if not flittin
from branch to branch, and the land-rail in the long gras
at the side of the wood are uttering their monotonou
cries.

A Strange Vegetable Parasite

The North Island of New Zealand contains a mos
singular plant, which is always found growing from th

body of a caterpillar. The native name for this twofold
being is the *aweto* ; but with the colonist it is known as
the 'bulrush caterpillar.' This strange plant is a fungus,
Torrubia (Cordyceps) Robertsii, which sows its spores on the
body of a living grub, and grows from that as if it were
from soil. The moth, whose caterpillar is thus victim-
ised, is of a species akin to our own ghost moths, which
are seen flitting across a flowery meadow in the twilight
of a summer's evening. The caterpillar of the New
Zealand species is said to feed on the leaves of a beautiful, scandent, flowering shrub, the 'rata,' near to the roots
of which it entombs itself prior to its metamorphosis into
the chrysalis stage. Whilst about to burrow in a soil
generally composed of vegetable mould, it receives some
of the minute spores of the fungus between the scales of
its neck, from which in its transitionary, sluggish state,
it is unable to free itself.

Nourished by the warmth and moisture of the insect's
body, then lying motionless, these spores vegetate, im-
peding the progress of normal change in the grub, and
the mature fungus latterly causes its death. The body
of the grub gradually becomes converted into a hard
tissue, and to all intents and purposes may be considered
the root of the fungus. Shortly after the inception of
the spores, the fungus appears as a slender rod emerging
from the ground. The vegetating process invariably
springs from the nape of the neck of the caterpillar, and
the under portion of the plant exactly fits and fills the
body of the grub. In the specimens now before the
writer, the caterpillars are about three inches long, and
the fungus on each nine inches high. The fructified
head, or apex, resembles the club head of a bulrush, and
the whole plant, without leaves and having a single stalk,
is like a bulrush in miniature—hence its name. The
plant matures its spores on a new generation of grubs,

and so it is propagated from year to year. When newly
dug up the substance of the caterpillar is soft. Most
specimens possess the so-called legs entire, with the
horny part of the head, the mandibles, and claws. The
Maoris eat the fungus, and likewise use it for tattooing
rubbing the powder into the wounds, in which state i
has, as might be anticipated, a strong animal smell.

Altogether this is one of the most striking example
of the life of a creature, higher in the scale of existence
sacrificed for the support of the lower; and one ex
amining specimens for the first time finds his curiosit
mingled with awe. The mistletoe and mushroom lev
their taxes on vegetables; the cuckoo steals a nest; th
hermit crab crawls into an empty shell; carnivorou
plants, like sun-dews, entrap insects; but here is
vegetable, not only destroying insect life, but convertin
the remains, first while living, and then after death, int
a permanent storehouse, so that its body is restraine
from going through those processes of change whic
would ultimately produce a winged insect flitting from
flower to flower. The destiny of the animal is foiled an
set at naught that a fungus may live and propagate it
kind. More than that, the grub is converted into wha
looks very like a part or root of the fungus itself.

CHAPTER VIII

DR GRIERSON'S MUSEUM, THORNHILL*

School Excursions to the Museum—(Poetry) *Hortus Doctoris*—
  Lines written in the Museum—The Cameron Statue in the
  Garden—Lines on a Specimen of ' Bos Scoticus '—Lines on a
  Column of Decayed Teeth.

A SCHOOL EXCURSION TO THE MUSEUM

PERHAPS a case favourable to the plea for the encouragement and establishment of local museums might be made
out by a simple statement of how an excellent private
museum, in a strictly agricultural and pastoral district,

---

* Dr Thomas Grierson, a scion of the Lag family, spent his life as
a medical practitioner and amateur antiquarian in Thornhill, and
died a bachelor in 1889 at the age of 72. He bequeathed the
museum (valued by G. F. Black † at £5000), and £1000 for its
maintenance, to the inhabitants of the district, to whose educational
interest he had devoted much time and self-sacrificing assiduity.
For many years Shaw was one of the doctor's intimate friends and
scientific associates, and he acted as one of the trustees under the
deed of bequest till his death. Dr Grierson originated the Young
Men's Society of Enquiry at Thornhill about 1877, in the discussions
of which Joseph Thomson, the African Traveller (whose monument
appropriately occupies a prominent position in the village), and
many other young men who have distinguished themselves in the
clerical and literary world, first cultivated the polemics of debate,
and practised the art of expressing original thoughts in science and
literature in the Queen's English. Dr Grierson has left a lasting
and befitting monument to a worthy memory for succeeding generations, but the present generation require no such talisman to re-

† Black, from the Antiquarian Museum, Edinburgh, and Joseph Blaset, A.R.C.S.,
Lond., arranged and labelled the collection, and prepared a complete catalogue,
published in 1894.

has, for a period of more than thirty years, acted as an educational influence. The population of Morton parish, in which the museum is situated, is not much over two thousand, but it is only one of a number of parishes which together make up the district of Upper Nithsdale. The population of the district is sparse, although the museum is one which well might grace a city. This is all the more remarkable as the objects of interest have been collected during the lifetime of Dr Grierson, the gentleman to whom they belong, and have been arranged and manipulated by his own hands. The Duke of Buccleuch made a free grant of the land on which the edifice was built and the garden laid out. The building is well placed at the termination of a boulevard-like street, planted on each side with lime trees. It crowns the summit of the moderate elevation on which the village of Thornhill is built, and the views from the garden are very wide and grand. The whole edifice consists of a dwelling-house and museum built on a plan well conceived for the purpose. The latter is rather low and oblong, consisting of ground floor and gallery, lighted by side windows. The gallery is very appropriately supported by the trunks of six oak trees, with the bark peeled off

mind them of the genial doctor and his never-ceasing and successful labours in the cause of science and humanity. At the death of Joseph Thomson, on whose short but brilliant career early association with Dr Grierson had no little influence, Shaw wrote his *Memorial Recollection* for the *Dumfries Herald*, August 7, 1895.

> Extinguished while thy sun was at its noon,
> Not Masai land with all its savage hordes,
> Not unknown mountains with their lion lords
> Appalled thee. 'Neath the red malarious moon
> Thy bed was sweet, as that of birds whose tune
> Awoke thee to new work. Men dark and wild
> Gazed, whooped, but harmed thee not, for like a child
> Thou play'dst with perils as with bees in June.
> Whether it was where stately Niger rolled,
> Or on the rugged Atlas mountains high,
> Calm, resolute, thou dug'st up bits of gold,
> Which men call knowledge. Shall we hope and sigh
> That thy brave spirit, though the corse be clay,
> Helps to lead heathen lands to holier day?

as brought from the forest, and are some of the last
specimens of the old oaks of Nithsdale. A light spiral
staircase connects ground floor and gallery. The débris
excavated for the foundation of the buildings has been
utilised to form a large conical mound in the middle of
the garden. The mound is grotesquely covered by blocks
of quartz crystals, conglomerate, and every kind of stone,
whose fantastic shapes or geological formation are apt to
excite curiosity, and the sides of this huge rockery are
clothed with a profusion of ferns and Alpine plants. The
top of the mound is reached by a cunningly devised winding pathway, beloved by all youthful visitors, and commands a fine view of the whole garden, which is quite a
botanist's paradise. There is no attempt to dazzle the
eye, or emulate the professional gardener, with the plant-
life it contains; yet it would be hard to find, in any other
equal area, such a variety of species. As might be expected, it is richest in that part of the British flora found
in the south of Scotland. The exotic species have been
chosen mainly for their botanical interest. Large objects
of art which do not suffer readily from atmospheric waste,
and for which room can be ill-spared within doors, such
as stone crosses, querns, baptismal fonts, canoes, etc.,
adorn the garden at suitable intervals. Nor is animal
life unrepresented. An ornate box, full of pigeon holes,
perched on a high pole, is the breeding place of numerous
starlings. A racoon or opossum roams restlessly in
an enclosure of wire-netting, and the garden has a hum
of bees around its old-fashioned hives. Harmless
reptiles, such as the slow-worm, newt, toad, and frog,
glide beneath the shrubbery or hop on the walks. Every
kind of snail and slug is gladly imported and may be seen
in suitable weather airing itself on walks or bushes.
The visitor may rest assured that no such phenomena as a
magpie's nest, a mole's run, or a wasp's paper hive will be

ruthlessly interfered with. At a former period, a monkey and a white peacock were denizens of the garden, but the former mischievously plucked off the gay flowers, and both were so troublesome that they were banished.

The collections within the museum are neatly arranged without being overcrowded. The area contains the natural history, and the gallery the antiquarian and industrial collections. In both sets, specimens belonging to the locality largely bulk. It is while looking at these that one is struck with the soundness of the views of those eminent naturalists who plead for local centres, towards which the natural history and antiquarian relics of a district may gravitate. Many an old pot, stone-hammer, obliterated coin, and curious fossil, not to speak of literary remains, have been preserved from destruction by the fact that there was a man ready to undertake a long journey in order to obtain them, and who was in possession of a repository in which they would be safe. Where else would ever have been deposited the old baptismal basin of the parish, the old village drum, the 'juggs' from neighbouring church-wall or market-cross, the balls got in the wall of the mouldering castle at hand, the bucket from its well, the Roman camp-kettle which a shepherd's wife had scoured and put up for a mantelpiece ornament?

Where else could be so securely placed the remarkable canoe, got from a neighbouring loch when drained at the time the concealed crannog became visible, or the enormous curling-stone of M'Call of Glenmannow, who, more than a century ago, was buried among the green hills seen from the museum garden? The Bibles and other relics of the persecuted Covenanters, the letters written in Robert Burns' own hand while in Nithsdale, and the portrait of Jean Armour come naturally to such a repository, and are gazed on with almost a personal interest by many an onlooker, who, if he never saw Burns, has seen many of the scenes celebrated in his songs, and whose winter evenings have been rendered less long by traditions of the sufferings and escapes of the Covenanters, or the prowess of the mighty Glenmannow. To the agricultural and pastoral district around is due the valuable collections in Teratology. Comparative anatomy is well represented, and the owner seems to know the biography of every domesticated animal whose skull, skeleton, or stuffed skin is under his keeping.

One great value of the collection is that of its being under the care of a gentleman whose lucidity in explaining, and enthusiasm in exhibiting, keep far away the usual museum-headache, apt to reach adults, and are a positive charm to the young. Every Saturday, during the summer months, the 'doctor' is at home, should any schoolmaster of the district express a desire to visit him with his pupils. Although so great a boon has not been taken advantage of as it deserves, still some schoolmasters within moderate distance have more than once performed the pilgrimage to this shrine of science.

A finer sight cannot readily be conceived than the assemblage of the sanguine boys and girls with shining morning faces, and decidedly primary colours of dress, as they trip from the lonely straths and shepherds' cots of Shinnel, Crawick, Skarr, or Cairn, whose streams with no laggard pace run Nithwards. The blue eyes, fair hair, and lithe, tall forms of the Saxon predominate, although the Celt has named their places of abode. Farm carts plentifully supplied with clean straw await them at the cross-roads, and are gradually filled, as lower levels are reached, with the children, who are considered eligible, of one or more parish schools. Should the time chosen be about midsummer, the delicious coolness of the morning, and the songs of many birds add to the glee of the children, who are drawn on this occasion by horses

known to be 'cannie,' whose harness is garlanded with
flowers or jingles with bells. As the procession gets
beyond the bound of the favoured parish, it attracts the
attention of many an old dame who gazes, wonder-struck,
on the threshold of her wayside cottage, and who is
noisily but courteously saluted. As the goal draws
nearer, the fun becomes livelier, for sight-seeing is only
part of the programme, and there is a vision of coffee and
cakes as well.

Then so indefatigable a collector as the doctor has not
failed to put as many as possible under contribution.
One little fellow has stayed up to eleven o'clock every
evening for a week, to gather glowworms for the doctor's
grass plats ; for these brilliant gems are found on some
Dumfriesshire roadsides. Yon demure girl is taking
charge of a teapot a century old. Her cousin has a large
turf on which the fern so appropriately named 'Adder's
tongue' is growing. Johnny Shanklang has a slow-worm—
got under the 'thruch-stane' in the kirkyard—safely shut
in a long-necked bottle. Watty Glencorse has got six
owl's eggs packed in soft moss. None of the gifts will
puzzle the doctor, but it may be new to him that mountain
melick, or the holly fern, grows on the hillside whence it
has been plucked. There is more chance of being original
with mosses, gall-nuts, or, above all, with beetles. Little
bottles containing in spirits specimens of *Coleoptera* are in
the pockets of the more knowing scholars, for they are
aware that a specimen, if new, will be labelled with the
donor's name and with date and place of collection.
Meanwhile, during the preceding week, every chest and
drawer has been rummaged in search of old 'spinning
whirls,' coins, rings, Bibles, letters, or newspapers ; so that
out of the *omnium gatherum* some trinket may represent to
posterity the name of its former owner. Barring tangible
gifts, the measurement of an erratic boulder or giant tree,

the date of the first appearance of a migratory bird, the
description of a squirrel or mouse's nest, are received as
a kind of paper currency, next in value to the genuine
article.

When the museum is entered it is generally arranged
that some obliging precentor or pianist be present to
diversify sight-seeing with music, vocal or instrumental.
Then each child in succession is introduced to the owner
of the collection by writing his or her name in a book.
The doctor then leads the procession, giving object lessons
as he proceeds. The delighted wonder of the children is
only surpassed by their eagerness to recollect what they
see and hear; for prizes are frequently promised for the
best essays descriptive of the contents of the museum and
garden. Sometimes these essays are more than dry
catalogues, and form quite pleasant reading. The life-
histories of animals in a state of Nature, or the sad
biography of some ass or horse, for which disease incident
to ill-usage has procured a niche, mingles in a promiscuous
manner with names of 'rusty swords and jingling jackets.'
The sensational element no doubt is popular. The scalping-
knife, or the model of the guillotine, the oblique arrangement of the sharks' teeth, or the length of the alligator,
seldom fails to be remembered. Poisonous plants, the sun-
dews, because like bad boys they catch and mangle flies,
the berberry, because its stamens leap when pricked, are
mentioned in the same breath with the 'juggs,' which in
olden times held to public gaze, by way of punishment,
drunkards and blasphemers, with the cat of nine tails,
the monster spiders, or the 'corby' crows. Yet with all due
deduction there is a great gain. Kindness to animals,
and a deeper interest in bird, beast, and blossom are
implanted. Curiosity in the past is aroused. A visit to
the local museum in boyhood is like the first reading of
Robinson Crusoe or the *Voyages of Columbus.* Especially to

children resident in lonely glens and shepherds' isolated
cottages it introduces a new world.   When the museum
has been formed and is presided over by one whose natural
tastes have made him an enthusiast, and when the objects
collected have taken no inconsiderable part of a lifetime to
bring together, we have the Columbus, who, through dark
days and sunny, with unflagging ardour and amid infinite
discouragement, has widened the mental horizon of the
locality in which he was born.—[25th February 1879].

HORTUS DOCTORIS

Soon banished from his lovely home,
Poor Man, where'er his foot might roam,
Shouldered his spade, and with goodwill,
Strove for a bit of Eden still.
The caged lark, to abate its grief,
Finds in a turf some small relief ;
The prisoned lion calmer grows,
To see a palm-tree at its nose :
The smallest garden ere we crossed
Reminds us of the great one lost—
A meteor frail, a glancing stone,
A fragment of an orb that's gone.
Just take this same nook in Thornhill,
Subjected to the doctor's will ;
Say, could a thousand miles of sea,
Suggest more thoughts to you and me ?
Could half Arabia show us more
Than this thin strip behind his door ?
Heather from hills much famed in song,
The Scottish thistle, rough and strong,
The clover, rose, and fleur-de-lis,
In odd assemblage here we see.
O'er ' Plato's ' grave a column stands,
Reared by its master's loving hands
(Hands sometimes bitten through the glove,
But the poor dog did all in love !)—
Here you have castle-stones in mounts,
And lakes in old baptismal fonts ;
And sturdy plants with steady pace,
Elbowing their neighbours out the race ;
Just as the cunning Saxon man
Dwarfs or destroys an Irish clan ;

Among the plants hop toads and frogs,
Such as St Patrick chased from bogs ;
Crawl snails, with shells, up every post,
Of wasps and beetles what a host !
Midges—the doctor knows their names—
And butterflies with wings like flames.
The misletoe, a thriving flunkey,
Grows on a row'n-tree near the monkey ;
An almond's tender branches wave
Above old ' Punchinello's ' grave.
Here you have plants of poisonous breath,
Whose sap fills up the cup of death ;
That hemlock, which the Grecian sage
Drank to appease a nation's rage :
And, passing from this grim array,
Flowers that might suit a bridal-day,
Or that sweet silent language shed
By lovers wishing to be wed.
With nose, and eye, and touch amazed,
And every wonder duly praised,
You ask yourself, when wars will close,
The desert blossom like a rose,
When man, renewed by love and truth,
Will win the Eden of his youth.

LINES WRITTEN IN THE MUSEUM

When man began, through mist and error,
To peep with wonder and with terror
Athwart the earth, and air, and ocean,
With something more than brute emotion,
He fixed upon some droll-shaped stone,
Odd shell, or fragment of a bone,
Invoking it for luck we see him—
This was the earliest museum.

Witches and warlocks knew full well
Each fetish charm, or hidden spell ;
As Tam o' Shanter saw, when fuddled,
What queer things were together huddled ;
And even to-day, with church and book,
At relics knees are wont to crook.

But, reader, all untouched with fear,
Gaze round on this museum here ;
And, ignorant still of many a cause,
Courageous learn great Nature's laws.

Go gliding backwards through the past
On yon array of fossils vast ;
These beasts beheld the morn's pale horn
Ere Adam's oldest son was born ;
These plants, as age on age did roll,
Have all got changed and turned to coal ;
Those flints were used, by savage men,
Long ere the days of sword and pen
(Though fighting then must have been fun,
Turn round and view that needle-gun) ;
That mummy cat perhaps adored
Ere Joseph saw old Egypt's lord ;
These halberts, swords, and habergeons
Flashed vivid once on tourney greens ;
These uncouth figures once were signs,
Though men write now with lightning lines.

Go gliding o'er the world's wide breast :
That tomahawk came from the West ;
Those ivory-gods from India's plain ;
These bright shells from the Spanish main ;
That parrot chattered, monkey swung,
Coiled serpent shot its forkèd tongue,
That curious dress first met the eye,
Where burning suns are riding high.
Whereas those birds so dun and white
Have cowered beneath an Arctic night ;
A man, like him in yon canoe,
Has flung his harpoon where they flew,
Then upon blubber dined forsooth,
Or startled at yon narwhal's tooth !
Far nearer, where the Nith may croon,
That otter fished beneath the moon ;
There's the first larch whose branches grew,
Soft nourished by Dumfriesshire dew.
See the old juggs, and older cross :
Glencairn smiles placid at their loss.

Hold converse next with souls of men :
A letter written by Scott's own pen !
Mark well the plain, bold, manly turns—
Autograph poem done by Burns !
Learn the expression in the lines
Of faces on those antique coins ;
The poet's and the artist's arts
Are those which best join heart to hearts.

Wild havoc fang and claw have wrought,
Fierce battles teeth and tusks have fought,
Much misery bow, and spear, and sword,
Have brought on peasant, priest, and lord.

What fights for *tuum* and for *meum*
Ere they all came to this museum !
Strange pictures of a world they give,
Yet 'tis the world in which we live,
And, bound by spirit and by letter,
Our duty is to make it better.

Dumfries and Galloway Standard, 1867.

THE CAMERON STATUE IN THE MUSEUM GARDEN

Here is the statue of no trimming slave,
Quaking between the cradle and the grave,
Saving himself from lash by dint of lies,
He died for Truth—died where the curlew cries,
Fell fighting, this stout soldier of the Cross,
In the broad, silent, dreary, grey Airdsmoss ;
And all around him with their brave hearts hot
Fought men who little feared the steel or shot—
Fearing a lie much more. 'He's down, he's dead,'
Cried Earlshaw's troopers—then they chopped his head
And hands from off his trunk, that men might know,
Who stroll at evening to the Netherbow,
Reading these ghastly signals, that no more
Should Cameron preach, whose fight on earth was o'er ;
No more, with Bible open and drawn sword,
Should hurl disdain at those who fain would lord
His conscience, and his right to preach and pray.

Five thousand merks were on his head, and they
Have got it—Bruce's troopers—well content.
The errand's done on which they had been sent—
Sent, but not sent by Christ, sent two to one.
'Twas on a July afternoon, the sun
Shone on the early heather bells, the bee
Hummed here and there ; no sheep, no bush, no tree
Marked the grim treacherous moss-hag with their shade.
The little Covenanting band had laid
Their bodies prone on a small patch of grass,
When forth from the horizon's line did pass
The marshalled troopers, nearer still they drew,
Shots now were interchanged, the steel glanced blue.

'Twas a brave fight, for Hackston led the van—
Stout heart and arm, and head that well could plan ;
And though the 'Whigamores' were beaten back,
Few dared to follow on their slippery track,
And most got refuge in that trackless moss ;
But of their killed by far the greatest loss

Was loss of him, whose statue now we see,
With bonnet broad, with breeches to the knee,
With plaid on arm, and Bible in his hand,
Just as in trying times the man might stand
In some Conventicle, with heart a-glow,
Among the hills two hundred years ago.

LINES ON A SPECIMEN OF 'BOS SCOTICUS'* IN THE MUSEUM

Dr Syntax in his school
Had told us of an Irish bull,
And on the wings of learning borne,
Had shown us a dilemma's horn.
When visitors came to papa,
Or softly dropped to see mamma,
To save ourselves the name of dunce,
The horn and bull were out at once—
'Twas high work to instruct and please
Fresh from Gamaliel Syntax's knees.

But here's a bull, whose horns, and muzzle,
And front, and cheeks, are all a puzzle ;—
Three guesses now to find his breed.
Well, you may guess an age indeed,
So cease your foreign names and bustle—
That bull's as Scotch as any thistle !
One of that Caledonian herd
Which never yet knew yoke or lord,
Whose great-grandfather tossed his head
Ere yet were Scots by Wallace led,
Whose startled sires round Mary wheeled,
When riding crazed from Langside field.
They stooped to no domestic cares,
And the wild Indian's fate was theirs.
Drumlanrig † sees them now no more ;
In truth, they're lost to wood and shore ;
And, like two islands in the sea
Where continents were wont to be,
In Hamilton's wide classic glades,
Or stately Chillingham's old shades,
Remain the last of all that clan
Which fought the pre-historic man.

* A head got from Cadzow Park, Hamilton, in recent years.
† Dr Ramage, late rector of Wallace Hall Academy, in his delightful and erudite work, *Drumlanrig and the Douglases*, 1876, records
the tradition that, about 100 years before, the last of the wild white
cattle were ' sold and driven off to Chillingham.'

And now, as modest as wood sorrel,
Permit us to append a moral :
Who will not work, they shall not eat,
Nor find space for their flying feet ;
Close even upon the strong and brave
Disease and death yawn like the grave ;
While sword and gallows, pit and net,
Are for the wild and lazy set—
From beast or body, man or wife,
Toil is the payment asked for life.

Lines on a Column of Decayed Teeth in the Museum

When Timour marched with fire and sword,
All Asia quaked beneath its lord ;
His lawless hordes poured west and east ;
The fight was first, and then the feast ;
When lust and rage at last grew dull,
By royal edict, every skull
Of those whom Timour's hosts had slain
Was reared upon the reeking plain ;
Such pyramids or columns shone
Amid the waste he called his own,
Amid the lonely blackened wild,
Where palace once and garden smiled.

In the Museum at Thornhill,
There's once more reared by subtle skill,
A ghastly column built of bone,
Which human heads once called their own.
By sword or axe they came not here,
No savage bore them on his spear ;
Tweezers and pincers of the mild,
Good doctor—while he coaxed and smiled—
Drew out these sad teeth from the jaw,
And doomed them never more to gnaw.
Ten thousand teeth, that once had racked
The wearers, stand now neatly packed,
Ten thousand grinders grind no more,
Snug kept within the doctor's store,
A trophy of the art which heals,
Fits men for work, and maids for reels.

Here, for some small ten thousand shillings,
Peace was restored to countless dwellings,
Smiles were given back to beauty's cheek,
Grim agony grew smooth and sleek.

X

One pull—perchance one uncouth roar—
One gush of blood—and all was o'er ;
The mouth which held the hornet's sting
Again could joke, again could sing ;
The jaw which felt the serpent's fang
Could crack its nuts and fear no pang ;
From cheeks swollen big the flannel's flung ;
The maid grows rosy, gay, and young.

True, Timour with a fiendish glee
Might laugh his pyramids to see ;
But here, with philosophic smile
One may peruse the doctor's pile,
And though at first inclined to start,
Soon bless the grand restoring art.*

A QUANDARY

Sir Francis Fire and Baron Fuel
Arranged that they should fight a duel,
For why ? Because their skin was thin,
And let a jest too deeply in.
Sir Francis from his horse alighted,
But knowing that he was near-sighted,
Quoth he, ' Now let each take his place,
Each pull his pistol from its case,
Each at the proper moment fire,
And honour bright, though both expire !
I'm handicapped by this short sight,
But here's my plan to put it right—
You'll take a rule, our seconds there,
And with that rule you'll measure fair
My distance from the Baron Fuel,
The regular distance for a duel ;
Then you'll allow that I should be
Nearer to him than he to me,'
' Agreed,' the Baron cries, ' Your hand ! '
Whereat the seconds schemed and planned,
Measured and corded, and zig-zagged,
Whispered and swore, and crouched and bragged,
And groped and fumbled o'er the land,
But ne'er found yet where each should stand.

* Written before the triumphs of modern dentistry had made
extraction of teeth almost a sin against humanity. The col[
being in an insanitary condition, was destroyed when the catal[
was made in 1895.

CHAPTER IX

Contributions of Special Scottish Interest

Dr Longmuir's Edition of Jamieson's Scotch Dictionary — Congresses—A Gowk's Errand—Wigtown Burghs Election—First Representations of Tartan and Philibeg—Scotland's Name and Scotland's Fame—Wanted a Dumfriesshire Dictionary for a Glasgow Man—The Dumfriesshire Dialect.

Dr Longmuir's Edition of Jamieson's Scotch Dictionary

Poor Tom Hood sings out in ecstasy :—

> ' I remember, I remember,
> The house where I was born,
> The little window where the sun
> Came peeping in at morn.'

But surely among all reminiscences that most deeply touch the heart are those of our mother-tongue, imbibed with our mother's milk. We are living in a century of great changes; and one of the greatest—albeit, the most silent—is the gradual disuse of the Scottish Doric. Indeed, it has been calculated that in another century the dialect of Lowland Scotland will be as good as obsolete, and be bound up in the works of Sir Walter Scott and Robert Burns, as early English is embalmed in Chaucer. Yet in the deep retired shore of childhood, in spite of a seven years' education, and almost all our reading being English, how pleasing it is to look back on the old names and to remember by whom and for whom they were uttered. Conning over the pages of this Dictionary is often like bringing up the dead from their graves; for in some cases there are words which we have not heard leap living from the tongue since the eyes of some old acquaintance were closed in death. The nursery once more opens its doors, and the toy-books and dolls of a primitive time flit before the mind's-eye as some other vocable is encountered. School life, with its noisy games when fun became almost deadly earnest, flashes up as we stumble upon some other, and we become for a moment young, supple, and ardent. Old faces at spinning wheels, old heads beneath blue bonnets, venerable patriarchs bending over Bibles, gossips with children at the breast circulating the latest tattle of the town, old carousals, the market, the house-heating, the wedding, seem all ready to be invoked and to appear at the magic rod of some of these little talis-manic words. There is much in a name, especially when that name is connected with scenes which were around us

'In life's morning march when the bosom was young.'

There are a number of Scotch words which we would like to see taken up, patronised, and put into English dictionaries—we mean these for which no synonym exists in the southern tongue. 'Gowpin,' * two handsful ; 'stoor,' dust in motion ; 'cawry,' left hand ; 'pinkie' or 'peerie,' little finger; 'flype,' to turn inside out ; 'whumle,' to turn or roll over; 'oxter,' armpit ; 'chuckie,' a quartz pebble; 'dover,' to slumber lightly, to be between sleeping and waking ; 'doddy,' a hornless cow; 'gleid,' a burning coal; 'o' or 'oe,' grandson or grandchild; 'primp,' to dress affectedly. These are words taken at random, and yet one is safe to say that the meaning they imply could not be indicated by less than two English words, or with-out using a compound. Words occurring in our dialect

* French *jointée*, *i.e.* as much as fills the 'bowl' made by the hands held out together.

may be looked upon as pariahs, tinkers, gypsies, or
'gaberlunzies.' Not being found in the register, they
wander about like orphans or stepchildren, and are left to
degenerate or fall in with luck very much as they may. No
attempt is made to adapt the vocal organs to them—they
must adapt themselves to the vocal organs, and hence
when you are in chase of a Scotch word you have often
in turning up this dictionary to go through the whole
list of vowels before you can find him. Take 'halock,' a
romp. I began by looking for 'hullock,' which is Renfrewshire, and at last caught 'hellock,' Dumfriesshire, from
which reference was made to 'halock.' Other instances
are common. Nor does one fare better with consonants.
The terminal dental is often dropped, as yaul' for yauld
and aul' for auld, and sometimes labials are interchanged,
according to the locality, and also the dentals and liquids;
while the position of that difficultly-sounded letter 'r' is
very indefinite, as 'girse' for 'gress,' 'grass.' Words in
one county lose whole syllables appertaining to them in
others—as 'showling,' Renfrew, for 'shillying,' Dumfries;
and words which are never heard but as adjectives or
substantives in the north are met with doing service as
verbs in the south, and *vice versâ*.

Looking for Renfrew 'hizard' or 'hezard,' a verb signifying to dry clothes by bleaching, one can only get 'rizard,'
a curious transposition of the 'h' and the 'r.' 'Y' is often
taken up and dropped, 'yin' in one county being 'ane' in
another; 'twau,' 'tway'; 'three,' 'threy,' etc. 'V' and
'u' and 'w' are interchangeable, as 'ubit' or 'oobit,' or
'vowbat,' or 'wowbat,' from Anglo-Saxon 'wigga,' a worm.
Besides these difficulties, there are local variations of
meaning equally perplexing. Words formed from sound
have a larger place in a Scotch dictionary than in an
English, and, indeed, there is a tendency to draw words
away from their original sound, and to make them more

graphic by imparting to them the imitative quality, so that
if language began by imitation, it sometimes also ends
there. Rustics delight in a little imitation, in alliteration,
rhyme, and gesture. These supply the place of training
and the severities of culture, and, in a rough and round
way, express well what is meant. They also make a more
marked use of accent. 'He came in "thud-thudding."'
'What are you "figgle-faggling" there at?' 'He ate it
"stoup and roup."'   'They were sitting "cheek for
chow"'—may be taken for examples which one need not
go far to find. Diminutives are also favourites with them,
as 'wee bit manikie.'

The proverbs of a nation are generally pretty well
gathered and stored in books, but there are phrases,
equally happy and national, which escape notice, and sink
into oblivion. Many of these are graphic, such as, 'As
blae's the blawart,' 'As mad's an ettercap,' 'Reeking like a
kilogie,' 'Though you're e'e were like the gowan, and the
gowan like the gowd.' We should have liked these
phrases to have been kept more in view in such a work as
a Scotch dictionary. Valuable little notes, however, are
sometimes added explanatory of games and old customs,
such as 'Tappy-tousie,'—'a play among children, exhibiting a memorial of the ancient feudal mode of receiving a
person as a bondman, by taking hold of the hair of his
forehead. Tappie, tappie-tousie, will ye be my man?
From "tap" and "tousie," dishevelled.'

Dr Longmuir has added six hundred and thirty words,
and in an appendix has given us more than a hundred
from Orkney and Shetland. He does not seem to have
any very special knowledge of Scotch, and has depended
much on contributors. The allocation of many of the
words is faulty. Nevertheless we are greatly indebted to
him for his painstaking as far as it goes.

CONGRESSES *

The world is wakening up. After the spate of big congresses in subjects of general interest, we are to have a flood o' wee congresses on topics o' particular charm.

In oor ain rural capital we have out posters announcing the speedy advent of the 'Corns and Bunions Congress,' wi' exhibits o' every kind o' saw that seeks the sair, o' every kind o' paring knife, boot-jack, elastic stocking, comfortable shoe, and docile slipper. In the Dreepdaily Burghs several congresses of considerable importance are arranged for. The 'Insecticide Congress' promises to be a great success. Weans that were lang shilpit will be shown sleek by using a comb of peculiar construction. The microscopist will throw magnified fleas on the screen, and it is not expected that the species will survive the proper exhibition of its bloodthirsty suctorial apparatus, especially if magnified three hundred diameters. An enthusiasm for the cannibals' destruction will then be sure to loup up.

The 'Capillary Congress' will be addressed by barbers and several fashionable hairdressers. Ventilated wigs, strops of great tenacity, perfumes, and razors, must give way in attractiveness to the new machine for cropping the head, made after the fashion o' the Australian sheep-shearing yin.

In the heaviest o' oor Dreepdaily Burghs we've already had our 'Toothache and Neuralgia Congress.' Burns' 'wee stool' that he 'kicked owre the muckle' in a fit o' toothache had been fortunately secured, and proved a great attraction. Dr Doze, dentist, showed a new mineral for fause teeth, and Dr Hornbook read a paper on 'The probable extinction, by natural selection, of the wisdom teeth.'

* The following two articles from the *Glasgow Bailie* appeared over the *nom de plume* of Robin Tamson.

'The Mouse and Rat Congress,' about to open at Minnihahi, will be one of engrossing interest. Several ladies will read papers on traps. The proper use of toasted cheese will be insisted on. The extraordinary jumps made by several women when a mouse crossed the carpet will be illustrated by moving puppets and the chairs leaped over exhibited. Kittens of one-mouse power, up to cats of ten-mouse power, will be exposed for sale. A curious paper will be read, by the learned Dr Zoo, on the waste of power in rats considering their high intelligence. It will be shown how docile they become under proper management if begun in infancy, and suggestions as to their education and future use will be thrown out. Could a dozen not be harnessed and draw, say, a wean's perambulator?

The 'Telephone Extension Congress' will meet a felt want. Not to speak of pipes carrying sermons to invalids, the nation will be asked to provide tubes carrying Parliamentary debates to all political clubs. The recitation and song of theatre or concert-room could also be screwed on as far as the West Highlands, under the auspices of contracting companies (limited). This week, Glasgow is labouring with the 'Trades Congress,' and next week she is to be enlightened (?) by the 'Journalists' Congress,' and yet she isn't a bit prouder than she was six months ago. O Morocco!

Congresses need think nothing accomplished as long as anything remains to be done. They, and the welfare of the future, are thoom and finger on the same han'. [7th September 1892.]

A GOWK'S ERRAND

I had an awfu' nicht o't, Bailie, on the first o' April. I got a neat note wi' a nice smell on the paper wi' that morning's post, purporting to hae come frae Mrs Geddes, saying that she would be glad, for the sake o' auld lang syne, if I would come owre to her house that nicht and drink a cup o' tea, and otherwise spend the evening.

Noo, Mrs Geddes, Miss Janet Jamieson that was, had been married twa or three years, but had nae family, and she had been a kinna auld lass o' mine. I had made her a present, yinst, o' a very nice pair of slippers, wrocht by my ain hand, and she had knit for me a pair o' socks and a pair o' red muffatees. We fell in wi' yin anither teaching in a Sabbath School, and after that we were for a while in the Salvation Army, and Janet was often the yin that spread the newspaper on the causeway o' the street when the pennies were expected at the end o' the services. She had a bonnie fresh face that the queer shovel o' a black bonnet couldna spoil, and as for mysel' in my war-paint, being fully the average size, I didna luk the warst in the processions. Janet never sermonised, but she could lead aff the spiritual songs like a mavis.

Although she married Geddes, aulder and richer than me, we never had had a fair cast oot. The fact is my social position was sair in my way. I tried to forgive and forget, although there set in a dryness between us. Geddes was a clerk on the railway, and spoke at political meetings, gied himsel' airs, and liked to be chairman. He cried 'One man one vote,' and I'm sure he thocht his one man one vote dooble the weight o' mine. He didna shake hands wi' us, but nodded, or said his 'Gude day,' naming me aye by my surname.

I put a fair face on at the loss o' Janet. I didna want the world to ken I was sick. I thocht to mak' her a wedding present o' a book named *How to be Happy though Married*, but feered that micht be construed into an affront, so I made it a Bible gae weel bound.

I had only been yinst in her house since she settled, and that was at a promiscuous tea handling.

My heart, therefore, as ye may suppose, gied a thump
when I got her note. I was that anxious about a clean
shave that I bled my chin. I put my silver sleeve-links
in my cuffs, pinned on my dicky neatly, put a loof-fu o'
hair oil on the tap, drew on boots wi' cheeping leather, as
having an aristocratic sound, an' stuck oot my hanky as
neat's a blackbird's bill looking owre its nest.

I gaed up the stair, knocks, a wee servant lass opens and
puts me into a weel-furnished room—sofa, mahogany side-
board, marble clock on the mantlepiece, and said I was to
tell my name. I replied that it was hardly worth while,
but my name was John Anderson, or in the register, John
William Anderson, being named for two uncles on baith
sides o' the house, as it was thocht I would be the last.
The Geddeses had flitted, ye see, and this was a cut
grander than whar they set up hoose-keepin'.

In cam' Mrs Geddes. She had newly washed her face,
and looked no a bit waur o' married life.

'Oh, Johnnie,' says she, rather taen-like, 'ye've been
an awful stranger, but I'm glad to see you. How's a' wi'
you ? Ye'll hae some news to gi' me. When are ye gaun
to tak' a wife?'

But wi' that the knocker o' the ootside door was struck,
an' in a meenit in comes Geddes, looking, I thocht, somewhat surprised to see me in the room wi' his wife.

'So, Anderson, you've come to see us at last,' said he.
'What do you think of our new house?' Then he blew
some stour aff the marble timepiece, and gloured at the twa
big oil-paintings, magnified fra photos, in big brass frames,
o' Janet Paterson and himself, wi' his watch chain painted
yellow, and Janet's marriage rings gae weel executed.
'Are you come to invite us to your wedding? Somebody
was saying ye were about to read the riot act.'

'Joking aside,' quo' I, for a new thocht had come into
my head, 'I am much obliged for the kind note I received

from your house this morning, an' if it's either boots or shoes ye want to be measured for, I'm sure I have recently acquired a stock of first quality leather, and shall be happy to serve you.'

I heard something at this. It must have been them winking to yin anither, for they had taen in the situation at a glance.

'Excuse me,' says she, 'I'll get you a cup of tea.'

The wee servant lassie came in, in a jiffy, and said that the master was wanted. As soon as Geddes went out she was in again, wapping a clean linen cover on the table, and giggling as loud's ye like.

'What's wrang wi' you, lassie?' says I.

'What's wrang wi' me,' quo' she. 'Do you no ken this is the gowk's day, and that I was sent for to a house where I wasna wanted, and that I'm jist giggling at my ain simplicity for gaun?'

I struck oil in a moment. I turned as white's a clout.

Getting up, says I, 'Would you tell your master and mistress that I've forgot to send awa a telegram? Excuse me, I'll rin to the office and send it off before the cups are set.'

'Ou aye,' says she, 'we can put the tea-pot in the cosy till ye come back.'

Since then, I'm up a close or crossing to the other side of the street, whenever I see Geddes coming forrit. [23rd April 1890.]

WIGTOWN BURGHS ELECTION

A DIALOGUE

Tam O'Shanter—Did ye ever hear the like o' this, Johnnie? Our freen, Mark Stewart,* after fechting his bit duel, bluidy i' the nose, his puff weel ta'en out o'

---

* Mark Stewart, afterwards Sir Mark J. M'Taggart Stewart, Bart., M.P. of Southwick.

him, and wi' a black e'e tae, is for up and trying M'Laren
again. I never heard its equal. He's as bauld as my
auld grandfather that keeked in at Alloway Kirk window
that nicht Doon was in flood. And M'Laren this time
hasna only himsel' weel lined and buffered wi' *Scotsman*
newspapers so as to break Mark's blows, but has got
a Lord-Advocate's horse-hair wig on his head. Man,
it'll look ill if Mark trips him up and the big wig lie
rowin' i' the dirt. It'll imbarraus the Queen's Government, to be sure. That's the only thing I'm vexed
for.

Johnnie.—I dinna think, Tam, ye may be muckle
vexed for that. The Queen's Government 'll no tak' a
meal the less. But it's an unco thing nooadays that
there's no a kintra gentleman or weel-educated man
can be sent up to Paurleement frae the toun or county
that he belangs tae if he dinna please the man that
writes the leaders in the *Scotsman* newspaper. I dinna
mean their funny man, for he's often very enterteenin','
but their ill-natured man that never says Lord Beacons-
field without saying, 'quack quack,' and that crosses
himsel' every time he has occasion to write the word
'Tory.' As sure's I hae an elshin in my han', I think
Ben was a bit o' gude ben-leather, and gied us a' peace,
and tied that Berlin treaty collar gey ticht about the
neck o' the big Roosian bear, and tugged him back just
as he was in sicht o' Constanteenople. I wush I had been
a lawyer, Tam. I wudna hae stuck at that word, and I
wud run a chance o' being an M.P. That's what naether
your grandfather nor mine i' Robbie Burns' time wud hae
aspired to.

Tam.—Hae lawyers sic' guid chances as a' that? Ye
mind how Burns describes their tongues in the poem
that made my respected grandfather grey wi' Olympian
dust? Noo, if they hae sic' gleg tongues for lees, I

think the fewer o' them we hae in Paurleement the better.

Johnnie.—That's the very reason they get in so easily. Man, if ye hae a mouth like a scented wind-bag it pleases far mair than a lassie's lug. This new Paurleement's sae peppered and sauted with lawyers that the *Times* newspaper—that's a gey decent, reliable paper—for the London Leeberal papers dinna gowl and screech, and tell lees sae heartily as their Scotch kintra cousins, but often write moderately and sensibly—as I was saying, this *Times* newspaper was allooing just the ither day that sae mony lawyers in the present Paurleement would mak' business drag, there would be such argle-bargling and splitting o' peas to gie neat wecht.

Tam.—Weel, Johnnie, I ken mair about markets than politics, but ye maun alloo that M'Laren promises a deal, and an advocate has a heap o' power. Now, us farmers are often sair wranged, and do ye no think, Johnnie, that it's every man's interest to look to number yin first, and if men o' M'Laren's way of thinking 'll gie us less o' hard times, and cheaper manures, and compensation for improvements, and the game in our ain hands, and sort our dykes, and put a wee bit tax, if it's needed, on tin-can meat and live kye frae America.

Johnnie.—Stop, Tam, your tongue's runnin' awa' wi' you. M'Laren's fixed with three words—'Peace, Retrenchment, and Reform. Noo, what's this Reform? It's to gie all and sundry a vote. I can tell you that if all and sundry get a vote, all and sundry 'll send up their ain candidates, and no ask leave to send up farmers' friends. I've heard wi' my ain ears in this souter's shop o' mine all and sundry grudging terribly that farmers should be compensated for cattle destroyed that time when rinderpest was in the kintra. M'Laren set ye a' richt! It's pure blafum. Somebody's been reading the *Scotsman* and made your head like a balloon. Noo, I hae a vote, and I'm gaun to vote for Mark Stewart. He understands farmers' questions. He's nae 'prentice M.P. And I hae some loyalty in me, Tammie, yet. I believe that if a man like Mark Stewart is faithful, as we ken he is, in that which is least, he'll no betray us in that which is greatest. I hae some loyalty in me, Tammie, my man. The *Scotsman* has 'leaders' they ca' them, but they don't just lead me by the nose.

Tam.—Weel, Johnnie, ye hae a gey lump o' a nose, and it's a wee cocked up tae, and ye would be far frae being a bonny object if ye were led by the nose wi' a ring in't, either through Stranraer, or Wigtown, or Port-patrick, let alane through the burgh toun o' New-Galloway. But to be ceevil wi' ye, ye ken I hae a bit thack house, fell to me frae the mither's side, in yin o' the aforesaids; and how mony gills will ye be awn me if I pledge myself to vote for Mark? For I think, after a', he's haimert-made and genuine.

Johnnie.—Pledge yoursel'! tak' my drink and then break your pledge! Do ye no ken the prophets and soothsajers hae been writing letters in the Dumfries Radical papers telling folk they see sma' harm in break-ing a promise made to a Tory. Noo, ye'll tak' my whusky, and afore the smell o't's oot your craigie, ye'll come to me telling me ye've sign'd awa' your sowl, for conscience sake, in the inside of a ballot-box. Ye Leeberals, what do ye care? Ye've got Bradlaugh, the Athiest, sent to Paurleement. Odd it should be a lang while afore I wud offer him a snuff oot o' my box.

Tam.—I'm no sic' a Rad as ye think, Johnnie, and, as for a promise, I promised to keep T.T., and I broke it—the mair's the pity, but a man can harrly get awa' frae his grandfather. But I promised to lo'e my wife and bring up my bairns in the fear o' Gude, and I do

think a promise is sacred, so, putting the buggy in below
the bed, and without saying whusky ava', I promise to
vote for Mark on the 18th; and then, Johnnie, ye'll be
your pint stoup, and surely I'll be mine, if Mark comes
up that day to the top o' the poll, and a gae greasy
poll it is, and needs yawl climbing to sprauchle up to the
tap o't.

First Representations of Tartan and Philibeg

I observed in a contemporary a sneer at the idea of a
Saxon originating the Highland dress.   No doubt painters
have been bold enough to go back nearly eighteen hundred
years to give us a picture of Galgacus all plaided and
plumed in his tartan array.   Yet John Hill Burton, discussing the subject of Highland costume, has advanced
arguments, not only showing how comparatively modern
Highland costume is, but also showing that the Saxon had
more to do with it than most people would imagine.   The
earliest notices of Highland dress show us that it consisted
chiefly of the skins of animals, with a saffron-dyed linen
shirt.   Bright colours are mentioned as a passion of the
people, but certainly they indicate no specific check or
heraldic character.

As soon as wool began to be manufactured in Scotland,
the checked plaid, shawl, or blanket came into use.   Early
in Scottish history women wore over their heads shawls
or screens, and over their shoulders mantles.   Sometimes
these were of one bright colour, sometimes of another,
and occasionally a check pattern was woven without any
reference to clanship in the disposal of the colours.

Every one of the Western Isles, according to Martin,
differed from another in the fanciful stripes of their plaids.
The Lowlander's plaid was generally of plain light and
dark squares; the Highlander, indulging the natural

taste of a lower civilisation, delighted in more gaudy
colours. The plaids of different districts might be known
from difference of hue or some favoured pattern, so that
a man might be known by his dress as to whether he
came from Argyllshire or Badenoch. 'It's impossible to
believe,' says Burton, 'that the rigid division into clan-
checks now attributed to the tartan could have existed
and remained unnoticed during the wars of Montrose and
Claverhouse,' although a beginning might then have been
made for mere convenience. It is not at all clear that
anything like the specific clan-tartans now exhibited
appeared either in the Jacobite Rebellions of 1715 or
1745. Almost the only notice of the '15 is one referring to the dress of Brigadier Grant's men, who were
'orderly paid at the rate of sixpence a day, well armed
and clothed, ordinarily in one livery of tartan, and
furnished with all other necessaries to defend them from
the rigour of the season.'

'It may be safely pronounced,' says Burton, 'that no
genuine picture of a chief or gentleman dressed in tartan
is producible of so early a date as Charles I.' In the
Black Book of Breadalbane, containing a series of full
length portraits of the chiefs of that house, *circa* 1620,
there is not a trace of tartan. The very word 'tartan' is
not Celtic, but from the French *tiretaine*, linsy-woolsy, or
peasants' dress. The Highland costume, as it is known
in later times, was perfected in the plaid and the kilt,
otherwise known as the philibeg. The most likely date
assigned to its definite introduction was half-way between
the two rebellions. The merit of the invention is thought
by Burton to belong to a man with a Saxon enough name,
Thomas Rawlinson, an English Quaker, a man of worth
and ability, who projected or managed the works for
smelting iron near Aberhalder, about two hundred yards
from the Caledonian Canal, where the ruins of the works

may still be seen, close to General Wade's old road, now
getting into disrepair.

Evan Baillie, of Aberiachan, Inverness-shire, says that
Rawlinson had a throng of men employed in his service,
and had become fond of the Highland dress as he then
saw it in its more generalised form. He resolved to make
it handy and convenient for his workmen. Accordingly
he directed the using of the lower part of their sack-
like clothes, plaited, as what is called a 'kilt,' and the
upper part was set aside. This piece of dress, so modelled
as a diminution of the former, was in Gaelic named *felie
beg* ('beg' means little), and in our Scots termed 'little kilt';
and it was found so handy and convenient that in the
shortest space the use of it became frequent in all the
Highland districts. 'Surely a Quaker in Highland costume,' says the historian, 'would be an exceptional phenomenon, even in the age of the restoration of the garb of
old Gaul.'

The sack-like original dress already alluded to is briefly
described as a plaid, buckled round by a belt, and the
lower part plaited, and the upper loose upon the shoulders;
a cumbersome, unwieldy habit to wear at work or while
travelling in a hurry.

Burton locates Rawlinson's works as in Glengarry, but
the writer of this, who saw the ruins of the works, is correct in his address of them. They are a little east of
Loch Oich and south of the Caledonian Canal, about three
miles from Glengarry, or at least from the district now
covered by the name. The tenant farmer of Aberhalder
at that time was an extensive farmer in Tynron, and he
once saw a large piece of cast-iron there marked with the
initials of Rawlinson. — *Dumfries Herald*, 15th February
1883.

Y

Scotland's Name and Scotland's Fame.

Auld Scotland, in her youthfu' prime,
  Held high her royal head ;
And they that daur'd affront her pride
  Wad rue the daring deed.
To free her from oppression's grasp
  On many a field she fought,
Where Scotland's name and Scotland's fame
  Shall never be forgot.

Where glorious Wallace led the way
  They followed, sword in hand,
And many a gallant blow was struck
  To free their native land ;
And then comes Bannockburn, it is
  A consecrated spot,
Where Scotland's fame and Bruce's name
  Shall never be forgot.

Old Scotland well may boast her Bards,
  Sweet followers of the shrine—
Adown the page of History
  Their names do brightly shine.
Saint Michael's, too, in fair Dumfries,
  Another hallowed spot,
Where Scotland's fame and Burns's name
  Shall never be forgot.

Thou fairy borderland, sweet home
  Of childhood's earliest dream,
Where many a saint and many a sage
  Have mused on holy theme.
And there comes glorious Abbotsford,
  The home of Walter Scott,
Where Scotland's fame and Wattie's name
  Shall never be forgot.

And long may that loved land produce
  The Patriot and the Bard ;
And peace and freedom find a home,
  Her safety and her guard.
Now auld Saint Fechan's fane receives
  Another noble Scot,
Where Scotland's fame and Carlyle's name
  Shall never be forgot.

May 1881.

Wanted a Dumfries Dictionary for a Glasgow Man.

They put me in a burble wi' their tone,
And at their queer unheard o' words, I groan.
To stamp a sheep wi' letters they ca' 'beust,'
And when a bodie's bien they say he's 'peust.'
A precipice they aften name a 'gairy,'
'Bask weather' means the weather's dry and airy.
To 'stell's' to stan'—jump and they'll say ye're 'yaul';
Point out a dam—they cry, oh, that's the 'caul.'
Their hens sit on a 'lauchter' o' gude eggs.
Instead o' whangs they've 'steekers'—licks are 'flegs.'
When the wee pan boils briskly on the ingle,
They talk about the 'laggan' o' the 'pingle.'
On 'bensel' days the wind blaws rough and cold,
'Liggats' and 'lunkies' a' their dykes hae boled.
'Twinters' and 'thinters,' sic like names for sheep!
To sprout's to 'chun,' to parboil is to 'leep.'
'Kirkwipe's' a word the Annan folk know well.
Rin 'widdershins'—against the sun—they'll yell,
For it's a cantrip they can nae mair stan',
Than pouring water, turning wrang yer han'.
They 'jib' their kye, feed them on 'orts' and 'locks';
Their weans rin out the sicht o' 'fremet' folks;
They talk o' 'tummocks' half grown o'er wi' 'spret,'
Where rashes for horse-brechams some folk get,
Slate-pen is 'caum'—a black-lead pencil 'waud.'
'Kinvalg'—what's that?—a tippet or a maud?
'Reeves' are their sheepfolds, and a 'stank's' their pool.
To play the truant is to 'trone' the school.
Pails 'stan'' in Ayrshire—in Dumfriesshire 'sit.'
The place they're hired for—they ca' that a 'bit.'
Near 'Sauterness' (1) they ca' a sow a 'swine.'
But then they kenna 'peever,' 'trundle,' 'byne.'
When Paisley folk say 'gots' (2), Thornhill say 'syres' (3),
'Clarty'—not 'clatty' wark is mucking byres.
They recommend 'road-ribbings' as gude mools;
They've got a 'gellic' in their list of tools.
Their corn's put up in 'stampcoles' and in 'thrieves.'
Kestrels are 'keelies'—Glasgow word for thieves.
Frae Seaton 'Sitlington' they somehow brew.
'Hairstanes' frae Hastings by some plan they screw.
'Hotson' frae Hewison they somehow drive,
And they've four ways o' spelling Minnyhive.
'Mingas' (4) and 'Trummle' (5), 'Gilkirs' (6), 'Frizle' (7), 'Greer' (8),
Wi' 'Dronnin' (9) and wi' 'Hot,' (10) go to 'Dusdeer' (11).
Better 'as' that—when sleeping wi' the dead,
They bear a heavy 'thruch-stane' ower their head.

1. Southerness. 2. Gutters. 3. Sewers. 4. Menzies. 5. Turnbull. 6. Gilchrist.
7. Fraser. 8. Grierson. 9. Drummond. 10. Howat. 11. Durisdeer.

WORDS, NEW TO ME, COLLECTED FROM THE DUMFRIESSHIRE DIALECT DURING THIRTY YEARS, 1864 to 1894.*

THE collection of words which I present has been gathered at intervals, as opportunity presented, or as curiosity stimulated. It is by no means exhaustive; indeed, I believe that with attention the number could easily be doubled. It is strange how few of them are to be found in the works of our more popular authors who have made us acquainted with Scotch characters and manners. The words here submitted may, to some extent, have been known in Renfrewshire, but they must either have become obsolete before my day, or been current in the parts of it away from those in which the first half of my life was spent. But, while Dumfriesshire dialect has introduced me to a great many new words, it at the same time presents blanks by not containing many old words familiar to me in childhood. Indeed, the obverse side of the shield should contain a paper on words in Renfrewshire new to a Dumfriesshire man. I fear, however, that unless work of this kind is attended to at an early date the crop will be a poor one. National education is upon us, and words not in the English dictionaries are treated as so much base coin. Powerful influences are at work in favour of the exclusive use of reputable words, and one of the most powerful of all is the open derision or suppressed laugh which assails the unfortunate individual who trips in his talk, and substitutes a word from the native Doric for one that has the patronage of the school-master. It is well for us that we have in Dr Jamieson's

* Read before the Dumfriesshire and Galloway Natural History and Antiquarian Society, and printed in its Transactions.

'Scotch Dictionary' such an excellent collection. Testing this collection by the words I have gathered, I am astonished, not so much at a few omissions, a sat the laborious and exhaustive collation he has made. Generally when I got a new word I opened his dictionary, and there, with a little painstaking, I found it in some form or other. With a few words my search was long-continued. Dialect is not under reins like the Queen's English. It runs a good deal loose at its own free will. Gaelic scholars tell us a Skye man could scarcely make himself intelligible in the Isle of Arran, nor a native of Sutherland understand the patois of Breadalbane; and it is the same with the dialects of English. Consonantal and vowel changes, depending on Grimm's law and on multiform divergent circumstances, changes like those so admirably discussed in Peile's introduction to Greek and Latin etymology, are to be met with in Scotch as elsewhere. Thus I look for 'Feume,' and I get it under 'Veem'; I look for 'Rauner,' and get it under 'Rander'; for 'Haizard,' and it is written 'Rizzard'; for 'Witter,' and it is under 'Otter'; for 'Kenches,' meaning 'favours,' and I get it under 'Kinchis,' a kink of rope; and just in the middle of the discussion on ropes, one of its meanings is 'unexpected advantages,' which I believe is my 'Kenches' thus cavalierly disposed of. My 'Gameril' is entered 'Cameril.' 'Yaupish,' meaning 'hungry,' is entered 'Yape,' or 'Yap.' Terminal *d* jumps in and out. The consonant *r* is of mercurial temperament, and you cannot predicate on which side of the vowel it will be found. In rare cases initial letters or syllables disappear, as 'Toush' for 'Cartouche,' and 'Orts' for 'Worts.' As for vowels, you are pretty much in the position of the student of those Hebrew manuscripts which have none. Peile says that there is much reason to believe Indo-Europeans begun with one vowel only, the sound of *a* in father, which has become, by the

law of least action, the father of the other vowels that
require a very little less stress to articulate.   In the
Scotch dialect *a* often betrays a tendency to escape from
itself; *e* and *i* change places, and altogether hardly a
single district abides exactly by the vowel sounds of
another. As to etymology, I have, with very few exceptions, let that alone. My impression is that the study of
dialects proves there is no Scottish nation distinct from
English.   The Anglo-Saxon in both countries speak
dialectical varieties of the same language.   I believe
there are more words of Celtic origin in the dialect of
Renfrewshire than in that of Dumfriesshire. ‘Taunel,’
a bonfire; ‘Oe,’ grandchild; and even ‘Beltane,’ denoting Whitsunday, are quite unknown, so far as I can
learn, to our Tynron shepherds; while several Dumfriesshire words not current in Renfrewshire are known in
the north of England, or may be found in old English
books. As to the sentimental notion that owing to the
long alliance of Scotland and France we have derived
many words from French, that notion must be received
with caution.   Max O’Rell, in *Friend Macdonald*, gives
a list of about forty of these words, a list neither complete
nor correct, as it can be shown that in great part they
are old English words, some still known to the English
peasantry, and going back to the days of Chaucer.   I
fancy that when words come to be despised as vulgar
they have a tendency to be put to humbler uses.   The
words ‘brisket,’ the ‘breast;’ ‘faiple’ or ‘firple,’ the
‘under lip;’ and ‘graith,’ ‘clothes,’ are instances of this
tendency. I seldom hear these words applied to human
beings. The ‘brisket’ of a sheep, the ‘firple’ of a horse,
and ‘graith,’ equivalent to ‘harness,’ are still current.
‘Don’t tell me I have “lugs,”’ said the schoolboy; ‘naebody but a cuddy-ass has “lugs.”’ Another peculiarity
in my list is one which might be expected; by far the

greater part of the words are monosyllables. Jaw-
breakers seem to have been avoided by our peasantry.
A few words supplied me by correspondents, but which
I have not myself heard uttered, are marked 'communicated.'

A

Adder-beads, small round
stones supposed to have been
formed by adders. Beads
from prehistoric graves, made
of dark glass.

Ark, a large chest for holding
corn or meal; E. English word.
[Common.] In Renfrewshire
we had no arks save those
mentioned in the Bible. In my
own kitchen I have an ark with
a partition, the one part holding oatmeal, the other flour.—
Waverley Novels.

Atherbell, or, in Tynron, *Etherbell*, the dragon-fly. ['Bell'
should be 'bill.'] Halliwell informs us that in the Isle of
Wight the sting or bite of a
dragon-fly is supposed to be as
venomous as that of a snake,
and there the local name is
snake-stanger. So the Dumfries Etherbell also has reference
to the snake or adder.

Aval or *Avil*, not spelt with
v in Jamieson, but with *w*, as
Awald or *Awalt*. The Dumfriesshire pronunciation agrees
with the history of the word.
A sheep lying on its back and
unable to right itself was said
to have 'fa'en avil.' I believe
it was applied to men lying
supine when intoxicated, and
even a man dying lying on
his back was said to 'die avil,'
vide Jamieson. Brachet, the
ablest French philologist, traces

the French word *aval*, meaning
'down-stream,' to the Latin *ad
vallem*, used of a river flowing
vale-wards. Its opposite is *ad
montem*, meaning towards the
hill. The verb *avaler*, literally
'to go aval,' signified at first to
descend, then became restricted
to 'to swallow.' From aval
comes the word *avalanche*, literally a mass of snow which slides
towards the vale. The word
was introduced from Switzerland. When in the vale of
Chamouni I heard the avalanche,
'that thunderbolt of snow,' I
thought how strangely the Swiss
and Scotch shepherds were connected by this word, one may
say, in the mouths of both. *Aval*
is not in Scott, Burns, Ramsay,
nor Ferguson. [The etymology
proposed, though ingenious, is
wrong. *Awald* is Saxon for 'on
the roll.' Common.]

B

Bairge or *Baird*, to scold.
[Banff.]

Bask, hard, dry. A bask day
is a day with a withering wind.
[Widely spread. Used by
Wiclif.]

Basket-hinger, the gold-crested
wren. Communicated.

Bat, state or condition. About
a bat—*i.e.*, about the same.

Baul or *Bauld* [bold, healthy.]
'Are you bauld?' signifies 'Are
you in good health?'

Beds, hop-scotch. The circular slate driven by the foot is called the bed-stane, but in Renfrewshire [and elsewhere, *e.g.*, Lothians] the game is known as the *Peeverals* and the stone the *Peever*, a word not given in Jamieson, but evidently allied to the Dumfries *peefer*, q. v.

Bee [or *Virl*], a metal ring round the foot of a staff. [Wiclif.]

To Beet or *Beit*, to help or mend by adding to. To beit a fire, to mend it; to beit a dyke [to rickle it]. Burns's *Cottar's Saturday Night*—'Or noble Elgin beats the heavenward flame.' [Common.]

Benner-gowan. I have heard this name applied to the feverfew of our gardens. [Benner = Bennert or Banewort.]

Bensel, force, violence, applied to a wild, stormy day. In N.E. bensel means to bang or beat. [Common as far S. as Lincolnshire.]

Bern or *Birn*, a scorched piece [stalk] of heather or shrub which can be used for kindling a fire. It is said of a niggardly frugal person, 'It's a queer brae that he couldna get a bern off.'

Berry, to thrash corn, or man, or child. In the Galloway poem of Aiken Drum, the Brownie says—

'I'll berry your crops by the light of the moon.'

In the N. of England the thrasher is a berrier, and the flail the berrying instrument. [Common.]

Borthy [i.e. *Birthy*], fruitful. Said of a plant, such as a rose, full of vitality and blossom.

Billy, brother. 'Waverley.' Allan Ramsay.

Bilter, a child. Common. A minnow. Dumfriesshire. Perhaps a generalised idea of 'a little one.' In Renfrewshire a thriving child was a 'big bilter.' [Rare, according to Wright]. [Also *Bilty*].

Bink, a bench, a long form used in schools. Allan Ramsay.

Bit, place. Have you got a new bit? Have you got a new place or situation?

Black - dookers, a Galloway word for cormorants.

Blaud, to strike.

Blearie, a buttermilk gruel. Probably from an older word *blear*, thin; given in Jamieson.

Bleez - money, money presented to the teacher at Candlemas. Some old people recollect when candles were lighted as a part of the ceremony.

Bluidy-fingers, fox-gloves; in Renfrewshire called Dead-men's bells.

Boiler, this is the common word for kettle.

Bowin, to take the lease of a farm in grass with the live stock on it. [Rather the sublet of a cow's pasture with the stock on it.]

Brand, a contemptuous name for a worthless person. Possibly a variant of *brat*. [Rather a reminiscence of the Biblical 'brand plucked from the burning.']

Brass, used in Dumfriesshire for money—in Renfrewshire 'tin.' Also, in the former it means 'coppers.' *Vide* Matthew's gospel.

Braxy, of or belonging to sheep that have died. [A fatal disease among young sheep.]

Breem, to burn with desire. E. England word. [English 'brim.']

Brisky, a chaffinch; also, *Brichtie*. Communicated.

Buckies, heps of the wild rose.

Buist, to stamp [with hot tar] the owner's initials on sheep.

Bull daisy, a wild orchis.

Bullering, making a noise, as with gurgling water in the mouth, more generally being rude and noisy or forward. Applied metaphorically to the quick bursting of buds by heat and rain, and to a great growth. 'Everything's bullering out.' [The Bullers of Buchan.]

Bullfit, the house-martin or swift. Communicated.

Bullisters, the fruit of the bullace tree. [Sloes.]

Burble, a state of confusion.

Burnbecker, the dipper or water-pyat. Communicated.

Bus, a cow-stall, N. of England, pron. Boose. [Common.]

Butterblobs, what James Hogg calls Lucken-gowans, the plant *Trollius Europœus*.

C

Cair or *Ker*, the left hand; Renfrewshire, *caury*. [In one form or other quite common.]

Cameril, a stick crooked so as to be inserted between the hind legs [hocks] of a carcase when hung up.

Capernoity, irritable. [Very common.]

Carritch, catechism. — Used by Burns.

Cashie, soft, succulent, delicate.

Caumstane, white stone for rubbing and marking the stone floor; slate-pen, which is called by my scholars *caum.*—*Waverley Novels*. [Common.]

Cawker, the sharpened under part of a horse's shoe. [The iron nailed to the wooden sole of a clog.] The slang word *cawker* [means] a dram.

Channel Stones, curling stones. [Common in Scotland.]

Charkers or *Cherkers*, crickets.

Choops, the *heps* of the wild rose. In Renfrewshire the hairy seeds inside were called 'lice' from the irritation they caused if they came in contact with the skin. [Same word as *hips*.]

Chun, a term applied to the sprouts or germs of barley, but as I have heard it, to the shoots of potatoes when they begin to spring in the heap. To chun potatoes is to nip off these shoots.

Cipher, a useless, diminutive person. [Of course this is merely 'cypher' = ' nothing.']

Clabber, tough mud on the highway. In Dumfriesshire to *clabber up* a dyke is to pile up the stones, in a temporary way, that have fallen down.

Cladscore, twenty-one sheep. [Highland black-faced sheep are numbered 21 to the score.]

Cleps, the handle of a pot. [The form which spans over it.]

Cleuch, a narrow valley. It is called a *clough* in N. England. [Common in both forms.]

Clink, alert. 'He was clink at it.'

Clyre, a gland in meat.

Cow-crackers, bladder-campions.

Crouzie, a long ladle for melting lead in. The lead was poured out of it into moulds or caulms for shot when country people had assembled for the purpose of a shooting match. A flat hat worn by women. A stand with three legs upholding a lamp.

Crock, an old ewe. In the

S. of England this is called a crone. [Very common.]

Crones, the small berries of the cranberry; evidently corrupted from *eran*, which in turn is from *erune*.

Crony, a potato. In Clarke's poem on the potato, often attributed to Burns.—Moniaive, 1801.

Crot or *Crut*, a short person. —S. Ayrshire. [N.E.]

Crottles, small fragments. The dry lichen of the stone dykes, apt to stick to clothes laid on them. [As 'fragments,' common.]

Cundy, a small opening to carry off water. Sometimes a rabbit-hole is called a cundy; evidently from conduit. [Common.]

Curbody, active courtship. Jamieson gives the following illustration of it—'She threw water at him and he an apple at her, and so they began curbody'—a lover's quarrel. [Perth.]

Curmas or *Kirmas*, a quarrel; evidently from skirmish. [Rather German and Dutch, *Kirmes, i.e.,* Kirkmass.]

D

Dabbies, shortbread for the Lord's Supper.

Daiman means rare [individual], occasional. Burns's mouse says:—

'A daimen-icker in a thrieve 'S a sma' request.'

Daised [or *dazed*], having lost its strength [stupid]; daised wood, rotten wood; a daised sack, one ready to burst into holes.

Daiver ye, confound ye. Perhaps allied to the Ayrshire *Taivert*, stupid.

Darg, a day's work. A field in Tynron parish is known as the four-darg; that is, it takes four days to plough [or mow] it. A corruption of 'day-wark.' In Scott, Burns, and Ruskin. [Very common.]

Dass, a column of the hay stack. Hogg, 'Brownie of Blednoch,' calls a dass a grassy turf growing in a stream. [English *Dess*, a layer, a stratum.]

Dazed bread in N. England means dough-bread, and dazed meat, meat badly roasted.

Dead man's creesh [*i.e.*, grease or fat], *Oenanthe crocata*, water hemlock.

Debate, struggle. He made a great debate, *i.e.*, he struggled well and kept up his head. In Chaucer it means to fight; and Gibbon calls the wars of the Crusades the World's Debate. [Obs. English.]

Deck of cards, pack of cards. [Shakespeare, etc.] In Mark Twain's *Huckleberry Finn* we read of 'an old ratty deck of cards.'

Deer's hair, the scirpus growing on the hills.

Deil's butterfly, the tortoiseshell butterfly.

Dock, the following entry is in Jamieson:—'Dock, a public walk or promenade in Dumfries on the banks of the Nith.' [Jamieson seems to be in error. The *dock* was the name given to the place where the ships lay, and afterwards to the land alongside of it. The word *port* is used in the same way in Dalbeattie.]

Doddy or *Doddet*, without horns, N.E. Scotland. [Common. Applied to a polled cow.]

Dollop, quantity. 'The whole dollop.'

Donneries, clothes' moths. I have not heard the word, but give it on the authority of R. Armstrong, Thornhill.

Dooth, shady. The dooth side of the hill is the side towards the north. *Douf,* benumbed.

Drachty, designing, cunning.

Draw-moss, the sheathed cotton sedge.

Dryne, driven, used by old shepherds. 'Have you ever dryne sheep over that road.'

Duffel, the name of a woollen cloth, dyed blue or various colours, used in Dumfriesshire for petticoats, and in Renfrewshire for cloaks or mantles for women. [Common at one time.]

Dymond or *Dinmont,* a wether in its second year.

E

Ebb, shallow, narrow.

Eek, sweat or damp from the body, as 'an eek from his head has stained the pillow.' [The dried sweat or yolk on the wool of sheep before washing.] We may recollect that the Greek word *ichor* means 'juice in the veins of gods.' *Vide* Skeat.

Eild yows, Renfrewshire *yell yows,* ewes that are barren. [Common.]

Ein, even. 'Draw the line ein,' *i.e.,* draw the line even. [Straight.]

Eizel or *Azle,* a hot ember, a cinder. [Common.]

To Ely or *Ailie,* to disappear, to vanish.

F

Faildyke, a wall built of sods.

Fawns, rough wet places on the hills; white spots on moorish or mossy ground. On the stone set up to commemorate the shooting of two Covenanters near where the parishes of Penpont, Tynron, and Dalry join at an elevation of 1500 feet, it is stated that the martyrs were shot on the adjoining 'Fawns of Altry.'

Feat, in the ballad of 'Aitken Drum' we are told of a newfangled wife fond of a' things feat, in the sense of nice, exact. In Shakespeare's *Tempest* we have the comparative degree, 'Look how my garments sit upon me much feater than before.' Allan Ramsay; Burns.

Feil, soft and smooth and warm.

Fern-year, last year. In Chaucer *ferne* means 'before.' Allan Ramsay. S. Ayrshire.

Fettel, condition.

Feuing, working or attempting. 'He's feuing well at the mawing.' He's making a good beginning.

Fiddering, fluttering. 'There's a badly spelled letter announcing her engagement. She would be fiddering'—*i.e.,* she would be in a flutter.

Firple, the Renfrewshire *faiple,* under lip (more frequently of a horse).

Fitchet, the pole cat. This is an old English word spelt *fitchew.* Shakespeare. The original meaning is 'the beast that smells bad.'

Flake, a bar [sheep hurdle.]

Flapper-bags, burdocks.

Flapperbags, butter-burs.

Flauchter-spade, a long two-handed spade [or breast plough], for removing the surface sod in the peat moss. Ramsay.

Fleem. Phlegm, spume. Chaucer. [The lancet used for bleeding cattle.]

To Fleg, to fly [or rush] from place to place.

Flichen, anything small or light, as 'flichens of soot.'

Flosh, a swamp, a bog. In this sense it is employed in the title of a popular English novel, *The Mill on the Floss.* Flosh is the name of a place near Gasstown, Dumfriesshire.

Flype, to turn inside out.

Foisonach or *Fushloch,* waste straw, dried grass, chips of wood, or refuse of that sort.

Foothy, in good condition, applied to cattle.

Fow, a pitch-fork.

Fow or *Fooze,* the house-leek. In the *Waverley Novels* it is spelt *fouats.*

Foy, an entertainment to a person about to leave a place.— *Waverley Novels.*

Frem or *Fremmit,* strange, foreign. Used by Burns, Ramsay, and Scott. Burns says—'And mony a friend that kissed his cup is now a fremit wight.' The word is spelt *fremde* in Chaucer, and *fremed* in Shakespeare.

Friggle, to work vainly, to work at trifles.

G

Gairies, steep, rough rocks; *gair* means side in the Scotch ballad of 'Burd Helen.' *Gair* seems to mean a rough place in the 'Brownie of Blednoch.' [Also means a green strip of grass below a spring.]

Gaishon [very lean], a skeleton. James Hogg's writings.

Galligaskins, rig-and-fur woollen coverings for the legs.—

Bennett's *Tales of Nithsdale.* [Common in both Eng. and Scot.]

Gangers, people on foot in contrast to those in vehicles.

Gaubert, a domestic cock that does not crow or lead out the hens gallantly.

Ged, a pike; an old English word allied to goad. The names both of pike and ged are suggested by the shape of its snout.

Gellock, an iron lever or crowbar. *Gellock,* the earwig; Renfrewshire, *gullacher.*

Gib or *Gibby,* a male cat. It is used in this sense in Shakespeare.

Gill, a leech.

Giyl or *Garel,* the gable.

Gled or *Buzzard-gled,* the buzzard. Communicated.

Gliff, a short sleep, a short while, a fright.

Goan, a wooden dish for holding porridge.

Goggles. 'To put the goggles on you,' to lead you a dance, to take your nap off one. Jamieson gives goggles as a name for the blinders of horses.

Gorlings, nestlings; in Renfrewshire, *scuddies.* This interesting word is allied to English girl and French garçon. Originally both girl and garçon were applied to young persons of either sex.—Ramsay.

Gorrach, to crowdy, or to mix, as porridge with milk, or to make mud pies.

Gowf, to flaunt about. A *gowf* is a foolish person; Chaucer, *gofish,* foolish.

Grain, the branch of a tree. [German, *Grein.*]

Grool, the ground refuse of coal or other material. 'To sweep out the grool' is to clean the outhouse.

Groozle, to speak huskily.

Grozzle or *Grozet*, a goose-berry.

Grushach, glowing embers.

Gryce, a pig. In Allan Ramsay and in several Scotch proverbs. Perhaps the swine-cry, *gussy gussy*, may be a degenerate descendant of *gryce*.

Guddle, to catch fish with the hand. [Eng. tickle.] Hogg gave the variant, *goupart*.

Gull. Jamieson says a 'chill.' I hear it more frequently when one is obliged to have a much lower estimate of any one. 'This incident was the first that gave me a gull at him.'

Gunner, the yellow-hammer. Communicated.

H

To Harp, to riddle; evidently suggested by the shape of the instrument used in riddling or separating sand and gravel, which is of an oblong shape, containing wires enclosed in a wooden frame.

Heather-bleet, the mire-snipe.

Hech-Kechan, making much ado about little. [The *ch* is aspirated.]

Hefted, domiciled, as of sheep that have got used to their pasture.

Hempie, the hedge-sparrow. Communicated.

Hewl, a cross-grained person.

Hindberries, raspberries.

Hirsel, a flock of sheep.

Hod or *Hud*, the back of the fire-place built of stone or clay somewhat like a seat; applied now to the spaces [shelves] on each side.

Hoshens, Renfrewshire, *Huggers*; stocking-legs used as gaiters in snowy weather.

Hummel, or *Hommel* to break the awns off barley. At a show of curiosities, Moniaive, I saw an oblong instrument with parallel bars which was once used for hommelling barley. [Common.]

Hummings, what is chafed and left by rats or other rodents. 'Give the wean a hum.' Chew a piece and feed it therewith.

Hurchin, an urchin or hedge-hog. Skeat traces the word to the Latin *horrere* to bristle, so that the initial *h* of the original is retained in Dumfriesshire.

Hurley Hurley, or *Hurley Hawkie*, a cry to cattle to bring them home from the field to be milked.

Hut, a square basket, which opened at the bottom for carrying manure into the fields—only known to old people, and that as a tradition.

I

Infestuous, extraordinary.

Innerlie, situated in the interior part of the district, snug, not exposed.

J

Jenny-spinner or *Jennynettle*, crane-fly.

Jib, to milk closely. [In small quantities as at last.]

Jibbins, the last milk milked.

K

Kade, [the six-legged] sheep-tick. [*Melophagus ovinus.*]

Kain, part of farm rent paid in kind. [*Kainer*, a dairyman who pays the farmer his rent in cheese.]

Karson or *Kerses*, the lady's smock or cuckoo flower. I

don't care a curse—*i.e.*, I don't care a kerse. [*Kerse* is rather a cherry.]

Kedgy, brisk, lively, amorous. E. English word.

Keelie, the kestrel hawk. A low word for 'thief' in Glasgow [and elsewhere.]

Keestless, tasteless, insipid.

Kenches, favours. In Jamieson entered Kinsches, 'unexpected advantages.'—*Waverley Novels*.

Kent, a walking - staff, a cudgel.—*Waverley Novels*.

Kork, to scold or nag.

Kat, irascible, quick tempered.

Kink here is a fit of coughing in chincough.

Kink, to twist a rope. *Kink*, a twist in a rope.

Kinvaig, a small plaid. So says Bennett's *Tales of Upper Nithsdale*. I have not met the word.

Kir, cheerful, fond, confidential.

To Kist, to enclose in a coffin. [Put in a chest.]

Kyaugh or *Kyaught*, anxiety. Mayne's *Siller Gun*.

Kyaw, jackdaw [or jackdaw's cry.]

Kyloes, Highland cattle.

L

Laggan-gird, the hoop [of a series] securing the bottom of a wooden vessel.

To Lair, to stick in the mud or snow. The piece of ground one purchases in a churchyard or cemetery.

Launer, a laundry-maid.

To Leam nuts, to separate the bunch of hazel nuts from the husk.

Led farm, a farm [not resided on by the tenant] held along with another [metaphorically, as if led like a spare horse.]

To Leep, to heat.

Leepit, par-boiled.

To Leese, to pass a coil of rope through the hand unwinding or winding it up again. [Also loosening the fibres of a rope.]

Let day, a day when you have little to do.

Liggat, a wooden gate.

Loper, to coagulate ; loper snow, snow in a state of slush. In Renfrewshire the word is *laper*, and only applied to blood. [*Lapper*, commonly applied to the curdling of milk.]

Lovenanty, O strange !

Lunkie, a hole in a dyke left for the passage of sheep.

M

Mankeeper, newt. Because it is believed that it waits on the adder to warn man of his danger. —Jamieson.

Mat, a door mat or bass ; in Renfrewshire a mat meant a thick woollen covering for the bed, generally wrought into a pattern.

To Mein, to pity, to bemoan.

Meroe or *Mercy* [that is, marrowy], ripe, applied to apples when they are sweet and mellow.

Minnie, mother.

Mochrum elders, cormorants. Communicated.

Moidart, stupid.

N

Nap, a wooden dish. 'To take your nap off one' is to befool him.

Nibbie, a walking-staff, a shepherd's crook [with a short handle].

Niddle, to work quickly with the fingers.

Nightingales, moths. Communicated.

Nocket, a luncheon.

Norrie, a whim.

Notour, notorious. Avowedly persisted in in spite of warning. —Bennett's *Tales of Nithsdale*.

Nups, the cloudberry. We have Nupberry hill in Closeburn —well named, for there the plant grows.

O

Oon, apparently a contraction of oven, but applied to a large shallow pan [metal pot], with suitable lid, in which the guidwives make loaves. Glowing peats are heaped on the top of the lid.

Orts, vegetable refuse. Wort is the old English word for vegetable. Plant is a more recent Latin word.

P

Paidle, a stake net. Communicated. [In East Lothian to hoe or thin.]

Paik, a low character.

Pan, the head. ' *Pan*, that piece of wood in buildings which lies on the top of the stone wall' Ray (1768). In Dumfriesshire the piece of wood in thatched houses joining the couples.

Papes, cherry stones.

Parrock, a small enclosure in which a ewe is confined when it is desired that she take to a lamb not her own.

Peefer or *Pyfer*, to whimper, to complain. *A Peefering body*, a trifling person.

Pensy, conceited. Ramsay. *Waverley Novels*.

Pettles, feet. This word occurs in Clark of Glencairn's Poems, 1801.

Picked calf, a [premature or] dead-born calf.

Pingle, a small tin goblet with a long handle, a pan.

Pingy, cold, not able to endure cold. [Fretful.]

Piskie, dry, shrivelled; applied to grass or to the hair of cattle.

Plut or *plout*, to put down with a plump.

Poulie, a louse; evidently from the French *pou*, a louse, *pouilleux*, lousy.

Pry, the carnation carex; valuable food for hill sheep.

Puddock-spit, or *Gowk-spit*, also cuckoo-spit. The froth secreted on stalks of grass around a small immature insect. [*Anthrophora spumaria*, and other species, belonging to the family ' Cicadellidæ.']

Puist, bien, in easy circumstances.

Pumrose, with Tynron peasantry takes the place of Primrose. Jamieson has *Pumrock*.

Puttock, the buzzard, a species of hawk.—Shakespeare.

Q

Quickens, couch-grass, allied [just as ' couch' is] to the old English word quick, living, used in the Creed, and here applied to this grass, whose vitality is marked. ' I am cut to the quick' means to the parts which are very sensitive, very much alive to the pain.

R

Rackingwage, too great a wage. Comp. E. rack-rent.

Ragabus, a tatterdemalion, a vagabond.

Ramps, Allium ursinum.

This is an old English word.
An old English word for March
was Lide.

'Eat leeks in Lide, and ramsins in May,
And all the year after physicians may
play.'

Raskill or *Rascal*, a young
deer. This is Shakespeare's
word for a young deer. In
Tynron we have Mount Raskill,
which I submit is 'Deer Hill.'

Red land, ploughed land, so
called by many who know it
is not red. *Vide* Gladstone's
misconceptions of Homeric in-
ability to distinguish colour,
founded on paucity of Homeric
colour-names. In old Scotch
ballads the fox and yellow gold
are red.

Reeves, a permanent sheep-
fold in Renfrewshire. *Ree* is a
court, an enclosed place for
coal—the coal ree. [*Reed* is a
court for cattle.]

Refeir, 'to the refeir,' in proportion. 'The cook has as
much work to the refeir as has
the tablemaid.'

Ressum or *Reisum*, a fragment, a small quantity. [Com-
mon.]

Rice or *Ryss*, brushwood.

' And thereupon he had a gay surplice,
As white as is the bloom upon the
rise.'—*Chaucer.*

Rien, contraction for riven.

Rile, Dumfriesshire contraction for ravle. To rile worset,
to entangle it.

Rime or *Rina*, hoar frost.
Ayrshire, *cranreuch*. It can be
shown that the two words are
variants from the same root.
Anglo-Saxon spelt it with an
initial *h*. Curtius connects
hrim with the Greek *krumos*,
frost.

Rip, a regardless fellow.

Ritocks, the [fibrinous] refuse

of tallow when it is first melted
or strained.

Rizzard, to dry, to bleach
clothes. In Renfrewshire the
word was *haizard*. 'This is a
fine day for haizarding the
clothes.'

Rizzards, red currants.

Road-riddens or *Road-ribbens*,
stuff cleared off the roadside and
banked up on the side. [Red-
dins from *red*, to clear up.]

Rookits, balls of minced meat
or fish with bread crumbs.

S

Sad, firm, steady. 'The
jelly is sad enough.' It means
grave or steady in Chaucer.
[Common.]

Saster, a pudding. An old
Moniaive man used this word.
In Hislop's collection of Scotch
prov., we have 'ye're as fu's a
stuppit saster.'

Scart, the Cormorant—of
Gaelic origin. *Waverley Novels.*

Scoory, disreputable in appearance. A 'scoory-looking
blade,' a broken-down looking
tramp.

Scowder, to scorch. [Com-
mon.]

Scrae, a thin turf.

Scrog, a stunted shrub.

Scuddy, naked, applied to an
undressed child or newly hatched
nestling.

Semmit, a flannel undershirt.

To shie, to start, as of a horse
at a strange object. E.E.
[Common.]

Shilbands, cart tops. [For
hay or grain.]

Shine, to fling or throw
violently. A shine is also a
quarrel.

Shoddie, a baby's shoe.

Shog-bog, a quaking mossbog.

Shore, to shore a dog on, to hound on a dog to cattle or sheep, perhaps with the intention of dividing the flock into separate parts [to scold].

Shott, an ill-grown ewe. [Inferior specimen removed from a lot of animals.]

Shyle, to make wry faces. Renfrewshire, *showl*.

Shyne, to fling from you as in anger. *A shyne*, a quarrel.

Sile, to pass through a filter. [As milk through a wire gauze.]

Silver-shakers, a very appropriate name for the beautiful grass, Briza media.

Sit, applied to any piece of crockery or furniture at rest. These *sit* in Dumfriesshire, but *stand* in Renfrewshire.

Skellie, to exaggerate, to narrate incorrectly. [To squint.]

Skelpy, a mischievous girl.

Skerry or *Scairy*, a shadow, a reflection, a metaphor. A woman was telling me how she had employed her Sunday reading in Revelation, when I began to corner her concerning the woman clothed with the sun, explaining how many thousand times it was larger than the earth, and so inconceivably hot that any woman would have melted in a moment, when she answered me rather pat — 'Oh ! sir, St John's account o' her maun be a scairy.'

Skly or *Skloy*, the place on which one slides.

Slid, slippery.

Slipshod. The meaning in Tynron is that the person is wearing slippers [or shoes] without stockings or hose. We all know its metaphorical meaning.

Snabbie, the chaffinch. Communicated.

Sneal, Dumfries cont. for snivel. *Waverley Novels.*

Snisle, half burned. A piece of hard soot is said to be snisled. Ham when singed in the cooking is snisled.

Snosh, comfortable. An old snoshie, a fat, comfortable old man.

Sonks, seats. *Waverley.*

Sosh, quiet, contented, applied either to man or dog. *Vide* snosh.

Soult or *Sault* or *Sout*, a leap, applied when the plough leaps up by striking a hidden stone. Also used when on a hay-stack. 'Give it a sout'—*i.e.*, leap up so as to press it down. The same word is in English. Summersault, originally written supersault (Skeat), being a leap up or a leap over.

Spang, to give a high leap. Ramsay.

Spelk, a piece of wood applied to a fracture, a little bit of thin wood that has run into the hand. Renfrewshire, *shelf*.

Spell, to add to a story, to exaggerate. In Chaucer spell means a narrative, and so in the word 'gospel.'

Spret, Juncus articulatus. [Jointed rush.]

Spry, active, nimble, lively ; also, smart in appearance and in dress. Added by Todd to Johnston. Given by Halliwell as a Somersetshire word, but certainly more general, since I find it both in Dumfriesshire and in Mark Twain's *Huckleberry Finn.* [Common.]

Spung, Jamieson says this is a Galloway word meaning to pick one's pocket. In Renfrewshire [and elsewhere] a spung was a purse, but the word was used chiefly as a synonym for wealth. 'A man with a good spung' was credited with having in his possession valuable deposit receipts.

Squair, the gentle depression between two heights. Possibly it may be a corruption of an older word swyre, applied to the neck in Chaucer. The Northumbrian proverb says—

'Little kens the guid wife, as she sits by the fire,
How the wind blaws caul' in hur-burl swire.'

Swyre is a place name in Dunscore. It is a hill-road in Selkirkshire. It means neck and hollow in the *Waverley Novels*.

Squeef, a mean fellow.

Squeel, 'on the squeel,' an expression signifying that butter-milk is becoming too sour for use.

Stalk, a quantity, as 'she has got a stalk of temper'—*i.e.*, is passionate.

Stampcole, a small rick of hay.

Stangs, to take the stangs, to have a fit of passion.

Stank-hen or *Stankie*, waterhen.

Stannerie [*Staneraw*], lichens yielding a stain or dye.

Starn, the pupil of the eye.

Steekers, boot or shoe laces.

Steep, Ranunculus flammula, from its acting like rennet.

To Stell, to place firmly. To stop, as when a horse 'stells' on the road. [A shelter for sheep; a support.]

Stog, to walk heavily.

Stool-bent, Juncus squarrosus.

Stoothin, lathing plastered.

Storm, applied to a period of frost as well as to wind and rain.

Stras Sonks, a wreath of straw used as a cushion or load saddle.
—Bennett's *Tales of Nithsdale*.

Striffen, film of thin skin.

Sturdied Sheep, sheep suffering from water in the head. [Gid.]

Surfeit, excessively cruel. When a parent cowhides his child it is surfeit.

Swab, a loose idle fellow, as 'a drunken swab.'

Swap, to exchange something. *To Swap*, used as to 'vouch.' 'I'll swap that's true.'

Swedged, grooved, applied to a horse shoe, or the iron of clogs.

Syke, a small rill. N. of England word. Also, the gutter in a street.

Syre, a sewer. Renfrewshire, *syver*. [Syver, common.]

T

Teem, to pour out. 'It's just teeming,' it's raining heavily.

Teep, to stint, to scrimp, to give out sparingly.

Teerer, a boy or girl employed to *teer* or stir the colour-sieve stretched (Fr. *tirer*) on a frame at printworks. Renfrewshire.

Tee-wheet, the lapwing.

Teuk or *Took*, a bye-taste, a disagreeable taste.

Than for then is universal with our peasantry.

The Tae-day, every other day.

Thruch-stane, a flat tombstone. [This through-stane. Common.]

Tings, tongs. Renfrewshire, *tangs*.

Tirr, crabbed. *Tir*, in Renfrewshire meant to strip. In this sense Burns uses it concerning the deil. 'While's on the strong winged tempest flying tirling the kirks.' Burns has an 'l' more, but that's neither here nor there.

Too-fa, a building annexed to a larger [as if leaning against it.]

Tove, to talk familiarly in a prolix manner. To flaunt about with girls.

A Tove, a coquettish person of either sex.

Trade, used as work. 'The craws are hauding a great trade' —*i.e.*, are busy building their nests.

Traik, dead sheep lying putrid, carrion.

Trauchle, to walk in a limping manner. [Rather dragging one's shoes.]

Tree speeler, the tree-creeper. Communicated. [Lit., tree-climber.]

Trone, a trowel. [Elsewhere, *truan.*]

To Trone the School, to play the truant.

Trounse, to beat, to castigate. A woman complained to me that the dogs leaped over and trounsed her flower-pot in front of her house. In the English Bible of 1531, Judges iv. 15 has, ' But the Lord trounsed Sisera and all his charettes.' Skeat connects this word with trunk and truncheon, and says it originally meant a thick stick for beating with.

Tummock, a tuft [as of grass], or small plat of rising ground. 'The road is kittle o'er thae hills in the dark, for there's sae mony tummocks that ye knock against ye're ready to be knocked down.'

U

Ug, to hate, to disgust. Ramsay. [Same root as in ' ugly.']

Uncos, news. An old man used to ask :—' What's the uncos to-day ? ' (Moniaive). [Common elsewhere.]

Unpurpose, untidy.

W

Wad, blacklead. My scholars apply it to a blacklead pencil. It is a N. of England word.

Wainted or *Weinted*, soured. A Northumbrian word.

Ware or *Vare*, spring. This is evidently the Latin *ver*. Of a cold day in summer it is remarked, ' it is as cold as a day in ware.'

Ware, the whole of the objects referred to. A variant of the English word gear, which means dress, harness, tackle ; but with us more frequently ' money.'

Weather-gaw, part of a rainbow seen, the greater part of the bow being intercepted. [Common, but rather in the sense of a blink of sunshine between storms.]

Weerstanes, in a state of hesitation.

Weir, a dam, a hedge. E. of England, a pond of water.

Weir, to herd, to keep watch over. To wear a gate at sheep-shearing, to open and shut it.

Withershins, in the contrary direction. Turning withershins, turning against the sun.

Witter, *Wutter*, or *Otter*, the barb part of a hook ; evidently a metaphorical word, it being, like an otter, apt at catching fish. [The tackle of a poacher for catching loch trout. Galloway.]

CHAPTER X

Abel's Love of Beasts—Cain in Eden—Adam's Dream—Adah sees the Serpent—Eve's Dream—Cain and Abel's Sacrifices—Destruction of Eden—The Sabbath.

SHAW's greatest poetical effort, *From the Expulsion to the First Death*, is a work of high merit extending to twenty cantos in the versification of Morris's *Earthly Paradise*, the reading of which probably inspired our author's muse to adopt this theme. It appeared in parts in successive numbers of the *Dumfries and Galloway Herald*, from 9th July to 31st December 1873, but was never published separately.

The tale opens with the ignominious and sorrowful retreat of our first parents from the Garden of Eden. The second canto deals with 'Abel's Love of Beasts,' and being characteristic of the author, we reproduce it *in extenso*.

> 'Twas mostly in the warm quiet autumn days,
> When the sun struggling reached them through the haze,
> When gold came on the small wild apple's cheek,
> And store of nuts was noway far to seek,
> That Abel loved to hear that tale twice-told,
> How that the beasts in days that now were old
> Thronged to the garden, each to hear its name ;
> He knew the story all, and how they came,
> What ones came first, and who were quiet and shy,
> And who were wroth and had an evil eye ;
> What mighty river-horse down Gihon swam,
> And how the bulky elephant and dam
> Rustled up from the reeds where Pison slept,
> And how the winged ones from the wide woods swept,
> Darkening the blue heavens with their wearied wings.

As Abel thought on all these wondrous things,
He cunningly caught many a beast, to try
If aught would love him with a kind bright eye;
And many a wounded young one nursed he too,
And hid them in soft places, safe from view
Of Cain, who cared not much for sport so tame,
Yea, each one of his small flock had a name;
And with a crested chatterer, green and gold,
You might him, in the morning sun, behold,
Or with two kids, tamed, round whose neck a band
Was wrought, of wild flowers, by his mother's hand,
Or with the weir'd bird flaked with white and jet,
Or with the cony whose fur ne'er was wet.
But most of all, to Eve he loved to show
These feeding from his hand.   His cheek would glow,
And his clear eyes, of his own mother's hue,
Wax round and larger with a deeper blue,
The greater grew the gathering and the noise.

Yea, and all beasts he knew them by their voice,
And loved to cheat them, calling their own cries,
Though scarcely guessed they of such roguish lies,
Until a stone-cast from him were they come.
In sooth, he could so like a wild bee hum,
That you would think the floweret's cup anigh
Swung 'neath the honey-seeker's golden thigh.
In all the lore of nests he was full wise,
And eager watched he when his mother's eyes
Peered in the dusky cup where eggs lay white,
Crowded, and warm—still more, if that her sight
Was met by open yellow bills and throats
Of hungry criers that, with downy coats,
Unfledged lay in the close and cunning nest,
Lined with the feathers of a mother's breast.

But more than all he prized his father's gift,
Who wearily one day did stoop and lift
An ass's colt, whereon a lion's paw
Had made deep wounds that were both red and raw;
And many a day he thought it soon must die;
Yet ever and anon kept Adam nigh,
Holding it warm within a little cave,
Which grew to be its home, where it would crave
Soft juicy grass, and eat it from his hand,
Till merrily it frolicked on the sand
That lay in a great reach beside the stream.
So on a morning what must Adam deem
But that its back, so soft and round and sleek,
Might hold his little Abel, and the meek

Beast stooped below the burden, light and warm,
Then trotted o'er the sand and wrought no harm.
And soon the boy repelled his father's hand,
And without bridle rode it o'er the sand,
Whereat Cain scowled, and struck it with a stone,
But Abel would not yield the world's first throne
On that first day of kingship, but made good
His way ere evening to a nutty wood,
And folding part of his small coat of skin,
Tied, with a grass thong, many a fruit therein,
Nor spoke of many a fall and many a fright,
But came home proudly with the waning light.

The following lines show the very different character
of Cain from that of Abel.

But as he grew in strength, the elder boy
Took to the hunt with such a weight of joy
That even the wild boar feared him, and in sleep
He hunted it in dreams. He learned to steep
His spear-point in the juice of evil plants,
Which grew in woods where scarce a sunbeam slants ;
But there, in the high branches overhead,
This supple climber was the stock dove's dread,
And for a prey brought home its eggs and young,
Or rifled honey from the bees that stung,
Or leaped the cataract foaming hoarse and white,
And with a club killed the wild goat outright.

One day an oak came down with sudden flood,
And on it, through the stream grown white with mud,
Was borne some poor four-footed beast, whose cries
Called both boys to the banks with much surprise :
So, when next day dawned calmer, Cain now knew
To cross the river on a tree trunk too,
And with him Abel reached the other brim,
Since that the younger boy could not yet swim.

Cain loses himself hunting, and after wandering many
miles, reaches the Garden of Eden, where he 'wriggles'
through the thick-set fence and enters, to find it in the
condition of a wilderness, and to encounter a monstrous
serpent.

Meantime a creature, venomous and bright,
Hooded and scaly, crawled right well in sight ;
Its neck was glistering gold and glistering blue,
And on its head a starry tire there grew.

And this, because its breath was fœtid hot,
Let the wind blow from Cain, but near him got,
And subtly, with its fascinating eye,
Looked at the boy, who shook, but did not cry;
Then licked its red jaws with its three-forked tongue,
And poised itself, and said or somewhat sung:—

· O, thou lovely human child!
I love thee for thy locks so wild.
Son of Adam, son of Eve,
Come not here to moan or grieve.
Child with eyes like heaven's own blue,
Lips like roses wet with due,
Finger nails like onyx stones,
Fairest form of blood and bones;
Child, be mine, and come with me,
Over earth and over sea;
Thou shalt wear the world's great crown,
Nor toil and sweat with skin so brown.

Cain. My father's cave I may not leave,
For he for me would moan and grieve,
But if you love me as you say,
O teach me how to find my way!

Serpent. Your way with me you shall not lose,
And you shall have whate'er you chose;
No brother shall divide your prize,
Nor snatch 't away before your eyes.

Cain. My brother, blinded with his tears,
Cries for me. Him my mother hears,
And both for my return now pray,
O dragon, show me on my way!'

Cain escapes from the garden by floating down the
Euphrates on a pine-tree. The family, after Cain had
wandered, becomes very anxious, and leaving Eve, the
elder daughter Adah, and the unweaned Zillah, behind,
Adam and Abel ultimately set out to search for the boy
in the direction of the lost garden, but on approaching
it they are overawed by the sights, and after offering a
goat for sacrifice, fall asleep.

And in their sleep there came a wondrous dream,
For Adam first beheld a rosy gleam,

And then an angel clothed with light came down,
And on his head he wore a golden crown,
His neck and face were white like milk—his locks
Dropped bdellium, such as falls on Pison's rocks ;
Who said, ' Fear not for Cain. The boy unwise
Gazed upon Paradise with longing eyes,
Then burst into that awful camp by force,
But that the rivers cried out loud and hoarse,
What might not then have been the serpent's gain !
Besides the words of promise are not vain.
Yet never more again to mortal eyes
Must Eden ere be seen—accurst it lies,
And evil dreams would haunt thee from its sight.
So changed is now that place of all delight
That I, one of the cherubim, the wave
Of whose grim sword proclaimed thee first a slave,
Full shortly will be eased from watch and ward.
For thee—thy pilgrimage shall still be hard,
Thou with thy wife and little ones must roam,
And shortly too, to seek another home,
A seven days' journey down Euphrates stream ;
And there upon your wearied eyes shall gleam
Glad eyes of Cain. There borne by many a flood
And quietly hid in cracks of the warm mud,
A little colony of Eden fruit,
With grain for man and beast has long ta'en root,
Let Abel watch the kids and tame beasts still,
As for the ground be it for Cain to till.'

On Adam's return, the whole family set out as directed,
and find Cain, and for a time all goes happily. Cain,
however, soon develops impatience of work, and envies
Abel's easy employment of tending his flocks and herds.

Adah, meanwhile, becomes very beautiful and otherwise attractive.

So Adah, always lively, quick, and bold,
Heeded not second thoughts, but straightway told
Zillah, who followed her as a fawn doth dam :
For Zillah, meek, and patient as a lamb,
Crouched to pick nuts when Adah climbed the tree,
And when she bathed scarce waded o'er the knee ;
While Adah, haughty, swam out like a swan,
Then, ere that Zillah could her dress do on,
Adah was decked, bright feather o'er her brow,
With gems around her neck and wrists enow,
Cain's favourite was she—yea, and Abel's heart
At every quarrel turned round to take her part.

An encounter which Adah has with the serpent is given in Canto XIII, as follows :—

> Zillah was hardly farther off than when
> The puzzled eye may think that beasts are men,
> When Adah, starting, thought she saw a glow
> Reflected near the river's brink, and lo !
> As if all precious stones in one bright band
> Were knit together by a cunning hand,
> She saw a lustrous snake, whose forehead shone
> With that sweet star which east and west do own.
> Its neck and soft round folds were jasper green,
> With streaks of sapphire mixed, and there were seen
> Topaz and emerald spots that interwreathed,
> And crescent glories sparkled as it breathed
> Or waved beneath great coils dark-hued like wine.
> Its crest was as an amethyst spun fine
> Into a purple mist, and on its tongue
> A sound made up of words and music hung ;
> But, as it spake out louder and more clear,
> Adah stood charmed despite of all her fear.

> *Serpent.* The sons of God live far away,
> Where all the year it shines like May ;
> But if they stood where now I lie,
> For you they all would pant and sigh.
> Fair hands must still for fair hands seek,
> And eye for eye, and cheek for cheek,
> What grievous grudge would pain his peers,
> Whose kisses caught thy falling tears !

> *Adah.* In sooth I scarce know what you mean,
> O brave bright worm in gold and green,
> What are they like—those sons of God ?
> Can you not bring them at your nod ?

> *Serpent.* Look in the water, and behold
> Your own hair, like a mist of gold ;
> Your eyes and hands as fair to see
> As fruit that hangs on Eden's tree,
> Your own face fashioned sweet and bright—
> The sons of God are such a sight.

> *Adah.* If thou be wiser aught than we,
> Upon the water look with me,
> And bring yon turtle dove to life,
> Whom late I slew with this sharp knife.

> *Serpent.* Who knows the secret things of death,
> Or all that fails with failing breath ?

How strong I am, how quick and lithe,
Ask the flesh-feeding beasts who writhe
Within my coils when all their bones
Give way, and vain are rage and groans ;
Yet, with great Death, I dare not strive,
Nor bring his pale-faced prey alive.
O shun great Death as ye would shun
A land forgot of moon and sun—
A land that knows not corn and wine—
A land that hates both thee and thine.
O speak not of a cold dead dove,
I come to speak of life and love.

Adah.   But live these sons of God afar ?
Or have they seen us from a star ?
Ah ! they are not so sweet as Cain
When his round face is washed with rain.

Serpent.   But Cain is sure a son of God ;
Have I not trembled at his nod ?

Adah.   Ah ! now you speak but painted lies,
For Cain is one of those who dies ;
No lore of life or death you teach,
Yet much I'm mazed that you have speech.

Serpent.   Yes, Cain, who dotes on you, shall die,
If you should live a painted lie ;
For know your father now has sworn
That Abel shall not live lovelorn
Of her he loves, who loves not him.
Ah ! wherefore should your eyes grow dim ?
To the far distant land of Nod,
Fly off with Cain, the son of God ;
There shall ye both much favour win,
In midst of all your glorious kin,
And Cain be free from hateful thrall,
While you shall reign great queen of all.

He ceased, for in the north, as set the sun
Beneath a bank of clouds wide spread and dun,
Thin as a hair and sharp, a line of light
Had filled the subtle creature with affright,
For doubtless naught else than the cherub's sword,
Coming as the vice-gerent of the Lord,
Had stopped his cunning wiles, or been enough
To make him haste to cast his painted slough.

Azrun, the third daughter, having been stung by a
snake, Abel sucks the poison from the wound, thereby

saving the life of the child, and makes a daring and
successful raid upon snakes generally. Referring to the
anxious mother the verse goes on :—

> Then when she thought the child would live, and sleep
> Fell on her eyes that now had ceased to weep,
> There came a dream ; and midway, in a ring
> Made of the dragons slain, a voice did sing,
> As of some kindly messenger and strong
> That, for a while, had left a seraph throng :

> > For mighty work comes mighty wage,
> > To feed thine Abel's righteous rage,
> > Close to his tent-door lies his prey,
> > A dragon slain for every day
> > It took to make the earth and sea,
> > And all the goodly things that be.

> > Shall aught redeem the tree of life ?
> > Shall nights of anguish—days of strife ?
> > Shall valiant friend, or vanquished foe,
> > Bring back one sweet day's vanished glow ?
> > O woe to thine, and woe to thee !
> > Long shall ye rue that glorious tree.

> > So walk with wary steps and slow,
> > Mindful that joys are mixed with woe,
> > That wine which cheers makes also mad,
> > That morning's mirth makes evening sad,
> > That the whole world is changed since ye
> > Set eyes upon the glorious tree.

Canto XVIII, in which Adam orders that the brothers
should sacrifice, opens with a description of the dream
of Cain.

> But unto Cain that night there also came
> Strange voices in his sleep, and like a flame
> Wavering from side to side, he thought he saw
> The snake that Adah on the sand did draw ;
> No longer spiteful, blotched with sudden fear,
> As in the garden it did last appear
> After the mighty rivers cried out hoarse,
> But sweetly swaying, veiling half its force,
> And making gestures like a captive king,
> Till it lay all around him, as a ring
> Begemmed with stones of fire and made of gold.
> Most subtle were its piercing eyes and old ;

> And when he heard the music of its tongue,
> He nought remembered of its fork that stung ;
> For in his heart such fancies sweet it nursed,
> That only silence seemed a thing accursed.

Cain is tempted to ask for the hand of Adah, and warned that his father is sure to favour the suit of Abel, who also is deeply enamoured of her.

Cain's sacrifices did not find acceptance.

> In vain, in vain, had Cain his altar decked,
> To him and to his gifts was no respect ;
> Great light on Abel's offerings shone that day,
> As in the hollow of God's hand they lay.
> But Abel, when he saw Cain's face at noon,
> Knew that his brother ne'er would ask a boon
> From God or man again. Knew there had come
> A crisis, as when starry skies and dumb
> Seem swept and garnished, so that some great blast
> Get room for all its cloudy hosts at last.

The brothers 'meet a-field that tide,' and after an angry altercation, Cain throws his spear at Abel and wounds him in the breast, and he bleeds to death. Abel's dog attracted Zillah, who—

> Went forth that day across the land
> With Owain and with Azrun in each hand.

On discovering Abel's body, she sought her mother's tent, and led her to the scene of the first death, where they were joined by Adam

> Ere daylight made the moonlight wane.

Cain does not come to the burial.

> Cain is a murderer, branded with a brand,
> Wandering through wilds with Adah by the hand.

Adam, near the close, accounts for the disappearance of the garden of Eden in these lines :—

> The cherubim before mine eyes did rise,
> And soaring rose to reach their native skies,
> Why should they stay ? That hour our son was killed,
> Eden was with the four great rivers filled ;

Deep waters sleep above the holy ways,
From whence our eyes first met the wondrous blaze
Of heaven's dear orbs, that like archangels shone.
The stones of fire that once we called our own.
Thou mindest them—gold, topaz, amethyst—
These, and the odour-laden milk-white mist
That floated round us, when we breathed the breath
Of that all-glorious tree which knew not death,
Whose fruit we ate on sacred seventh-day feasts,
These, and the garden filled with loathsome beasts,
Haply lie drowned so deep, that angels, mazed,
Fret no more seeing beauty so abased,
For beautiful is death compared to shame,
And like a star doth shine my Abel's name.

THE SABBATH

Thou art a cooling, desert well,
 Most musical and sweet,
Where weary pilgrims dip their shell,
 And bathe their burning feet.

Thou art a lovely isle of light,
 Amid a cloudy sky,
Through which the sunbeams issue bright,
 To which the wild birds fly.

The fabled mermaid of the deep,
 While storms vex sea and shore,
May in her crystal caverns sleep,
 Nor hear their dashing roar.

The little child, with care and pain,
 With weary thoughts opprest,
Hides, until all be well again,
 Deep in its mother's breast.

And so the poor man's soul is kept
 From care and trouble free,
And all the ills which round him crept,
 Are scared, blest day, by thee.

Then let us watch, as holy ground,
 Amid all common ways,
The path which leads to bliss profound,
 The sacred 'Pearl of Days.'

APPENDIX A

The Cat and the Sparrow

(Adapted from the Norse.)

Tremble all ye hosts of rats,
Progress has got hold of cats,
And he who now to London goes
At times may see the great cat shows :
May see Tom with his tortoise shell,
May see Bess with her silver bell,
May see the Scotch wild cat, whose eyes
Glare with war's brightest, fiercest dyes ;
May see the Persian clad in silk,
With orbs as soft and mild as milk ;
May see the tailless cats called Manx,
With rather longer hinder shanks ;
May see cats red, and grey, and brown,
And black and white, from every town.

If there's no cotton in his ears,
He'll ne'er forget what then he hears—
Caterwauling, hissing, purring,
Growling as they'd got the murrain ;
Mewing with uplifted paw,
Sharping nails like sharping saw.

Long ago, in Egypt, puss
Put the people in a fuss,
There she was the nation's god,
And they watched her every nod ;
When her eye would glow like coal
While she watched a mouse's hole,
When full dry and'in the dark
You stroked her wrong and made her spark,
The priests would stand in circle round
And read the auguries most profound.

Still there was a habit which
Puzzled all, both poor and rich ;
It seemed, before Manetho's time,
According to an ancient rhyme,
That cats in Egypt were so good
That ere they thought of tasting food
They washed their face, and then fell to.
But now 'tis the reverse they do.
Well, an old priest, as bald's a stone,
With beard that like a cataract shone,
Explained the matter. He had found
In an arched passage, underground,
A manuscript without a date,
Which the whole matter did relate.

In Memphis once a cat had caught
A sparrow, that turned round and sought
One minute's grace ere it should die.
' One minute only—dear me, why,
You can't refuse't—think of your face,
'Tis still to wash.' In such a case
Puss, with her paws for sponge and tow'l,
And with her mouth for ewer and bowl,
Began her temples to bedew,
When off at once the sparrow flew ;
And now, since then, it is the case
For cats to eat, then wash their face.

The Biter Bit

A thief got once into a dairy,
And tripped along as soft's a fairy ;
With furtive eyes he viewed the cheese—
When, hark ! he heard the farmer sneeze,
Twinkling all round him like a rat,
He popped some butter in his hat ;
Then turning round, says he : ' Good-day,
Farmer ; I've rather lost my way,
I want a talk about the swine.'
Says farmer Jones : ' Come first and dine.'
The goodman placed him near the fire,
And piled on logs till it blazed higher.
' Sir stranger, you're amazing fat,
'Twould cool you to take off your hat.
No, no—don't rise—we have some broth ;
You'll take it, and some mutton both.'
The butter melting with the fire,
Had made the thief's whole face perspire ;
Great beads were forming on his nose,
Adown his chin it oozed like brose ;

At length he jumped up like a trout :
' Don't stop me, for I will be out.'
Quoth Mrs Jones : ' You're in a flutter ;
But, oh ! your sweat smells like my butter.'

March 1864.

Two Sides to a Question

I.—HAME'S AYE HAMELY

Hame's aye hamely ; what a seat
For wearied shanks and blistered feet
Is the arm-chair near the glede,
No far frae the cradle head !
Next your richt hand there's the bole
Fu' o' serious books and droll ;
For the chair a cushion's made
Frae the wrack o' some aul' plaid ;
The ham's aboon you on the cleek,
The tea-pot's keeking through the reek,
Great ferlies glitter on the brace,
The eight-day clock ticks in your face.
That's *your* seat, gudeman, and hark !
Collie kens you—yon's his bark,
Yon laich star's your window's licht,
Ye ope the door and sic a sight !
Bairns come tumbling to your knees,
Fat wee hands your coat-tails seize,
Chubby cheeks and dimpled chin,
How they deave you wi' their din !
Cat it purrs, and kettle sings,
Bird in cage spreads out its wings.
Mither gi'es the fire a knock,
Lowe loups up and starts the clock,
Dishes on the rack smile bricht,
House-fly thinks it's day outricht,
And bizzes brisk, while in the pan
The ham skirls out—' Come in, gudeman,'
Fremmit folk ha'e prettier claes,
Fremmit folk ha'e polished ways,
Fremmit folk ha'e lots o' gear,
Hame has a' the heart holds dear.

II.—FAR AWA FOWLS HAE FAIR FEATHERS.

A land o' honey and o' milk,
A land o' satin and o' silk ;
That is the land ye'll never see,
By riding on your ain roof-tree.

Sitting like an aul' singed cat,
Watching pigs' meat in the pat,
Doodling sleepless weans, and see!
Paid for't by the nurse's fee!
Aye some rotten thing to men'
Either in the but or ben;
Thack blawn aff—the riggin' doon,
Rats a' swarming in the toun:
That's within—without's the same,
Workin' till ye're stiff and lame,
Nose at grindstone, late and air,
Toiling a' days, foul and fair;
Into bed, rheumatic, damp,
Through your sleep roar wi' the cramp.

O that I were ten years younger!
Would I live in fear o' hunger,
Fear o' tailors' bills or grocers'?
Question gets plain answer—'No, sirs.'
I'd off to the backwoods at once;
Beyond the dub baith gleg and dunce,
Cast off richt soon baith care an' cark,
Wi' fair day's wage for fair day's wark.
Yestreen the sun set i' the west,
And when its glede was at its best,
I saw the bonny clouds divide,
And soom like goold-fish by its side,—
Soom and swoon, and seem to thaw,
Owre bens and fells and far awa';
And there was opened in that west,
A road to islands o' the blest,
A road for wings, but I had nane,
I sighed, for nocht my lot would sain.
But when I slept, frae angel's breast
I got a dream I saw the west;
And golden laks in deep blue skies
Roused me wi' a sweet surprise.
There were groves, and grass like balm,
And flower-wreathed trees that made me calm,
And humming birds flew in a trice,
Like bits o' rainbow through the ryss.
Instead o' hag moss beat wi' sleet,
Were miles on miles, rich holms o' wheat;
And when I woke I cried wi' pain,
'O let me dream that dream again!'
For I was waukened wi' a roar,
'There's gryce to kill, and still ye snore!'

A land o' satin and o' silk,—
A land o' honey and o' milk,—

2 A

That is the lan' ye'll never see,
Though tiptoe on your ain roof-tree.

III.—A BRAW BRIDE'S EASY BUSKIT

I've seen a lassie harping san',
Wi' cheeks as rosy as the dawn;
Yin a' soap-suds I've thocht as braw
As Venus ris'n frae waves like snaw.
There's Bessie Morrice o' the glen,
Frae a thack house—a but and ben,
In a douth place that lassie's e'e
Breaks like the sunlicht thro' a tree.
Mud couldna fyle that maiden's face,
Nor duds deprive her shape o' grace;
Whether she tak's to bake or brew,
Her aul' claes look like maist folk's new;
Catch her dancin', catch her spinnin',
Her neck was aye like cam'ric linen,
Her e'e as clear's a drap o' dew,
Her feet were wings when past she flew.
At morn she's blyther than the lark,
At gloamin' after a' her wark
Sae yawl—she seems to wear a charm,
Altho' an aul' toosh hap her arm.
Ye meet her ankle-deep in glaur,
She seems to say ' dance gin ye daur.'
This day a budget's on her back,
And O! between you and the sack,
There's sic a rose-bloom strapping queen,
Ye hardly daur to trust your e'en.
Neist day, wi' plaid thrown owre her arm,
She climbs the hill ayont the farm.
And her feet, clean, without a smutch,
Whiten the gowans that they touch.
Her hair's a' taffled—what o' that?
Her thin and weel-worn gipsy hat
Sits as it ocht to sit, you'll vow,
Like crown upon a lady's brow.
E'en when she flytes her face is fair,
E'en when she pouts her lips are rare—
Rare as geans, not ripe, but red,
Hanging temptsome owre your head.
Smiles or sighs alike become her,
Winter wild or sunny summer.
But O! when pleased she hums a tune,
The very man that's in the moon,
Tho' caul' and far, could he but hear,
He'd warmer grow, and draw mair near;
For Bessie's claes they ne'er need sortin',
And Bessie's face is Bessie's fortune.

IV.—FAIR FEATHERS MAK' FINE FOWLS

Ye see yon pookit pyfering face;
Yestreen when in a cloud o' lace,
Below the gas-licht bobbing braw,
It bore the gree amang them a'.
Her arms and neck, the servants say,
Are made o' unco bruckit clay;
Below the e'en as blae's a yeddar,
And yet the captain's gaun to wed her;
Hair no her ain, but then as bricht
As blue skies in a starry nicht,
Wi' diamonds and wi' gowd that glows,
And scented like an open rose;
Her gown—the like was never seen,
Nae peacock's tail thick set wi' e'en
Could match it, trailing wi' a sweep,
That made the hearts o' lovers leap;
The bracelet on her arm would buy
Some dizens sic as you and I;
The fan that aired her was a treasure;
And when she rose to dance a measure,
Her earrings, set wi' little bells,
Dangled down like a witch's spells,
And shot a' roun' a silver licht,
Like that that mak's a lily bricht;
Her very name has naething plain—
'Tis Mary Ann Christina Jane.
Then when she's in her carriage seen,
Sae saucy—veil drawn owre her e'en,
An ostrich feather on her pow,
A shawl wrapped roun' her like a lowe,
Mauve gloves that smell wi' some sweet water.
Ye quite forget the servant's chatter
About her wizened skin—na, mair,
Ye're e'en get dazzled as ye stare;
And let the day be bask or bensel,
Ye fain would draw her wi' a pencil;
Ye rather like the Roman nose,
Ye think the lily beats the rose,
Ye think the thin hand beats the plump,
And sae to catch it fain would jump.
Sic cantrips can fine feathers cast,
They tak' by storm maist hearts at last.

V.—A ROWIN' STANE GATHERS NAE FOG

What's come o' Jock the tailor's bairns?
Their heads had aye mair hair than hairns;
Below their bonnets bees were bummin'
New-fangled tunes their tongues aye hummin.

Wi' goose, wi' lapboord, and wi' thummle,
They made but aye an unco bummle.
' To sit cross-legged and shape and sue,'
Quoth Rab, ' that's what I'll never do.'
Sae owre the muckle dib he swam,
And after him his brither Tam
Landed ae day in New South Wales ;
And there wi' goads at oxen's tails,
They started in the carryin' trade ;
And when the spates cam', had to wade
Knee-deep in roads as saft as broze;
Wat to the bane through hat and hose ;
And when the drouth cam', then their e'en
The burnin' saun pricked like a preen,
Bush-rangers cam' and took black-mail,
Left them as toom's a tumbled pail.
Quoth Tam, ' Rab, this will never doo,
What sall we put our han' to noo ? '
' Diggings,' said Rab ; ' Agreed,' said Tam.
Sae aff they set and raised a dam,
And bored and riddled, toiled and moiled,
Wi' hair unkempt and claes besoiled.
Wee bits o' goold, like midge's lug,
For days they frae the quartz-san' dug :
At last they faun' them big like flaes,
And hid them far ben in their claes :
Ae day a nugget like a clock,
Tam chucked fra oot its native rock,
There baith began to bore and wummle,
And bits cam' oot as big's a thummle.
Sleeping wi' pistols in their belt,
Wi' skin as broon and rough as felt,
In tent like dowg's-hatch, watching dowgs
And keelies sneaking roun' their lugs,
Dreaming they heard revolvers crack,
Catching rheumaticks in their back,
Munching their everlasting mutton ;
Quoth Rab, ' This life's no worth a button,
Our stane man tak' anither row,
I'll seek hame wi' my gowd, I trow.'
Came hame'—got wife—rented a shop,
Sell't fowl and fish—dressed like a fop ;
But sell't his hens on rainy days,
Wagered and had unsettled ways,
Turned bankrupt—kenna whaur he's noo—
Jock Tamson's bairn—the story's true.
But what o' Tam?—na he stayed still,
Till some yin robbed him, then the gull
Flew aff—to Boston was't? The war
O' North wi' South—the bloody spar

O' Grant wi' Lee was then gaun on ;
Tam listed in the North ; anon
He got promotion—then a shog
Into a ditch—nae signs o' fog
On either stane yet ! though they say
He row'd aboot for mony a day
On crutches wi' an empty wame,
Writing his freens to take him hame.

VI.—A SITTING BIRD BUILDS NAE NEST

When yae thing fails ye try anither,
That was the way me and your mither
Gathered our gear and filled our purse.
It disna do to sit and nurse
Your sorrow, or gae roun' and roun',
Like gin horse on a road that's soun' ;
For never venture never win ;
Bare feet maun look for empty shoon ;
Will ye sit still and sook your thoom ?
The burn's in spate, ye canna soom,
Sae up and trot and tak' the hills,
And save yirsel frae threatening ills.
The very birds they rove and roam ;
The nichtingale that's noo at Rome,
Will be in England in the simmer :
It's no when suns but glint and glimmer
The gowk sits still—it changes bab,
Dae ye sae in ill weather, Rab,
When ice gets flooded, change your tee,
Nor stan' in water to the knee.
Follow whaur trade's gude, markets high,
Bounce to a new place—don't be shy,
Look to thae emigrants, a' flaes
And dirt, wi' duds instead o' claes,
Packed up like herrings in ship's hold,
Owre the Atlantic's waves they're rolled ;
Labour is high on th' ither side,
They push, get on, and soon they ride
In coaches, wha were beggars here.
We sit by neuk and cry it's queer.
Queer ! There's Will Watson jist at hame,
That was a lad ye couldna tame.
Dashed into Glasgow—took a shop,
Put goods in window—noo he's top
Hatter, they tell me, in Stockwell ;
Got married to his handsome Nell,
Whase tocher micht hae filled a kist.
Will left us and was never miss't ;
Had he stayed on—weel, at the most,
He'd clauted roads or run the post.

APPENDIX B

ADDER-BEADS AND CHILDREN'S RHYMES [*]

ABOUT a week ago I visited an old lady who is between 80 and 90 years of age, resident in Tynron, and from whom I procured the adder-bead which I now produce. It was an heirloom in her family. The story of its finding is that a shepherd, she believes, in the parish of Closeburn, had observed a number of adders very fierce and very agile. He got alarmed, and hastened from the place, throwing off his plaid, which tradition says is a good plan to divert the ferocious attack of either adders or weasels by taking up their attention for a while. Next morning he returned to the spot, to discover that his plaid was pretty much eaten, or, as the old lady said, ' chattered.' The adders were gone, and while gazing on the knoll on which he had seen them he discovered this bead. The Tynron lady's grandmother wore it around her neck as a charm or amulet. The same lady's father once got the offer of £5 for it, which he refused. I may say that I have already been offered more than I paid for it. A Dumfries naturalist told me they were common, and that a friend of his had nearly a score, but on inquiring at aforesaid friend I found his were spindle whorls of stone. I believe they are very uncommon, at least in Dumfriesshire. There is not one in the Grierson Museum, as you may see from the catalogue. Looking at this bead, it might with more propriety be called a glass ring. The best account I find of them is in Brand's *Popular Antiquities*, Vol. III., p. 286, edition 1888. Pliny, the Roman writer, refers to them. Pennant, in his *Zoology*, says the tradition is strong in Wales. The wondrous egg, or bead, was considered a potent charm with the Druids. It used to assist children in cutting their teeth, or to cure chincough, or to drive away an ague. Camden gives a plate of these beads, made of

[*] Communicated on 14th February 1896 to the Dumfriesshire, etc., Antiquarian Society, and printed in the Transactions, 1897. *Vide* also a paper by J. R. Wilson, Sanquhar (p. 27 of the 1898 Journal), in which the existence of other Dumfriesshire beads is chronicled.

glass of a very rich blue colour, some of which are plain and others streaked. The *ovum anguinum*, or Druid's egg, has been frequently found in the Isle of Anglesey. It has been found in Cornwall and most parts of Wales. The Welsh name for them is *serpent's gems*. Mr Lloyd says they are small glass annulets about half as wide as our finger rings, but much thicker, usually of a green colour, though some are blue and others curiously waved with blue, red, and white. Pliny says they are hatched by adders. These beads are not unfrequently found in barrows. Bishop Gibson engraved three found in Wales. In Brand's *Antiquities* no mention is made of them being found in Scotland. The tradition that they have been produced by serpents is current in all the districts in which they have been found.

Folk Riddles

John Corrie, member of this Society, has collected a number of Folk Riddles from the parish of Glencairn (*vide* Transactions, 1891-92). It struck me that I might supplement that paper with examples of a few more current in Tynron, but I fear destined soon to become unknown. I shall also give examples of other rhymes, but take the Folk Riddles first.

What is it that you have, and I have not, and I use it more than you do? Ans., Your name.

What goes through the wood and through the wood and never touches the bushes? Ans., A sound.

What goes through the wood and leaves a brat on every bush? Ans., Snow.

> As white as snaw, but snaw it's not;
> As red as blood, but blood it's not;
> As black as ink, but ink it's not;

Ans., A bramble, whose blossoms are white, and its fruit first red and then black. It equally well suits the gean, or wild cherry.

> Through the wood and through the wood,
> And through the wood it ran,
> And though it is a wee thing,
> It could kill a big man.

Ans., A bullet, which runs through the wooden tube of the gun.

> I have a little sister, they call her Peep, Peep,
> Over the waters deep, deep, deep,
> Over the mountains high, high, high,
> And the poor little creature has just one eye.

Ans., A star.

What is it that God never saw, kings seldom see, and you and I see it every day? Ans., Your equal.

What goes up the water and up the water and never comes to the head of it? Ans., A mill-wheel.

There was a man who saw a pear tree, and pears on the tree. He stretched out his hand and plucked, but he neither took pears nor left pears on the tree. This is a verbal quibble. The explanation is that he took *one* pear and left *one*.

Here is a riddle we have upon a beetle, or, as the children call it, a 'clock.' The description is quaint and graphic.

> Wee man o' leather / Gaed through the heather,
> Through a rock, through a reel, / Through an old spinning-wheel,
> Through a sheep shank bane, / Sic a man was never seen.

The following is a curious piece of natural history: There was a leak in Noah's ark. The cat tried to stop it with its paw, but in vain; then the dog tried to stop it with its nose, but in vain; then the women tried to stop it with their knees, all in vain. Noah's wife prayed, and it was stopped; but the cat's paw, the dog's nose, and women's knees remain cold unto the present day.

The following is a reminiscence of the time before bridges: What goes through the ford head downmost? Ans., The nails on a horse's shoe.

The next riddle gives us a glimpse of drudgery which sanitary engineers are rapidly rendering obsolete. What goes away between two woods and comes back between two waters? Ans., A woman, when she goes with her empty wooden stoups to the well and comes back with them filled.

The following riddle is rather gruesome:—What is it

that waits with its mouth open the whole night in your
room for your bones in the morning? Ans., Your shoes.

The following verbal quibble is confusing enough when
first heard:—Whity looked out of whity, and saw whity
in whity, and sent whity to turn whity out of whity. The
explanation is that a white woman looked out of her
white 'mutch,' or head-dress, and saw a white cow among
the white corn, and sent a white dog to turn it out.

London brig appears in one of Mr Corrie's riddles; it
also appears in the following:—

> As I gaed owre London brig, / I let a wee thing fa';
> The haill folk in London town / Couldna gather't a'.

Ans., A pinch of snuff. This reminds us of the Scriptural
expression of 'water spilt upon the ground which cannot
be gathered up again.'

> Mouthed like a mill-door, / Lugged like a cat;
> Though you guess till ne'rday, / Ye'll no guess that.

Ans., Potato pot.

The following riddle has a very wide range:—

> Come a riddle, come a riddle, / Come a rot, tot, tot;
> A wee wee man wi' a red red coat,
> A staff in his hand and a stone in his throat.
> Come a riddle, come a riddle, / Come a rot. tot, tot.

Ans., A cherry.

The following I first heard in Annandale:—What is it
that is very much used and very little thought of?
Ans., A dish-clout.

Children's Rhymes

I used to feel rather melancholy at the following narrative, sung in a low monotonous tone.

> No a beast in a' the glen / Laid an egg like Picken's hen;
> Some witch wife we dinna ken / Sent a whittret frae its den,
> Sooked the blood o' Picken's hen. / Picken's hen's cauld and dead,
>   Lying on the midden head.

As I grew older I was warned away from straying in
woods by the description of a hobgoblin. Folk-lorists are
endeavouring to show that Shakespeare's 'Caliban' was
suggested by no books of travel, but by the legends
current about the men of the woods and caves, who ex-

isted in Warwickshire in the dim dawn of history. I am sorry that I retain only four lines descriptive of my terror, but they are graphic enough :—

And every hair upon his head / Is like a heather cow ;
And every louse that's looking oot / Is like a bruckit yow (ewe).

The following rhyme was given in autograph by Thomas Carlyle to a friend, and has been published in *Notes and Queries*. It is dated Chelsea, February 1870.

Simon Brodie had a cow,
　He lost his cow and couldna find her ;
When he had done what man could do,
　The cow came home wi' her tail behind her.

Carlyle also gives his reminiscence of an old Scotch song given at the same date.

Young Jockey was a piper's son,
And fell in love when he was young ;
But a' the tunes he learned to play,
Was over the hills and far away.
And it's over the hills and far away,
The wind has blown my plaid away.

The Dumfriesshire magpie gets more lines than usual :—

One's sorrow, two's mirth, / Three's a wedding, four's a birth,
Five's a funeral, six is snaw, / Seven draws the dead awa'.

When boys saw one they used to spit hastily three times to spit away sorrow. In *English Folklore*, by Thiselton Dyer, other three variants are given, but not the one above.

The children's Hogmanay rhyme in Dumfriesshire is more polite than its Renfrewshire version.

Hogmanay, troll lol lay,
Gie's a piece o' pancake / And let us win away ;
We neither came to your door / To beg nor to borrow,
But we came to your door / To sing away sorrow.
Get up guidwife and shake your feathers,
Dinna think that we are beggars,
But boys and girls come out to play, / And to seek our Hogmanay.

There is a children's game beginning with a rhyme. The rhymster touches alternately two boys, beginning :—

As I gaed up the apple tree, / A' the apples fell on me.

And ending with the lines :—

Bake a pudding, bake a pie, / Stand you there out-bye.

The last touched stands aside until only one remains, who is obliged to bend with his head against the gable, blindfolded. The first boy puts his hand on the back of the one blindfolded. The rhymster puts his hand uppermost and asks, 'Where will this poor fellow go?' So the blindfolded boy sends half a dozen or more to different places, all within easy distance. Then he and the rhymster clap hands, and the fun is to see all the boys running back to the gable. The one who comes in last has to submit to be blindfolded in turn.

Another rhyme runs thus. The girl or boy points to one and says :—

Hey Willy Wynn, and ho Willy Wynn, / This night I must go home ; Better alight and stop a night, / And I'll choose you some pretty one. He replies—Who will that be, / If I abide with thee? She answers—The fairest and the rarest / In a' the country side.

The fun consists in suggesting some one likely to be obnoxious to the aforesaid Willy Wynn.

This rhyme was dinned into the ears of poor girls who were too proud :—

Lady, lady, landless, / Footless and handless.

The following is an invocation to rain and sleet :—

Rain, rain, rattlestanes, / Don't rain on me ; Rain on Johnny Groat's house / Far ayont the sea.

Another one comes nearer midsummer :—

Sunny shower, sunny shower, / You'll no last half-an-hour.

This being St Valentine's Day, I give the rhyme I best recollect concerning it.

The rose is red, the violet's blue, / The lily's sweet, and so are you, And so is he who sent you this, / And when we meet we'll have a kiss.

The following is the full text of a rhyme used for the purpose of diverting children in the nursery. It was obtained by a friend of mine from his grandmother, who resided in Dumbartonshire. She had learned it in her childhood, about 1795 to 1800. The gentleman who gave it to me set it to music, and it was sung at a children's concert in Aberdeen. I have only heard part of it in Dumfriesshire. It is worthy of *Alice in Wonderland.*

> As I gaed up the Brandy hill, / I met my father wi' gude will,
> He had jewels, he had rings, / He had monie braw things,
> He had a hammer wanting nails, / He had a cat wi' ten tails.

> Up Jock, doon Tam, / Blow the bellows, old man.
> Peter cam' to Paul's door / Playing on a fife.
> Can ye shape a Hielandman / Out an auld wife?
> He rummelt her, he tummelt her, / He gied her sic a blow,
> That out cam' the Hielandman, / Crying, trot, show!

> Man wi' the skinny coat / Help me owre the ferry boat;
> The ferry boat's owre dear, / Ten pounds every year.

> I've a cherry, I've a chess, / I've a bonnie blue glass;
> I've a coo among the corn, / Haud Willie Blackthorn.

> Willie Blackthorn had a coo, / Its name was Killiecrankie,
> It fell owre an auld dyke / And broke its neevie nankie.

> Ink, pink, sma' drink, / Het yill and brandy;
> Scud aboot the hay-stack / And you'll get sugar-candy.

The man with the skinny coat in charge of the ferryboat is worth taking a note of. Will he be very much prehistoric?

In conclusion, we have a few puzzles got from transferring the accent, of which the best and widest known is the one :—

> In firtaris, / In oaknonis,
> In mudeels is, / In claynone is.

The only new one I have runs thus :—

> Leg-à-mouton, / Half-à-gous, / Pastry-ven-i-son.

Leg of mutton, half a goose, pastry venison.

APPENDIX C

REFERENCES TO LITERARY CONTRIBUTIONS BY SHAW
NOT CONTAINED IN THIS VOLUME

THE subjoined list is far from comprehensive, as time has not been available to make a thorough search in the numerous periodicals to which Shaw was a casual contri-

butor. Such a search would have been made with difficulty,
and would have been unsatisfactory in any case owing to
his practice of appending to letters and articles 'S.',
'J. S.', 'Tynron,' or 'Dumfriesshire,' in place of his
name. Even in the cases of valuable articles, because
unsigned, the general indexes to periodicals were of no
assistance.

By the kindness of Robert Service we are able to give
the following references to letters by Shaw which appeared in *Nature*—'Right-handedness,' page 605, Vol. I;
'Philology of Darwinianism,' page 55, Vol. II (this letter,
signed J. S., is acknowledged on the fly-leaf of what was
his own copy of *Nature*); 'A Local Museum' (Dr
Grierson's), page 61, Vol. XV; 'Yellow Crocuses,' page
8, Vol. XVI, and 'The Future of our British Flora,' page
550, Vol. XVI (this is a specially interesting contribution); 'Explosive Gas in a Lake,' page 435, Vol. XXIII,
and 'Sounds of the Aurora,' page 484, Vol. XXIII;
'Birds singing during Thunder, page 101, Vol. XXIV,
and 'Singular Behaviour of a Squirrel, page 167, Vol.
XXIV; An Insect attacking a Worm,' page 574, Vol.
XXVI; 'Inverted Images,' page 461, Vol. LIII, 'A
Daylight Meteor,' page 581, Vol. LIII, and 'Late
Nesting,' 1895.

Service also supplies the names and dates of a number of
papers (mostly unpublished) read by Shaw before the
*Dumfriesshire and Galloway Natural History and Antiquarian
Society*, with brief reference to them, extracted by him
from a copy of an old Minute Book of the Society,
formerly in his possession.

'January 2nd, 1866:—"The Appreciation of Beauty
by Animals." This gave rise to considerable discussion
as to its bearing on Darwin's theory of Natural
Selection in the Preservation of Species.

'April 3rd, 1866:—"The Growth of the Taste for Beauty
in Objects of Natural History." He showed by various
quotations from the writings of successive poets, ancient
and modern, how gradual had been the development of
the faculty of appreciating the beautiful in objects of
Natural History for its own sake.

'May 1st, 1866.—"Words Peculiar to Dumfriesshire." [Incorporated in Chapter IX.]

'April 2nd, 1867.—"Some Popular Errors regarding the Habits of Animals."

'January 7th, 1868.—"Right-hand Superiority"—which contained a great deal of interesting observation and speculation on the subject.

'May 5th, 1868.—"The Influence of the Human Period on the Sagacity of Animals." In which he cited numerous illustrations in support of the theory that association with man, or warfare against him, had gradually educated certain species of animals to a higher degree of intelligence and brain power—this quality being transmitted hereditarily through successive generations. Considerable discussion followed.

'April 5th, 1870.—"Notes on some Large Boulders in Tynron and Keir." Interesting details were given of boulders examined by him in the bed of the Shinnel Water and its affluents, and also in the burn course near Barndennoch, Keir. These boulders are principally of whinstone and conglomerate, very numerous, and some of very large size. He also produced sketches of a rock of a very peculiar shape in Appin Glen, and showed small specimens of the rocks described.

'April 4th, 1871.—"Local Words in Dumfries and the West not found in Jamieson's Dictionary." [Incorporated in Chapter IX.] The paper was much appreciated, and elicited a number of instructive remarks.

'April 9th, 1872.—Shaw exhibited two articles found some time ago in Tynron—one apparently the remains of a small iron dagger, and the other in the shape of a dog collar, though evidently too small for that purpose.

'April 8th, 1873.—Shaw showed ten large and beautifully executed photographs of a variety of objects in the British Museum, illustrative of ancient art, part of a complete series of such photographs now in course of publication by authority, with the view of rendering such matters familiar to persons who may not have any, or sufficient opportunity of examining the objects represented.

He then read a number of "critical remarks" in reference generally to the state of Art at the period of the execution of the Sculptures, principally Egyptian, portrayed in the photographs, and pointed out the use to which the art of photography might be put for the preservation of views of our local ruins, objects of antiquity, curiosity, etc.'

It is gratifying to notice that the British Museum has at last (1898) adopted on a national scale the proposal which Shaw made in 1873.

'March 2nd, 1877.—"Fertilisation of Flowers by Insects." Illustrated by reference to a large number of diagrams showing the various ways in which flowers are fertilised by insect agency.

'December 7th, 1877.—"Lessons from the English Names of Animals and Plants." Showing how most of the names of our domestic animals had been preserved almost unchanged in many languages since they had their origin with the Aryan people, who at a remote period inhabited the Highlands of Western Asia. The names of a great number of plants and animals were also explained and their history given.

'April 5th, 1878.—"Modern Theories of Colour in regard to Animals." In which he showed, with the aid of coloured illustrations, how in many cases the colours of insects, animals, and birds had assumed a protective resemblance to the objects among which they live.'

In 1882 Shaw supplied many contributions to the excellent 'List of Flowering Plants of Dumfriesshire and Kirkcudbrightshire,' compiled by James M'Andrew, schoolmaster, New Galloway, and read to the Society.

Additional Samples of Contributions to Periodical Literature:—

An Article for 'Boys and Girls,' and another on 'Wild Fruit.'—*Good Words,* 1881.

'Health and Happiness of Animals.'—*Gráphic,* 12th February 1890.

'The Raising of Lazarus.'—*The Agnostic Journal,* October 1894.

'Theology and Playing Cards.'—*People's Friend* (Holiday Number), 1895.

'My Holiday Veesitors.'—*The Bäilie*, 23rd September 1891.

The following are a few of the more interesting of Shaw's writings, mostly in his own 'hand,' which will be found in Dr Grierson's Museum, Thornhill—a presentation from his relatives at Barrhead :—

1. 'From the Expulsion to the First Death.'
2. Numerous other verses on various subjects.
3. 'Carinus and Rienzi : a tragedy in five acts.'
4. Lectures on 'John Knox,' 'Sir Walter Scott,' and 'Thomas Carlyle.'
5. Several Lectures on 'Vacation Rambles,' including 'My Tours through Switzerland, Germany, and The Low Country.'
6. 'Sketches of Obscure Persons,' 'The Tailor,' 'The Sweep,' etc.
7. 'The Story of Belle Antonnette,' in eight chapters.
8. 'The Murder Hole,'—a Galloway tale.
9. 'Bothwell : a tragedy, by Algernon Charles Swinburne.'
10. Short Essays on 'The Scottish Shepherd,' 'Annals of our Parish,' 'William Wallace,' 'Samuel's Half Hour,' 'A Bathing Incident,' 'Thomas Jordan's Taunt,' 'Moses Potts, and our Pleasure Excursion,' 'Passages from a Life,' 'Recollections of Old Sermons,' 'Adventures of a Dancing Master,' etc., etc.

APPENDIX D

BIBLICAL CRITICISM :—A LETTER TO THE REVEREND DAVID MORRISON ON THE 'EPISTLE TO THE HEBREWS.'

Tynron, 25th Nov., 1888.

'Dear Friend, as C.'s exegesis is quite unsatisfactory, I have taken steps to inform myself about this *Epistle to the Hebrews* which you thought "rather rhetorical." Your judgment, then, appears to me quite correct. I think it is the "Macaulay" of the *New Testament*.

'The writings of the Apostolic Fathers are silent on the point of Paul being the author. Irenæus did not attribute it to Paul. Tertullian (A.D. 240) denies the Pauline authorship. Marcia excludes it from his canon. Cyprian does not mention it. The Pauline authorship was not disowned in the West until the beginning of the fourth century. Jerome (A.D. 420) and Augustine favoured the opinion that it was written by Paul. Origen (A.D. 254) often employs it as a Pauline writing. His own belief was, that while the sentiments were Paul's, another wrote them down. Afterwards he adds, " God alone knows who wrote it."

' Summarising—the Western or Latin Church did not consider it Apostolic until the fourth century. In the Eastern Church tradition was early and uniformly in favour of its Pauline authorship.

' Having looked at the External evidence, let us glance at the Internal.

' The want of a title or inscription is striking. The name of the writer does not appear, contrary to Paul's method.

' The manner in which the *Old Testament* is quoted differs from the Pauline. The writer knows the *Jewish Scriptures* only in the Septuagint version, which is cited, even where it has words added to the Hebrew text, as in I. 6 from *Deut.* xxxii, 43 ; and also where the meaning of the original is entirely deserted, as in x, 5-7. Paul seldom quotes the LXX, and his citations agree with the Vatican text, whereas the *Epistle to the Hebrews* uniformly follows the Alexandrian one. One illustration must suffice. Thus I, 7 is from the LXX Alexandrian copy ; the original Hebrew meaning is that God makes the winds his messengers and the lightnings his servants. But in the Greek rendering which our author follows, the sense becomes, " He makes his angels winds, and his servants flames of fire," implying that the angels are changed into those elements by God to do his pleasure.

' None of the introductory formulas and quotations, so common with Paul, such as, " as it is written," " for it is written," " the Scripture saith," appears in our Epistle.

' The writer betrays an imperfect knowledge of the Tabernacle and Temple. The pot of manna and Aaron's rod are put in the Ark of the Covenant, which is opposed to I *Kings* viii, 9, II *Chron.* v, 10, where it is expressly declared that the Ark had nothing in it but the two tables of stone.

' The golden altar of incense is put in the Holy of Holies, whereas it was in the first apartment, towards the Veil that separated the one from the other.

' In the Tabernacle Aaron's rod and the pot of manna were *before*, not *in* the Ark (*Exod.* xvi, *Num.* xvii).

' It is a mistake to say (*Heb.* ix, 19) that the blood of the sacrifices was mixed with water ; so also the statement that the Tabernacle was sprinkled with blood (ix, 21) is incorrect. It was sprinkled with oil, as we learn from the *Old Testament.*

' His spiritualising of the person of Melchizedek reminds us of Philo and the Rabbins.

' Paul shows that the law cannot bring a man to righteousness, because he is unable to fulfil it. The writer of the *Hebrews* blames the defects in the priestly arrangements. Paul says Judaism is unsatisfactory not because of the law, but because of man's relation to it. *Hebrews* says the defect is in the constitution of Judaism itself.

' In *Hebrews* the sacrifice Christ offers is himself, so that he is both priest and victim. This is not Pauline.

' In *Hebrews* Christ is a higher pre-existing being than in the Epistles of Paul. According to Paul He ultimately delivers up the dominion to the Father; in the *Epistle to Hebrews* his dominion is everlasting. He is not yet, however, elevated to the Λόγος of John.

' The Pauline idea of the death of Christ is that it is an expiatory sacrifice ; that of the *Hebrews* a sacrifice of purification.

' Paul delivers from punishment because of imputed righteousness. *Hebrews* delivers from a guilty conscience. *Hebrews* does not connect the work of Christ with his death on the cross, but with his appearance in Heaven where he discharges his interceding priestly duties.

' What is " faith " ?

' Paul answers, an inward appropriation of Christ's righteousness imputed to us. *Hebrews* answers, the invisible world viewed as real and as future.

' The Pauline idea that Christ is the first member of a " renewed humanity," the second Adam, is not in our Epistle—" The Apostle and High Priest of our profession." Epithets unknown to Paul.

' Every reader feels that the style is unlike Paul's. The periods are regular and rounded ; the rhythm oratorical and smooth. Exact sentences—without Paul's abruptness, full-toned expressions, words of a poetic complexion—are abundant. Instead of the Apostle's dialectic method, his fiery energy and impassioned style, we have the stately and polished eloquence of one who built up rhythmical periods. In single words less common are preferred to colloquial ones. " Effulgence," and " express image," are employed instead of " image of God " ; " μισθαποδοσία " for " μισθός, μεγαλωσύνη " not " μέγεθος," etc.

' Why in an *Epistle to the Hebrews* should Paul write purer Greek than in his unquestioned epistles written to Greeks ?

' Hoping that this finds you well.—Remain yours faithfully,
' JAMES SHAW.'

INDEX

Printed in the United States
125218LV00004B/126/A